THE L

1934: a 13-year-old Jewish boy escapes Nazi Germany to become the highest decorated WW II Palestinian soldier in the British Army.

2010: a top Israeli computer scientist searches for the favorite artist of her youth.

From the rise of the Nazi Party through the formation of the State of Israel, across a sea of time to present day, their worlds collide in

LOVE PASSION WAR

PART 1

ERIC HAUSMAN-HOUSTON

(Based on a true story)

Part 1 ends at El Alamein, North Africa, July 3, 1942, when the Nazis had won the war, they just didn't know it. For the over 100,000 Allied soldiers who needlessly died in North Africa, it's time for the truth to be told.

(I have filled in the blanks and made slight adjustments, such as the merger of minor characters to ease the read, but overall I have tried to relay the story and those involved as close to the truth as possible.)

For photos visit Facebook: THE LOST ARTIST

"A page-turner! Revealing important insight into little-known history of pre-state Palestine and World War II, this fascinating journey of a remarkable man is a rip-roaring story from beginning to end. I recommend it to everyone. "
Rabbi Mark S. Golub, JBS TV, jbstv.org

THE LOST ARTIST

LOVE PASSION WAR

PART 1

Special thanks to Art Proulx, for the wonderful cover design, and to Mary Beth Marschik and Renée Bradley for their insightful editing. All have refused payment, insisting that their work goes to the recovery of the stolen medals. To them I am extremely grateful

Cover photo (top): Fred Hausman, 1945, (bottom R - L) Clay Proulx, Lance Irwin, Patrick Ollila

To my father, Fred Hausman, and Einat Amitay.

May they inspire others as they have me.

TABLE OF CONTENTS

FORWARD - THE STOLEN MEDAL

In 1944, Fred Hausman (Fritz Sigmund Hausmann) was awarded the Distinguished Conduct Medal (DCM), the highest honor given to a non-British citizen in the British Army. It is the only one awarded to a Palestinian soldier, making it the most important WWII medal to Israel. The medal was recently discovered to have been stolen by a crime ring within the British Ministry of Defense (MoD). Taking in all of the known facts, so far that is the only plausible explanation.

Before his untimely death, Norman Palmer QC CBE, legendary in British restitution law, along with Hunter solicitor, Hetty Gleave, represented this case on a mostly pro bono basis. Because of lawyer confidentiality I've been advised not to include Norman Palmer's and Hetty Gleave's correspondence. But included at the end of the book is my communications with Scotland Yard, the MoD, and Lord Michael Ashcroft, current possessor of the stolen medal, so that you, the reader, may judge the facts for yourself.

Each book sold will help fund a full investigation to end the theft of these medals from within the MoD and unite all stolen medals with their rightful owners. We will then donate my father's medals to a worthy cause, such as the Ben Shemen Youth Village, which saved my father's life and I believe still takes in orphaned and refugee children. Any extra money will go to non-profit veterans organization, such as Homes For Our Troops, Fisher House Foundation and UK's The Soldiers' Charity so that they may be the ones to benefit from these crimes.

With your help these brave soldiers, who risked and gave their lives for our freedom, may finally be shown justice.

THE LOST ARTIST

LOVE PASSION WAR

PART 1

CHAPTER 1

Spring 2009:

EINAT TOOK A MOMENT as she got off the phone with "THE VOICE OF ISRAEL." There was hope again for her search. The show (literally translated "THE SEARCH FOR FAMILY") had become a huge hit. With all of the turmoil that Israel had faced, family and friends were often lost to each other. Now, on the radio for fifteen minutes everyday, from 4:45pm to 5:00pm, people found missing loved ones. Sometimes Einat (as she explained, "Pronounced like 'a-nut',") would listen while driving. At particularly moving moments when long lost friends, brothers and sister, parents and children were reunited, she would glance at the drivers in the cars around her to find both men and women drying their eyes.

She knew they wouldn't be drying their eyes for her. Hers was an unusual case. Not only was she unrelated to the man she was looking for, she had never met him nor knew of anyone who had.

The classic Israeli children's book, AND THERE WAS EVENING, published in 1949, was in its forty-second edition. Referred to as the pearl of Israeli children's literature, many Israelis could recite its opening lines by heart, "Blue evening sky, clear evening sky, sailed around by a bright moon..." Now in her mid-30s, Einat, and most of her friends, could still recite the entire poem. Its rhythm left such an indelible impression, its beloved images still etched in her mind. But its illustrator, Haim Hausman, remained a mystery. Who he was and what became of him always led to the same answer: "He must be dead. The book is too famous. We've been looking for him for sixty years, if he were alive we'd know it."

She hesitated to even contact the show; assuming the producers would feel her search was inappropriate for them. But the mystery must have also peaked their interest. "Write down everything you want to say on-air and keep it with you at all times so you're ready when we call you in four days." Four days? It could take years to get on the show and she had just put her request in the week before.

She suddenly felt unprepared, though since the time in her teens when she wanted to become a kindergarten teacher she had been collecting information on the children's culture of the Kibbutz. So little was known of the artists who had created

Israel's first children's books. 'AND THERE WAS EVENING' was illustrated before there was an actual State of Israel. They were fighting for something that wasn't even a country. The British they had fought with in World War II, who had pushed Jewish immigration into Palestine through the Balfour Declaration of 1917, were now economically shattered by two world wars. With Britain's citizens still on food rationing, they had no option but to pull out of the nightmarish situation they had created.

For many of the Jewish refugees who had risked everything to immigrate to Palestine, there was now nowhere to go. Most of their families had been wiped out in Europe. They were now illegal immigrants in fear for their lives. Einat's father was six-years-old at the onset of the Jewish/Arab Palestinian War of 1948. He would tell her of how there was no money for food or shoes, they slept on dirt floors, and when shot at, they used dug out holes in the ground for bomb shelters.

But amidst all of this chaos: bombs, killing, starvation, there were artists creating children's books. Did they even consider themselves artists? At the time, there was no Hebrew word for "illustrator." They were just people who drew. She wondered how someone could even publish and distribute children's books as if there were no war going on. 'AND THERE WAS EVENING' has no death. It's innocent, and very humane, as were all Israeli children's books of that time. They seemed to have understood that terrifying witches, giants and monsters had no place for children in need of relief from the nightmare.

Did Haim Hausman have children? Had he struggled to create some sort of normalcy for them? He must have known that a child's survival, physical and emotional, relies on the nurturing protection of a loving adult. Perhaps that's why the book remains so eternal.

It seemed wrong to her that he had become famous, yet nobody knew who he was. Without those people who had left everything to risk their lives on a daily basis, there would be no Israel. Was he still alive? Did he know the impact his illustrations had on so many? In 1948 he was part of a Kibbutz. How could he disappear?

She decided that it was time to find out. Though people had been looking for him for sixty years, unlike Einat, they hadn't been creating search engines for the last ten of them.

CHAPTER 2

May, 1934

A FEW WEEKS AFTER FRITZ'S thirteenth birthday, he left the protection of his loving family in Germany to make the long trip alone to Palestine, not knowing when or if he would ever return. On the day of his arrival, the 'Disturbances' broke out as Arab revolutionaries attacked several buses transporting Jews. The Haganah (Underground Jewish paramilitary) retaliated while the controlling British tried to maintain order with an iron fist. At the Ben Shemen Youth Village, Fritz's destination, teachers hid with children in shelters as Arab snipers shot at the school. The bus driver assured Fritz, "Not to worry. This happens. Welcome to the Promised Land." Fritz showed no emotion. Having experienced the rise of the Nazi party, he was accustomed to living under constant threat.

When the fighting finally settled down, late at night under the cover of darkness, the bus pulled into Ben Shemen. Driving with the lights off, guided only by the moon; the dry land, barbed wire fence and sterile white buildings of the compound were a cold welcome.

As the pale, lanky boy with a full head of dark curly hair stepped off of the bus carrying only his suitcase, Dr. Siegfried Lehman introduced himself in German as Professor Lehman. Lehman had emigrated from Berlin, Germany in 1927 to found the youth village and agricultural school. Now in his early 40's, he attempted cheerfulness as he took Fritz's bag saying, "We made sure to have an exciting day for your arrival. I hope the trip wasn't too taxing." Fritz, sensing the weariness in the thin man's waning smile, shook his head 'no.' Lehman led him to the front door of the main building where two men sat holding rifles. Lehman jested, "Several professors have stayed up to greet you." He introduced Fritz to Professor Melnick, a tall, handsome biology teacher, and Professor Pearlman, a shorter, stout math teacher and one of the foremen of the farm. Their stern nods made it clear to Fritz that, after the events of the day, their sole purpose for staying awake was to protect the compound.

Lehman led Fritz inside, resting his suitcase in the entryway. Knowing that Fritz must be hungry, he brought him to the kitchen where he prepared a sandwich. "Everything is grown fresh here. Have you ever worked on a farm?" Fritz shook his head: "My father has a vineyard but his farmers work it for him." Lehman raised an eyebrow: "Oh, did you bring your father's farmers?" Fritz shook his head again. Lehman shrugged: "Well, then I'm afraid you'll have to work the farm along with the rest of us."

Though it wasn't to his taste, Fritz felt obliged to eat the sandwich of vegetables and dry bread as Lehman explained the workings of the youth village. Based on the communal ideals of the kibbutz, each child was under the supervision of four adults; a homeroom teacher focusing on their education, a 'house mother' of the dormitory for maternal care, a youth leader for peer guidance and social activities, and a foreman to work under on the farm for four hours a day. "One of our many mottos is, 'working the earth purifies the soul'," Lehman smiled as he added, "I'm guessing your father never taught you that." Fritz shook his head, knowing those were the last words his father would ever utter.

Lehman brought Fritz to a separate building of communal showers and toilets, where he brushed his teeth and changed into pajamas. They then walked to a large, narrow, wooden structure. "The dormitory," Lehman announced. Fritz said nothing, though it looked more like a shack than the white stucco building advertised in the leaflet. Considering admission was donation only, he was in no position to complain. "There are four groups in you're building; A, B, C, and D. You're in group D. Have you ever shared a room with three other boys?" Fritz shook his head. Lehman cracked a smile as they entered the building, "So, this shall be an adventure."

He brought Fritz to room D, quietly leading him to his bed, the only light coming from the moon through the window. The four beds of each room were made of horsehair mattresses resting on low wooden platforms surrounded by thick, high wooden planks to protect the children from rifle fire in case of Arab attacks. Lehman put down Fritz's suitcase, indicated the bed, and after a slight nod goodbye, so as not to wake the other boys, he quietly disappeared out the door. Fritz could just make out the three other boys asleep in their cots. One boy, snoring loudly, suddenly sat up and spoke to him in a foreign language. Fritz, unable to understand, gave a shrug. The boy lay down again, and was soon back to snoring.

Fritz, climbing into his bed, disturbed several rodents that scurried between the walls. Staring off at the small functional room, it seemed far removed from his large, comfortable home in the town of Bingen am Rhein, Germany, where the river Rhine cuts through the mountains of the lush, green valley. To Fritz, it would always seem like the most beautiful place on earth.

His early childhood was sheltered by his loving mother, Klara, their cook and governess, Martha, their maid, Toni, and Fritz's outspoken sister, Lotte, eight years his senior. His father, Julius Hausmann, five-foot six-and-a-half-inches, the same height as Napoleon Bonaparte and perhaps as temperamental, was responsible for Fritz's discipline. Always feeling guilty after giving Fritz his weekly spanking, he would try to make it up to the boy by talking to him. The conversations inevitably turned into lectures on the one subject in which Fritz showed no interest: running a successful business. But Julius did his best to set a good example for his son, and always brought him a present when returning from a business trip.

The name "Hausmann" was traced back to a Jewish Roman admiral. Jews were often the sailors and commanders in the Roman Navy. To prevent rebellions, Rome made sure to retire high-ranking officers far away from their homeland, and many Jewish Roman naval commanders ended up in

Germany while their German counterparts were often retired in Romania.

In 1911, Klara had turned 21 and was expected to marry. A mutual friend of the family, believing that Julius, at age twenty-six, would make a good match, introduced Klara's family, the Wohlgemuth's of Budenheim, who were also traced back to Roman naval personnel, to the Hausmanns. The parents met several times before agreeing to the arrangement.

At the couple's first meeting, Julius found Klara to be an energetic, intelligent, striking girl with dark curly hair, and at five-foot two-inches, an acceptable height. Klara was less certain of Julius, who appeared somewhat rigid and proud. During the men's private negotiations, Klara's father was shocked by Julius's suggestion that the dowry be increased. "If you feel my daughter is unworthy ..." Julius cut him off assuring, "No, not at all, Sir. You have an extremely charming and beautiful daughter. I would be lucky to have her with no dowry, but it is important that I provide a life worthy of her." Klara's father shrugged off Julius's brazenness to his youth. But as Julius methodically laid out all of his finances, his plans for the vineyard, and what it would take to make it a success, to Julius's surprise, Klara's father agreed.

After the meeting, it was Julius who confided with pride to Klara what he had accomplished. Klara was taken aback. Julius asked with concern, "I hope I haven't spoken out of turn. I believe I was acting in both of our best interests." Still dumbfounded, a slight smile crossed her face as she shook her head,

"No, if you can part extra money from my father, I believe you capable of anything." As they both laughed, Klara was won over.

Both accepted their parents' decision, and a few months later they were married. Their first years were happy ones. Through Julius's hard work and careful planning of the vineyard he was able to become a successful wine merchant. And in 1913, with the birth of Lotte, their world seemed complete.

But that world would soon shatter.

June 28, 1914:

The Black Hand, a secret underground Serbian organization, assassinated the Austrian Archduke Franz Ferdinand. The German Emperor, Kaiser Wilhelm II, upset by the murder of his friend, triggered the inevitable series of events that would begin WWI. Pushing Austria-Hungary to attack Serbia, Russia, in treaty with Serbia, was forced to mobilize troops in Serbia's defense. When Russia refused to cancel its mobilization, Germany declared war on Russia. Knowing that France was bound by treaty to Russia, Germany invaded neutral Belgium in order to reach Paris by the shortest route. Britain then declared war on Germany to honor its treaty with France and Belgium. Japan, honoring its agreement with Britain, also declared war on Germany. Italy, allied to Germany and Austria-Hungary, was able to declare neutrality because of a clause committing them only in the event of a 'defensive war', but a year later, in 1915, they turned on their former allies and joined the allied forces against Germany. With Germany's policy of unrestricted submarine warfare threatening America's commercial shipping, and with the huge debt that would not be repaid if the Allies lost, in 1917 the United States entered the war.

Julius was enlisted as an officer and fought for the next four years without leave. Due to its technological advances, The Industrial revolution had changed the world, creating a war on an unprecedented scale. Over twenty million people died, many from disease and malnutrition.

For the four years that Julius was away, Klara raised Lotte on her own while maintaining the vineyard. Having lived a sheltered life, she was still not far from a girl herself. What little free time she had was spent volunteering as a nurse to help the wounded soldiers at the local hospital. There was little machinery left on the farm, as much of the metal had been confiscated and melted down to build arms. With supplies increasingly short, strict rationing was enforced. Wine and raisins, being less perishable, were in high demand and the German government appropriated a good amount of what the vineyard produced. On November 11, 1918, Germany fell to defeat, leaving the country devastated. There was no "Marshall" plan, no aid for reconstruction. The world believed that Germany should pay for what it had done.

The German's, having lost all faith in Kaiser Wilhelm (even President Woodrow Wilson gave up working with him on peace negotiations) called for his abdication. But Wilhelm refused, claiming it was England, Russia and France's fault by exploiting Germany's treaty with Austria to connive a war of annihilation against him. Wilhelm finally consented when it was made clear that even the German army would not defend his throne. He was forced into exile in the Netherlands, ending the German monarchy.

The Treaty of Versailles provided for the prosecution of Wilhelm "for a supreme offence against international morality and the sanctity of treaties", but despite demands from the allies, Queen Wilhelmina of The Netherlands refused to extradite him. King George V of England, Wilhelm's cousin, wrote that Wilhelm was "the greatest criminal in history", but he opposed the calls to "Hang the Kaiser!" Wilhelm blamed his dysfunctional family in part by saying, "To think that George and Nicky (Nicholas II of Russia, also a cousin) should have played me false! If grandmamma (Queen Victoria) were alive, she would never have allowed it."

But he would put the bulk of the blame for his actions upon the Jews. In 1919, Wilhelm wrote denouncing his abdication as the "deepest, most disgusting shame ever perpetrated by a person in history." The Germans were "egged on and misled by the tribe of Judah (Jews.) Let no German ever forget this, nor rest until these parasites have been destroyed and exterminated from German soil!" He advocated a regular international all-worlds pogrom à la Russe (induced riots to kill Jews and destroy their homes.) He wrote that was "the best cure" and further believed that Jews were a "nuisance that humanity must get rid of some way or other. I believe the best would be gas!"

In the 1930's, enamored with Hitler, Wilhelm petitioned through his wife for the Nazi Party to revive his monarchy. But Hitler's lust for power and scorn for the man whom he held responsible for Germany's greatest defeat, kept Wilhelm in exile. Wilhelm's admiration for Hitler's work, however, never faltered. In 1940, he wrote to his sister, Princess Margaret, "The hand of God is creating a new world & working miracles... We are becoming the U.S. of Europe under German leadership, a united European Continent ... The Jews are being thrust out of their nefarious positions in all countries, whom they have driven to hostility for centuries." And in 1941, shortly before his death, Wilhelm wrote that the English ruling classes were "Freemasons thoroughly infected by Juda... British people must be liberated from Antichrist Juda. We must drive Juda out of England just as he has been chased out of the Continent."

It's a mystery why anyone would think that the Jews would start a war over the death of Archduke Ferdinand. But Wilhelm, believing his monarchy to be the land of Christ, was convinced that it had to be the Jews who were responsible for his demise, World War I, and World War II. (The Jews were also undoubtedly to blame for his deformed right hand and his extreme weight gain.)

CHAPTER 3

IN 1918, after four years of hunger, cold, and near death in the trenches, Julius returned home to face bankruptcy for back taxes and huge debts that the vineyard had incurred to stay afloat. But even though Germany was now in a massive depression with soaring inflation, he realized that the victors would thrive, demanding fine wines, such as German Rieslings. With no jobs to be found, the farmers were willing to work for food and board, and within two years he was able to pay all of their back wages and turn the vineyard profitable again. As a sign of better times, on April 27, 1921 Fritz was born.

But Julius couldn't show the same exuberance for the birth of his son as he had eight years before with Lotte. He had seen too much. The humor that Klara once easily pulled out of him seemed to have vanished. His sole focus now was on building a successful business that would protect them from the threat of any such repeated disaster.

Klara, on the other hand, was able to put the past behind her and focus her energy on raising Fritz. She took him everywhere; collecting berries, building dams, skating, skiing, hiking in the nearby forest, and teaching him to draw. Fritz rarely played with other children. The class division of the time separated them from the underpaid Jewish workers in town, while being Jewish kept them apart from Bingen's upper class. But he loved his pet frogs, turtles, lizards, and Klara would help him tend any wounded birds or abandoned baby animals they would find. Klara was more than his mother. She was a leader, a best friend, and he would do anything for her.

Since Klara was afraid of lightning, so was Fritz. They would huddle together in the hallway during thunderstorms, shuddering at every bolt. When she lit candles and prayed in the nearby monastery, a practice passed down from her Catholic nanny, Fritz did the same. It made no sense to him. They were non-religious Jews, but since it pleased her, it pleased him.

When she took him for trips on the train, he was shocked by the personal questions she would ask the other passengers in their compartment, "Do you have a girlfriend? How's your sex life? How much money do you make?" What amazed Fritz the most was that they would always answer, usually in explicit detail. So, he became outgoing. At the age of six, when a kind, elderly woman smiled at him on the train, he asked, "How's your sex life?" The compartment broke into laughter. As an embarrassed smile crossed the elderly woman's face, Klara assured, "I'm sorry, he doesn't know what he's saying." He would be more careful next time, but Klara's reassuring arm on his shoulder showed approval for his effort.

Friday afternoons, Klara would take Fritz to a little café on the river. "I think it's the happiest place on earth," she would tell him. He didn't understand why she was so enchanted by the seemingly ordinary café, but he would never begrudge her a pleasure.

There, they would see her friend, Rudolf Schank, "Onkel" Rudy to Fritz, a tall, handsome, friendly man who appeared to take a special interest in Fritz. Several musicians played waltzes and popular songs of the day while Fritz ate ice milk and Klara and Onkel Rudy laughed and sometimes even waltzed. Klara told Fritz, "We don't have to tell father about this. He probably wouldn't appreciate our little café and we don't want him to feel left out." Loving to see his mother happy, as she was never so relaxed as when they were there, he would keep their secret.

Since Julius considered it inappropriate for children to dine with the adults, Fritz ate breakfast and dinner with Martha and Toni in the kitchen. But when Julius was away, Fritz would happily sit by Klara's side. "You are the man of the house now," she would tell him. "So it's okay for you to eat at the dinner table."

Having had little contact with other children, Fritz was terrified of his first day of school. Lotte, then fourteen, advised, "Just be sure to make a good impression or they'll kill you." Over dinner, Toni, whose parents worked for Klara's family in Budenheim, tried to reassure him. "School will be fun. You'll make lots of friends." Toni was blonde, pretty, and too kind to take seriously. But the older, stricter Martha would be straight with him. When he asked her about school she scowled, "Well, we all somehow survive it." Survive it? Was it that bad? What if he was the first to not survive it?

He walked into school the next morning shaking at the expectation of being beaten, tortured, and humiliated. As it turned out, it was very pleasant. The other boys were friendly, they played together outside during recess, and the only odd moment was at lunchtime when he noticed several of the boys gazing at his food. Not knowing what to do, he asked if they wanted to share his lunch with him. Instantly, the boys crowded around as he divvied up his sandwich and passed around his apple for each boy to take a bite.

At the end of the day, Klara, Martha and Toni made the short walk to the school and waited outside for him to exit with Lotte. They quickly hovered around asking, "How did it go?" "Did you make friends?" What did you learn?" He shrugged, "It was okay. But I'll need a bigger lunch. School makes me very hungry." Martha's jaw almost dropped: "You? The boy who won't eat anything?" Toni gently cut in, "How many sandwiches do you think you'll need?" Fritz counted on his fingers before answering: "Six." Klara and Martha were dumbfounded. But Toni gave an imploring nod, indicating with her eyes towards some of the raggedly dressed children: "Children get hungry." Klara, catching on, nodded to Martha: "Of course, you'll make as much as he needs." Martha, in disbelief, instantly barked: "Six sandwiches? Are you mad? The boy can't eat..." Klara cut her off with a gentle hand on her shoulder, "He's a growing boy. It's okay." Nothing was ever stated, but Martha must have figured it out. The next morning, while handing him the large bag of six sandwiches and fruit, there was a glint in her eyes as she said, "Now make sure you eat it all."

With plenty of food at home, he would usually give away his share and forgo eating lunch. From then on he spent most of his free time playing with his gang. They would build forts, then defend them and invade other gangs' forts. Sometime they would excavate beautiful ancient glass and pottery in the former Roman garbage dump, or climb up to the quarry to unearth petrified prehistoric sea creatures from the Jura Sea before it broke through the mountains to form the River Rhine. The highlight of their excavation was at the end of the day when they would smash all of their findings on the rocks, never considering their value.

It was a happy time in his childhood, only slightly tainted by the fact that the boys called each other by their first names while they referred to Fritz as "Jew." It wasn't meant offensively. Sometimes, when they would call out, "Hey Jew, come here and help us!" he would call back, "Okay Christians, I'm coming!" But it never deterred them.

His closest friend, Hans Egert, was the only one of the gang who called Fritz by his actual name. Shortly after they started school together, Hans's father, a driver for a competitive winery, was killed in an auto accident. Their friendship helped Hans cope with the loss. Fritz always made sure to save Hans one of the sandwiches that he brought to school each day. And Fritz's house became a second home to Hans. They knew each other over two years before Fritz saw the inside of Hans's home. Hans had always avoided Fritz from visiting by explaining, "My younger brother and sister will just get in the way." But one day, Fritz joined Hans when he went home to drop off his books. Though Hans was hesitant to have him come up, curiosity got the better of Fritz.

Entering the small, rundown one-bedroom apartment, Fritz hid his shock to find no furniture. Boxes were used for chairs, a larger box was the table, and several old mattresses on the floor sufficed as beds. Hans, his mother, younger brother and sister didn't seem distressed by their living conditions, but until then, Fritz had no idea what poverty meant. Most of the families were too proud to let anyone know of their living condition. As soon as Fritz left, Han's mother was furious: "How dare you let that wealthy kid in here! If you're father was alive he would beat you!"

That night, Fritz told his family about it, expecting them to be as shocked. "Let that be a lesson to you," Julius sighed before going back to his paper. But what lesson? To use boxes when you can't afford furniture? Klara seemed much more affected, immediately arranging work for Frau Egert. Lotte pulled Fritz aside: "They haven't told you this, but a lot of your friends live like that, even worse." Seeing the surprise in Fritz's eyes, she added, "I know, it's horrible. But I'm making sure things will change." Despite their father being a devout Capitalist, Lotte had secretly joined the socialist youth movement in her school. She decided that it was now time for Fritz to take up the cause.

The next day, he was standing on the sidewalk in front of Bingen's Grand Hotel handing out leaflets for an upcoming meeting of the National Manufacturer's Association when he suddenly looked up to see that he had just handed a leaflet to his father. Furious, Julius dragged Fritz home to give him the worst spanking of his life. Thus was Fritz's introduction into politics.

By the late 20's, there were three combatant groups in Bingen, The Socialist, Communist and Nazis. Every Sunday they would march to the main square where a huge fight would erupt. Fritz came to accept that as the norm, even looking forward to one day joining the Socialists in fighting the Nazis. But Julius was determined that his children would have no part in any radical political movement. Not long after the leaflet incident, Lotte was sent to boarding school in Darmstadt, Germany. The night before she left, she gave Fritz the most fantastic pillow fight of his life. He couldn't wait for her to come home so they could do it again. But it would never be. After boarding school, Lotte went on to the university in Freiburg, Germany, and for the rest of his childhood he rarely saw her.

Fritz was accepted into the realshule (secondary school) when he turned ten, and was then allowed to sit at the dining room table with Julius. The day of his acceptance, Julius paraded Fritz down the main street showing off his new uniform of white and red bands. To not offend Julius, now an important local businessman, the men took off their hats as they passed, forcing Fritz to constantly tip his deep purple cap and visor to them. Julius thrived on such display, but it made Fritz want to disappear.

Embarrassed by his father's pompousness and pride, he swore to never be like that. Fritz finally asked, "Father, can we go home now?" Julius questioned, "Why, are you ill?" Fritz shrugged, "No, but we shouldn't do this. We're Jews." Julius was dogged, "You must be proud of who you are, and your accomplishments. Holding your head up high makes people respect you. That's how you change attitudes."

But no matter how high Julius held his head, attitudes in Germany only worsened. Fritz started hearing singing in the streets of songs such as, "NOTHING WILL BE BETTER TILL JEWISH BLOOD SPRITS FROM OUR KNIVES." He was the only Jew left in his realschuler. Though the others were too afraid to go, he wanted to become an engineer, and had the support of his gang.

During one recess, Werner Heydrich, the local Nazi leader's son, threw a rock at Fritz, hitting him on the back of his head. Fritz, stunned, struggled to get up as Werner scowled, "Dirty Jew, go back where you belong!" Fritz, feeling the back of his head, looked to see the blood on his hand. Regaining his equilibrium, he turned to Werner, "I don't bother you. Why do you bother me?" Werner sneered, "'Cause your stink bothers me. Go back where you came from, Dirty Jew." After years of abuse, Fritz finally exploded, lunging at Werner, throwing him on the ground and knocking the wind out of him. To assure a fair fight, Fritz's gang circled around keeping Werner's gang from interfering.

Hearing the commotion, their professor broke through the boys to find Fritz with Werner pinned down beneath him. Grabbing Fritz by the collar, he pulled him up while yelling, "Stop that! Immediately!" Werner, lifting his head, cracked a smile as the professor dragged Fritz into the school while reprimanding, "You're in serious trouble, young man!" Inside his empty classroom the professor anxiously turned to Fritz: "Do you realize what you've done?!" Fritz replied, "I didn't do anything. He started it." Seeing the beads of sweat on the professor's forehead, Fritz realized that it wasn't a matter of right or wrong. The professor was terrified. What if the Nazi leader retaliated against him and the school for allowing such a thing to happen? Fortunately, the incident passed without a mention. Undoubtedly, Werner didn't dare tell his Nazi father that he had been beaten up by a Jewish boy.

From then on, almost everyday on his way to school, Werner and his gang or some other Nazi youths were waiting for Fritz. He developed a system of taking off the heavy leather belt with a metal buckle that he had commandeered from Julius's WWI uniform, wrapping it around his wrist and whipping it in the air so that he would slash anybody who got too close. He usually beat them up. Sometimes he got the worst of it, but the Nazi boys actually became afraid of him.

By the time he was twelve, Hans was his only friend. They spent most of their free time together. One afternoon, they found a pack of cigarettes on the ground with one cigarette left inside. "What should we do?" Hans asked. Fritz replied, "Must be meant for us." Amazed by their extraordinary luck, they snuck up to the top of the abandoned lookout tower built on the old Roman fortress to share their first cigarette. They coughed, felt sick, and loved every minute of their entry into manhood.

Time slipped by, and suddenly realizing that they would be late for dinner, they raced each other through the town back to Fritz's house. Julius was a stickler for punctuality. "It is the first thing someone notices about you," he would say. They made it back to the house only a few minutes late. But fearing that Julius would know that they were smoking, they tried to sneak upstairs to quickly change clothes and rid themselves of any cigarette smell. The fourth step's creek gave them away. "Fritz, is that you?" Julius called from the den. Hans froze as Fritz responded, "Yes, Hans and I were just playing. We're changing for dinner." Julius, appearing in the entry hall, sternly looked up at them: "You're covered in sweat." Fritz apologized, "We climbed the mountain, to see the view." Julius admonished, "And you look filthy. You are young men now. Your appearance is important." Fritz nodded, "That's why we're changing." Before they could escape up the stairs, Julius added, "A little play is good, but these are important years. Don't forget that." Fritz nodded, "Yes, father." Hans also sheepishly nodded. Surprised that his son so easily agreed, Julius nodded towards the stairs, "Okay, go get ready for dinner." As nonchalantly as possible, they walked upstairs. Once on the landing, they ran to Fritz's room, ecstatic to seemingly have gotten away with it.

But racing through the town together proved to be a mistake. As Hans walked his usual route home that night, he turned a corner on a quiet street to see Werner Heydrich, in his brown Hitler Youth uniform, appear from a doorway. He turned to go back, but three more Hitler Youths blocked him from the other side. "We've been waiting for you," Werner said as his gang closed in.

The next day, Fritz heard a knock on the front door. Expecting Hans, he ran to open it. Hans stood there frozen, black eyed and bruised. "What happened? You okay?" Fritz asked. Almost trembling, Hans choked out, "I'm not allowed to see you any more. The Nazis said if they catch me playing with a Jew again they'll kill both of us." Fritz somberly nodded. Hans said, "If we just make sure they don't see us …" Fritz shook his head, "No, it's too dangerous. We'll wait. My Father says this will blow over soon."

That was the last time they ever spoke. Several times he saw Hans looking at him as they passed each other in the street, but he quickly looked away, not wanting to get his friend into trouble.

To fill the loneliness, Fritz built a Bavarian fort in his backyard where he would read, learn to play the guitar, and spend much of his time sketching. He had always loved to draw. In elementary school he had challenged himself to sketch an entire children's book about a little bee named Queen Maya. It was a sad moment when his teacher, admiring it, asked if he could have it and Fritz felt obliged to give it to him.

As often as he could, he went to the movies. He had been given one mark a week to see a film, but under the circumstances, his parents became more generous. He would sit in the dark, transported into different worlds by his favorites; war movies, such as the German 1932 film, 'F.P.1 DOES NOT ANSWER' starring Hans Albers, and the 1930 American anti-war film, 'ALL'S QUIET ON THE WESTERN FRONT'. In this militaristic time, both films caused an uproar. He also found the cartoons that preceded the main attraction equally mesmerizing, especially the Disney animation. Going early, he would stay as long as possible until he would have to go home for dinner.

After riding a German Shepherd on Martha's farm when he was very little, he had begged his parents for a dog. Julius finally conceded, but the dog kept jumping up on people, and a heartbroken Fritz watched as the dog was given to a farmer in a different town. Having recently had the chance to hold a trained pigeon in his hand, his parents had seen how much he was taken by the bird. He hadn't believed in the possibility of having one of his own, but to Fritz's surprise, Julius had a pigeon coup built for him. Fritz spent hours with his birds, loving that these beautiful, gentle creatures trusted him enough to rest on his arms and shoulders as he fed them.

To make new friends, Klara enrolled Fritz in the Jewish Boy Scouts. Feeling like an outsider, he eventually quit, but what he learned of the Zionist movement stayed with him. Founded in the late 19th century, named after Zion, a hill of Jerusalem, the movement's goal was to liberate the Jews from persecution by reclaiming their home in the land of Israel, the Biblically divine "Promised Land" of the Jews. (In the 2nd century CE, the Romans crushed a Jewish revolt and renamed the land 'Palaestina', [probably after the 'Philistines'] to lessen Jewish identification with the land of Israel.) In the late 19th century, it was a small mandate under the powerful British Empire, and the Balfour Declaration of 1917, stating British support for the Zionist movement, helped to make the movement a reality. To the upper class British, it seemed like the best solution of what to do with the Jews. But Balfour, giving little thought to the thousands of Palestinian Arabs displaced by the massive influx of European Jews, helped to create the overwhelming Mid-East conflict that exists today.

Zionism had never been discussed in Fritz's home, as Julius was far from eager to have his family farming in a kibbutz, their only opportunity in Palestine. But to Fritz, the possibility of living in a land where he would be accepted, even embraced, seemed like a dream. He suddenly became very religious, dragging his parents to synagogue every Friday night and Saturday morning and making sure they kept every Jewish holiday.

When Hitler came to power in 1933, Lotte and her boyfriend, Harry Ostreicher, both Socialist student leaders at the University of Freiburg, knowing they would be arrested and likely killed, escaped by fleeing over the border to Switzerland. They were then able to study at the University of Bern until transferring to a university in Bologna, Italy.

That morning in 1933, Fritz woke up and checked on his pigeons to find that someone had given them poisoned seeds. Some were already dead, but seeing a few of his favorites struggling to breathe, he picked them up and sat down under the stairs crying as he held his dying friends. He couldn't understand why anyone would do something so cruel.

Martha and Toni, being Christians, were no longer allowed to work for Jews. Though Fritz was the closest either had come to having a child, both were determined to remain stalwart on their last day. Martha hugged him goodbye assuring, "It's just for a short time, Fritz, until all this craziness passes." But Toni, nodding in agreement, broke into uncontrollable tears, and Martha consoled her as they left.

It was now up to Klara to take care of the house. One "high holy day", Fritz looked at Klara in shock as she came home with a large ham. She assured him, "Don't worry, it's Kosher." Knowing it was a lie he ate it anyway, and soon lost interest in religion. But he didn't forget what he had learned about Jewish history. Beginning an all-out campaign to go to Palestine, he would argue with his father, "Our people belong there! It's our home!" Julius scoffed, "Two thousand years ago it was our home, and even then we were glad to get out!"

With the Nazis prohibiting Jews from owning land, three Christian families were soon assigned to move into their home. Julius, Klara and Fritz stayed in rooms on the second floor, while a teacher from Fritz's former nearby high school moved in with his family on the first floor, a choir master took over the third floor with his wife and two small children, and a teacher of engineering, with Nazi affiliations, lived with his wife and daughter on the fourth floor. Having only one kitchen, and with Martha gone, Klara was forced to do most of the cooking, becoming a servant in her own home. To help cope, she tried to view all of the families as guests.

The families were fairly respectful, making the situation tolerable, but when all Jewish employees were terminated from German government positions, Fritz knew that it was time for him and his parents to leave. Julius, determined to protect their home and business, refused to go.

The only way Fritz saw of getting his parents out of Germany was to pave the way by going to Palestine himself. He continued his campaign, but even with Klara's support, Julius stood firm.

Then one day, Julius's locksmith, a Jewish man, found his eight-year-old son hanging from a tree behind their house, a red swastika painted across his bare chest. There were no arrests, no suspects, nothing in the papers. It was as if no crime had been committed. Julius, shaken into reality, realized that could have been Fritz. He agreed to let Fritz go, but only to England where he could eventually study at Oxford or Cambridge.

For the past three summers Fritz had been sent to summer camps in different countries; first Sentimier, Switzerland, where he came back fairly fluent in French, then to Tuscany where he learned Italian, and last to Kent to learn English. He hated being sent away from his home. But it gave him a larger view of the world and the confidence to travel. What he discovered in these other counties was that they may have been more tolerant of the Jews, but he was still an outsider. The distinction of Oxford or Cambridge meant nothing to Fritz, and Julius finally consented to Palestine.

The challenge now was getting an exit visa. The Nazis knew that large numbers of fleeing Jews would increase the chance of an international boycott on Germany, and a mass exodus of Jewish laborers would drain the economy. Even with Julius's money, the exit visa remained elusive.

In 1933, Haim Arlosoroff, the young Zionist leader in Palestine, came to Germany to meet with Adolf Hitler. It must have taken great courage for Arlosoroff to place himself defenselessly in the center of the Nazi party, but in very different ways, both Arlosoroff and Hitler saw the British Mandate of Palestine as a land of opportunity. The Nazis wanted an easy way to rid themselves of Jews while keeping their property without creating an international embargo, and Arlosoroff wanted to fulfill the Zionist dream of a Jewish nation.

On 25 August 1933, the Haavara Agreement, an agreement between Nazi Germany and Zionist German Jews was signed. Jews immigrating to

Palestine would put their money in a special bank account, used to purchase German goods for export, and a percentage of the proceeds of the sale of the goods would go to those Jews when they arrived in Palestine. So, to the rest of the world, it was the Jews themselves importing the goods.

Because of the Haavara Agreement, about 60,000 German Jews escaped inevitable death in Nazi concentration camps and approximately $100 million was brought into Palestine during the height of the worldwide depression of the 1930's to help establish the Jewish nation. Nazis ended up deeply regretting the Haavara Agreement. Paradoxically, Hitler turned out to be a great help in forming the State of Israel.

Still, chances of procuring the exit visa for Fritz, or any German Jew were slim. Because of Arab demands, the controlling British severely curtailed Jewish immigration. But at that time, the Nazis wanted legal ways to rid Germany of politically active Jews. Because of Lotte's affiliation with the Socialist Party, they may have been inclined to remove her potentially political younger brother. For a price, Julius was able to obtain the coveted exit visa. Plans were made for him to take Fritz by train to Bern, Switzerland, where Fritz would travel to Palestine with a young Jewish couple and their baby daughter.

The night before Fritz left, Klara made a dinner of his favorite foods. Determined to remain positive, she pretended as if he were only going away to summer camp. But at the Bingen train station, not knowing when or if she would ever see her son again, she broke down into tears as she hugged him goodbye. At thirteen Fritz was now 5'6", Julius's height, and four inches taller than his mother. As they held each other, she could feel him also begin to choke up. Trying to regain her composure she wiped her tears away while saying, "Silly me, I just love you too much." She caressed his cheek one last time before sending him off on the train. "We will see each other soon," she said, but each knew better than to trust those words.

On the trip to Bern, Julius attempted conversation with his son. Fritz loved art, animals, adventure, the outdoors. As Julius explained every possible pitfall of running a successful winery, Fritz's eyes glazed over. Eventually, Julius read the business news while Fritz drew in his sketchbook.

At the station in Bern, Julius found the couple with the baby that had been arranged as Fritz's travel companions to Palestine. Once in Palestine, they would part ways as the couple was going to a Kibbutz located in a different direction. They seemed pleasant enough, though very quiet. Julius thanked them for looking after his son, and they awkwardly nodded. Perhaps they were surprised that Fritz, at thirteen, was already as tall as his father. When it was time to board the train, Julius, believing that Fritz was now too old to hug, firmly shook his son's hand goodbye, "Not to worry, we will have you home soon."

"How could he be so blind," Fritz thought. But as the train pulled out of the station, Fritz saw Julius drying his eyes with his handkerchief. Never having seen his father cry, it made him realize that, as different as they were, his father actually did love him.

From Bern, they arrived by train in Triesta, on Italy's northeastern coast, where they boarded a ship. Rather than going directly to Palestine, the ship went down around the heel of Italy's boot and up to Naples, picking up passengers along the way. The young couple, not having had Klara as a mother, left it up to Fritz to make conversation. "Are you excited about going to Palestine?" he asked. They momentarily looked at each other before nodding slightly. He continued, "Have you been out of Germany before?" They hesitantly shook their heads, wondering where this interrogation was headed. Doing his best to put them at ease, he asked them where they were from, what they did there, and anything else he could think of other than their sex-lives. They confided that it was their first time out of their small village south of Stuttgard, Germany, where Nazis had set fire to their house and killed a neighbor's boy by tying him to horses and pulling him apart. They were some of the lucky few in their town to receive exit visas.

Their parents, only having enough money for their passage, insisted that they go, promising to follow as soon as possible. Feeling their anxiety, Fritz assured them, "Don't worry, I was nervous the first time I went abroad, but you can relax. I'll take care of everything." They smiled at this odd boy. Since they only spoke German, they were grateful that Fritz did all of their communication with the Italian crew.

On their arrival in Naples, Fritz's learned that the ship would be docked for two nights. He excitedly told the couple, who couldn't understand how being stuck in port on a ship for two days was good news. With no private cabins, they were forced to sleep sitting up on benches in the large lower deck. But Fritz was thrilled for the chance to see the lost city of Pompeii. With his travel money, he arranged for a guide, inviting the couple to join him with their baby. "I think we better not," the wife said. Fritz, dumbfounded, exclaimed: "But it's a preserved Roman city, buried up to twenty feet in volcanic ash from the eruption of Mount Vesuvius in 79 AD!" Getting little reaction, he added, "They have plaster casts of people buried alive!" Oddly enough, even that didn't tempt them. The wife regretfully shook her head: "It doesn't sound safe. We promised your father we would look after you."

It was their choice not to go, but they would not deter him. The couple, never leaving the boat for the entire trip to Palestine, anxiously watched as Fritz set off. Early that morning, as his guide drove him to Pompeii, he felt the rush of independence. With little tourism back then, he could wander almost freely in and out of Pompeii's grand buildings and maze of streets. His main objective was the casts of frozen bodies. They were everything he expected; people and animals ducking in terror as the ash came down upon them. But to his surprise, what he found most extraordinary were the beautiful wall-covered frescos of the villas. The massive murals at the House of the Vetti were his favorite. Never before had he seen rooms so transformed by art.

After a lunch in town, he hired another guide with a boat to take him to the Island of Capri to see the remains of Tiberius's Villa Jovis. The guide, impressed by Fritz's Italian, happily answered every question that Fritz could think of, even the personal ones. With a smile, the guide finally inquired, "So young man, what about you? Do you work or are you a man of leisure?" Fritz thought momentarily before affirming, "Man of leisure." After all, the week before he was given a quick Bar Mitzvah, proving that he was now a man. The ruins, with no volcanic ash to preserve the massive complex, had suffered two thousand years of decay, but Fritz was still thrilled to walk in the footsteps of one of the most notorious Roman emperors.

After climbing to the Villa's top terrace to see the view of the bay of Naples, the guide affirmed: "Beautiful, isn't it?" Fritz nodded in amazement. With a glint in his eye, the guide added: "But to see true magic, there is the Blue Grotto. The light will soon be perfect."

Taking the boat to the northwestern corner of the island, the guide helped Fritz into a small inflatable raft and they floated into a tight opening in the large cliff wall jutting out of the sea. The brilliant blue water illuminating the cavern dazzled Fritz. He had never seen such iridescence. The guide explained, "It is because there are two sources of light, one below water level you can not see." With an impish smile the guide asked, "Do you swim?" Fritz nodded enthusiastically. Stripping down to his shorts, Fritz jumped into the lustrous blue water. The guide laughed as the boy screamed from the piercing chill. But once adjusted to the cold, Fritz swam in the aquamarine world, diving down between glistening rocks. As the sun began shifting, causing the brilliant blue to darken, the guide pulled Fritz back up on the raft and wrapped a towel around him.

After visiting several more sights, the guide left him off at a little seaside café. There, on the terrace overlooking the bay of Naples, he ordered Linguini di Mare and a bottle of local white wine made from grapes grown on the slopes of Mount Vesuvius. Being eleven when he went to camp in Italy, he never had Italian wine before; much less an entire bottle to himself, but the waiter seemed unfazed by the thirteen-year-old boy's request. "This country is fantastic," Fritz thought. Aided by several glasses of wine, he struck up a conversation with an attractive young Neapolitan couple at the next table. Intrigued by this outgoing foreign boy, they accepted his offer of wine and invited him to join them for dessert and espresso with Sambuca.

Fritz swaggered back onto the ship, still feeling the liqueur. On greeting the couple with the baby, the wife exclaimed, "Where have you been? We were so worried." "Nothing to worry about," he slurred while falling onto the bench facing them, "I've been everywhere." Before relaying much of his adventure, he passed out. But for the rest of their trip, Fritz attempted to draw from memory the sites he had seen in order to show the couple all they had missed.

CHAPTER 4

AFTER A SIXTY-YEAR search, Einat knew that her chances of solving the Haim Hausman mystery were slight, but it had now bordered on an obsession. Having worked on search engines, she came to believe that some questions wanted to be answered, while others didn't. The ones that were to be kept secret were always a struggle, ending with her giving up in frustration. But with Haim Hausman, everyone she spoke with invariably wanted to help, suggesting places to search, people to talk to, leading her in different directions, opening more doors. She began bringing up Haim Hausman with everyone she met. It seemed as if the search had become a part of her.

Perhaps she needed to focus on something other than the true battle she was facing, to focus on something where the stakes weren't life and death. Her therapist, a keen-eyed, caring woman, splitting her time between patients and teaching at a university, was the one to first encourage her. After discussing the project, Einat admitted, "I don't know why I'm doing this. He seems like a lost cause." Her therapist agreed, "He very well may be, especially if you give up on him. But if it excites you, why stop before you've even started?"

Later, when Einat hesitated to contact the Radio show, her therapist argued, "Never let the fear of rejection deter your success. It may not feel good, but it's healthy. You're putting yourself out there, making things happen. Do you want to be a slug on the side of the road watching life pass you by?" Einat shrugged, "It's never been a particular ambition." "Good, so call them!"

Einat began therapy after her breast cancer returned. Being in her mid-thirties, the cancer would grow faster than in someone older and the cancer cells that had survived the first round of chemo were now more resistant to the medication. Odds were against her. But she was determined to be there for her three small children and husband she loved. On days that she could hardly get out of bed she would remember her therapist prodding, "You don't feel well, it's okay. You rest. But you keep going. You think of your next step, your next project, your next passion. You do not give up. New adventures!"

But what adventures could there be for her now?

At sixteen, she had wanted to stay on the Kibbutz and become a kindergarten teacher. "You're too smart for that," Her father admonished, "The future is computers, technology. You need to get out of here and study." She laughed in disbelief, "So, only stupid people should mold our youths?" Her father grumbled, "Don't twist my words." She shook her head: "I don't think I am, unless I don't understand what you're saying, which means I'm plenty stupid to teach." Her father responded soberly: "The Kibbutz is Communism at its best. Our survival depended on it. But things are different now. You should now see the world before deciding where you belong."

Having to go out into the world was not unexpected. By the age of nine, she knew that, like most Israeli men and women, she would be serving in the armed forces after high school. The army was her call of duty. Still, as a teenager, it was difficult to leave her family and friends within the protection of the Kibbutz. Its large support system was the only life she had known.

But adjusting to army life ultimately helped her gain a clearer sense of her potential. Learning to fight and defend a nation became empowering. She discovered that she was strong, could stand up for herself and be independent.

And the army is where she met her husband. He had grown up in a nearby Kibbutz, but they hadn't met until they both enlisted. Having similar backgrounds, both separated from family and friends, and both being young adults getting to know themselves in ways they never had before made it natural for them to become friends. It wasn't long before they realized that what they felt was much more than friendship, that they were in love and wanted to spend their lives together. A woman is discharged if marrying while in the army so they waited until they both completed their two years seven months of service.

Einat had resisted when her father pushed her to go out into the world, but after the army she and her husband decided to study in Haifa, Israel. Her focus was on French and English linguistics. Then, on scholarship from Microsoft and a sponsorship from the US Navy, they went to Attenborough, Scotland for their masters. From there they went to Australia for their PhD's in computer science.

In 2001, three-and-a-half years later, they moved to the north of Israel in the Galilee where she worked for IBM Research, primarily on internal search engines. Eventually, she was given a chair. Instead of a Kibbutz, they made their home in a sort of settlement with no farming, less than 30 kilometers (20 miles) from Palestine. The five hundred or so families weren't deemed much of a threat to the Palestinians and a fence around the community seems to still suffice for their protection.

Einat had always been a hard worker. She was raised that way. It became part of her identity. Raising a family and working full time was the life she had wanted. After the initial shock, she viewed the breast cancer as just a temporary glitch. She told herself that she was too young, had too much to live for, and like many women, she would survive it. For her husband and children she was determined to remain positive. She got through the first round of chemo and happily picked up her life where she left off.

She was ill prepared for the cancer to return two years later. The heavy dosages of the second round of chemo were crippling. She hated the way she looked as she gained weight and lost her hair. However, as challenging as it was, she kept up with her work at IBM. Her therapist had convinced her that working was crucial to her survival, "It's an insurance against the insurance."

One day, while feeling particularly weak from the chemo, she received a notice in the mail that her position was terminated. Stunned, she spoke to her boss, but it was clear that there was no room for discussion. The decision was made. After all of her years at IBM, she had expected at minimum some compassion. Perhaps they felt that it was inconsiderate of her to put them in the awkward position of having to fire her. "Evidently," she thought, "sick workers should simply walk off and die on their own, like an elephant." She left IBM, never to return.

Losing her Chair was a low point, but her therapist encouraged her: "There is more to life than internal search engines. Find something else that excites you. Even if you can only work one out of four days, you keep going."

Weak and dispirited, she stayed in bed for two weeks until she finally asked herself, "Okay, what do I do with my life?" After being fired from IBM, she decided that she would only work on something that really mattered to her.

Through the chemo she did all she could to give her children a sense of normalcy. 'AND THERE WAS EVENING' was the perfect book for a child to escape the larger problems of the world. While reading the book to her youngest child one evening, still entranced by its words and images, she chose her mission.

Her initial plan was simple: document the early Israeli artists to give some insight into their lives. There was little to go on, but she knew how to search. She went to the library to find all of the books that came out of the two Kibbutz publishing houses. The three classic Israeli children's books of Fania Bergstein were the favorites. Their simple beauty seemed to transcend time.

There was little online about Fania Bergstein. Born in Poland in 1908, she joined the Zionist Youth Movement, immigrated to Palestine in 1930 with her future husband, Aaron Wiener, and became part of the Kibbutz Gvat, where she introduced rural farming culture into Israeli children's books. After a prolonged illness she died of heart failure on September 18, 1950, one year after "AND THERE WAS EVENING" was published. She would never know of its success.

Einat hoped that some insight on Fania might emerge through the illustrators of her books. There was only the same nominal online information about Ilse Kantor, the illustrator of her first book, 'COME TO ME, SWEET BUTTERFLY,' published in 1945. But when she looked up Haim Hausman, the illustrator of her favorite drawings, other than illustrating 'AND THERE WAS EVENING,' she found nothing. It was as if he never existed.

She soon discovered that she wasn't the only one looking for him. But even with an ongoing search since the book had become a best seller starting in the 1950's, every lead had gone dead. Nothing was uncovered; no date of birth, not even the area where he was from. She asked herself, where do you start searching for someone who apparently doesn't exist?

NORTH BAY

RETIREMENT COMMUNITY

OFFICE 707 552 3336

NORTHBAY@COGIR.NET

2261 TUOLUMNE ST | VALLEJO | CA 94589

WWW.HAPPYLIVINGBYCOGIR.COM | LIC. #486803810

HAPPY LIVING BY cogir

CHAPTER 5

FRITZ LAY IN BED with his eyes closed wondering why people were in his bedroom in Germany speaking in a foreign language. Only his mother, Martha or Toni would come in that early in the morning. Resisting waking up to the nudging on his shoulder, he finally opened his eyes to find three thin, tanned, strange boys around his age standing over him. Having barely slept during his long trip to Palestine, it took him a moment to focus in on the room where Lehman had left him the night before. The oldest and more outgoing of the boys said something to him in a foreign language, the same thing he had said the night before. Realizing that it must be Hebrew, Fritz wished he had studied more, but he had always learned a language once he was in the actual country. In each respective language, he asked, "Do you speak German? French? Italian? English?"

"English!" the boy exclaimed, "We must learn language of enemy." "Enemy?" Fritz questioned. He thought of the Nazis as the enemy, and after his arrival in Palestine, perhaps the Arabs, but the British? "Yeah, they bad. They take our weapons so we can't protect ourselves. They send Jews back after making long trip here so they die. Everyone hates British here, even Arabs." The boy introduced himself, "I'm Avi, from Ukraine. This is Sasha and Mica. They twins from Czechoslovakia. They don't speak English good." The brothers nodded to Fritz. Avi asked in English then Hebrew, to help Fritz learn the language, what he had asked before, "Who are you? Where you from?" Fritz nodded, "I'm Fritz, from Germany." Avi cracked a smile, "Fritz, from Germany?" Sensing that he had said something wrong, Fritz gave an awkward nod. Avi, smiling to the brothers, extended his right arm to Fritz in the Nazi salute, "Heil Fritz of Deutschland!" Sasha and Mica broke into laughter as they followed suit with the Nazi salute, "Heil Fritz!"

Fritz gave a slight obliging laugh. Having been an outsider in Germany for being Jewish, would he now be an outsider in Palestine for being German? He had heard that immigrant students were teased for not speaking Hebrew and wearing strange, long, dark garb, but he was unaware of the animosity still felt towards the Germans over WWI and now for the rise of the Nazi Party. Even though he was Jewish, being German, especially from a good family, by implication meant that he had some part of it.

"Hurry, get ready," Avi exclaimed, "Or we late for breakfast." The boys spoke to each other in Hebrew as they quickly dressed, laughing several times while glancing at Fritz. Fritz, pretending not to notice, uncomfortably changed out of his pajamas as he sat on his bed with his back to the boys. After years of Julius drilling in the importance of appearance and making a good first impression, he struggled over what to wear. Finally deciding on something casual, he stood to face the boys. They stared at his pressed beige shorts and shirt until Avi asked, "You go on safari?" The twins laughed as Avi indicated Fritz with a wave of his thumb, "Yekke."

Fritz shook his head questioning, "Yekke?" Avi smirked, "It means you good German. Is that how they dress for work in field there? What you feed cows? Beer, sausage?" Fritz shrugged, "I've never worked on a farm." Avi feigned shock, "No? Big surprise. Is okay, you learn. You work 'Falhar' with horses, tractors, growing wheat, or cow stable. You no work flower garden, vegetable garden and chickens. That only for girls. Come! We late!"

This was the first time Fritz was exposed to the new breed of Jews in Palestine. They prided themselves on being different than the Jews of the Diaspora (Jews dispersed throughout Europe after their exile from The Holy Land.) Even most poor Jews in Germany were intellectual professionals, rarely working the land. But these new Jews would not lie down like lambs for the slaughter. They proudly worked the earth with sweat and muscle, and seemed to him ready to kill anyone out to crush them. Sensing that his artistic aspirations would not be appreciated, Fritz decided that for his time at Ben Shemen he would keep his drawing to himself.

With no running water in the dorm, the boys headed for the lavatory building. As they walked with other boys from the dorm, Avi introduced Fritz to a smaller, skinny, freckled boy around their age. "Fritz, this is Hillel. He from Germany too. Maybe you make sausage together." After initial greetings, Fritz, happy to speak German, asked Hillel, "What's a Yekke?" Hillel nervously whispered back in German, "A stuffy, slow German. Speak Hebrew. They don't like German here." After quickly relieving themselves in the communal boys' lavatory, they rushed to the commissary.

Inside the large white stucco hall, they grabbed seats on benches in front of long tables set with Army regulation plates, forks, knives and napkins. Fritz took a place next to Hillel as Avi, Sasha and Mica sat across from them. The hall filled with a cacophony of young voices chattering in Hebrew as metal bowls of fresh cucumbers, scallions, radishes, tomatoes, kohlrabi and green peppers were placed on the tables along with bottles of oil, vinegar, salt and pepper. Students over the age of fourteen were selected alphabetically on a weekly rotation system to help with the meals. Each student was served a single hard-boiled egg and small glass of milk. Avi introduced Fritz to several other boys and girls qualifying, "He no speak Hebrew," which seemed to translate to, "Don't waste your time with him." Seeing how nervous Hillel was to speak German in front of the other kids, Fritz hoped to find a time alone with him.

Lehman stood up and banged his spoon on the table until the children quieted down. He then announced in Hebrew, "Boys and girls, we have a new student here today, Fritz Hausman." He continued in German indicating Fritz, "Please stand, Fritz, so that everyone can get to know you." Embarrassed by his 'safari' outfit and wishing Lehman hadn't addressed him in German, Fritz awkwardly stood. Avi, pretending to sneeze, let out, "Yekke!" The children all laughed. Lehman immediately banged his spoon on the table. "That's enough," he said in Hebrew. "It is all of our jobs to make every new student here feel welcome." After a quick blessing of the food, Lehman invited the children to eat.

Fritz observed the students politely vying for tomatoes and vegetables. Far from a free-for-all, manners were evidently important. The children then sliced up what they had selected and flavored it with oil, vinegar, salt and pepper. Fritz took an unclaimed cucumber, the only vegetable of the bunch that he liked. He hated tomatoes and kohlrabi, never understanding why his father would force him to finish them at the dinner table when he would later only throw them up. Fritz watched as Hillel cracked his egg on the table, removed its shell and ate it while washing it down with the milk. Trying to do the same, Fritz almost spat out the pungent, non-homogenized milk. "How can you drink that?" he asked Hillel in disgust. Before Hillel could respond, Avi jumped in, "You no like? I take." Fritz shrugged, "It's yours." Hillel looked at Fritz with concern, but held his tongue. Avi downed the milk, slapping the glass on the table as he told Fritz first in Hebrew then English, "Good stuff."

Lehman came over to ask Fritz first in German then in Hebrew, "Are you getting along okay?" Fritz nodded politely. As if fishing for a compliment, Lehman probed, "And how is you're breakfast?" Imitating Avi, Fritz stated in Hebrew, "Good stuff." Lehman smiled, "I see you're catching on." Avi cut in, "We teach him." With a slight nod, Lehman smiled to Avi before telling Fritz, "Come by my office when you're done. There are a few things I'd like to go

over with you." Fritz shrugged, "I'm done now."
Lehman looked at the half eaten cucumber on his
plate. Avi assured in English, "It's okay, we finish and
take away plate for him."

∞

Leading Fritz through the compound, Lehman
pointed out the different buildings. Once inside his
office, Lehman sat behind his desk, motioning Fritz
to take the chair facing him, as he matter-of-factly
stated, "So, let's get down to business. Maybe you
have sensed that being German here can be a bit of a
challenge." Fritz, wondering how he could change
his background, nodded awkwardly. Lehman smiled,
"I should know, even though everyone has to be nice
to me. But it might be a good idea for you to use your
Hebrew name. Were you given one at birth?" Fritz,
having no idea, shook his head with a shrug. "Would
you like to have one?" Lehman asked. Not having
thought about it, Fritz gave an uncertain nod.
Lehman smiled, "Good, any in mind?" Fritz shook his
head again. Lehman asked, "Well, is there someone
with a Hebrew name that you particularly admire?"
After a moments thought, Fritz stated, "Haim
Arlosoroff," though he wasn't even sure that Haim
was a Hebrew name. Lehman nodded, "He was a
great man. It's a tragedy that his life was cut so
short."

On June 16, 1933, only a week after negotiating the
Haavara Agreement with Hitler, Haim Arlosoroff
was assassinated while walking with his wife, Sima,
on the beach in Tel Aviv. He was only thirty-four
years old. There are many theories to his unsolved

murder, but the two major Jewish parties of the Yishuv (the Jewish people of Palestine before the State of Israel) seemed most likely responsible. Surprisingly, of all the groups, the Nazis were never suspected.

To Fritz, Arlosoroff was a true hero, paying with his life in his battle for peace between Arabs and Jews. Lehman affirmed, "Haim is good. It means 'life'. So, Haim, your Hebrew name is decided?" Haim gave a nod, adding, "If I dropped the last 'n' in Hausmann, would that make it less German?" Lehman shrugged, "Perhaps." Looking at Haim's form in front of him, he added, "But it appears that I already omitted it. If you want, I can put it in." Fritz shook his head, "No, that's good."

As Lehman led Haim to the schoolhouse he advised, "It may be best for you to focus only on Hebrew this first week." Inside the building, Lehman summoned the Hebrew teacher out of her classroom, and explained that Haim would be staying for all four of her morning classes. The teacher and Lehman then spoke briefly in Hebrew before he took off.

"Class, this is Haim Hausman," the teacher articulated in Hebrew to the children of mixed ages. "What do you say?" "Shalom Haim," resonated from the class. In Hebrew, the teacher told Haim to take a seat, pointing to a free desk in the back of the room. For the next four hours, knowing that his life there depended on learning Hebrew, he struggled, as he never had before, to pay attention to the teacher.

At noon, after the last class, with the fundamentals of Hebrew swirling around in his head, the teacher was able to make Haim understand in Hebrew that he was to follow Sheila, a pretty girl in his class, to the farm.

As they walked, he deduced through broken Hebrew that Sheila had come alone from Russia the month before. Unlike some, having survived a dangerous, oppressive world taught Sheila to be strong, to fight for what she wanted. And Haim immediately respected the strength emanating for within her. He followed her to the shed of the flower garden where a large, burley man was working with seedlings. Sheila introduced Haim to the foreman, who handed her a brown bag and she went off to the other girls working in the garden.

Haim, still in his pressed shorts and shirt, nervously stood in front of the looming figure in ragged, dirt covered work clothes. Handing Haim a large tray of seedlings, the foreman said in Hebrew, "Follow me." Fritz, frozen, choked out, "Wait! Do you speak English?" The foreman nodded, "A little, why?" Haim asked, "What part of the farm am I to work?" The foreman, confused why he would ask such a question, shrugged, "Here, of course." Haim practically stuttered, "But, I can't. Only girls work the flower garden." Raising an eyebrow, the foreman asked, "Do I look like a girl?" Haim nervously shook his head. The foreman asked, as if knowing the answer, "You work farm before?" Haim glumly shook his head. The foreman, picking up a small brown bag, said, "Follow me." He spoke in Hebrew as they walked. Haim, unable to understand, nodded whenever seemed appropriate.

The foreman had Haim put down the tray by a small patch of land, explaining with a mix of Hebrew and English how to plant the seedlings. "After finish job, take half-hour lunch break." He handed Haim the brown lunch bag and headed back to the barn.

Haim quickly finished the planting, and made his way over to Hillel in the field of the nearby vegetable garden. "Want some help?" Haim asked in German. Hillel shook his head: "Are you working in the vegetable garden?" "No, the flower garden," Haim said as if it left a bad taste. "But I'm on my lunch break. Maybe we can eat together." Glancing around to check that no one was watching, Hillel nodded and picked up his brown lunch bag: "From now on eat all your breakfast. It has to last you all morning." Haim shrugged, "Then I hope it's better tomorrow." Hillel looked at him quizzically: "If you didn't like it today you won't like it tomorrow. It's always the same." Though disappointed, Haim had never cared much about food. He shrugged it off, glad to at least be speaking German.

With his clothes already dirtied from planting the seedlings, Haim gladly dirtied them more as they sat on the ground eating their lunch. Having had nothing but water since his small breakfast, he realized how hungry he was. "This isn't bad," he said with surprise. In Germany, he would never have considered eating a chickpea sandwich, but for some reason, it tasted good. When he told Hillel his new name, Hillel nodded as if the change was expected.

Haim asked, "Do you mind working the vegetable garden? I thought only girls worked our jobs." Hillel only shrugged. Surprised by Hillel's calm reaction, he asked, "Will I get made fun of for it?" Hillel gave a slight nod of resignation, "Sometimes, and you get tricks played on you, but you get used to it." Haim admired Hillel for not caring, but knew that he couldn't feel the same. "Too bad we're not in the same group." Hillel nodded: "They try to split us up so we learn Hebrew."

As they talked, Haim discovered that Hillel's father had been a math professor and his mother a music teacher. They left Germany to stay with a cousin on a new moshav (similar to a kibbutz) about an hour from Ben Shemen. His father's years of analyzing equations and his mother's flute training from the Hochschule Conservatory did little to prepare them for the heavy manual labor of building a new farm. Leaving for the fields before dawn, only returning after sundown with aching bodies and hands blistered, left Hillel mostly on his own. As difficult as it was to break up the family, his parents decided it was best for Hillel to be at Ben Shemen, where he would not only be safer, but would also receive an education, guidance and supervision. And they could visit as often as possible.

Haim sensed that Hillel kept a certain distance from him. Was it because he was a newcomer, didn't speak Hebrew, or just didn't fit in? Perhaps, like Haim, after having to leave everything behind in Germany, Hillel was reluctant to get close to anybody. Whatever the reason, Haim didn't blame him. If his own family was nearby, he might have also been more guarded, as he had been in Germany. As they finished their lunch, Haim said, "I should probably go back to the flower garden." Hillel responded with a nod, and the boys returned to their respective chores.

For the rest of the day, Haim pushed wheelbarrows full of cow manure the half mile from the stables to the flower garden, where the girls would spread it out. Nodding to the foreman whenever seemed appropriate proved to be a mistake, for at the end of the day, the foreman made him stay late to finish everything he had unknowingly agreed to do. When he was finally allowed to leave, he joined the last group of boys heading to the communal shower.

Haim watched anxiously as the boys stripped down to nothing. As filthy as he was, his heart pounded at the thought of being seen naked. Only his doctor had seen him without any clothes on since he was a very small child. Trying to hide his embarrassment, he quickly took off his clothes, hung them on a hook like the other boys, and rushed under the shower hoping to be seen for as short a time as possible. With all of the healthy looking tanned boys, he felt like a skinny, white frog. To his relief, no one seemed to take much notice.

Surviving the showers, he made his way back to his room, relieved that Avi and the twins had already left for dinner so that he could change in private. On his bed he found a small pile of folded clothes with a note pinned to them: "A student outgrew these. You may find them useful." The "L" for the signature undoubtedly stood for "Lehman". Holding up the clothes, they looked more like rags sewn together than shirts and pants. Cracking a smile, he thought of his father and how he would look if he came down to dinner in them. Leaving the work clothes on the bed, he put on his most casual long pants and shirt and headed to the commissary.

On entering the hall, he was pointed to a serving table where he picked another cucumber from a large bowl of vegetables and a student dished out a bowl of stew for him. Avi, with the twins in the same seats as at breakfast, immediately called out, "Hey Fritz, we save you seat!" Haim, making his way over, squeezed into the small space Avi made available. "Why you no wear new clothes?" Avi asked. Haim, taken aback, questioned, "New?" He had thought they were only meant for work in the fields. Avi shrugged, "Yeah, you get clothes like us." Having been so concerned about his own appearance, Haim hadn't realized that the rags Lehman left for him were similar to what all of the boys were wearing. Avi smirked, "You like flower garden, Fritz? See you work late." Haim shrugged, "It's okay. And my name is now 'Haim'." Avi, nodding with approval, raised his glass of water, "Le Haim! To life!" The boys toasted. Avi smiled, "Haim, good name. Who tell you to pick it?" Haim shook his head, "I did, after Haim Arlosoroff."

Avi practically spat out his water, "Arlosoroff, the coward? Ben-Gurion kill that traitor." Momentarily stunned, Haim asked, "Coward? He risked his life to negotiate with Hitler. If it weren't for Arlosoroff I wouldn't be here." In a mix of English and Hebrew, Avi fired back, "Arlosoroff no risk life. He friends with Hitler. He friends with Arabs. Ben-Gurion knows better. He kill Arabs and Nazis before they kill us." Haim asked in disbelief, "How? Arabs outnumber us ten to one." Avi shook his head, "No matter, only good Arab is dead Arab." Haim scoffed, "That's what the Nazis say about us." Avi slammed down his fist. "You and Arlosoroff want everyone to hold hands and walk off in sunset. I from Ukraine. I know better. In Ukraine, we no say 'please and thank you.' We fight to live. I no negotiate. I kill Hitler if I get chance!"

Haim shrugged, "Great, go kill him?" Avi firmly nodded while pointing, "If I there, I do it, 'cause I no coward like you and Arlosoroff!" Haim retorted, "You're no genius either. If Arlosoroff walked in there and tried to kill Hitler he'd be dead in seconds." Avi stared at Haim trying to figure out if he really just called him stupid. Though the same height, Avi, a year older, was clearly stronger.

After Arlosoroff formed the Communist Mapai Labor party, he and Ben-Gurion, its leader (and the future first Prime Minister of Israel) strongly clashed. Both men dreamed of establishing a Jewish State, but Ben-Gurion pushed for mass Jewish immigration to settle the land in order to lay claim to it, while Arlosoroff argued that ignoring British policy could strengthen Arab-British alliance.

Though some believed Ben-Gurion capable of doing anything to achieve his goal, radical members of the Revisionists, the Zionist right-wing nationalist party and Mapai's opposition, were probably to blame for Arlosoroff's assassination. Arlosoroff had spoken out against their attacks on the British, and since they considered negotiating with Nazis as unpardonable, Arlosoroff had crossed the line with the Ha'avara Agreement, no matter how many Jews it saved. Perhaps worst of all, in April of that year, Arlosoroff organized the historic first Luncheon of Zionist and Arab leaders at the King David Hotel in Jerusalem. Those opposed to Jewish/Arab relations and a bi-nationalistic state viewed it as treason. Some Revisionists even openly questioned Arlosoroff's right to live, and the Mizrachi, the main party of religious Zionism, demanded that he resign from his post.

Haim Arlosoroff's wife, Sima, the only eyewitness, identified two members of the Revisionist Party as the hit men, one of whom was found "guilty" and sentenced to death. But he was later acquitted, undoubtedly because of the many high-ranking Revisionists in the Yishuv's court. Many Revisionists, however, blamed radical Arab leaders for Arlosoroff's death, while other Revisionists claimed that Ben-Gurion and the Mapai committed the murder in order to frame them.

Whoever was responsible, it seemed a sad commentary to Haim that Arlosoroff was apparently murdered by his own people after dedicating his life to the Zionist cause.

CHAPTER 6

EVEN THOUGH AVI was stronger, it looked to Haim as if there was no choice but to fight. He would never agree that Arlosoroff was a coward, and Avi seemed determined to bend Haim to his will. If Haim didn't stand up to him now, the intimidation would never end. He wished he had worn Julius's WWI belt for defense, but it didn't matter. Years of dealing with Nazi Youths taught him that, in the long run, accepting a possible beating was better than cowering. Seated on Avi's right, Haim brace himself for the first strike as Avi swung his arm backhanded towards his chest to knock him off of the bench. Haim instinctively threw up his left arm, blocking Avi's fist while grabbing the dull regulation army knife with his right hand and aiming it at Avi's neck. The other children went silent as the boys locked eyes.

Professor Melnick, alerted by the sudden hush, abandoned his dinner to make his way to the boys. As Melnick approached, Avi's grimace turned into a cracked smile. "Okay, you like Arlosoroff for being friends with Hitler and Arabs. Maybe someday you learn, is important to pick right friends." Haim, relaxed by Avi's sudden change, shrugged slightly saying, "Maybe." "Everything okay here?" Melnick asked. Avi smiled, "Sure, we play. He good. Has me going."

For the rest of the evening, Avi acted as if nothing had happened, as if they were the best of friends.

Though it was a friendship Haim wouldn't trust, he couldn't help but question if there was some truth in what Avi had said. Why didn't the Jews in Germany kill Hitler? Why didn't he? Hadn't he fantasized of disguising himself as a Nazi Youth, infiltrating Nazi headquarters and killing Hitler along with the rest of the Nazi leaders? But never considering that he might actually get away with it, it remained a fantasy. Did that make him, as Avi said, a coward?

Still deprived of sleep since his long journey to Palestine, Haim had trouble sleeping again that night. Not only because of his fight with Avi, but due to the hot sun he had taken his shirt off while pushing wheelbarrows full of cow manure. By nighttime, his back had turned lobster red, and with the burning pain he could find no comfortable position.

Lying awake, he wished that he were back home in Bingen. But his home was now in Palestine. He had to make the best of it. It was his only chance of getting his parents out of Germany. And he had grown to admire Ben Shemen's lack of pretension. If his father could only appreciated it, they might have been there together. Why was his father so rigid? Why did he have to hire somebody to do such simple tasks as winding a clock or hanging a painting? To Julius, those jobs were beneath him. Maybe Palestine would teach him to enjoy doing things on his own.

Haim knew better than to ever mention that in his letters home. Haim's description of Ben Shemen to his parents was similar to propaganda: "Palestine is our homeland. I know how happy you'll be here. You must come to see for yourself." Knowing that Nazi officials would probably burn the letter before it ever reached his parents, he continued writing on the hopes of one getting through.

∞

Those first weeks passed slowly as Haim adjusted to the routine of four hours of class, lunch in the field, four hours of working the farm, a stew, soup or casserole for dinner, and a full night's sleep from utter exhaustion. After standing up to Avi, both kept a certain distance. He had hoped to make other friends, but the language barrier seemed to separate him from the other students. He told himself that it didn't matter, he was used to being on his own and once he learned Hebrew things would be different.

With determination, and no distraction from family or friends, he focused as he never had on his schoolwork. In Germany, he considered himself lazy, content to spend the rest of his life just playing with his gang. It terrified him to think of actually having to one-day work for a living. His father had drummed into him the importance of school for his future, even hiring a tutor who came everyday to help with his homework. But Fritz quickly learned that by procrastinating the tutor would eventually just tell him the answers.

However, he did love to read, mostly the fantastical novels of Karl May. May, incarcerated for theft and fraud, made good use of his time in jail by writing adventure stories covering the history of the foreign lands he wrote about, all of which he learned from books in the prison library. Late at night under his covers with a flashlight, so that his father wouldn't know he was awake, Fritz was transported by May's books into exotic lands. Whether it was Morocco, Kurdistan, or America, Fritz then studied them on the map, and at school they became his best subjects.

But at Ben Shemen he learned how to learn. And classes became interesting, even exciting. On the night of his arrival, Haim was impressed by Professor Melnick's stoic demeanor as he sat with a rifle protecting the compound, but as a biology teacher Melnick shined. Though Haim began excelling in mathematics, Hebrew and Palestinian Arabic, he fell in love with biology. Instead of engineering, as he had wanted to do in Germany, he decided that biology would be his calling.

At Ben Shemen, he also became healthier. After several months of working in the flower garden, he was moved to the vegetable garden. A far cry from working at the Falhar with horses, tractors and machinery, but a step in the right direction. His first day in the fields, a Lithuanian boy he was working with (a cousin to Ariel Sharon, the future prime minister of Israel) suddenly picked a full, ripe, red tomato, cut it in half with a knife that he grabbed from his belt, sprinkled it with salt from a shaker that he pulled out of his pants' pocket and handed it to Haim. "Here, try this," he said before taking a large bite out of the other half. Haim, liking the boy and not wanting to offend him, took a bite even though he knew that it would make him sick. To his surprise, he not only found it delicious, he felt no nausea. He would never know why. Perhaps the illness was psychosomatic. But from that day on, he was never again sick from eating vegetables.

After learning Hebrew and tanning like the other boys he still didn't have any close friends. He assumed that the "Yekke" label had stuck, but he told himself that it didn't matter. He would work hard and once his family joined him there, things would be different. He never complained to his superiors for fear that his father would find out that he wasn't fitting in. So, his write-ups continued: "He's quiet … keeps to himself."

CHAPTER 7

FOR SEVERAL WEEKS, Einat carried with her the notes of what she planned to say on the radio. 'THE VOICE OF ISRAEL' had already postponed her interview several times. She didn't mind. She was receiving chemo every three weeks, and the last postponement gave her time to recover from a recent treatment. It also gave her time to gather more information, though her therapist assured her that she had enough. But knowing that the show might be her one chance at finding Haim Hausman, she continually ran over what she had uncovered to see if she had missed anything.

Her initial quest to document the life of Fania Bergstein brought her to the daughters of Ilse Kantor, Fania's close friend and illustrator of her first book, 'COME TO ME SWEET BUTTERFLY.' Ilse, born in Prague in 1911 to a wealthy Jewish family, narrowly escaped the Nazi occupation of Czechoslovakia in 1939. Living in a tent for her first year in Palestine at the Kibbutz Gvat, she helped replace the men off to war by learning to fix kerosene stoves, farming tools, machinery, and doing anything else that was necessary. At night, after long, exhausting days, she drew stories for the children.

Ilse met her husband, the German conductor/composer, Abraham Deus, at the kibbutz in 1941, and was pregnant with their first daughter, Teresa, in 1944, around the same time that the newly formed KM Press (the kibbutz publishing house) agreed to publish Fania Bergstein's poem, 'COME TO ME SWEET BUTTERFLY'.

Fania had become a seamstress for the kibbutz when her heart condition, first diagnosed when she was eighteen, forced her to stop heavy manual labor. Though fabric was hard to come by, for the esteem of the children she took extra care in the clothes she made, as she had with her poetry. Far from searching for an artistic breakthrough, she introduced farming culture into Israeli children's literature to help bring the children pride and joy in their life on the farm. With Fania's influence, Ilse's art also reflected their life on the kibutz.

When Fania asked Ilse to do the illustrations for 'COME TO ME SWEET BUTTERFLY' Ilse practically stammered: "But, I can't. I'm not a real artist." Ilse had loved art since early childhood. She even studied at the renowned Academy of Fine Arts in Paris. But the harsh critiques from the teachers of the Academy discouraged her from a professional career. Fania encouraged her: "Of course you are. You're the only one I would trust with this. You know these children. This for the them." Ilse, loving Fania's poem, worked late at night painting illustrations of the daily lives of children and adults of the kibbutz, all in clothes that Fania had sewn.

The book was published in 1945, not long after Ilse gave birth to Teresa. And Fania dedicated it to the child. After the horrors of WWII, as Fania and Ilse had hoped, it seemed to bring the children some pleasure and normalcy. Little thought was given to its wider circulation. Now in its 55th edition, known for it's beautiful poem, it has become the most popular Israeli children's book of all time. Fania, Ilse, their families and their kibbutz have never received a penny for it, nor ever expected to.

Searching online, Einat was able to locate Ilse's daughter, Teresa, who was living at a nearby kibbutz. During their initial phone conversation, Teresa felt comfortable enough to ask Einat if she would like to come over to see the original 1945 illustrations of "COME TO ME SWEET BUTTERFLY." Hoping to have an exhibition of the early kibbutz artists, Einat jumped at the chance: "Of course, when is convenient for you?"

A few hours later, while looking at the original illustrations in Teresa's simple, but comfortable home, Einat felt the thrill of glimpsing back into a world that so intrigued her. Turning the last page, she asked, "Do you have other original drawings of your mother's works?" Teresa showed her eight magic lanterns; picture stories drawn on long strips of paper lit from behind by a candle. One of the magic lanterns was of 'AND THERE WAS EVENING.' Einat looked at it, bewildered, wondering why the drawings were so different than the famous Haim Hausman illustrations. She couldn't help but ask, "Why did your mother do the magic lantern for the book and not the actual illustrations?" Teresa sighed, "She did the illustrations. And against Fania's wishes they were replaced with Haim Hausman's. I don't think my mother ever got over it." Einat was taken aback, "I'm sorry. I had no idea. Do you have the originals?" Teresa shook her head. "My sister has those. To see them, you'll have to ask her. We no longer speak."

Teresa explained that Fania not only dedicated 'COME TO ME SWEET BUTTERFLY' to her, but also a translation of 'WEE WILLIE WINKY' into Hebrew. Teresa's father then set it to music and it became the famous 'TERESA'S LULLABY'. Einat knew it well. Teresa shrugged, "So, I got the lullaby and the illustrations for the book that was published, while my sister got no lullaby and the illustrations that were never published. Unless I give her the illustrations, she won't be happy. But if I give them to her, I won't be happy. So, there you have it."

Einat left puzzling over how the seemingly innocent act of dedicating a lullaby could destroy the relationship between two sisters. She immediately contacted the younger sister, Tamar, in hopes of seeing the unpublished illustrations of 'AND THERE WAS EVENING'. Tamar seemed delighted that Einat showed interest, and promised to send her photocopies. Like her sister, she also had no idea of the identity of Haim Hausman or why his illustrations replaced her mother's. "The one thing I do know," Tamar stated, "was that Fania wanted my mother's illustrations. She even refused to submit the translation until my mother was finished so they could be submitted together as a final product." Perplexed, Einat asked, "The translation?" Tamar sighed, "Yes, few people know this, but the classic Israeli children's book 'AND THERE WAS EVENING' is actually based on an excerpt from an obscure

Hans Christian Andersen story." Einat was stunned. She had always thought it to be the original work of Fania Bergstein. Tamar assured her, "Don't blame Fania. My mother said that Fania hated the publishing house for omitting Andersen's name. But even though it may not have been Fania's original story, to her credit, nobody knows of the Andersen story, and Fania's beautiful poem has become a timeless classic."

Einat, more perplexed than ever, contacted the publishing house to find out why they didn't credit Anderson and why they chose Haim Hausman's illustrations over Ilse Kantor's. They had no marketing division with children's focus groups back then, so some adults had to have made the decision. "'COME TO ME SWEET BUTTERLFY' is a best seller," said one of KM's children's book editors. "I can't imagine any publisher rejecting the illustrator's next work." "Then how do you explain it?" Einat asked. He considered, "Maybe Haim Hausman switched the illustrations himself." "Is that possible?" Einat asked, intrigued. "How would he have done it?" The editor pondered, "Maybe he wasn't a he. Maybe Haim Hausman, like George Eliot, was an alias for a female artist." Einat, confused, asked, "But how would that explain how the illustrations were switched?" The editor mused, "Maybe she slept with the publisher." Einat, giving up, added, "Or maybe Haim Hausman was a mobster who had the mafia put a horse's head in the publisher's bed." The editor laughed, "Maybe." Einat was passed on to other editors at KM, but they also appeared to be in the dark.

CHAPTER 8

HAIM'S HARD WORK paid off. After six months of working in the vegetable garden, he was moved to the Falhar. Having had more than his share of tricks played on newcomers, he believed those days were now over.

For his first day at the Falhar, Avi told him that it was tradition to haul the chicken manure to the vegetable garden foreman, "To say thanks and make him feel good for all he teach you." As Haim rolled the wheelbarrow piled high with the dark, porous, smelly chicken excrement he smiled to the foreman: "Hi, this is to thank you for everything. Where do you want it?" The foreman stared at the pile in disbelief. "Back in the chicken. What would I do with it?" Haim hesitantly asked, "It isn't tradition for me to bring it to you?" Suppressing a laugh, the foreman shook his head. "No, take it to the back of the compost. Eventually it'll break down into fertilizer." Seeing Haim downcast from another prank, the foreman picked up two freshly harvested apples from a large basket and tossed them to him. "Here, thanks for the shit." Surprised, Haim caught them.

As he began walking the path from the compost to the warehouse to get supplies for the Falhar, he took a bite from one of the tart, fresh apples, putting the other in his pants' pocket.

Finishing the apple, he stopped as he saw a majestic black Arabian stallion galloping in one of the fields.

With his upturned nostrils and high tail, Haim had never seen a horse as beautiful. In Bingen, horses were heavy, built for pulling carriages and plows. Though lighter, this one looked as if he would sooner break a plow than pull it. The horse came to a halt as Haim climbed over the fence and began slowly walking towards him. When within ten yards, the young stallion bucked and reared, showing off his strength. Haim stood frozen, mesmerized, watching in awe at what looked like a charger to the gods. The stallion, calming down, looked directly at Haim, and letting out a huff, trotted over to him. Haim was too frozen to run.

The horse halted a few steps in front of him. Haim stood there, uncertain what to do. Perhaps sensing the boy's admiration, the horse took a step closer. Transfixed, feeling the horse's breath, Haim slowly lifted his right hand to gently pet the tip of his nose. The horse lifted his head and Haim patted his strong, shiny neck feeling the bits of dried mud caked into his coat. "Good boy, why are you alone out here?" The horse lowered his head again as Haim scratched behind his ears.

Remembering the apple, Haim took it out of his pocket: "You hungry?" The horse began nibbling at it. "Careful, boy," he said, concerned that the powerful horse would bite his hand. But the horse got the apple between his lips, swallowing it after a few short grinds in his powerful jaw. Sniffing around Haim's pants' pockets, he began looking for more. Laughing, Haim said, "Whoa, that's it boy." As the horse kept sniffing his pants, Haim said, "Okay, I'll see what I can get for you."

Haim ran back to the vegetable garden, pulled a bunch of carrots out of the ground, and dusted them off as he ran back to the horse. Seeing Haim coming from around the bend, the stallion let out a whinny and galloped to him. Haim climbed over the fence and carefully fed him the carrots until they were all gone. The horse sniffed around his pants' pockets again. "Sorry, boy, I'll get in trouble if I get caught stealing any more." The horse nuzzled Haim as he affectionately pet his neck. "Don't worry, I'll try to get more after work. I'm sure a horse as nice as you deserves it."

Suddenly, a farmer ran towards them in the field yelling, "Get away from that horse! He's a killer!" Haim stepped back as the horse violently reared up. The Farmer's eyes widened as the horse turned and charged him. Quickly hightailing it back, the farmer made it over the fence just before the horse could get to him. The stallion pranced threateningly back and forth warning the farmer to stay back. The farmer yelled to Haim, "Jump over the fence. I'll distract him!" Antagonizing the horse, the farmer sneered, "I'll turn you into glue you dumb beast!"

Haim ran towards the horse, calling to the farmer, "Stop it! You're upsetting him!" The horse went to Haim, burying his head in his chest as he comforted him. "It's okay, boy. He didn't mean to scare you." In disbelief, the farmer quipped, "Scare him?" Haim snapped, "Yeah, how'd you like it if someone ran at you screaming you're a killer?" The farmer shrugged, "If I was this crazy horse I'd agree." Haim continued calming the horse as he said to the farmer, "You're the one who looks crazy to me."

The farmer, perplexed, watched as the horse nuzzled the boy. "Never seen him let anyone touch him before. We can't even get him in a stall." Haim called back, "Try not threatening turning him into glue." The farmer, still shocked, asked, "How long you known him?" Haim shrugged, "We just met. What's his name?" "Amon," the farmer said, still perplexed, "after the Egyptian king of the gods." Haim smiled at the horse while gently holding his head. "Amon, king of the gods. That suits you." The farmer smirked, "I could think of better." Ignoring the comment, Haim asked, "Who owns him? Why can't they touch him?" The farmer, still calling from the other side of the fence, explained, "He was a gift from King Abdullah to Haim Arlosoroff. After Arlosoroff died, the widow Arlosoroff donated him to the school."

King Abdullah, the Emir of the British mandate of Transjordan (renamed Jordan in 1949,) only became a recognized king by the West when Jordan gained its independence in 1946. The only Arab leader considered a true moderate by the West, he remained an ally throughout World War II, maintaining order in Transjordan and helping suppress a pro-Nazi uprising in Iraq. His friendship with Arlosoroff, and willingness to work with him, was undoubtedly another reason for Arlosoroff's assassination.

Haim's eyes widened as he asked, "He was Arlosoroff's horse?" The farmer shook his head.

"When he was a colt. Not like this. If Arlosoroff's widow knew anything about horses she'd never allow this monster near children."

Haim quietly assured Amon, "Don't listen, boy. You're no monster." Then calling to the farmer, "Maybe he's just unhappy here and wants to go home. Maybe he'd be different if you treated him better." Haim may have been projecting, but even though Amon was full-grown, he sensed that he was too young to be taken from his mother and left in this desolate land. Perhaps Amon sensed the same of Haim. Whatever the reason, he somehow trusted this boy. "Who takes care of him?" The farmer shrugged, "No one. We put food out for him. That's it." Haim gently pet Amon's head as he quietly assured, "I'll take care of you, boy." He then called to the farmer, "Who do I talk to about doing it?" The farmer scoffed, "You? Not possible. He's too dangerous." But Haim's mind was set.

∞

After finishing his work that first day at the Falhar, Haim gathered as many apples as he could fit in his pockets from the orchard. Amon whinnied and galloped towards him when he saw Haim coming down the path. While feeding him several apples from the other side of the fence, Haim took a few bites himself. He then climbed over to play with Amon in the field. Amon trotted after him trying to get the apples, running in circles around him as Haim held them behind his back. When the last apple was finished, Amon followed Haim back through the field to the edge of the path where Haim climbed up on the fence to pet him more easily.

Somewhat blinded by the setting sun, Haim could just make out two men walking towards them. He soon saw that one of the men was the farmer, and the other was Professor Pearlman, the stocky, bowlegged man who was guarding the compound with Professor Melnick that first night. As the men came closer, Amon became agitated. Haim jumped off of the fence to calm him, "It's okay, boy. I won't let them hurt you." The men stopped, watching as Haim gently calmed Amon.

Sensing not to get any closer, the farmer called out, "I told the foreman you want to take care of the crazy horse!" Haim called back, "Just 'cause he doesn't like you, doesn't mean he's crazy!" The two men suppressed a laugh. "So can I?" Haim ask. Professor Pearlman called back, "You think that's a good idea? He's too much for any of us to handle." Haim nodded, "Yeah, it's a good idea." The men shared a smile. Pearlman called back, "We'll have to talk about it. I doubt Professor Lehman will approve. What if he hurts you?" Haim shook his head. "He won't. He's nice, if you're nice to him."

Haim tried to have Amon befriend the two men. But as they got close Amom became too skittish. The men soon gave up, and went to wash for dinner.

Arriving late that evening at the mess hall, Haim sat alone to quickly eat and get back to Amon. While scarfing down his stew, he suddenly saw Lehman standing by his side. "Professor Pearlman tells me you want to take care of Amon." Haim asked hopefully, "Can I?" Lehman gave a somber shrug. "Come to my office when you're finished."

Haim, concerned, watched anxiously as Lehman walked away. He turned as he heard Avi from behind: "Pretty funny today with the chicken shit, wasn't it?" Haim shrugged, "Yeah, you got me." "You not mad?" Avi asked nonchalantly. Haim shook his head, "No, forget it. It's probably the smartest thing you've ever done." Avi smiled before asking uncomfortably, "You just tell Lehman?" Haim shook his head again. "Don't worry, you're safe." Avi smiled, "You're okay. What Lehman want?" Haim shrugged, "Nothing. I may get some work at the stable. That's all." Haim went back to eating signaling Avi to leave.

In reality, Haim wasn't angry with him. If it hadn't been for the prank, he may not have met Amon. But rather than risk being made fun of for his friendship with a horse, he preferred keeping it to himself.

∞

Through the open door of the office, Haim saw Lehman in discussion with Pearlman. "Come in," Lehman sternly said. "Take a seat. We were just discussing the problem." "What problem?" Haim ask, readying for battle. Lehman qualified, "Of what to do with the horse." Haim, taken aback, insisted, "It's no problem. You need someone to take care of Amon, and I want to do it. I'll get up early, stay late. I promise, it won't take any time away from my work." Lehman explained, "We're more concerned for your safety…" Haim interrupted, addressing Pearlman, "But you saw him. You know he won't hurt me." Lehman interrupted, "Even if that's true, we weren't planning on keeping him." Haim's eyes widened, "Where's he going?" Professor Pearlman cut in, "This is a poor land. Where do you think horses go that can't work?" Having no idea, Haim shook his head. Pearlman stated, "The slaughterhouse." Haim blurted, "But, you can't, you can't kill him! He was a gift from King Abdullah." Pearlman nodded, "That's the only reason he's still alive. We offered to give him back, but the King's secretary told us returning a gift would be an insult. He said we should do with him as we please. Still, killing him might be taken as an offence."

Lehman tried calming Haim. "I'm sorry, until today, we didn't think he could be trained. Maybe…" Pearlman cut in, "And he probably can't. Even if he's not crazy, even if he was only abused or something, no farmer in Palestine, Jew or Arab, wants a horse that can't work. He's a plaything for the wealthy. Which means here he's worth more dead here than alive."

"I'll buy him!" Haim stated. "I'll work extra, eat less, do whatever it takes to cover his cost." Lehman shook his head, "You must see that you can't have a pet horse. Everybody in Ben Shemen contributes, even the animals." Haim asserted, "He'll work." Pearlman scoffed, "At what, steeple chases, trotting around in a circle?" "No, plowing fields, with me!" Lehman shrugged to Pearlman, "Amon may not have been intended for work, but it appears that Haim will never forgive us if we don't give him a chance to pull his weight." Haim's eyes widened with hope. Before he could say anything, Lehman warned, "You have to understand, this is extremely unusual, but we are allowing only a very short trial. If he continues to appear to be a danger, that will be it." Haim, exhaling, smiled to Lehman and Pearlman, "He won't. I promise."

∞

That night, guided by the moon, Professor Pearlman walked the path to the field. As he suspected, Haim was with Amon. Seeing Pearlman, Amon began to shy. Haim quickly calmed him, "It's okay, boy." Pearlman, shaking his head, said, "You've got your work cut out for you," Haim shook his head: "You don't know him." Pearlman asked, "So, what's your secret? You give him apples?" Haim answered, "No, he was nice to me before that." Pearlman smirked, "So you did give him apples." He took Haim's silence as a "yes." Pearlman reproached, "Everything on a kibbutz is communal property. When you give him apples you're stealing from everyone." Haim countered, "He lives here too. If it's communal, why can't he have them?" "Because he hasn't worked for them! That's why. From now on, he eats what he's allowed!" Haim begrudgingly nodded. Pearlman asked, "You ever train a horse before?" Haim hesitantly shook his head. Pearlman nodded, "You have any idea what you're getting yourself into? He probably likes you 'cause he knows you're a sucker. How do you expect to train him?" Haim shrugged, "We'll figure it out. But he won't do anything he doesn't want to." Pearlman scoffed, "Okay, make him want to go in a stall."

Though uncertain, Haim nodded confidently, "Sure. Come on, boy," Amon followed Haim as he walked in the direction of the stables. As Haim began walking faster Amon kept up until he was trotting by Haim's side. Pearlman cracked a smile as he watched the boy and horse disappear into the darkness.

Making it to the barn, Haim caught his breath. After Amon drank from the water trough, he followed Haim towards the barn. Seeing Amon shy as they got too close, Haim assured, "It's okay, boy. You don't have to go in." Amon took a few nervous steps back and watched as Haim slowly entered the dark barn.

Finding a kerosene lantern hanging on the inner doorframe, Haim lit it with matches resting nearby on a horizontal beam of the exposed wall. As he investigated, he found two large plow horses asleep in their stalls. Hay was stored in the stall next to them. The remaining three stalls were empty. Finding an old rake and shovel, Haim hung the lantern on the inner doorframe of the free stall nearest to the entrance, so that Amon could look out if he wanted to, and began clearing the old bedding and dried manure. As he went to get the wheelbarrow outside of the barn's entrance, he saw Amon's head peaking in watching him. "Hey, boy," he said, as he stopped to pet him. "I bet you'll like it here when I'm done." Amon, standing just outside the entrance, watched as Haim got the wheelbarrow and pushed it back into the stall.

Walking the longer route of the path, Pearlman saw light coming from inside the barn and focused in on what looked like a shiny, black horse's hind-end sticking out of the entrance. After passing some tall brush, he saw that the shiny black hind-end was gone, and questioned if his eyes were playing tricks on him.

Haim was laying down bedding when he heard hoof steps from behind. He quickly turned to see Amon at the stall's entrance. "Good, boy! You did it!" He slowly stepped backwards, leading Amon into the stall. "See, it's not so bad." With Amon fully inside, he patted him again. "How 'bout we clean you up?" He picked up an old horse brush and began removing dried mud caked into Amon's coat and mane. "If you want, I can stay here with you tonight." From outside, he heard Pearlman answer, "You'll sleep where you're supposed to."

CHAPTER 9

EINAT LOOKED to the illustrations in 'AND THERE WAS EVENING' for some answers as to Haim Hausman's identity. The use of light and the professional style, never seen before in Israeli illustrations, made clear why both critics and artists admired them. But Einat was particularly taken by the playful character of each animal and the sensitivity shown towards the little girl's relationship with her father and the moon. Whoever drew them must have loved children and animals. The love of fantasy, especially Disney animation, also implied that Haim Hausman was a young man when he painted them. An older artist at that time would have probably worked in a more conventional style. Which would mean that he had probably been a soldier, as was the norm for all young Jewish men in Palestine at that time. He also came from Germany; not only because of the name 'Hausman,' but in the drawings she felt a culture familiar to her through her grandparents.

In 1936, Einat's granduncle was stabbed to death while walking home from work in their hometown of Kassel, Germany. He was only 18. There was no investigation. Again, it was treated as if no crime had been committed. Her great grandparents, devastated by the loss of their only son and fearful of what might happen to their three daughters, sent Einat's grandmother, sixteen at the time, and her two younger sisters, one by one, to Palestine. Her great grandparents, unable to get exit visas for themselves, remained in Germany to eventually die in a concentration camp. If given the choice, it's questionable whether they would have left. Their home and business were in Kassel, and not knowing how bad things would get, most Jews procrastinated leaving until it was too late.

At seventeen, Einat's grandfather made the trip to Palestine alone, meeting Einat's grandmother en route when he was placed in her group of youths for the voyage. On their arrival, the group decided to stay together at a nearby kibbutz. Two years later they formed the kibbutz where Einat's father, and then Einat, were born and raised.

She always felt that her grandparents came out of the same world as the father and daughter in 'AND THERE WAS EVENING.' Their groomed hair and pressed clothes were so unlike people raised on a kibbutz. Looking at the illustrations with a more analytical eye, she now saw it as a beautiful, elegant cartoon of a little German girl in a strange land. Perhaps, like Dorothy in OZ, the girl being so out of place added another dimension to the intrigue of the drawings.

Fania purposely omitted the girl's blue eyes from Andersen's story to make her more like the people of the Kibbutz. In reaction to Nazi aesthetics, blue eyes and blonde hair were frowned upon in Israeli children's books. Having felt like an outsider for being fair, Einat was keenly aware of that. It's doubtful that, working for a kibbutz-publishing house, Haim Hausman would refuse the writer's wishes and demand that she be the Nazi ideal of the

Aryan blue-eyed blond beauty. Fania also omitted the number of baby chicks in her poem, but Haim Hausman drew eleven, as Andersen specified. Why would he only be shown the English or German translation of Andersen's story and not Fania's poem?

She searched the illustrations for more clues to Haim Hausman's identity, but all she could come up with was that Andersen gave no description of the father. So, if the old adage is true that "artists draw themselves" perhaps the drawing of the father was, at least in part, a self-portrait. If so, Haim Hausman was tall, handsome, and possibly fair-haired. The fair-hair was questionable. Since the daughter in Fania's poem was blonde/blue it would follow for an artist to give the father the same coloring, but as for the rest, why couldn't Haim Hausman have modeled the father on himself?

If so, a young, tall, handsome man, born to a good Jewish family in Germany in the early 1920's, fled to Palestine as a teenager where he would probably become fluent in English and Hebrew before fighting for the British in WWII, and returning to Palestine after the war, where he eventually illustrated a children's book for a new kibbutz-publishing house.

When Tamar's photos arrived of her mother's illustrations for 'AND THERE WAS EVENING' Einat was impressed by how different they were from Haim Hausman's. It was as if two artists were given the same subjects with no idea of the other's approach.

Einat was also surprised to see that, along with the illustrations, Ilse Kantor hand wrote Fania's text illuminating the first letter on each page, showing their complete collaboration. On the cover, under a moon smiling through sheer clouds, Ilse wrote, "'AND THERE WAS EVENING' by Fania Bergstein, after Hans Christian Andersen, illustrated by Ilse Kantor." So, it was true. Fania had included Andersen's name. Einat questioned why the illustrations were rejected. There was a beautiful tenderness between the father and daughter in the last of Ilse's illustrations, but only two of the illustrations contained the moon, and instead of evening, all of the drawings appeared to take place on a warm, sunny day.

After hours of searching in the archives of Fania Bergstein, Einat found a letter in response to poet Benjamin Tene's letter complementing Fania on the book and illustrations. Fania wrote, *"I'm glad you approve of 'AND THERE WAS EVENING' but of the artist who did the illustrations, I know nothing. They were done without my approval or knowledge, and I can't explain why. Publishers often do strange things. Certainly you know something of that."*

Einat then found another, uncharacteristically fiery, letter from Fania to KM Press asking them to stop the publication in order to add Hans Christian Andersen's name as the source of the story. So, Fania was angry with the publishing house for not giving Andersen credit. But does that mean she had seen an actual proof of the book with Haim Hausman's illustrations? Had she agreed to them? In any case, her wishes were again ignored, and Fania, perhaps too weak from her heart condition, was unable to put up much of a fight.

How could even Fania Bergstein have no idea of the identity of her illustrator? Maybe, as some believed, he was a phantom, or a pseudonym for a famous artist. Einat posted on her blog what she had uncovered along with Ilse Kantor's illustration of 'AND THERE WAS EVENING' and the two letters of Fania Bergstein, ending with five questions:

Does anybody know the original Andersen story and if it has a similar set of illustrations?

1. Who is Haim Hausman?

2. Who decided to have him do the illustrations?

3. Why?

4. Where are the original Haim Hausman illustrations?

By putting it out there, she hoped that all would be quickly answered. The only answer she received came from one man who informed her that the story was based on an excerpt of the Hans Christian Andersen story 'WHAT THE MOON SAW.' But the flood of questions that poured in told her that she wasn't the only one bewildered as to why there were two such different sets of illustrations. Several people asked what it said in the contract. "The contract?" Einat had to laugh. How different the world was then. What would the contract have said?

"The undersigned agrees to work for nothing." But the question that came back most was, "How is it possible that nobody knows the identity of such a famous artist?"

With KM's approval, Einat looked through their records, many of which hadn't been touched for nearly sixty years. She found a dusty 1946 payroll report including Haim Housman. His salary of about $16 dollars a week put him in line with an average paid worker for KM. The spelling of his name was slightly different, but again, that was common for German to Hebrew to English translations. In keeping with her theory that he was away in the war, there was no indication of him working there before that.

After a week, Einat gave up hope of getting any more answers through her blog when someone posted that he had seen a booklet on botany that Haim Hausman illustrated in Ben Shemen for one of the teachers. Calling the Ben Shemen Youth Village, the woman in charge of the archives gruffly told her, "No, never heard of a Haim Hausman. Don't know anything about the booklet either." Einat insisted, "Haim Hausman is a famous artist. It would be good for the school to know if he went there." The woman responded, "The man who told you this is probably very old and confused. There's no Haim Hausman in our computer."

If he was old and confused, he was alert enough to respond to her blog. Through an online search and many phone calls, Einat found that the National Library in Jerusalem had a single copy of 'Anatomy and Morphology of the Plant' by Dr. Zechariah Gottlieb, published in 1941, with illustrations by Haim Hausman. "Would it be possible to see it?" she asked the librarian on the phone. He explained, "It's restricted. But for a small fee we can send you photocopies."

The photocopies arrived about a week later. It was clear that the pamphlet had been frugally printed. The illustrations and what looked like typewriter type were printed in the cheap, standard, blue ink, probably the same ink used to save money for the blue and white illustrations in 'AND THERE WAS EVENING'. But the delicately drawn plants and the clean, simple lines of the hand drawn title could definitely have come from a young Haim Hausman. To Einat's surprise, on the inside cover it said, "Illustrated by Haim Hausman, a graduate of Ben Shemen Youth Village."

Published in 1941? Did he enter the war after that, or had he finished the drawings several years before they were published?

Einat called the woman in charge of the archives in Ben Shemen, explaining what she had found. The woman exhaled dismissively, "We have no records of a him. I don't know why the book says he's a graduate. It's probably a misprint." Einat didn't back down: "Maybe the name was changed in the translation from German to Hebrew. Was there a 'Huzman' or 'Housman' or any similar spelling?" The woman, barely hiding her frustration, said, "I can check again, but it will take time." Einat offered, "I don't mind looking myself, if that's okay." The woman buckled, "No, we can't allow that." Einat added, "I believe he was born in the early 1920's and arrived as a teenager, so you might want to start from 1933 up to the beginning of the war in 39."

Shimon Peres, the Israeli president, had graduated from Ben Shemen. His wife's parents had also been teachers there. If they could verify that Haim Hausman had been a student, the archivist at Ben Shemen might take her more seriously. Einat was able to get through to Shimon Peres's daughter, who asked her father and grandparents, but they had no memory of Haim Hausman. She then tried all of the ministers and administrators, who were at Ben Shemen during that time, but the few still alive were extremely old, and she again had no luck.

To Einat's surprise, the woman in charge of the Ben Shemen archives called a few days later to tell her, "Well, like I said, there's no Haim Hausman." Einat thanked her and was about to hang up when she continued, "But I did find a file for 'Fritz Huysman'. He seems to have arrived maybe in 1934. It's hard to tell. There was a fire and a lot of files were lost from that period. There are notes on him from 1935." Einat said with hope, "That's fantastic..." The archivist interrupted, "Don't get excited. It's a different name. It's probably not him. But it's all we have. I can't tell you what's inside the notebook because it's personal, so don't ask." Einat immediately probed, "Can you at least tell me where he was born? Was he from Germany? Did he come from a good family? Did he fight in the war?" The woman grumbled, "I told you, don't ask." hesitantly adding, "But it seems he was very secluded."

She explained to Einat that when young Jews came to Palestine at that time without family or friends, they were considered orphans and treated almost as if they were criminals. So, most of the notes are, "He doesn't have many friends," or "He keeps to himself." Einat asked, "Is there anyone you can think of who might know about these friendless criminal orphans?" The archivist recommended someone that she thought might be helpful, adding, "But call around. Your guess is as good as mine."

CHAPTER 10

ASLEEP ON THE HAY BEDDING in Amon's stall, a horse blanket covering him for warmth, Haim woke the next morning to find Amon anxiously backing up in the stall. Haim quickly turned to see Professor Pearlman at the stall door, demanding: "How long have you been here?" Haim nervously answered, "I woke early and wanted to check on him." Pearlman narrowed his eyes: "You came right back here after I brought you to the dorm, didn't you?" Haim admitted, "I didn't want him to be alone his first night in here." Pearlman reprimanded, "Never again. From now on, you sleep where you're assigned. We need to know where you are."

Knowing that students were not allowed out past curfew, Haim nodded respectfully. The older students, aged sixteen and up, rotated lookout shifts throughout the night. When Arab rebels snuck in to shoot at the school, Haim and his roommates grabbed rifles from under their beds and fired back through holes carved out in the walls. Knowing that you could give yourself away with just a lit match, Haim made sure to wear dark clothes and used no flashlight as he snuck to the stables.

After the grooming from the night before, Amon's dark, shiny coat glistened in the morning light. Pearlman gruffly admitted, "He looks good." Haim shrugged, "He just needed brushing. I thought you didn't like Arabian horses." Pearlman shook his head, "Just this one. But they're actually bred for intelligence and speed for battle in the desert. All great horses have some Arabian in them. Do you know the Arab legend?" Haim shook his head as he stayed close to Amon, stroking his neck to keep him calm as Pearlman continued. "They say Allah called to the South Wind, 'I want to make a creature out of you. Condense.' And the wind swirled down to form the Arabian horse. 'You shall fly without wings,' Allah said. Too bad Allah said nothing about him pulling a plow."

Pearlman took Haim through the horses' morning routine: feeding, grooming, letting them out, and mucking their stalls. Haim then went to watch Amon run in the field, releasing his young stallion energy. Seeing Haim, Amon immediately trotted over to him. Haim tenderly pet his head saying, "Hey boy, I have to go, but I'll be back on my break." Haim climbed over the fence and hugged Amon's head one last time. Amon stood watching until he disappeared around the bend.

∞

At 7:30 am, Haim entered his room to find his suitcase rummaged through on the floor and Avi and the twins looking through his sketchbook: "What are you doing? Who said you could go through my stuff?" Avi shrugged, "We look for clues where you are." Haim, incredulous, asked, "In my sketchbook? Hand it over." Avi gave it to him, assuring: "Sure, why you upset? It good. You real artist." The twins nodded obligingly. Haim stuffed the sketchbook in his bag warning as he left, "I stay out of your stuff. From now on, stay out of mine."

He ate breakfast alone while finishing his homework from the day before. He didn't take "You real artist" as a compliment, just one more way to point out how he was different. But now that they had seen the sketchbook, nothing was stopping him from drawing. He had wanted to capture Amon on paper, but from then on he would be more careful and burn each sketchbook as it was finished.

After class, Haim ran back to Amon. They played together in the field as they made their way to the shade of an olive tree where they shared his lunch. It reminded him of his days in Germany when he would share his lunch with his gang. He then sat down and began sketching. Analyzing Amon's lines and curves, he felt a certain thrill as he made him come to life on the page.

After working at the Falhar that afternoon, he went back to Amon. They played for a bit more before he sat in the field to sketch again, taking extra care in the placement of his legs and hoofs in his walk, trot and canter. He then settled in to do his homework as Amon grazed nearby.

The next afternoon, Haim sat on the fence petting Amon as he asked, "What do you think, boy? Want me to try riding you?" Amon turned to nuzzle him. "Hope that's a yes," Haim said as he stood on the fence putting his right hand on Amon's far shoulder. Amon nervously pulled away stretching Haim until he fell to the ground. Amon immediately came nuzzling Haim's head.

Back on his feet, Haim patted Amon's neck and went back up on the fence for another try. This time he made it onto Amon's back. Amon shuffled anxiously, trying not to throw him. As they both relaxed, Haim slowly sat up, straddling Amon with his legs. "Good boy," he said with relief as he patted him. "Want to try walking?" With slight knee pressure, Amon took a few awkward steps forward. Soon, he was walking naturally.

As he broke into a trot, with no saddle or reigns, Haim bounced around holding on to his mane until Amon went into a slow canter. Haim held on, leaning in, learning to move with him. He could feel Amon's desire for speed. The charger in him was bred for it. But suddenly fearful of falling off, Haim said, "Whoa," while gently pulling on Amon's mane until he came to a stop. He had never felt such a rush. Amon seemed equally excited. He could almost feel the adrenaline running through his veins.

∞

That evening, Pearlman watched in disbelief as Haim rode Amon casually up to the barn. "Hey, what you do with the crazy horse?" Haim called back, "What crazy horse? You must be delusional." To Haim's surprise, Pearlman encouraged him to ride. With war looming, perhaps he felt it was best for the boy to have every advantage. Having no saddle or bridle at Ben Shemen, Pearlman suggested using the plow harness for reigns, "If he's going to work the fields, he'll have to get used to them sometime."

Haim waited until he and Amon were alone that night to try on the harness. Amon shied at first, but after Haim put the harness over his own head, to reassure him, Amon allowed Haim to put it on him without pulling back.

The next morning, Haim woke again in the stall to find Pearlman holding an apple out for Amon, "Take it, you crazy horse. I don't bite," Amon, agitated, wanted the apple but refused to get that close to Pearlman. Surprised that Perlman didn't reprimand him for sleeping there again, Haim immediately went to calm Amon: "It's okay, boy. It's for you." He slowly led Amon to the apple. Leaning in nibbling at it, Amon finally got it between his teeth. As Amon chewed, Haim said to him: "Professor Pearlman must really like you, or he wouldn't have stolen that apple from everyone in the entire village." Pearlman conceded, "Okay, it's an apple, not the crown jewels."

The horse that no one could touch was soon plowing more fields than the other horses, and without ever being forced. He and Haim were best friends, working together, doing whatever they could for each other. Amon would still only allow Haim near him. He even became more adamant about it, but because of the extra land they cultivated, no one complained.

With only the plow harness for reigns, Haim rode Amon bareback every day. He could feel how much Amon loved it, getting excited when realizing it was their time to ride. Amon loved speed, letting out his young stallion energy as he galloped with Haim on his back through the fields. But Haim was careful to never let him overdo it, always slowing him down when he felt him pushing too hard, and walking him afterwards until he was fully cooled.

Had it not been for his relationship with Amon, Haim might have worked harder at his friendships with the other students, and perhaps his life there would have been better. But Haim didn't see it that way. He only felt lucky that for some reason Amon had chosen him as his friend.

CHAPTER 11

FOR HUMAN INTERACTION, HAIM could always talk to the farmers about feed, fertilizer or the never ending discussion of which worked better - the moshav with each family owning their individual farms in the collective, or the kibbutz with all of the farms merged together as one. Their world was a living experiment, a collaboration to form a better life. Their survival depended on working together.

Haim found that no one was criticized as long as they did their best. But laziness, viewed as stealing, was the major source of gossip. News quickly spread that Meni, a young farmer, got out of harvesting because of a sprained ankle, but was caught that same night dancing with Yehudit.

Such transgressions were low on Haim's list of concerns. believing that he was a man when he turned thirteen, even shaving then though he had no facial hair, by Spring of 1935, after turning fourteen, he decided that it was time for him to make his mark. The question was, how?

David Ben-Gurion was giving a lecture near Ben-Shemen, and Avi pushed Haim to go. "It's good for you. Maybe you learn something." As the leader of the Mapai (the right-wing Zionist labor party, though still a leftist organization) since 1930 and recently becoming the chairman of the executive committee of the Jewish Agency, Ben-Gurion was essentially the leader of the Yishuv (the future State of Israel.)

Haim had heard how Ben-Gurion wanted to be friends with the Arabs when he first arrived in Palestine, but in 1909 an Arab shepherd stopped him on a path to ask for a match. When Ben-Gurion obliged, the shepherd pulled out a knife, wrestled Ben-Gurion to the ground, and stabbed him in the hand before running off with his bag. Avi told Haim as they walked to the lecture with the other students, "That scar tells him the true heart of the Arab. Trust him, he stabs you in the back." "Or the hand," Haim thought. But wasn't that what the Nazis said about Jews. Haim didn't understand why one thug shepherd should be the example of all Arabs. But by now he knew better than to argue with Avi.

Having heard so much about Ben-Gurion, Haim expected him to rant and rave on the evils of the Arabs as Adolph Hitler had of the Jews. But to his surprise, Ben-Gurion was a quiet, thoughtful, professorial type, and though only five-foot three-inches, possessed a commanding presence.

As Haim listened, he found himself getting caught up, even nodding as Ben-Gurion explained, "Everybody sees the problem in the relations between the Jews and the Arabs. But not everybody sees that there is no solution to it. There is no solution." It was true. Haim had been so concerned with finding a solution he hadn't considered that one might not exist. Ben-Gurion continued, "I don't know any Arabs who would agree to Palestine being ours, even if we learn Arabic. And I have no need to learn

Arabic. On the other hand, I don't see why an Arab should learn Hebrew. There is a national question here. We want the country to be ours. The Arabs want the country to be theirs." The only solution as Ben-Gurion saw it: "We must expel Arabs and take their places." And with a firm but collected demeanor, he concluded, "We are finally now responsible of our own destiny."

The crowd went wild. Haim found himself seduced by the euphoria. Before the lecture, he would have never considered kicking people out of their homes and country as something to cheer about. He knew all too well how that felt. But for the first time he found himself elated by not being the victim, but by being the aggressor and reveling in the power to control his fate. As they walked back to the dorm, he didn't even mind Avi putting an arm over his shoulder saying, "See, I told you he open your eyes."

In his letter to his parents that night, he wrote telling them to join him, that Palestine would soon be theirs. As he lay in bed, excited by the thought of having his family back together, he began to wonder how 200,000 Jews would kick out more than 800,000 Palestinian Arabs, not to mention the millions of other Arabs that would come to their defense. It didn't matter, Ben-Gurion made it clear that it would happen. To appease the Arabs, the British limited Jewish immigration into Palestine to 15,000 a year. Ben-Gurion said to ignore that and bring in as many yolim (Aliyah Bet, illegal Jewish immigrants) as possible. "By changing the numbers we change our destiny."

The next day, Haim went to Lehman to see what he could do for the cause. Lehman gave a disheartened shrug, "Ben-Gurion is of one view. You once believed in the work of Arlosoroff." Arlosoroff's desire for unity with the Arabs now seamed as idealistic as German decency prevailing over the Nazis. The Grand Mufti, Haj Amin al-Husseini, was gaining strength as he joined with Hitler to make Palestine a purely Arab nation. His following increased as his gangs raped, tortured and killed Jews. Not wanting to play into the Grand Mufti's hands, Ben-Gurion urged a policy of restraint. If the Jews retaliated then, a war they were ill prepared for could wipe them out. Preparing, creating a strong underground army, was the only way to eventually take control.

"There is something you can help with," Lehman conceded. Haim anxiously asked, "What? Name it." Lehman hesitantly added, "You have to understand, secrecy is imperative." Haim firmly nodded. Most of the other students worked hard to fit in, joining in extra curricula activities, singing patriotic songs full voice around the nightly campfires. But seeing that Haim was more of a loner and how quiet he had been about his relationship with Amon, Lehman decided to take the chance of confiding in him: "I received word that yolim have arrived. It would be a help if you could hide one of the boys for the night." The importance of secrecy was driven home by the fact that, after being there for almost a year, Haim had no idea that Lehman had any connection to the underground.

"He's safe with me," Haim assured. "No one will find out. Where should I hide him?" Lehman shrugged, "Where do you go when you leave your dorm at night?" Haim's eyes anxiously widened. Before Haim could make up excuses, Lehman cut him off: "It's okay. I know." Late at night, rifle in hand, Haim often snuck from his dorm room to the stables, watching out for Arab snipers as he slipped unnoticed past the older students on guard duty. Having told Avi and the twins that he was guarding the stables from possible Arab attacks, they agreed to keep quiet.

He never discussed his relationship with Amon. Any flaunting might jeopardize it in some way, and silence made it less likely to become a topic of discussion. But at one breakfast, when several students asked Haim to join them for a race that afternoon, Avi smirked, "He can't. He has to play with his pet horse." Haim's eyes narrowed as he corrected, "We have no pets here. I work the stables. If you want, you're welcome to clean horse shit with me." Avi never brought the subject up again.

Haim wouldn't have blamed his roommates for informing on his sneaking out at night. Keeping quiet meant also putting their necks on the line. But it was more likely Professor Pearlman who told Lehman. As the stable foreman, he may have even brought Lehman to watch Haim sleeping in Amon's stall. Perhaps after discussing it, they decided that Haim seemed as safe there as in the dorm, and decided to let it go.

Lehman now advised, "Wherever you hide him, it's best I not know." Haim nodded, "Where is he going?

Maybe I can bring him there." Lehman shook his head. "It's best for you to not know. If the boy is caught, the British will send him back to Europe, which will probably mean his death sentence. You have no record. You can say you found him wondering and took him in for the night. But that will be the last time you can help. A second offense could have you deported back to Germany and our school locked down." Haim assured, "I'll die before they get anything out of me." Lehman cracked a smile, "That's comforting, but try to first play dumb."

After nightfall, Haim waited with Amon at the end of the small path leading away from the west field. "Stay low and keep out of site," Lehman had warned. They hadn't discussed bringing Amon, but a black charger could be their best chance of escape. Hours passed with nothing but the occasional lights of the British patrols passing by on the distant road. Having lost his struggle to stay awake, Haim was startled when Amon was excited by a large, black car, with no lights on, turning onto the unpaved path. The car stopped about twenty feet in from the road, probably to avoid puncturing a tire. As there were few newer models like that in Palestine, Haim guessed that they chose a vehicle least likely to break down.

The car signaled by flashing its lights three times. Haim signaled back with his flashlight. He then jumped on Amon and galloped to them. With only a crescent moon for guidance, Haim could just make out a darkly dressed woman and boy with a suitcase standing in the path. He pulled on the reigns of the harness whispering, "Whoa!" The boy and woman looked terrified as Amon came to a halt practically on top of them.

Without taking the time to comment on the horse, the woman whispered anxiously in Hebrew, "Do you speak Polish?" "No," Haim whispered back as he dismounted. The woman continued, "You won't understand each other then, but no matter, the less spoken the better. He has eaten, but will need food in the morning. His cousin will pick him up here tomorrow at 10:00 am." Haim asked apprehensively, "In daylight?" The woman nodded, "It is less suspicious for a woman and boy to travel then. She will have another boy's papers in case they are stopped. We had no choice but to travel tonight as the British have begun searching homes along the coast." Haim could just make out the silhouettes of other yolim in the car.

On the main road, he spotted the lights of a British patrol heading their way. To keep Amon quiet, he covered his eyes with a cloth while stroking his neck. The woman put an anxious arm around the boy's shoulder as the lights of the patrol neared the path. If the patrol spotted the car, Haim was ready to put the boy on Amon and gallop off with him.

They held their breath as the patrol slowly passed. Exhaling with relief, the woman determinedly whispered, "When you see his cousin, you will ask her if she is lost. She will say that she is looking for her little brother who has run away. Do not turn him over unless she says that. Do you understand?" Haim nodded. As she turned to leave, Haim asked, "Can he ride a horse?" The woman asked the boy in Polish. The boy shook his head "no." Haim shrugged, "It may be a good time to learn." The woman translated and the boy looked up at Amon, terrified. The woman advised, "He made it this far. Please don't kill him now." With that, she hurried to the car leaving the boy with his suitcase.

They watched as the car slowly drove off with no lights on to disperse the other yolim presumably throughout the nearby moshav. Haim guessed the small, thin, pale, blond boy to be around eleven years old. With his long side locks, stiff-round-black-felt hat and long, dark garb he looked as out of place as he must have felt. Haim took the suitcase, and led the boy up the path as Amon walked on Haim's other side. Haim was proud of Amon. A stranger in such close proximity would have normally upset him, but he seemed to understand that this boy needed their help.

With every distant crack and sound, Haim became increasingly anxious of Arab snipers. Had they also been alerted of the yolim's arrival? If so, at the boy's slow pace, the long walk through the open fields could prove fatal. Near the field's entrance, Haim hid the suitcase under some brush, and led the boy to Amon. Realizing what was expected of him, the boy pulled back in fear. Without a word, Haim firmly held the boy's shoulders, looked into his eyes and nodded as reassuringly as possible. The boy remained frozen as Haim got him up on Amon's back. He held onto Amon's mane as Haim jumped up behind him. Haim picked up the reigns and they started off into the field.

As Amon broke into a trot, the stiff, terrified boy would have bounced off had Haim not held him firmly between his arms. When Amon broke into a canter the boy's hat was blown off by the wind. Haim could feel the boy stiffen, too frightened to look back for it. Haim's firm hold told him that it would have to be left behind.

The boy was more relaxed by the time they trotted up to the barn. Haim helped him dismount, and after walking Amon to cool him down from the run, they brought him to his stall without lighting the lamp. Haim brought the boy back outside of the dark barn and offered him some bread, vegetables and water that he had stored for him. Though the woman said that the boy had eaten, he finished everything off.

To slip by the British undetected, he would have to fit in. Even with only the light of a crescent moon, the boy's clothes were a dead give-away. Haim had him change into an extra set of his farming clothes that he had brought along. Though much too large for the boy, by rolling up the cuffs and sleeves, and tightening the rope belt, he would get by. Haim then pointed to the boy's long side locks. Picking up a pair of grooming sheers that he had taken from the barn, he nodded to the boy. As Haim clipped, the boy remained unresponsive, emotionless. He didn't know if the boy was traumatized watching his side locks fall to the ground or if had understood that it for his protection, but all that mattered was keeping him alive.

Haim led the boy behind bales of hay in the barn's dark storage stall, where he had him lie down on hay bedding and covered him with a horse blanket. Exhausted, the boy soon fell asleep. To snore as loudly as Avi could have given them away, but fortunately, the boy slept quietly.

∞

Haim planned to stay awake on guard duty all night, but hearing the rooster crow he opened his eyes to find streaks of sun glistening through the barn's wood panelling. He quickly looked over to find the boy also waking. After making sure no one was around, Haim brought him to the nearby outhouse before hiding him again behind the stacks of hay.

As Haim finished mucking the stalls, Pearlman arrived. "You're here early," he said warily. Haim shrugged, "Yeah, couldn't sleep. You can take off if you want. I'm almost done here." The boy moved slightly, rustling the hay in the storage stall. "What's that?" Pearlman questioned? Haim shrugged, "Probably a mouse. Think I saw one earlier. I'll take care of it." Knowing that Haim had furtively made pets of the mice, even feeding them grain, Pearlman cracked a smile, "Yeah, you'll take care of it, like a mother." Because of Haim's hard work, and with the mice having plenty of natural predators to keep their population in control, Pearlman decided to allow it: "I'll help finish up here and we'll go to mess hall together." Though Haim hated leaving the boy alone, unable to come up with an excuse, he agreed.

As they walked away from the barn, Pearlman expounded on his plans for the fields as Haim, concerned for the boy, struggled to listen.

Seeing Pearlman and Haim enter the mess hall together, Lehman immediately went to them. "Everything okay?" Haim affirmed with an anxious nod. Checking his forehead for a fever, Lehman said, "I don't know. You seem flushed, and a little warm. You better go see the nurse." Catching on, Haim turned to go, but Lehman stopped him. "Here, take some food, in case you get hungry." Lehman quickly made up a bag for him. If their conversation seemed odd, Lehman's conversations often seemed odd, and as the head of Ben Shemen few questioned it.

Rushing back to the barn, Haim was relieved to find the boy where he had left him. Sitting together on bales of hay, they ate the bag of food Lehman had made for them, and the boy seemed to enjoy feeding Amon carrots with a flat palm, so as not to be bitten. When they finished, Haim tied a bag of the boy's clothes and a canteen of water to his back. He then put the harness on Amon, helped the boy up onto him, jumped up behind, and they comfortably trotted out of the barn and into the field. Soon breaking into a cantor, Haim kept the boy firmly between his arms to make sure that he was safe, but the boy now seemed relaxed enough to stay on by himself.

At the other end of the field, Haim stopped Amon to retrieve the boy's hat, and Amon carried the boy the rest of the way with Haim walking by their side. After finding the suitcase where Haim had hidden it,

Amon grazed as Haim and the boy weeded around the fence, intently watching each occasional passing car on the main road. A half hour passed when an old ford pickup stopped about fifty yards past the path. It slowly reversed, turned in, and a young, attractive, dark-haired woman got out anxiously looking around. Haim signaled the boy to stay hidden in the brush. He then jumped on Amon and galloped to her. "Are you lost?" he asked in Hebrew. Not expecting a horse, she stammered, "I, I'm looking for my cousin, I mean, little brother. He's like a brother. He ran away." To make up for the mistake of referring to him as her cousin, she added, "He has a scar of the Star of David on his left arm. Boys in Poland cut it into him." Having made a point of not watching him change, Haim hadn't noticed the scar. But he felt confident enough that she was the boy's cousin. Cracking a smile, he nodded, "Wait here." The woman smiled back with relief.

Haim found the scar of the Star of David on the boys left arm, just as she had said, and a short time later, the woman was surprised to see her small cousin, suitcase between his arms, sitting on Amon in front of Haim as they trotted to her. Haim helped him dismount, and the boy ran into her arms. Tears swelled as she spoke to him in Polish. Nodding to each of her questions, the boy then pointed to Haim. She explained, "I asked who taught him to ride a horse?" Haim shrugged, "I just put him on. He did the rest." Admiring Amon, she added, "And such a magnificent horse, I think Jacek is very lucky to have you both as protectors." Somberly looking down on Jacek's head, she questioned, "Are you the one who cut his hair?" Haim uncomfortably nodded. She conceded, "It looks good, as if he belongs here. Thank you."

After Jacek whispered with his cousin, he went to Haim, extended his right hand and in stilted Hebrew said, "Thank you." Haim shook his hand saying, "My honor." Jacek then turned to Amon, thanked him in Hebrew, and gathering his courage, pet him on the nose. Amon seemed to tolerate it, but before he could shy, Haim handed Jacek his bag of clothes, "You're very brave. We are lucky to have you here." The cousin translated, and Jacek seemed emboldened as he smiled back in gratitude.

Haim watched them drive away. With no idea of where they were going, he wondered if he would ever see them again, if they would be safe. He then understood why the woman who brought Jacek to him seemed to remain so emotionally detached. But after helping Jacek, he knew there was no turning back. He and Amon were meant for more than just plowing fields.

CHAPTER 12

Eɪɴᴀᴛ ᴡᴀs ᴄᴀᴜɢʜᴛ off guard when the radio show called her cell phone during a morning therapy session. "Can you do the show now?" they asked. She had carried with her the paper of everything she wanted to say on air, but each time they had called it was only to say, "We can't record it today. Are you free tomorrow?" Finally resigned to being postponed indefinitely, she now listened to the producer explain, "Don't worry about going over. We're not live. We can edit later. The most important thing is that you sound relaxed and natural. If you freeze, we probably won't use it." She hadn't considered freezing. But that was now all she could think of.

Her therapist encouraged, "It's fine. I'll make lunch. You have the office to yourself." Specializing in 'Second generation after the holocaust' (children of holocaust survivors) she had a deeper understanding of Einat's quest to find this person who had survived so much war. Seeing Einat's bewilderment, she firmly insisted, "Talk to them." Einat appreciated the support, knowing how easy it would be on her own to give up. "New adventures," her therapist reminded as she left the room.

The search itself had also been encouraging. People were still responding whenever she wrote or talked about Haim Hausman, usually leading her to someone else. Not that much had come of it yet, but something about the mystery seemed to also intrigue them. It helped her move forward, reinforcing the idea that she was looking for something that wanted to be found, that an outside force was urging her on. She found herself even talking to Haim Hausman, asking questions, "Where are you now? Did you change you're name from Fritz to Haim?"

Giving Einat space to talk on the radio, her therapist went to the kitchen. Excited to see her out of the session, her energetic, two-year-old Rottweiler mix excitedly brought her his squeaky toy. Acquiescing, she went out with him into the backyard to play.

Alone in the office, Einat pulled out the worn paper from her purse. Having gone over it so many times, words at creases were practically illegible, but she now worried that it wasn't fresh enough in her mind, that she would freeze and lose her best shot of finding him. Trying to maintain her composure, she began reading. "Everybody knows Haim Hausman, but nobody knows him. Can anyone out there help solve the mystery?"

At that moment, the Rottweiler, hearing Einat's voice, dropped his squeaky toy and ran barking through the yard to the office window. Afraid of interrupting the radio show, her therapist tried catching him without calling out, making the dog only more determined to let her know that someone was alone in her office. Even the squeaky toy failed to distract him.

Hearing the barking, Einat wondered what was going on out there. Had an animal gotten into the yard? Wanting to help, but afraid of interrupting the interview, she continued talking over the dog's barking. She first recited Fania Bergstein's poem. Flubbing a few of the lines because of her nerves and noise, she slowly relaxed as she discussed everything from Haim Hausman's possible background to what she had discovered from the daughters of Ilsa Kantor, Fania Bergstein's letters, the book on botany that Haim Hausman was credited with illustrating, which claimed that he was from Ben Shemen, and the publishing house's payroll record.

After fifteen minutes, just as Einat was finishing the call, her therapist finally caught the dog. The producer seemed pleased, assuring her, "Don't worry about the barking. You sounded good. We should have it edited and ready for this afternoon's show." As Einat came out of the office, her therapist profusely apologized, explaining what had happened. She then admonished the dog. "You owe Einat a big apology." Einat assured her and the dog, "He was just doing his job." The dog put down his squeaky toy in front of Einat, presumably for her to throw to him. But her therapist shook her head: "So, you are now presenting your squeaky toy as a peace offering."

Einat listened to the show that afternoon with her husband and children. Her husband said with certainty, "That should get you some answers." Her children agreed, but most of their discussion was on how to stop a dog from barking, suggesting spraying him with water to giving him a steak.

Einat then called the number that the show had given her to retrieve her messages, and entered the code, hopeful when she heard that there were already twenty-seven messages. Most of the messages only said that they were surprised she was looking for somebody so famous. Others assumed that she hadn't looked hard enough. One man told her that Haim Hausman was in Degania Alef, the first kibbutz, established in 1910. Einat contacted the kibbutz but was told that many of their records had been destroyed during the Arab rebellions or the war of '48, and had no luck in finding him there.

Most people assumed Haim Hausman was dead. "Everyone knows the book. If he were alive he'd come forward." A few told her that Haim Hausman was an alias for a famous artist who didn't want his name on a children's book. Einat questioned why someone like Picasso would come to Palestine, illustrate a children's book and sign it Haim Hausman.

Because the book is such a classic, many thought of it as always being there, never considering that there was an actual writer and illustrator. People listening to the radio show now discovered that it was based on a Hans Christian Andersen story. Some were offended, others just disappointed. "It's not even a Hebrew classic? It's Christian?" Einat explained, "It's based on a small excerpt from an obscure Hans Christian Andersen story, but the beautiful poetry is Fania Bergstein's. If a story's origin determines its nationality, then Cinderella is Greek or Asian."

Over the next few days, she responded to the several hundred people who called or wrote in. But nothing led to Haim Hausman. Though her instincts still told her that someone had to know who he was, she began losing hope.

She then received an ominous message from the renowned illustrator, David Polonsky: "I believe I have the answer to your question, but you may prefer leaving it alone." In a friendly voice he ended by leaving his number and asking her to, "Call anytime. Just ask for David." Einat knew David's work. With her first online search for Haim Hausman, David's brilliant illustrations for 'Moonless Night' came up. Inspired by the classic Haim Hausman illustrations, they earned David his second win of the prestigious 'Israel Museum Award for Children's Book Illustration.' All of the finalists' works that year were impressive, but Einat found David's to be extraordinary. Though David's love of the Haim Hausman drawings was evident in his illustrations, she never considered contacting him in her search.

Listening to his message again, her first instinct was not to call, as a small part of her feared that Haim Hausman was erased from history for a reason. In that case, ignorance might be bliss. What if the truth would destroy the popularity of the book? Or what if David's theory was wrong but Einat believed it and unjustly slandered Haim Hausman? After a restless night, curiosity got the better of her.

In their friendly phone conversation, Einat confirmed that she had a DVD player. David ended by saying, "I'm sending you a video. Let's talk after you've seen it." As Einat hung up the phone she thought, "What could a video reveal? Is there footage of Haim Hausman committing some horrendous act or exposing himself?"

The video arrived two days later accompanied by a short note stating: "This is the 1937 Norwegian Phillips light bulb commercial 'How the Light Came Anyway When the Sun Overslept,' animated by the German artist, Hans Fischerkoesen. Interested to know your thoughts."

Einat anxiously put the DVD into the player and began watching the animated commercial of little human-like stars unable to wake the sleeping sun. Daylight comes anyway because, to the little stars' surprise, a large Philips light bulb sits on the sun's throne in the clouds.

The resemblance between the Fischerkoesen and Hausman stars was unmistakable. Haim Hausman must have seen them, unless they both based their stars on the stars of another artist. Einat had thought Disney to be the main influence for the Haim Hausman illustrations. But what did it matter if the main influence was actually Fischerkoesen?

Searching Hans Fischerkoesen online, she found that after 1936 the German film industry became a branch of the Nazi regime. With no films from Jewish dominated Hollywood allowed into Germany, the clubfooted Nazi Propaganda Minister, Paul Joseph

Goebbels, set up film studios, including an animation studio, to make up for the loss of Disney and other American animation, which had become extremely popular in Germany. Many top German animators had already fled to America, and the Nazi's were determined to show that they could produce equal, if not better, animation for their people.

The 45-year-old Hans Fischerkoesen, (originally Hans Fischer, adding his home town of Koesen to make his name more distinctive) was the most prominent remaining German animator that the Nazi's evidently trusted. At Goebbels orders, he moved his studio closer to Nazi headquarters to make children's animation for the Third Reich.

Though Fischerkoesen was somehow able to keep Nazi propaganda out of his animated films, at the war's end he was arrested by the Russians as a Nazi collaborator and sent to Sachsenhausen concentration camp in East Germany. In 1948, after three years in prison, he was finally exonerated by proving that he had actually worked against the Nazis as a member of an underground resistance group of artists.

After being released into Soviet controlled East Germany, he was only allowed to work on assignments in the state-controlled DEFA studios. Later that year, he and his family successfully made a dangerous nighttime escape to West Germany, where he established a new animation studio. The studio was a success, garnering many awards. He even appeared on the cover of *Der Spiegel*, Germany's equivalent to *Time* magazine, and

Fischerkoesen worked up until several years before his death in 1973.

"So, what do you think?" David asked Einat on the phone after exchanging friendly hellos. Seeing the similarity of the stars, but not seeing anything else that was taken from Fischerkoesen, she questioned, "Why wouldn't Haim Hausman study cartoons with stars and moons for inspiration? No one can hold that against him?" David sighed, "What if it's more than inspiration?" Einat, confused, asked, "What are you saying? It's not as if Fischerkoesen drew the Haim Hausman illustrations himself." David somberly asked, "Are you sure?" Einat, taken aback, shook her head: "It's only the stars on the first page. Nothing else is similar or copied. Maybe I'm biased, but I actually like the Haim Hausman stars more. They have more character, and I find the Hausman illustrations more beautiful."

David agreed, "They are more beautiful. And nothing is copied. That's why it's an issue. The Haim Hausman illustrations were done eleven years after the Philips light bulb commercial, and is much more in the style of Fischerkoesen's later work for the Nazis. Look at his 'Snowman' of 1944." Einat argued, "So, he was influenced by them too?" David exhaled, "Something has always bothered me about the Hausman illustrations. When I saw the Fischerkoesen video, I knew what it was. They're just too good. They look like they came out of a major studio. Haim Hausman's characters, perspective, use of light and color, even in only blue and white, inspired me."

Einat conceded, "I have too much respect for your work to question your judgment, but…" With a slight laugh, David interrupted, "But you're about to question my judgment." Einat explained, "Fischerkoesen was in a Soviet prison camp in East Germany when 'AND THERE WAS EVENING' was illustrated." David corrected, "He was paroled and escaped that year to West Germany. If Fischerkoesen, or somebody close to him, was friends with someone at KM Press they could have asked him to do the illustrations. Or maybe he just offered. Communications were open then between Germany and Palestine." Einat argued, "But they were supposed to use only artists from the kibbutz, and they couldn't have paid him." David reasoned, "The kibbutz publishing house cared about quality. Fischerkoesen was a great cartoonist and animator. Since Fischerkoesen worked for the resistence, maybe it was his way to make up for the work he did for the Nazis. In any case, it wouldn't have been for the money. Where are all of the other Haim Hausman illustrations?" Einat, puzzled, asked, "What other illustrations?" David nodded, "Exactly. Artists have a large catalogue of work showing their progress. Where are his other works?" Einat had no answer. David continued, "Fischerkoesen explains why there's no trace of Haim Hausman, or his work, why even Fania Bergstein and Ilsa Kantor knew nothing of him, why they look so Germanic, why the blonde hair, blue eyes, and the crotch shot weren't changed, and why they're so good. It explains it all."

Einat took a moment to absorb what David was saying. She never considered the quality of the illustrations as being an issue. It would take an artist of David's caliber to see that. "So, who was Haim Hausman? Why was he on the publishing house's payroll? Why was he given credit for illustrating the book of botany?" David proposed, "They wouldn't give credit to Hans Christian Andersen, so why would they give credit to Fischerkoesen, the Nazi's animator? Fischerkoesen probably knew and didn't care. And if Haim Hausman illustrated a book on botany, why not give credit to him, a young artist working for the publishing house who may have been killed in the war? It was after all 1948."

After her conversation with David, Einat couldn't look at the illustrations in the same way. There was no proof. David had contacted Fischerkoesen's family, but it was too long ago. Nobody knew anything about it. She tried to grasp what it implied. For the Israeli children's classic to be illustrated by an artist who worked side by side with one of the most notorious Nazis, Hitler's devout follower, close friend and confident, Paul Joseph Goebbels, that just couldn't be good.

CHAPTER 13

LEHMAN REPRIMANDED, "You made Amon part of the underground?" Haim shook his head, "No, it was his choice. He wanted to." Lehman raised an eyebrow, "The horse volunteered?" Haim nodded: "I don't make him do anything. I ask, but he does what he wants." Frustrated, Lehman conceded, "So the horse was recruited." Haim gave an uncertain nod. Lehman admonished, "If I knew you were bringing him, I never would have allowed it. I asked to only know as little as possible about the boy, his whereabouts. Not about you bringing along a dangerous animal. What if he hurt that boy?" Haim assured, "He didn't. He wouldn't. He can go anywhere, outrun the British, and with his black coat, if I dress dark we'll be like a shadow in the night. Think how much we can accomplish." As determined as Haim was, Lehman would still have none of it.

Palestinian Arabic was a requirement at Ben Shemen. Unlike Avi and most of the other students, Haim had taken it seriously, studying up to several hours a day. Since Ben-Gurion made it clear there was no point to communicate with the Arabs and there would be no working together for one common goal, Haim could now use that time for training.

His 20/20 vision made him a naturally good shot. To make himself indispensable to the Haganah, he began building his strength by swimming laps and holding his breath in the water tower that was filled each day to irrigate the fields at night. Soon, he was able to swim underwater for up to several minutes. For Amon's strength, Haim continued to ride him each day, gradually increasing their speed and distance. At the far end of one field, Haim would place a dummy to act as a yolim (illegal Jewish immigrant.) In no time, they were like a well-oiled machine as Haim would easily remount Amon with the dummy, and they would gallop off.

∞

In late August 1929, five years before Haim's arrival in Palestine, riots broke out over access to Jerusalem's Western Wall, a holy site for both Jews and Arabs. Over a week period, 133 Jews were killed, many more were injured and a considerable amount of property destroyed. The British intervened, killing 110 Arabs before the riots subsided.

From that point on, Jewish defense in Palestine changed. Most adults over sixteen in Jewish settlements and many from the cities were recruited into the Haganah. Foreign arms were covertly acquired, and training camps were set up where they were taught to fight, defend and make hand grenades, along with other weapons and equipment, transforming an untrained militia into a skilled underground army.

Determined to protect the students of Ben Shemen, Lehman kept most of the younger students out of the Haganah. But with Haim being tall for his age, and his voice already changing, he could pass for older. After seeing Haim and Amon train together, Lehman was swayed. Allowing them to work together, Lehman made an exception, and on the condition that Haim would not recruit other students, he was allowed to enter into the Haganah at the age of fourteen.

Ben-Gurion, along with other leaders, dictated the official Haganah policy of restraint (havlagah.) Haganah members were there for defense only, not to instigate attack on Arab rebels or their villages until the Jews were prepared to win. But Haim made it clear that he and Amon had not volunteered to just be guards. They were there to help yolim. His commanding officers accepted his right to speak for Amon, but before Lehman would agree, Amon would have to pass more tests proving that he would not become a liability.

Until Amon passed all of the requirements, with rifle over his shoulder, Haim and Amon scouted in the afternoons, helping the Haganah create maps of routes, secret paths and hiding spots for the yolim's journey in from the sea.

∞

One day, while scouting to the northeast of Ben Shemen, Haim and Amon came upon an Arab boy around Haim's age pulling on a mule carrying a large load. His clothes were plain, a turban of old cloth for protection from sun and sand and a cloak that at one time had been white. Haim watched furtively as the mule limped a few steps and stopped. Looking like a good practice opportunity for Amon with strangers, Haim called out, "Do you need help?" The startled boy, not understanding Hebrew, ran to hide behind a large rock.

Haim called in Arabic, "It's okay. I won't hurt you." The boy called back in Arabic, "What do you want?" Haim answered, "Your mule is hurt. My horse would like to help." The boy cracked a smile, "What if your horse is just saying that in order to steal my grain?" Haim called back, "That's impossible. He is a poor horse, but he never lies." Sharing a laugh, the boy hesitantly came out from behind the rock. Seeing that the boy appeared to be unarmed, Haim rode over to him on Amon, stopping within ten feet. Avi had drilled in, "Never trust an Arab," but he felt no threat. The boy froze as Haim dismounted and slowly took the rifle off of his shoulder. As Haim threw the rifle to the ground, the boy relaxed. In return, the boy pulled a knife from his back pocket, and threw it into the ground in front of him.

Haim approached holding out his right hand. "I am Haim. This is Amon. Pardon him for staying back. He doesn't appreciate strangers." They shook hands as the boy introduced himself: "I am Khalid." Haim asked where he was headed. Khalid pointed to the nearby hill, the village of Beit Nabala. Haim knew it well. Some of the Arab rebels who shot at the school were thought to come from there.

When Lehman was planning the Ben Shemen Youth Village he had spoken with the village heads in the area, including Beit Nabala. Since the land was acquired legally and his objective was to save children (mostly from the pogroms in Russia and Eastern Europe) most were amenable. But followers of the Grand Mufti, Amin al-Husseini, believing that it was part of a master plan to take over Palestine, began scare tactics to stop construction.

However, "Go away Jew!" or "Go back to where you came!" written in Arabic late at night on the side of a building was nothing compared to the atrocities happening to Jews in Europe, and since by then there was nowhere else for Lehman to build his school, construction went forward.

By 1931, a more militant group of the Haganah broke off to form the Irgun. Dissatisfied with the policy of defense only, the Irgun set up ambushes and counterattacks to protect the school. With several casualties on both sides, both swore vengeance. The British intervened, arresting both Arab rebels and members of the Irgun, making it clear that any insubordination would not be tolerated, and any instigators of future attacks would be tried and executed. By the time Haim arrived in 1934, the fighting was reduced to the occasional late-night rifle fire, which neither side reported to British authorities, as they feared the British strong-arm approach would only make matters worse.

Considering both boys' histories, Haim was surprised that Khalid seemed to trust him enough to check his mule's leg. Haim affirmed, "It's sprained. He won't make it with this load." Seeing the concern in Khalid's eyes, Haim went to Amon and stroked his neck as he asked in Hebrew, "Do you want to help them? We won't if it upsets you."

Haim put the rifle back over his shoulder, and Amon followed as he walked to the mule. Seeing that Amon was still relaxed, Haim began untying the burlap sacks of grain. "Help me get these off," he said to Khalid. "But stay on the other side of your mule so you don't get too close to Amon." Once the bags were untied, Haim secured them onto Amon. Without the heavy load, the mule was now able to limp behind as they began their ascent up the path.

"Thank you," Khalid said. "I didn't think you'd want to help me." Haim asked, "Why, because I'm a Jew and you're an Arab?" Khalid nodded. Haim shrugged, "Amon is my best friend, and he's Arab. We always help each other." Khalid walked a few steps before asking, "Are you sure your horse isn't Jewish? He acts Jewish." With a slight laugh, Haim asked, "How so?" Khalid answered, "Well, he doesn't like Arabs." Haim shook his head, "He doesn't like most people." Khalid said, "Oh, so he's British," The boys laughed, helping them become more comfortable with each other.

Haim was surprised by Khalid's sense of humor. Weren't Arabs supposed to be cold, suspicious and full of hate? But Khalid was a boy not much unlike himself. "What did you think I was going to do to you?" Haim asked. When Khalid only shook his head, implying that he didn't know, Haim said, "We hear you want to rape and kill us." Khalid admitted, "Yeah, that's what they say about you." Haim nodded, "So how many Jews have you raped and killed?" Khalid laughed as he bashfully shook his head again. Haim nodded, "Same here. If we agree not to rape and kill each other, maybe we can be friends." Reading the anxiety in Khalid's eyes, Haim added, "It's okay. No one has to know. But we could help each other. We both know different things." Khalid smiled slightly as he nodded.

At first, Khalid hardly looked Haim in the eyes, but that slowly changed. During their half hour walk, they seemed to talk easily about anything, even with Haim's stilted Arabic. For Haim, it felt good to have a friend his age, especially one that didn't judge him as an outcast orphan.

In Khalid's village of six hundred, there were few boys his age that he could talk to. The small group that attacked Ben Shemen pressured him to join, but his father warned, "If you kill the innocent why shall you not be killed? And perhaps all of us punished and our farm taken away." Most other children his age, like their parents, had little interest in the outside world. But Khalid was different. He admired Haim for having the courage to go out on his own.

It gave Haim hope of Jews and Arabs living peacefully together, if they could only communicate. But with the Grand Mufti and Ben Gurion each determined to rid the area of the other, there seemed little chance of that.

As the outer wall of the ancient village of Beit Nabala appeared through the trees, Haim warned, "You better go alone from here." Khalid nodded awkwardly, embarrassed for not being able to invite

Haim inside. Both boys knew that it could prove dangerous if they were seen together.

Khalid helped Haim untie the sacks from Amon. Seeing that Amon remained relaxed, Haim said, "See, he likes you. He usually won't let anyone else get that close to him." Khalid smiled, "Okay, so maybe he's only part Jewish." As the boys shook hands goodbye, Haim asked, "Do you know anyone I can talk to about helping our people get along better?" Khalid, uncertain, shook his head, but offered, "I'll ask my father. How do I find you?"

∞

The next day, as arranged, Haim found Khalid waiting alone at the same rock he had hidden behind when they first met. After making sure no one else was around, Haim rode up to him. Khalid then led Haim and Amon to a hidden, shady spot off of the path where the boys sat down to eat their lunch.

As Haim emptied a small sack of apples and carrots for Amon, Khalid said with surprise, "Jewish horses must be happy." Haim laughed as he shrugged, "Sure, when they're not persecuted for their beliefs." Intrigued by each other's lunches, the boys decided to trade. Khalid had never had a fresh farmer's cheese sandwich with sliced vegetables on homemade European bread. Realizing after the first bite that it was not to his taste, he confessed, "We don't have to trade if you don't want to." But enjoying Khalid's unusual homemade pita stuffed with fresh goat cheese, olives and dried fig, Haim shook his head assuring, "No, it's okay. Go ahead."

It seemed strange that they lived in such close proximity, yet their worlds were so different. Lehman had reached out, always inviting the heads of the nearby Arab communities for holiday dinners. Several times a week Mahmud came from Lydda to barter with his cart of fruits and vegetables. And once a year, the students of Ben Shemen visited schools in the Arab communities, including Beit Nabala, where they joined them for lunch. Arab students would also do the same at Ben Shemen, but culturally, little was exchanged. Besides a few local foods and customs that were introduced into Ben Shemen, the new world they were creating was almost entirely based on what they had learned in Europe.

As they ate, Haim asked, "Did your father know anyone I can talk to?" Khalid hesitantly nodded, "There's an Arab café he delivers produce to in Tel Aviv. He says men are always talking politics there. If you're serious, I'd better go with you. Anything happens to you now, I'm responsible." Haim shook his head, "That would be too dangerous for you." Khalid said nothing, but knew he was right. Extremists in his village allowed the organized visits between Jews and Arabs, but if they knew he had befriended Haim, they may scar his face as a traitor, as had been done to others. Avi and the more radical bunch at Ben Shemen may not have liked Haim befriending an Arab boy from Beit Nabala, but it's doubtful they would have gone to that extreme. Haim assured, "Don't worry. I'll be okay. I was fighting Nazi youth gangs for years back home in Germany."

Suddenly hearing footsteps heading towards them on the path, the boys remained hidden as Haim pet Amon and covered his eyes with the cloth to keep him quiet. Glimpsing through the brush, they made out several men with kufi caps and rifles slung over their shoulders. If they were the Grand Mufti's henchmen, they were known to slit the throats of Jews. And who knew what they would do to Khalid for befriending one.

The boys froze as the men passed less then ten yards away. As their footsteps disappeared into the distance, they exhaled with relief. Haim asked, "Did you recognize any of them?" His heart still racing, Khalid shook his head. Haim cautioned, "I'd better go. If they come back, we may not be so lucky." "When will I see you again?" Khalid asked. Haim shrugged, "Saturday's my day off. If we meet Sunday I tell you how it went in Tel Aviv." Khalid nodded. Watching Haim gallop off, he worried what he had gotten him into.

CHAPTER 14

HAIM SPENT EARLY SATURDAY morning with Amon before walking the two miles to the bus stop in Lydda (now Lod.) Knowing that rocks were sometimes thrown at the Ben Shemen school bus as it passed through the town, Haim wore Julius's WWI army belt and buckle for protection. Bracing himself, he approached several Arab men and women waiting at the bus stop. Gathering his courage, he politely inquired in Arabic, "How are you? Are you going to Jaffa?" With the harsh desert sun and wind etched on his face, an elderly man glanced his way with a slight nod. "Thank you," Haim said with a smile, hoping to strike up a conversation. But none would follow.

Boarding the bus and walking back to find a seat, Haim noticed that only the small children looked back at him. All of the passengers appeared to be poor and Arab. They must have known that he was a Jew. No British in Palestine would ever wear such ragged clothes. But there were no dirty looks, no under-the-breath derogatory remarks. Perhaps there would have been an issue had he been a woman without a hijab (head covering.) During the entire bus ride, hardly a word was spoken. He had hoped to start a dialogue, but sensed there was a stricter code of privacy than in Germany. He missed his mother. He believed Klara would have somehow had them all talking, though judging from the solemn group, maybe not about their sex lives.

As everyone descended the bus in Jaffa, Haim asked the driver in Arabic for directions to Tel Aviv. Without a word, the driver pointed towards a street. Haim thanked him and with Khalid's roughly drawn map in hand, he began the two-mile trek to the café. Taking in the sand-colored stone streets and buildings of the ancient city, he felt a certain elation walking in the footsteps of ancient Kings, Pharos, and Emperors.

Some claimed Jaffa to be the oldest port in the world, founded by Japhet, one of Noah's three sons, after the Great Flood. Archeological evidence showed the strategic location repeatedly sacked and rebuilt since first inhabited in 7,500 BCE. Ramses II, King David, Alexander the Great, Richard the Lionheart, Saladin, were just a few of its rulers.

In 1799, Napoleon Bonaparte besieged the walled city, sending in French messengers with an ultimatum of surrender. After the messengers were tortured, castrated, decapitated with their heads impaled on the city wall, Napoleon, infuriated, breeched the city's wall by commanding his troops to pull down one of its towers. In retribution for the slaying of his messengers, he allowed his men two days of slaughter and rape before ordering the execution of the Turkish governor and thousands of Muslim soldiers. When the French troops ran out of bullets, they finished the massacre with a bloodbath from bayonets.

Napoleon then released hundreds of local Egyptians to spread the word of Jaffa's fall. But as Napoleon attacked to the north, instead of being intimidated, the enraged Syrians rallied in defense, fighting back Napoleon's troops. Due to the horrid conditions, Bubonic Plague soon broke out, decimating the French Army and local population, forcing Napoleon to end his conquest of the Ottoman Empire.

On his retreat, for fear that they may be turned informants, Napoleon ordered the poisoning of all of his troops too ill to be evacuated. But unbeknownst to Napoleon, the doctors refused, and rumors of the ordered poisoning quickly spread throughout France. To contradict the rumors, in 1804, the year of his coronation as Emperor, Napoleon commissioned Antoine-Jean Gros to paint, "Les Pestiférés de Jaffa," (The Plague Victims of Jaffa.) The large work of Napoleon tenderly comforting the victims still hangs in the Louvre. But since compassion was a trait rarely associated with Napoleon, the painting quickly became a target of ridicule.

Under Ottoman rule, Jaffa was rebuilt. And with the influx of Jewish pioneers, for a short time at the end of the nineteenth century, Arabs, Christians and Jews lived peacefully together there. But the population soon swelled. By 1909 the dirt and squalor of the overcrowded streets, along with a Turkish decree forcing Jaffa Jews to move their living quarters once a year, pushed 66 Jewish families to buy a plot of land in the sand dunes north of the city. There, Tel Aviv was built with gardens, playgrounds, street lamps, and running water in the hopes of creating a modern city free of persecution.

In WWI, Turkish Ottomans, allied with Germany, expelled the Jews from Tel Aviv and Jaffa, forcing them to live in makeshift camps. But with the end of WWI and the Ottomans' rule, under the new British Mandate, Jews were allowed back into the cities. Arab riots soon broke out in Jaffa pushing Jews to flee for Tel Aviv, and by 1935, as Haim walked through Jaffa's maze of streets, he saw that it had been reduced to a poor, small, almost exclusively Arab town.

Children stood in doorways staring as if Haim were some strange alien creature. Not one adult made eye contact with him until he came upon a sidewalk café where several Arab men sat drinking coffee and a handsome, bearded, middle-aged man returned his gaze. Tempted to join them, Haim thought better of it, as the man's glare could have easily meant, "You are not welcome here." The man turned back to the conversation with his companions, and Haim continued on as planned to Tel Aviv.

∞

The white city of Tel Aviv was unlike anything Haim had ever seen. Designed by refugee German Jewish architects trained in the modern Bauhaus school, their large, glass structures, for bringing in warmth and light in the colder climate, were now redesigned for shelter from the hot desert sun. To Haim, the white concrete buildings, layered with balconies of recessed windows, stood like ships in the desert.

With over 100,000 Jews already living in Tel Aviv it was easy to get directions in Hebrew or Arabic, and

Haim soon found the café. Its Arab male clientele was seated outside under the awning of the unassuming white building. Haim took a seat next to one of the more animated tables.

A stern looking Arab man in a uniform immediately headed his way. Afraid that he was about to be thrown out, Haim anxiously took out his identification papers. "What can I get for you?" the man asked in Arabic. Realizing that he was a waiter, Haim relaxed and ordered a coffee. It only cost about a penny, but making half a pound a month, it was all he could afford. When the waiter returned with the coffee, Haim nonchalantly took a sip, practically spitting it out. He had never tasted coffee that strong. But wanting to fit in, he choked it down.

Perhaps the men at the next table assumed that Haim didn't speak Arabic, or they were just indifferent to him, but he listened in as they complained of their Jewish clientele. When a stout older gentleman finally said, "Problem is, Jews are cheap! They want something, but they don't want to pay for it!" Haim countered in Arabic, "So, why not just sell to Arabs?" The stout man reacted as if Haim had always been part of the conversation. "They are worse! You give an Arab something for half its value they still say you rob them. Americans, that's what you want. Tell Americans a price, you know what they say?" Having no idea, Haim shook his head. Attempting a Texan accent, the man chortled, "By golly, what a steal!" Haim laughed respectfully. The man asked, "So, my young friend, what brings you to these parts?" Haim shrugged, "I live in Ben Shemen and want to make sure Palestine is safe before having my family join me here."

The men all laughed. "Good thinking," the stout man said. "Make sure it is safe for all of us. As merchants, we need a protector." Having bartered a good part of their lives, these men enjoyed conversing. The stout man introduced himself and the other men at the table before warning: "But make sure your family knows that no one comes to Palestine to get rich. Everyone here is poor. Jews are poor and Arabs are poor. It is a hard life." Haim shrugged, "It doesn't look so hard for you." The man laughed while patting his large stomach, "We are but the fortunate few. Having younger family members looking after our shops gives us the luxury of free afternoons." Haim offered, "Maybe it would be an easier life if we all worked together." The man commended: "Excellent idea! Now why didn't we think of that?!" Slapping his hand down on the table, he picked up his drink and toasted: "To Haim!"

As they talked, Haim discovered that these men were open to unification. Having a mostly Jewish clientele it would be good for businesses. Another man exclaimed, "Arabs and Jews should kick out the British and work out Palestine between ourselves." While another added, "And crazy Arabs and Jews should kill each other off so we can live in peace. You know it's only a small minority of extremists creating the problem." Haim was surprised by these men's belief that most Arabs and Jews wanted to live together peacefully. Haim asked, "But what if the extremists kill us first?" The man remarked, "Yes, that would be unfortunate."

Haim enjoyed talking with them. They reminded him of Lotte and her socialist group arguing late into the night. When it was time for Haim to leave, they all gave him a warm goodbye: "To the next time."

Walking back through Jaffa, Haim came upon the same sidewalk café where the bearded man had glared at him. This time the man glared while giving a slight nod. Haim nodded back, and gathering his courage, went to sit a nearby table. Raising his hand to silence his companions, the man looked at Haim with dark, piercing eyes as he asked in Arabic: "Why do you come here?" Haim awkwardly answered, "For coffee." The man reproached: "This is no place for you." Haim stood his ground, "Why? I've done nothing wrong."

The man's glare softened slightly: "If something were to happen to you, there could be repercussions." A smaller companion explained: "See, he likes you. He's protecting you. That glare is actually his smile. His name is, Shihab. It means, Fire. Too bad they didn't name him, Smiley. I am Rasul, the owner of this fine establishment." Rasul introduced Haim to the other men at the table. Shihab contested, "I do not glare. I try to understand why the boy comes to a place that is unsafe." Rasul argued, "He's young. He doesn't know." Rasul added to Haim, "You are very welcome here, young man." Haim countered, "I do know. I came here to change things."

"You can do nothing," Shihab grumbled despondently. Rasul countered, "That's not true. He can assassinate the Grand Mufti, his followers, Ben Gurion, the radical Revisionists..." smiling to Haim, "Don't kill King Abdullah. He is our friend." Haim relaxed a little knowing that King Abdullah was for unity and moving the nation into the twentieth century. Shihab countered, "The boy is no assassin. He is for peace. He will do nothing. That is why Hitler, the Grand Mufti and Ben-Gurion will thrive."

These men were different than the poorer Arabs Haim had seen in Palestine. Though they may not have been like the Sheiks he had seen in movies and newsreels, they were better dressed, groomed and more refined. The inn of the café also seemed nicer than the typically rundown buildings of Jaffa. Haim was surprised to hear Ben-Gurion grouped with Hitler and the Grand Mufti, but wanting to hear what they had to say, he didn't argue.

When the waiter asked Haim what he would like, Shihab ordered, "A coffee. Put it on my tab." Not wanting to offend, Haim thanked him and insisted on getting the next one: "I was told everyone in Palestine is poor, Jews and Arabs." Rasul corrected, "Most are poor. Eight or so families rule Palestine. A bipartisan state is in their best interest. That is why only the Grand Mufti gave immediate support for Hitler. And you can imagine what Hitler, the lover of blue-eyed blonds, really thinks of our Grand Mufti."

Shihab cut in, "But it is the Grand Mufti everyone hears. He who squeaks loudest the masses will follow, like sheep for slaughter." Rasul explained that during the Middle Ages Arabs were the greatest thinkers with the most advanced culture. "The compass, the Sextant, where do you think Arabic Numerals came from?" Haim shrugged, "Arabs?" Rasul laughed, "How did he guess?" Shihab interjected, "We are now reduced to feudalistic peasants, fearful of anything new, forcing Jews out of Jaffa to go off and build Tel Aviv. A city we are too backward to comprehend."

Haim offered, "You don't seem so backwards." Rasul interjected, "You mean, for a feudalistic peasant." Shihab offered, "I am a former administrator to the mayor. I know what goes on. I can tell you, there will be war. These Arabs may lack nationalism. Why should they care about a government that only takes? But they have fear, enough to fuel the Grand Mufti and Hitler."

Haim was surprised that these men seemed more impressed than antagonized by the Jews in Palestine. As one said, "With no money Jews build a government with an underground police force in a country that isn't even theirs. While the Grand Mufti rounds up gangs." Haim countered, "That's how Hitler started." Shihab corrected, "Germans are different. They organize. They work together. Here, Arabs don't trust, don't smile, won't even look you in the eye. And the landowners don't care. They will sell to whomever gives the highest price, Jew or Arab. So, how will they stop Zionism? They can't. But with so many Arabs, war may be inevitable, and eternal."

Rasul smiled at Haim, "As you see, we keep Shihab here to lighten our spirits. Trust me, young man, it is not so dour. King Abdullah believes that together, Arabs and Jews can build a great nation." Shihab interrupted, "And how will that happen? Once a war is declared, it is too late." Harun, a heavyset man at the table asked Haim, "Your friends at Ben Shemen, are they religious?" "What does that matter?" Shihab questioned. Harun answered, "No religion, you are corrupt, like Soviets. Too religious, you're backwards. I ask the boy, the Jews who build Tel Aviv, the children at Ben Shemen, are they the same Jews in Europe now being slaughtered?" Aware of the difference from his first day there, Haim shook his head. The man nodded, "So, you see, Shihab, war may not go on forever. It may change these Arabs into fighters. They may win."

Haim had never associated the European Jews with the poorer Arabs of Palestine. But was a Hasidic felt hat any different from an Arab turban? And the young couple with the baby traveling with him on the boat to Palestine, rarely smiling, avoiding eye contact, too fearful to even get off the boat to see Naples and Pompeii, were they that different than the poorer Arabs of Jaffa? Had working with others to build a new life in a foreign land changed them? Would they now fight for their new home? During that one night Haim spent with little Jacek he had seen a change in him. Jacek was learning to survive. Would the Palestinians Arabs do the same?

On the bus home, Haim sat in silence wondering how Ben-Gurion could be likened to Hitler and the

Grand Mufti. But hadn't he disassociated himself from the Arabs, as Hitler and the Grand Mufti had of the Jews. If Arab leaders were to speak with him they would have do so in Hebrew, English, Turkish, French, Polish, Russian, Greek, or Spanish. Was learning a ninth language really that tasking, or was it more telling that a Jewish leader in Palestine refused to learn the native language? Ben-Gurion had said that ridding Palestine of the Arabs was a necessary evil. How different was that from Hitler's view of the Jews? Before Haim had met Khalid, he may not have asked those questions.

That Sunday, while Amon ate his apples and the boys shared their lunches, Haim spoke of his trip to Jaffa and Tel Aviv. "You went to the table of a strange man glaring at you?" Khalid asked in disbelief. Haim shrugged, "You'd do the same if you wanted to talk to him." Khalid laughed, "Not if my only weapon was a belt. What could you do with it, spank him?" Haim assured, "A belt is actually safer than a gun." Khalid cracked a smile, "What war is won with belts?" Haim argued, "That's different. If I pull a gun out at a bus stop, someone might shoot me. But pull out a belt, they all stand back." Khalid shrugged, "Or laugh." Haim nodded, "Either way, it's better."

Suddenly a man's voice called out in Arabic, "Who goes there?" The boys froze. Through the brush, they could see several Arabs, rifles in hand, heading their way. Haim quickly got Khalid onto Amon and jumped up behind him. As they galloped off, the man yelled in Arabic, "Stop or we shoot!" Glancing back,

Haim saw the men lift their rifle. Just in time, Amon galloped into the forest, sheltering them in the trees.

With their hearts still racing, they made it to the path towards Beit Nabala. From there it was a short walk for Khalid. Though the men probably didn't see Khalid's face, it upset Haim to have put his friend in possible danger. "I'm sorry," He said. "We better be more careful next time." Khalid assured, "It's okay, they can't catch Amon." Their hiding spot now compromised, the boys agreed to meet in the same place where Haim had met little Jacek. Haim assured, "Amon and I will go there each day for lunch until you can make it." Khalid took off his turban and handed it to Haim, "Wear this. If you're spotted they'll think you're Arab." Taking it, Haim asked, "Don't you need it?" Khalid laughed, "No, it's just a rag. I'll make a new one when I get home." Haim put the turban on his head and got back up on Amon. Khalid watched with concern as they disappeared into the woods.

To avoid the Grand Mufti's guards, they took a longer route home. As they came to the border of a field, Haim had Amon step out slowly checking to see that no one was around. "You like going fast, boy? Here's your chance." Loosening the reigns and leg pressure, Haim gave a slight tap with his heal and hung on as Amon charged out into the open field.

As they galloped, Haim spotted the Arab guards at a far distant edge of the woods. Ducking behind Amon's neck to hide his face, he pulled on the left halter whispering, "Turn, boy. They can't know where we're going." They had fled Arab guards and British police before, but never while Haim was wearing a turban. If they recognized them, who would they think was riding the Arabian stallion now? They galloped towards Beit Nabala. Once out of sight, Haim had Amon turn and start back on an even longer route home.

At Ben Shemen's east field, concerned that the Arab guards were sent to watch for them, Haim decided to make one last run for it. Galloping into the field, Haim looked back to see that they weren't followed.

Suddenly, he felt Amon falling out from under him. With Amon being such a strong runner, he had never considered that he could lose his footing. But tired from the long ride, he had tripped in a brush-covered hole. Haim went flying through the air, his young body hitting the ground, bouncing and tumbling to a stop. The wind knocked out of him, Haim gasped for air as he lifted his head to see Amon lying twenty yards away.

Panicked that Amon had broken a leg, Haim struggled to his feet. In Bingen, Haim could never forget witnessing a workhorse being shot after falling in a trench. Klara assured him that there was no choice. The horse could not survive with a broken leg, and killing him quickly was more humane.

Still gasping, Haim ran to Amon. Just before reaching him, Amon jumped up on all fours. In utter relief, Haim hugged Amon. He then checked Amon's legs. Besides a few scrapes and bruises, it appeared that they had both survived the fall. Amon nuzzled Haim as he scratched him behind his ears. By his unusual affection, Haim could see that Amon was also shaken.

Haim spotted the turban on the ground. Having forgotten that he was still wearing it, he picked it up: "What would they think if they saw me riding into Ben Shemen wearing this?" He put the turban in his pocked, so that he could return it to Khalid, and got back up on Amon. Still concerned about being followed, he and Amon went much more cautiously to the stables.

∞

Haim went back to Jaffa and Tel Aviv the next Saturday to talk politics with his new friends in the cafés. He brought homework to pass the time on the bus, but soon found himself capturing on paper a small child on the neighboring bench sleeping against her mother. As he studied her lines and curves Haim noticed the girl's mother curiously looking at him. Turning his work pad towards her, so that she could see what he was drawing, he asked in Arabic, "Would you like it when I'm done? Otherwise, I'll just throw it away." Somewhat wary, she hesitated before giving an uncertain nod. When he finished the drawing, he tore it from the pad, handed it to her and went back to drawing. Relaxing as she realized that he expected no money, she carefully placed it in her bag so as not to wrinkle it.

Haim then asked to sketch the careworn man that he first attempted talking to at the bus stop in Lydda. With only a slight nod, the man agreed. But when

Haim showed him the finished drawing a large smile of many missing teeth spread across his face. Haim began a second sketch of the man, but this time, he began asking simple questions in Arabic as he drew. "Were you born in Palestine?" "Do you like it here?" "Do you go to Jaffa everyday?" Haim discovered that the man's family had worked in the Jaffa citrus groves since the early nineteenth century. Citrus exports had become Palestine's largest revenue with Jaffa exporting over ten million crates of oranges a year. "Do you enjoy working outside," Haim asked as he handed him the second portrait. The man looked bewildered, as if he had never pondered that question. A woman sitting next to the man interjected, "It is for the pennies they give us that we work all day in the hot desert sun, not for the pleasure." Understanding, Haim nodded adding, "At Ben Shemen they tell us that working the earth purifies the soul." The woman jeered, "Then we will go to heaven. Hopefully there are no orange groves up there."

Each Saturday, Haim continued sketching the passengers. As the weeks passed, he could feel himself improving, more easily capturing their shapes, light and depth. They always seemed pleased as he handed their portraits to them. Several even began smiling and nodding as he boarded the bus.

While sketching a frail, older woman, she confided that she had worked in the same textile factory since the age of five. Surprised, Haim asked what a five-year-old can do. With a smile, she mimed sewing. It was the only education she had known. Children, considered apprentices, were paid practically nothing, but it was important to her family that she learn a trade. He soon discovered that all of the children on the bus were working. Sabah, the little girl that he first drew sleeping by her mother, Luja, was only four-years-old but already training as a servant girl in the café where her mother worked. Several other children worked as sharecroppers in the citrus groves. An eight-year-old boy was an apprentice in construction. His twelve-year-old brother, who had gotten him the job, was recovering after a beam fell on his right foot. With no workers' benefits or healthcare, their family would have been ruined had the townspeople not helped to pay for the boy's medical bills.

Child labor laws introduced under the British mandate were apparently only put in place to appease the League of Nations. To keep labor costs down, wealthy Palestinians used their influence to make sure that the laws were never enforced. Margaret Nixon, the British government welfare inspector, who at first supported child labor regulations, ended up advocating nonintervention. She was somehow assured that Palestinian children enjoy working long hours in terrible conditions, concluding her term of office by stating, "A white British adult couldn't possibly understand what a black, Bedouin girl servant felt."

If the money the children earned helped to pay for their schooling, then one day they could possibly find a better job. If it went to helping their families, as it usually did, they would remain illiterate, like most of the adults on the bus.

Haim understood having to do what it takes to survive, but he didn't see why Arabs and Jews couldn't work together to have the same benefits that the Jews had set up through the Histadrut? Established in the 1920's as the labor organization of the Yishuv, the Histadrut acted as a trade union, bank, insurance company, pension fund, job placement agency, and with its own health care, educational system, newspaper, publishing house, and even a theatre group, it was a state within a state. While pushing its advantages to his new friends, Haim made sure to leave out that it also headed the Haganah and all illegal Jewish immigration.

"We may all be poor, but working together we can change things for our children." As odd as they found this strange boy drawing their pictures and talking of their children's future, they couldn't argue against free health care, education and a better life. Though few believed it possible, they continued opening up to him. Haim found that his friends on the bus felt no animosity towards him for being Jewish. But as Shihab claimed, "Those for blood squeak loudest."

At the café in Jaffa, Shihab questioned Haim sardonically, "You think that poor Arabs will join Jews to form a trade union? They won't even do that for themselves." Rasul shook his head as he smirked, "It is an excellent idea. Since Haim refuses to assassinate the Grand Mufti, educate the masses so they do it themselves." Harun contended, "They don't want education. They have religion." With a slight clearing of his throat, Shihab silenced them: "It's not lack of religion that keeps poor Arabs from organizing. Over centuries there have been too many invasions and corrupt governments for them to trust any."

Haim argued, "I don't see it that way. They want to work together to have a better life." Shihab stared through Haim with steely eyes: "They talk to you because you talk to them. When you are not there, what do they say?" Uncertain, Haim shook his head with a shrug. Shihab nodded, "That is right. They say nothing. They look off in silence, just as you found them. They may help an injured local boy, but they will not give to strangers. Years have taught them that any regime only takes, never gives." "Maybe things are different now," Haim argued. Shihab countered, "The only difference now is that a bus ride makes it easier for these workers to get to their thankless jobs."

Few argued with Shihab, too intimidated by his glare. But unwilling to give up on his new friends, Haim would persist in their heated discussions.

∞

"How do you get away with it?" Khalid asked, shaking his head in disbelief. "If I told everyone we should join the Jews to make a new country, I'd be killed." Haim shrugged, "Not if you first drew them." Khalid laughed before soberly warning, "Just be careful. And never mention Amon. The Mufti's men were asking if anyone knows of a boy with a black horse."

Haim had been secretive of Amon with everyone but his friends at the café in Jaffa. When they asked what his friends at school thought about unity, Haim answered, "My best friend is an Arabian horse. So naturally he's for it." Their curiosity sparked, he explained his relationship with Amon. The men at the café seemed so far removed from his life at Ben Shemen he didn't think it could matter, but he never mentioned Amon again.

Over the next few months Haim continued making friends on the bus and in the cafés. Rasul, the innkeeper in Jaffa continued joining their discussions. During one heated exchange, Haim expected to be told to quiet down as Rasul came over. But with a gentle hand on Haim's shoulder, Rasul bent down to whisper in his ear, "My friend, there is a gentleman who would like to speak with you."

Haim followed Rasul into the small, dark café. Glancing over Haim's farming clothes, Rasul asked, "Did you bring anything else to wear?" Haim uneasily shook his head. Rasul shrugged: "His eminence will understand." They walked across a small courtyard to a large wooded door where Rasul cautioned, "Remember, there is no reason to speak of this to anyone." Opening the door, they entered a large, imposing room, almost ostentatious compared to the rest of the inn. In the Arab culture it was not uncommon for such opulence to be hidden.

In the center of the room, a distinguished gentleman sat on an embroidered silk pillow resting on an impressive Persian rug. Two cups of coffees resting on a round, silver tray were placed in front of him. With his cotton white robe and face that seemed familiar, topped with a perfectly wrapped white silk turban, Haim guessed him to be an important religious figure. Rasul indicated with his right hand to the more modest pillow on the other side of the tray facing the gentleman, "His eminence, Sei Sendi, wishes you to sit."

Sensing not to speak until spoken to, Haim sat down and waited. As long as he was silent he hadn't made any mistakes. The gentleman neither smiled nor frowned before finally pointing to the cups of coffee and taking the one closest to him. Haim picked up the other coffee and waited for the gentleman to sip first. When Haim tasted the coffee, he was shaken by its strength. It was even stronger than the coffees he was still getting used to. But he struggled to appear unaffected. The slight smile that cracked on the gentleman's face showed that Haim fooled no one. Each time the gentleman sipped, Haim did the same, and gradually the coffee became more bearable.

"I hear that Amon is very fond of you," the gentleman finally said in Arabic. Haim's eyes widened, anxiously wondering how he knew of Amon. Had he been told of them scouting together? Haim nervously explained, "We're just good friends. He likes to be ridden." The gentleman acquiesced, "And how did he have the luck to find you." Haim cracked a smile: "We found each other. He was a gift of King Abdullah to Haim Arlosoroff. When Arlosoroff was killed his widow donated him to my school." The gentleman seemed satisfied with the explanation: "And is he a well trained horse?" Haim nodded: "He's the best plow horse at Ben Shemen." With a raised eyebrow, the gentleman questioned, "An Arabian plow horse?" Haim nodded awkwardly, concerned that he done something wrong: "He doesn't have to. He wants to. We just do what we can for each other." The gentleman offered, "To persuade such horse to plow fields speaks very highly of you."

Amon was all they talked about until the gentleman said, "I understand that you would like us to have a common state." Haim nodded: "Arabs were once the greatest thinkers. They're hard workers, like Jews. Together we could make a great nation." The gentleman looked at Haim askance: "Do you believe that to be possible?" Haim nodded, "Arlosoroff believed it. I want to continue where he left off. Unfortunately, those against squeak loudest." They discussed little else, and Haim, as Rasul instructed, walked out backwards so as not to turn his back on the gentleman.

∞

Several days later, Haim sat in the mess hall with his roommates when he noticed the gentleman's picture on the front page of a newspaper. Seeing Haim's eyes widen, Avi asked, "What's with you?" "That's King Abdullah?" Haim said in disbelief as he read the article of the emir's trip from Jaffa to Cairo. Avi shrugged, "So?" Haim shook his head, "Nothing, I thought he looked different." Avi laughed: "What you expect, pitchfork, tail? They say he's not as bad as most of them." Believing that he was a religious leader, had Haim addressed him in the wrong way? Called him 'Your Holiness'? How foolish he must have sounded bragging that Amon was a gift of King Abdullah. He tried to remember anything else he might have said to offend the king of Transjordan. Not knowing if he would ever see the king again, (much less the greater role that he would one-day play in his life) Haim cracked a smile thinking, "Too late now."

CHAPTER 15

SHORTLY AFTER TALKING to the artist, David Polonsky, Einat went through another treatment of chemo and radiation. Nearing the end of this round, she found it harder to bounce back from the strong dosages. Considering the gravity of any cancer cells surviving now, the dosages would have been even stronger had her doctor felt her body could handle it. After several days in bed, she finally saw her therapist, anxious to discuss her conversation with David.

"I never thought I'd be upset that the illustrations are too good," Einat said as she watched her therapist study the illustrations of 'AND THERE WAS EVENING.' Acquiescing with a nod, her therapist added, "But if Fischerkoesen was also a victim of the Nazis, people might understand." Einat gave a slight laugh, "They were upset just finding out the book was based on a Hans Christian Andersen story. How will they react to the illustrator being Goebbels' top animator?" Directing her eyes from the book to Einat, her therapist asked, "What frightens you most about this?"

Einat took a moment before shaking her head, "We don't know how much time I have, but whatever it is, shouldn't I focus it on my husband and children?" Her therapist shrugged, "None of us know how much time we have. If you think waiting all day for your family to come home is best for you..." Einat argued, "No, but why search for someone who may destroy the reputation of the book? What good would that do?" Deep down, Einat hated giving up the search. Finding this artist who had undoubtedly suffered so much war had become a passion. And it had made her feel she was moving forward, focusing on something other than her battle with cancer. Her therapist questioned, "Have you thought of posting David's theory on your blog?" Seeing Einat's bewilderment, she continued, "Present it as a slim possibility. The reaction may help you know how to go forward."

The next morning, still weak, though feeling slightly better, Einat hesitantly hit the send button as she posted the Fischerkoesen video with David's theory and the questions:

"...Could it be that Haim Hausman was actually this well known German animator? Could he have illustrated the book to make up for the films he had made for the Nazis? Since he was released from a Russian prison by showing that he was a member of the German resistance, should we embrace this artist who also suffered at the hands of the Nazis?"

The hate mail poured in. "Embrace Goebbels' top animator? Are you insane?" "Why would a kibbutz-publishing house hire an animator for the Nazis?" "Fischerkoesen could have copied the stars from the same place as Haim Hausman. It proves nothing." Several people wanted to know what Fischerkoesen did for the Jews while in the underground. Besides keeping swastikas and Nazi propaganda out of his films, Einat could find nothing.

Disheartened, she went back to her therapist, who admitted, "As a psychologist, I usually don't recommend suppressing the truth, but this may be the exception." Seeing Einat's anxiety, she asked, "What do you think? Is Fischerkoesen the artist?" Not having considered her own feelings, Einat was momentarily taken aback. "David Polonsky believes so. Who am I to argue?" Her therapist nodded: "That's true. After all, you are just a puppet in David Polanski's hands." Einat laughed slightly while shaking her head: "No, but..." Her therapist encouraged, "What does your gut tell you?" Einat closed her eyes and thought of the Fischerkoesen videos she recently watched on YouTube, and then of the Haim Hausman illustrations. Conceding, she said, "I'm probably too crazy to accept the facts, but I just don't believe it." "Why is that?" her therapist pressed. Einat took time to gather her thoughts: "It feels as if they were drawn by someone who knew this land." Her therapist waited, allowing Einat to continue. "The father and daughter are German, I see that. But the vegetation, the houses, the chicken coup, they're from here. People have even tried to find Haim Hausman by looking for the actual house in the illustrations. I always thought *they* were crazy." Her therapist asked, "Couldn't Fischerkoesen have drawn them from photos?" Einat nodded, "Of course, but 'Snow White' and 'Pinocchio' were made in Hollywood, and because some of the animators were German and Swiss they look Germanic. How could Fischerkoesen, who was never in Palestine, have drawn like that?" Her therapist shrugged: "Sounds like a sane question."

With a slight laugh Einat added, "Here's where you may think I'm crazy." Einat explained her theory of how some questions wanted to be answered, and some didn't. "Whenever I talk to people about Haim Hausman, doors open. I don't think that would be the case if Fischerkoesen were the artist. The doors would stay shut, keeping the secret safe. But then David's right. The drawings are too good. It doesn't make sense." Feeling Einat's anxiety, her therapist cracked a smile, "So, forget about it. Move on." As Einat looked at her in disbelief, she added, "Or, make sense of it."

CHAPTER 16

Summer, 1936:

NO WORDS came out of Haim's mouth as he tried to order his Haganah troops. Even though he was still the youngest in his unit, their commanding officer was sick, and having scouted the area with Amon for the past year he knew the land better than any of them. It was now up to him how they would sneak in the newly arrived yolim (illegal immigrants/Aliyah Bet.) A naked light bulb hung from the ceiling as he stared at the large map spread out on the table. With the Great Arab revolt of 1936-1939 well underway, Arab-Jewish relations had spiraled downward. The wrong choice of routes could easily send them to their graves.

In 1930, the Muslim preacher, al-Qassam, had recruited hundreds of Arab peasants as militia for what he named, The Black Hand. After months of training, a jihad (holy war) was declared on the Zionists and British in Palestine. Soon, three members of Kibbutz Yagur were ambushed and killed, followed by the attempted bombings of Jewish homes outside of Haifa, the killing of several members of a northern Jewish settlement, and the murder of a Jewish father and son by throwing a bomb into their home.

As al-Qassam and his followers became more violent, blowing up newly constructed railway lines, even the Grand Mufti pulled away in favor of a more political approach to ending Zionism. But in October of 1935, a large shipment of arms destined for the Haganah discovered in the Jaffa port, stoked Arab fears of a Jewish military takeover.

A British constable was soon murdered near Ein Harod. Search parties went out to capture their most likely suspect, al-Qassam. For ten days al-Qassam and twelve of his followers were on the run, hidden by local followers. British police finally surrounded them in a cave near Ya'bad. But instead of surrendering, al-Qassam ordered his men to die as martyrs, and opened fire on the British. By the end of the shootout, al-Qassam and three of his men were dead.

His last stand made him legendary as a symbol of resistance. Thousands of Arabs mobbed al-Qassam's funeral in Haifa, crashing through police lines to get nearer to his body. "For the first time, the Arabs have seen someone give their life for the cause," Ben-Gurion warned. "This will give the Arabs the moral strength they lack."

From 1931 - 1936, the Jewish population of Palestine had more than doubled to 370,000, 27% of the total population. To placate Arab demands, the British severely cut back on immigration. With the increasing persecution by the Nazis, many Jews considered illegal immigration their hope of survival.

In 1934, two kibbutz residents had secretly traveled to Greece to arrange for the passage of the Velos, the first large ship to transport illegal immigrants to

Palestine. The 340 passengers, mostly young adults and children, used aliases in case the British uncovered the plan. Terrified of being intercepted, the older ones quietly comforted the children during the several days journey from Athens to Palestine. Landing safely, the Haganah slipped the yolim in under the radar of the British, giving them forged papers and dispersing them throughout Palestine.

After the success of the Velos, a second voyage was arranged. The British, however, trailed this one to Palestine, and forced them to return to Greece. They wandered from port to port until the Polish government finally accepted them back. To survive, they would have to escape again, but the next ship, the Wanda, sank in the harbor of Danzig (a free city state from 1920-1939.) Though none of the passengers drowned, from then on smaller boats were used, carrying only 20-30 yolim. Yolim also entered over land from the north through Beirut and Damascus, but with Ben Shemen twenty miles from the coast, Haim's unit primarily focused on those arriving by sea.

It's estimated that 40,000 yolim entered Palestine by 1939, and up to 100,000 by the end of WWII. With the need for extreme secrecy, it's still unknown how many were saved by illegally sailing to Palestine, slipping ashore, and disappearing into the Yishuv.

As the Jewish population increased, so did tensions with the Arab communities, causing the Yishuv to push its exclusivity program of hiring only Jewish workers. The worldwide depression had already taken its toll on the Arab workers. With even fewer jobs available more Arabs were left impoverished and idle. It was only a matter of time for tensions to explode.

On April 15, 1936, shortly before Haim's fifteenth birthday, the Great Arab Revolt began when Arab rebels attacked a convoy of trucks, shooting and killing two Jewish drivers. In revenge, Irgun gunmen (ignoring Ben-Gurion's defense only stance until the Jews were strong enough to take the country) shot and killed two Arab workers sleeping in a hut. A few days later, riots broke out in Tel Aviv during the funeral for one of the Jewish drivers. The British drove in with armored cars and opened fire to keep out the Arab mobs. A wildfire of news spread throughout the Arab villages and towns that Jewish rioters were destroying Arab property and beating their children. Soon, more riots followed in Jaffa and Tel Aviv.

The Arab Higher Committee was formed to gain national Arab independence. With the Grand Mufti as president, they fought to stop Lord Peel's plan for partition of Palestine into a small Jewish state, a residual Mandatory area, and a larger Arab state linked to Transjordan. Furious over the proposal to transfer 225,000 Palestinian Arabs from their homes in the Jewish state to the Arab state and Transjordan, they demanded the end of all Jewish immigration and land sale to Jews. Until that time, The Arab Higher Committee called for a general strike, shutting down municipal governments and forbidding Arabs to pay British taxes. Riots spread throughout Palestine. Arabs from neighboring countries crossed the border to join in the revolt.

The British placed Jaffa under curfew, as it was considered the origin of the strike and the rebellion's epicenter. Its maze of dark narrow streets, overcrowded tenements and underground sewer system made for easy escape from the British army, while also allowing Arab snipers good cover for attacking Tel Aviv and Jewish vehicles.

With military reinforcements from Malta and Egypt, the British barricaded off Jaffa's old town, cut off municipal services, and covered all access roads with shards of glass and nails. British bombers then dropped leaflets in Arabic warning the inhabitants to evacuate the city that same day.

On June 17, 1936, a British warship sealed off any escape by sea as 1,500 British soldiers blasted their way into Jaffa, blowing up ancient buildings from east to west, cutting a large path of destruction through the heart of the city. On June 29th, another path was blown through from north to south. The British claimed that the operation was to modernize the old town, but few were deceived. Its obvious purpose was to take control of the town by allowing British military vehicles better access. Almost 6,000 Palestinian Arabs were left homeless, most ending up destitute.

Upset by the news, Haim set out to find his friends at the café in Jaffa. With no buses running from Lydda since the beginning of the revolt, some of his Arab friends on the bus allowed him to join them in the back of a pickup. Tarek, a lean, handsome Arab labor worker in his mid 30's handed Haim a turban: "Wear this. And when we are stopped, say nothing." With seventeen of them crammed into the back of a large pickup, they jostled down the dirt road. Haim sat next to Tarek's wife, Luja and their daughter, Sabah, the little girl that he first drew on his trips to Jaffa. Over many bus rides they had become good friends, and Luja had saved all of Haim's drawings of them. In order to protect him, Luja and Tarek had Sabah sit on Haim's lap to make him appear as part of their family.

Several miles outside of Jaffa, they were pulled over by an Arab patrol in search of Jewish terrorists attempting to enter the city. Haim did as told and remained silent. Luja pressed closer to him, sliding Sabah onto both of their laps. While an Arab guard questioned the driver, two guards held machineguns on the group. Avoiding eye contact with the guards, Haim focused on calming Sabah, who was now five-years-old and had already learned to fear the guards. With his dark hair, deep tan and turban he blended in enough to pass through with the others.

On the outskirts of town they were stopped again, this time by a British patrol searching for weapons. Haim knew better than to be armed. He didn't even wear Julius's WWI army belt for fear that it would give him away. For his own protection, an unarmed Jewish boy was as likely to be kept out of Jaffa as a Jewish terrorist. But he was again passed through with his friends.

After half an hour of carefully walking over the shards of glass and nails blanketing the roads, he finally made it into Jaffa's old town. The once overcrowded streets, clattering with tradesmen selling their wares, were now deserted. The only sounds now were a dry, desolate wind and distant bulldozers clearing out the demolished buildings.

As the café came into view, Haim exhaled with relief. It was still there. Though fortunate to be out of the path of destruction, the building appeared to be abandoned. Haim slowly opened the door and entered. Suddenly hearing the click of a cocked gun, he froze. Turning his head, he saw the barrel of a rifle aimed between his eyes.

"Haim, are you crazy? Why are you here?" Shihab sternly demanded. Though Haim sensed Shihab's relief as he lowered the rifle. Appearing from behind Shihab, Rasul, the innkeeper corrected as he eyed Haim's turban. "You are the crazy one. This is not our Haim. This is some handsome, young Arab boy, so much more attractive than that skinny Jewish kid. What brings you here, o' handsome one?" Haim cracked a smile, "I wanted to make sure you were all right." Putting an arm over Haim's shoulder, Shihab led him to the bar. "And if we weren't, what then? You would fight off the British singlehandedly?" Rasul put his arm over Haim's other shoulder. "You are crazy, and a good friend."

Haim asked apprehensively, "Where is everyone?" Shihab assured, "They left, in time. Like idiots we stayed to protect this miserable place." As if affronted, Rasul corrected, "It is my miserable place. Which means you are the idiot."

While Rasul made coffee, Shihab confided to Haim, "The few who tried to resist quickly fell in British gunfire. The rest watched in silence as their homes were crushed. Most who lost everything had no desire for revolt. Their greatest hope was for their children to have a better life. Now they starve in camps."

When it was time for Haim to return home, Rasul stayed behind to protect the inn as Shihab walked Haim out of town. When Haim pointed to the pickup truck back to Lydda, Shihab warned, "Do not return until the buses run again." Before Haim could argue, Shihab insisted, "This is not a request. It is for all of our safety. Until then make no attempt to contact us." Haim nodded begrudgingly, and turned to go. Shihab called to him: "Haim, come here." Over the year of heated discussions, the handsome man's harsh glare had softened. Seeing the strong man's protective eyes now well up as he spread his arms, Haim ran back to him. As they hugged goodbye Shihab offered, "Thank you, my good friend."

From the back of the pickup, Haim watched Shihab disappear into the distance not knowing if he would ever see him again.

∞

"Where have you been, young man?" his housemother scolded as Haim entered the mess hall 15 minutes late for dinner. Flustered, he stammered, "I, I sprained my ankle. I was soaking it down in the creek." "Is it better?" she questioned. With a short nod he assured, "Yeah, see, not too bad now."

He knew that his father would have pushed him for the truth and severely punished him for dressing up as an Arab to check on his friends in a war zone. At the worst, his housemother would write him up and nothing would come of it. Though he enjoyed the independence he felt in Palestine, it was also a constant reminder that he was on his own. But in his letters home, he assured his parents that he was safe and secure at Ben Shemen, never mentioning the illegal work he was doing for the Haganah.

By mid-summer of 1936, thousands of Jewish-farmed acres and orchards had been burnt and destroyed. With increasing murders of Jewish civilians some communities fled to safer areas. But even with the Arab revolt, after seeing how the Germans embraced the Nazi movement, Haim believed that his family was better off in Palestine. Most poor Arab workers distrusted the Palestinian ruling class, making it harder for them to organize, and with the revolt, things were changing for the Yishuv.

The British, in need of troops, were now forced to recognize, and even train, the Haganah. The first thing Haim learned was how to imitate a British officer. When his troops were slacking off he would call out in a British accent, "On your feet you bloody rookies!" Those who didn't see him quickly stood at attention. The rest laughed as Haim asked the ones standing, "Righty 'o old chaps, seen any yolim scurrying about?"

Openly building an army would one day prove invaluable to the formation of the State of Israel, but at the time for Haim it made bringing in the yolim even more dangerous. To appease the Arabs, the British became more diligent in capturing and sending back illegal Jewish immigrants. Those caught helping them were often imprisoned and deported, and being caught by the growing Arab militia often meant immediate execution.

Haim was informed that three small boats carrying 43 yolim had arrived off of the north coast of Tel Aviv. Haganah units would wait until after dark to slip them ashore. Early on, Haim learned the importance of planning missions for nighttime, when it was easier to disappear. At night, just keeping perfectly still behind some brush made one virtually invisible. Once the yolim were moved into safe houses along the coast, Haim's unit would receive a call from a Tel Aviv bakery communicating their mission in code.

The call came about 8:30pm. "Excuse me, I lost the address of where we are to deliver the 11 loaves of challah for the Friday night seder?" Haim understood that his unit was responsible for distributing 11 of the yolim into different farms of the Ben Shemen Moshav. From there, the yolim would receive forged papers and be moved deeper into Palestine.

He had tell them quickly where the yolim were to be dropped off. Unnatural pauses could alert British and Arab militia, listening in on wiretaps, to a possible covert Haganah operation. Their lives now depended on how relaxed he sounded. Wiping the sweat from his forehead, he told them as casually as possible the address of the farm, adding how much they were looking forward to the challah. The farm was in close proximity to the other farms of the Ben Shemen moshav, but the yolim would not stay there. Now that the address was given out, they would only be dropped off nearby, and three Haganah teams would take them to other designated farms. Haim picked the teams, half expecting an argument to ensue. Being the youngest, he was surprised that they seemed to respect his authority, usually agreeing with whatever he suggested.

Haim scouted ahead with Amon to the drop off point. Once confident that the coast was clear, he signaled with a flashlight for his men to come to the entrance of the farm. They then waited behind brush on the narrow dirt road as Amon grazed in the nearby field. Shortly after 1:00am Haim was drifting off to sleep when he was alerted by a bus heading towards them. It signaled with three flashes of its lights, and Haim quickly signaled back.

The 11 yolim were quietly dropped off, and the bus quickly continued on its way. Haim had hoped that they would all be changed into local clothes. The ones in long dark garb were always a dead give away, but there was rarely enough time or resources at the safe houses to give them a full transformation. Their respective farms would have the task of making them look like the new Jews of Palestine. Moving fast, Haim pointed to the yolim each team would be responsible for, grouping the smaller children with his stronger men in case they had to be carried. He then mounted Amon, wrapped a large black scarf around his head and face, exposing only his eyes, and scouted ahead as the teams with the yolim trailed behind.

Things were going as planned until Haim and Amon, turned a corner to come upon five strong, young Arab militia. The Arabs, as surprised to see Haim and Amon, went for their rifles. Knowing his teams would have a hard time getting away from them, Haim loudly ordered the Arab militia in his British accent, "Hurry up, you swaddies! Illegals are making a run for it!" Confused, the men moved out of the way as Amon trotted past them. Haim called back, "Hurry up! No dawdling, rookies!"

Haim rode Amon fast enough to keep out of the their reach while making sure not to lose them. It didn't matter whether they were following Haim because they believed he was a British agent or a Haganah in disguise. The longer he kept them on his trail, the more chance the yolim had of getting to safety.

When he finally reached the border of the woods, Haim called back to the winded Arab militia, "Sorry, old boys, much too slow! If I don't break off now, the illegals will get away! Cheerio!" Catching their breath, the men watched as Haim and Amon galloped off into the woods.

∞

The next day, nothing seemed out of the ordinary as Haim did his chores, went to class, worked on the farm and spent time with Amon. His men, alerted by his loudly calling out to the Arab militia in his British accent, used alternate routes to bring the yolim to their designated farms. To avoid being followed, Haim took Amon a long way back through a shallow creek to cover their trail.

It wasn't until after supper that Haim was summoned to Lehman's office. Apprehensively walking in, he found Lehman and Pearlman meeting with a British officer and three middle aged Arab men.

Lehman immediately introduced Haim in English, "Ah, here's our stable boy. Maybe he can help." As if talking to a child, Lehman asked, "Do you know anyone who might have ridden the black stallion last night?" Haim anxiously stared at Lehman before shaking his head. Lehman continued, "It seems that someone pretending to be a British officer may have led Arab guards on a wild goose chase. Do you know anything about this?" Haim nervously shook his head again. Khalid had warned him that there were rumors of a black stallion helping the Haganah. Since the young Arab militia from the night before wouldn't dare show themselves to the British during the height of the revolt, Haim guessed that these men were acting for them.

Haim continued staring, too frightened to speak, as Lehman explained to the men, "I'm sorry, his English isn't very good. He's been here a year, but he's a little slow." With a friendly hand on Haim's shoulder, Lehman smiled, "He fits in well at the barn though." Lehman then asked Haim in German, "Do you think that anyone could have ridden the crazy horse last night, the crazy horse that no one can ride, to help bring in illegal immigrants?" Haim anxiously answered in stilted English, "No, no one ride crazy black horse. He killer."

"Like we told you," Pearlman affirmed. "The horse is dangerous. Nobody can ride him." Lehman intervened, "Since it was dark, how do you know it was a black stallion? Maybe it was a bay or even a chestnut?" One of the Arabs despondently shook his head: "This horse has been seen before. There can be few like him in Palestine." The British officer intervened, "It is a good point though. In the dark it's hard to be certain."

Lehman assured, "As you've heard, no one can ride our horse. If he hadn't been a gift of King Abdullah, we would've gotten rid of him long ago. In fact, if you want him he's yours. You'd be doing us a great favor by taking him." Hearing that, Haim's heart raced. He was about to speak up when Pearlman cut him off, "That would sure make the boy happy. The horse attacks him. See how scared he looks just at the mention of the crazy horse. He has to wait till he's out in the field just to leave food for him." Though panicked, Haim had no choice but to remain silent.

The British officer nodded, "See now, if you had any doubts, they're giving you the horse. That should settle it." Surprised by the offer, the Arabs talked briefly amongst themselves before acquiescing. Lehman patted Haim's back reassuringly as he led him out, "You can go back to your dorm now. We'll take these men to the barn."

Doing as told, Haim went to the dorm, but only to get his rifle. Perhaps Lehman felt he had to sacrifice Amon, but Haim wasn't about to. He blamed himself. Amon would not have been in danger had he not taught him to trust people. Besides a few yolim children, Haim was the only one to pet him, but he had grown comfortable around Pearlman and the men of his Haganah unit. With Pearlman joining these Arab men at the barn, would Amon also trust them?

"What you doing?" Avi asked, looking up from his card game with the twins. "Saving a friend," Haim briskly responded as he loaded ammunition into his sac. Avi began to get up as he asked, "Need help?" Already heading out the door, Haim shook his head, "Not yet. I'll let you know." He appreciated the offer, but nothing could slow him down. It seemed as if his only choice was to escape with Amon from Ben Shemen.

∞

Hiding behind brush, Haim anxiously watched as Lehman and Pearlman led the British officer and the three Arab men into the barn. Wherever they took Amon, Haim would follow, wait until it was safe and make it look as if Amon broke out on his own. From there they would hide at one of the farms used as safe houses until his Haganah unit could help move them deeper into Palestine. Caring about his education, Haim hadn't wanted to leave Ben Shemen. But education would have to wait. After all of the fields Amon had plowed and countless yolim he had helped to save, they were sure to find a kibbutz to take them in.

From inside the barn, Haim heard Amon let out a terrifying whinny. Wood planks were hit and cracked as the men yelled to each other to hold him back. Haim was about to move in when he saw Lehman and Pearlman run out of the barn with the British officer on their trail. More commotion and yelling came from inside the barn before two of the Arab men helped out the injured the third.

"The mad horse broke my rib!" Haim heard the man cry out in Arabic. Lehman encouraged, "Maybe once he gets to know you..." "You crazy as horse!" the man screamed at Lehman. Pearlman shrugged apologetically: "We tried to tell you." As they laid the man down on the ground, Pearlman cautiously slipped inside the barn's entrance to put out the lantern. Judging from the terror on his face as he quickly reappeared, Amon must have begun charging him. Wasting no time, Pearlman locked the door by pushing a long 2x4 through the metal bracket.

Haim watched as they carefully place the injured man on a wooden plank, lifted him onto a large cart and rolled him towards the infirmary. They disappeared into the darkness with the man crying out with every jostle.

Haim stealthily made his way to the barn, unbolted the door and carefully stepped inside. In the darkness, he could hear Amon's heaving breathing. Haim assured, "It's okay, boy. It's me." He lit the lantern to see Amon rear up, blood dripping down his left shoulder. "Whoa," he said, trying to calm him. Amon anxiously backed up as Haim went to him. Spotting a pitchfork on the ground with bloody prongs, Haim's heart sank: "What did they do to you?" He waited patiently for Amon to calm down. When finally able to go to him, Haim carefully pet Amon's neck. Amon, still shaken up, nuzzled his head into Haim's chest. Gently petting Amon behind the ears, Haim assured, "It's okay, boy. They're gone."

After cleaning and dressing Amon's wounds, Haim made up a bed of hay in the stall so that he could stay with him that night. Just as he was drifting off to sleep, Amon became agitated. The sound of a creaking door jolted Haim up. He listened, frozen, as footsteps entered the barn and the lantern was lit. Quietly getting his rifle, Haim kneeled on one knee as he aimed at the stall's entrance. The footsteps came closer until Lehman stepped into view with Pearlman right behind him. Amon became more agitated as he tried to back up with nowhere to go. Haim ordered the men: "Stay back." Lehman jested with his hands raised, "We come in peace."

Seeing that Haim had no intention of lowering his rifle, Lehman ordered, "Put the gun down, now. Do you want to kill somebody?" Holding the gun firm, Haim ordered, "Go away. You've upset him enough." Lehman awkwardly shrugged, "He upset our friends even more. Now put the gun down." Haim conceded, and Pearlman cracked a smile: "We looked for you at your dorm. You're roommates were concerned, but I had a feeling we knew where you'd be." "You didn't know," Haim corrected. "If Amon wasn't hurt we'd be gone now." "Hurt?" Pearlman questioned with concern, noticing the bandage in the dim light. Haim sneered, "You're *friends* stabbed him. He'll need time to heal." "It's not all their fault," Pearlman shrugged. "It was self-defense." Haim glared at Lehman: "I don't blame them." Lehman nodded, "You're upset, but you should be proud of Amon. He played his part beautifully."

Refusing to make eye contact with Lehman, Haim turned to comfort Amon. Lehman understood that Haim was serious about leaving: "It may be that I have more faith in Amon than you." Those words only heightened Haim's anger. Instantly knowing how disingenuous they sounded, Lehman soberly offered, "My job is to protect the students. They have to come first, always."

∞

"They call him, Nightmare," Khalid laughed watching Amon nuzzle Haim as they shared their lunches. "The one injured says no one can get near him, much less ride him." Haim asked, "So, what horse do they think they followed into the woods?" Khalid shrugged: "Not this crazy one. One elder says he's the Devil's horse. Get too close and he'll steal your soul." Haim stroked Amon's head, "Hear that, Nightmare? They're on to you."

It was only then that Khalid found out that Haim had been helping to bring in the yolim. Without knowing specifics, as Haim felt the fewer details Khalid knew the better, Khalid seemed to understand that Haim was risking his life to save innocent people: "I would do the same." Khalid confessed that many in Beit Nabala were impressed by what the Jews were doing in Palestine: "But most know better than to speak out."

Some Palestinian Arabs, such as the Druze, would even fight on the side of the Yishuv and serve in the Israeli army. But to avoid being killed as a traitor during the Arab Revolt of 1936, silence was necessary.

Several weeks later, when the incident seemed far behind them, late at night Haim woke to a light tapping on his window. Looking out into the darkness he focused in on Khalid. Stealthily getting up, so as not to wake his roommates, Haim went to the door. "Where you going?" Avi yawned. Without turning, Haim whispered over his shoulder, "Checking on something. Go back to sleep."

Outside, Haim signaled Khalid to keep quiet as he led him away from the dorm. As they crouched behind a stonewall, Khalid blurted out in a whisper, "They will kill Amon tonight. You must stop them," "Who will?" Haim anxiously asked. Knowing that time was crucial, Khalid struggled to get out the words: "The men who followed you to the woods. One is the son of the injured man." Haim shook his head trying to understand, "But they think Amon is a different horse." Khalid insisted, "No matter. They want revenge. If he is a crazy horse, no one will care. If he is the phantom ..."

Khalid's eyes suddenly widened as he looked up. Haim turned to see Avi and the twins aiming their rifles at Khalid's head from over the wall. Avi demanded as he moved in, "Who is he?" Haim's eyes narrowed as he stood to block Khalid from their line of fire: "A friend, risking his life for us." Haim turned to put a grateful hand on Khalid's shoulder, "You must go. Can you get back safely?" Khalid nodded, "They'll be coming from the north. Be careful." As Khalid slipped off into the darkness, Haim blocked Avi and the twins from going after him: "There's no time to explain. Arab snipers are about to attack the horse stable." Moving quickly, he had the twins go for backup while Avi helped him bring munitions to the stable.

Winded from running, Haim and Avi dropped their sacks of weapons on the stable floor. Haim had Avi fill buckets of water as he quickly checked on the horses. Relieved to find them safely in their stalls, he helped to carry in the buckets of water before having Avi climb up into the lookout. Haim was about to lead Amon and the other horses to a hiding spot in the woods when Avi fired off several shots. "What happened?!" Haim anxiously whispered up to the lookout. "Snipers!" Avi whispered back. Grabbing his rifle, Haim spied through a hole in the wall several silhouettes hiding behind the fencing. As one crept closer, Avi let off several more warning shots. The sniper quickly scuttled back. Though it was dark, from his agile movements Haim guessed him to be one of the young Arab militia he encountered several weeks before.

As the snipers began firing at them, Haim and Avi fired back, aiming low. Besides ending the relative peace that they had enjoyed with their neighboring Arab communities, serious consequences would follow if anyone on either side were killed. For the Arab militia, getting rid of a crazy horse was one thing, but with British intolerance for insurrection at its height, their communities would be put under strict curfew and swift action taken.

With ammunition running low, Haim contemplated breaking through the back of the barn to sneak out Amon and the other horses. The twins finally crept in with reinforcements. Haim breathed a sigh of relief. With seven of them now defending the stable, the Arab snipers realized that they were outnumbered. The shooting had stopped, but just as the boys began to relax, Haim spotted flames from the other side of the fence. A barrage of flaming arrows (cloth-wrapped-arrows doused in kerosene and set on fire) began raining down on them. Most of the arrows burnt out in the dry dirt paddock. But from up above in the lookout, Avi struggled to throw buckets of water on the burning arrows that landed on the barn's large wooden door. The boys shot back with their rifles pushing the snipers back until they finally retreated.

There was no time to relax as the boys fought to put out the flames. With the last embers out, they finally cheered their victory. But the celebration was brief as one of the twins called out, "Smoke! Coming from the offices!" In the rush to get to the stables only the sleeping quarters were secured. With the offices left unguarded, the Arab militia, angered by their defeat, shot their last flaming arrows into the unprotected building before escaping into the darkness.

CHAPTER 17

RECOVERED FROM her most recent treatment, Einat went back to Ben Shemen to see if there was anything that she had missed. Though many of the files for the years Einat was searching had been lost in a fire, someone there had to know something. It was much too hot for the scarf Einat wore on her head, but hiding her hair loss seemed to help make people be more relaxed. The surly archivist greeted her with a forced smile, more cooperative now that Einat had been on the radio. "You might want to try talking to Livna," she suggested. "She was a housemother here for years. If anyone knows anything about your artist, she would."

Having started at Ben Shemen in the mid 1950, after Haim Hausman had disappeared, Livna suggested talking to Enoch Weitz. "He was here before me. But I must warn you, he can be a little off."

∞

Driving onto Enoch's farm, Einat saw a thin, elderly man gathering tomatoes in a field. Guessing that it was Enoch, she parked the car and walked out to him carrying a copy of 'AND THERE WAS EVENING'. Enoch, in his early nineties, alertly responded to her inquiry of Haim Hausman: "Sure, I remember him. Gave art lessons after school in the village. He was a Yekke." Einat laughed slightly at hearing "Yekke," encouraged by the implication that Haim Hausman, like the father in the book, wore pressed clothes due to his stiff, proper German background.

Excited to finally meet someone who actually knew Haim Hausman, she began bombarding Enoch with questions. "How well did you know him? Was his name originally 'Fritz?' Was he young, old, tall, short?" Enoch happily restated, "He was a Yekke." Unfortunately, he didn't seem to remember anything else. Einat probed further: "Do you have any idea what happened to him?" Her hopes rose as Enoch happily nodded, "Sure. He disappeared." Einat sighed, "Yes, I know." Showing him the book, she asked, "Do you know if he did these drawings?" Enoch confirmed with another nod. Hopeful again, Einat asked, "Are you sure? Did you see him working on them?" Enoch pointed to the book's cover: "No, but it says so right there."

From their conversation, Einat only surmised that at the time of publication, Haim Hausman was a Yekke who gave art lessons in the village. Whether the father in the book was a self-portrait, or whether Haim Hausman even drew the illustrations still remained a mystery.

She went home, questioning if the doors had finally shut on her search. But as she listened to her messages, there was one from Ayala Gordon, the founder of the Ruth Youth wing of the National Israel Museum: "I hear that you're looking for Haim Hausman. Perhaps I can help..."

Founded in 1965, the National Israel Museum has one of the leading collections of art and archaeology in the world. The Dead Sea Scrolls, a carved female figurine considered the oldest artwork in the world, the foremost Israeli artists, along with masters such as Rubens, Rembrandt, Chagall and Picasso, to name a few, are all part of its permanent collection. With the Ruth Youth wing providing classes to over five thousand art teachers and fifty thousand students each year, it wasn't long before Einat's quest was brought to their attention.

"It's not a simple answer," Ayala, a bright, nimble older woman said as she took Einat through the impressive, newly renovated complex. "Did he die in the war of '48? Was he missing in action? Did he not want to be found?" Walking through a long sublevel of the archives, Einat was overwhelmed by the seemingly endless works in storage. "We've been asking those questions even before the museum was opened. Until your blog, we had no idea he was a graduate of Ben Shemen, or that 'he' was even a 'he.'"

In a climate-controlled room, Ayala showed Einat a series of magic lanterns. "Before they were donated to the museum in the late 1990's, they travelled between kindergarten classes telling stories to the children. Fortunately, they must have realized they were special as they took very good care of them." "They're beautiful," Einat said, overwhelmed as she looked through the almost one hundred drawings. Ayala added, "We attributed these to the style of Haim Hausman, but Lotem Pinchover, from the Hebrew University in Jerusalem, recently wrote an article arguing that they're not only in the style of Haim Hausman, but that they were actually drawn by him. She even found the signature of 'Haim' on one. We know of no other artist from that period with the same name."

Though the drawings were executed much quicker than the finished paintings of 'AND THERE WAS EVENING', by their use of light, perspective, smiling suns and moons, and distinctive characters, Einat could feel the hand of Haim Hausman. "Do you know of any more of his works?" Ayala shook her head, "But there had to be many more. No one can just draws like this." Einat affirmed, "They are very good, aren't they?" Ayala casually nodded. Einat qualified, "I mean, would you say they could have come from an important studio, like Disney?" Ayala assured, "In my opinion, yes. But considering the quality of the illustrations in the book, one would expect that."

Einat was particularly taken by a drawing of a smiling young man standing on a cart quickly pulled uphill by a smiling horse. She then saw another one of the same young man and horse plowing a field. When Einat asked if those drawings were based on a story, Ayala shrugged her head, explaining, "A smiling horse must have some story, but we don't even know the dates they were drawn. It was probably after '45 when he worked for the publishing house. If you're right that he was born in '21 or '22, he was only a teenager before the World War II. It's hard to believe that he could have drawn them then, but not impossible."

Relieved, Einat explained David Polonsky's theory of Fischerkoesen being the actual artist. Ayala assured, "Lotim's point was that none of the other artists at that time, as wonderful as they were, could have done these. Maybe it's all we have, but he definitely existed. It would be wonderful if you found him. We'll help in any way we can."

Leaving with a catalogue of Haim Hausman's magic lanterns, Einat rushed home to email them to David Polonsky. Soon after, the phone rang. She picked up to hear David chime, "The veil is lifted!" Einat exhaled with a smile, "This is all they have, but Ayala assured me there had to be many more." David agreed, "Thousands more! But where are they?" Einat shrugged, "Considering the time, they may have been used for kindling. But of course, now we're back to having no idea of who he was." David countered, "That's not true. You've ruled out Fischerkoesen, so only about six billion more people to go."

CHAPTER 18

BY OCTOBER 1936, the British had temporarily contained the Arab uprising. With trains and buses running again, Haim could see his friends at the café in Jaffa, and they picked up where they left off with the usual heated arguments. Life at the café was getting back to normal, but their attitude towards Haim had changed. Since risking his life for them, he was now considered one of them.

His friendship with Khalid had also grown stronger, but they took greater care in keeping it hidden. If the Arab Militia discovered that Khalid had informed on their plan to kill Amon, he would be killed as a traitor. Fortunately, with the elders also upset by the attempt to kill a gift horse from King Abdullah, the young Arab Militia conceded to leaving the crazy horse alone. However, late night shootings at the Ben Shemen dorms became more common.

In the summer of 1937, when Haim was 16 and used to commanding troops, Lehman summoned him once again into his office. Though Haim hadn't fully forgiven Lehman for allowing the Arabs to try and take Amon, an Arab patrol had discovered a boat carrying 40 German Jewish refugees attempting to land off of the Tel Aviv coast. "I believe one of the boys on board was destined for here," Lehman confided. Haim attempted to hide his surprise. He had never known Lehman to take in any illegals. If discovered it could jeopardize the entire school. But the boy, Ivan Sachs, was the son of old family friends, and knowing that the Sachs family had risked everything to get the boy to Palestine, Lehman felt compelled to help.

When Ivan hadn't arrived as planned, Lehman was informed by the underground about the small boat from Greece now under British and Arab patrol off of the Tel Aviv coast. It was impossible to plead Ivan's case to the British authorities without giving away his involvement in illegal activity, and with the High Arab Council insisting that Jews had exceeded their quota, there would be no point. Ivan would not legally be allowed to stay. Lehman shook his head despondently: "To make it so far, just to be sent back."

Knowing the likely outcome for a refugee Jewish boy sent back to Germany, Haim offered, "What can I do?" Lehman shook his head. Since Arab and British patrols knew of the boat, a dinghy going out to get the yolim would be too easily spotted. But Haim had proven to be resourceful, and Lehman hoped that he might have an idea.

Haim found it frustrating knowing that the yolim only had to jump deck and swim ashore. But with no idea of where to go, they inevitably stayed on board to return to what would be certain death. Having conceived no plan, Haim asked, "Can the boy swim?" Hopeful, Lehman perked up: "Maybe."

At best, that was wishful thinking. Residents of small German Jewish communities rarely learned to swim. But Haim tried to come up with a plan that evening with his Haganah unit. They immediately shot it down: "Too dangerous. We can't take out dinghies." Agreeing, Haim countered, "But what if I quietly swim out, sneak on board, and just point out where they have to swim to?" A senior soldier warned, "If caught you'll be killed or deported." Haim assured, "They won't catch me. I swim fast and can hold my breath for several minutes. All you have to do is hide out in the dunes and bring any yolim that come ashore to safe houses." Another argued, "What about the ones who don't make it? If we wait too long, we'll be sitting ducks."

Though he was still the youngest, they usually agreed to his plans. But this apparently had been tried before, and failed. Haim assured, "It will be dark, with only a crescent moon. If you sense any danger, abort. Don't worry about me. I'll just point them in the right direction and go. It's up to them if they want to save themselves."

Shortly after 2:00 am, about a mile up the coast from where a British guard was keeping watch on the boat, Haim began his swim wearing only a pair of thin shorts. It was easy at first in the warm, shallow water. But to avoid being spotted, he swam further out doing the breaststroke to avoid splashing. The rougher, cold waves became more of a challenge, but with an eye on the distant figure of the guard watching from the dock, Haim pushed forward. Stroke after stroke, he slowly moved towards the dark shadow of the boat.

After half an hour the boat was finally within his reach. Judging by its distance from the shore, Haim had to be extremely careful not to splash in order to remain hidden in the large, black sea. Gliding quietly to the back of the boat, he grabbed hold of the ladder attached to its side. Exhausted, he took a moment to catch his breath before climbing up to peer over the edge. About a dozen passengers were asleep on deck, as the boat was clearly too small to comfortably sleep all forty passengers below deck.

Seeing no guards onboard, Haim quietly slipped on deck and found a sleeping boy about his age. Giving the boy a careful nudge, the boy woke with a start. Haim silenced him with a finger to his mouth before whispering in German, "I'm here to help. Do you understand?" To Haim's relief, the boy nodded. "Do you know Ivan Sachs?" The boy nodded and pointed to a fair, smaller boy about Haim's age sleeping nearby. "Ivan, wake up!" the boy called out in a whisper. Slowly coming to, along with the other passengers on deck, Ivan focused, confused to see this tall, lean, wet almost naked teenage boy.

Haim was assured that no British or Arab guards were on board. The Greek captain and his two mates were asleep in their quarters. Since they didn't speak German, Haim could speak freely without being understood, but on the small boat they would have to speak softly. After three years, it felt strange to speak German again. Though he was anxious to find out whatever he could of condition at home, there was no time.

Pointing out the distant spot on shore where they were to swim, Haim explained, "Haganah troops will take you from there to safe houses. Otherwise, in the morning you go back to Germany." Frustrated that no one moved, Haim ordered, "Go! Put lifejackets on and swim!" They still remained immobile, bewildered.

Unwilling to waste any more time, Haim went below deck to try his luck with the rest of the yolim. After waking them up and explaining the situation, they gave him the same mystified gaze. "Hurry up," he ordered. "My troops will leave before sunrise." When they still didn't move, Haim became angered to have risked his life for these idiots. He had promised his unit to immediately swim ashore after giving the information. His mission accomplished, it was now their choice to live or die. As he turned to leave, Ivan and the other passengers from above, following him down, were now blocking his way. Aggravated, he told them again while demonstrating, "Go! Swim! Do only the breaststroke so you don't splash. The slightest sound could give you away."

Pushing his way to the stairs, Haim was stopped in his tracks at seeing an anxious, young couple holding a baby, their fear palpable. "Shit," he thought. "A crying baby, just what they need." "Can you swim?" he asked the parents. Both the husband and wife awkwardly shook their heads "no." Haim assured, "It's okay. You won't sink with life jackets on. Put the baby up high on your husband's back, so you can swim behind to keep the baby quiet." As Haim turned to go, he finally took in the anxiety on the other yolim's faces. Some were only children. His heart sank as he saw his quick escape disappearing.

"Who here can swim?" He asked. Nine of the yolim slowly raised their hands. Haim commanded, "You are now team leaders, responsible for getting your groups to shore."

Haim had them put on life jackets while organizing them into nine groups. As he was fitting a life jacket onto a child a powerful hand suddenly grabbed him by the wrist. Haim turned to look up at the large captain snarling something at him in Greek. Seeing that Haim didn't understand, the captain then demanded in broken English, "What you do?" Freeing his wrist, Haim defiantly stated, "Helping them escape. They will leave everything they have to pay for the life jackets, and your silence." The passengers had taken what little of value they could, but everything else from their former lives would have to be left behind.

The captain softened as he shook his head, "They already pay." To Haim's relief, the captain was working with the underground and had no desire to bring them back to Germany. "What else you need?" the captain asked. Haim explained: "I saw a large rope on deck. About 40 yards should hold us together. I'd prefer not having to steal it." The captain patted Haim's back: "Is yours."

On deck, the yolim were placed in a line with the stronger swimmers at the back of their groups. Haim then tied one end of the rope around his waist as the captain fed the other end through each passenger's life jacket until finally tying it around the waist of the last yolim, whom Haim had guessed to be the strongest of the swimmers.

Wasting no time, Haim climbed over the deck, down the ladder and into the water, forcing each yolim to follow in turn. The father with the baby on his back was next, followed by the mother. The baby began crying when dragged into the cold water, but from the back of the boat the cries appeared to go unnoticed by the guard on shore. By the time everyone was in the water, the mother had calmed the baby by playing with him as if he was in a bath.

It was shortly after 3:30am when Haim exchanged a grateful wave to the captain, and began to swim off. The rope around his waist immediately tugged him back. The yolim, afraid of making a sound, were paralyzed in the water. Haim whispered back, "Each person has to tell the one behind to swim, but no splashing." He struggled to get them moving, gasping for air each time he was pulled down by the rope. After several minutes, they were finally paddling behind him. Understanding the seriousness of the situation, barely a sound came out of any of them. To Haim's relief, even the baby remained quiet.

After swimming for at least ten minutes, the boat was still not far behind and Haim was already exhausted. How would they make it to the landing point in time? Why had he turned down the captain's offer of a life jacket? Was it foolish pride, or did he just not want to impose? Haim had said that it would slow him down, but when dragging 40 yolim, speed was hardly an issue.

They slowly forged ahead, with each stroke the rope around his waist pulled him down into the choppy sea. He regretted ever coming up with the ridiculous plan. No wonder his unit had been against it. Through sheer determination he somehow continued, but by the halfway point his strength was giving out, and he had lost all sense of time. How long had they been swimming? An hour? Two hours? Swimming past sunrise at 5:30 am would make them easy targets. If spotted, Haim was now far too weak to untie himself and escape. He saw no choice but to land early and sneak up the coast.

Just ahead was a section of the beach that jutted out, today called Tel Baruch Beach. Landing past it would give them cover from the guard. But as Haim struggled to bring them in, an undertow began pulling them out to sea. If he couldn't get them past the undertow, they would be dragged out to sea to either be picked up by patrols or drown. With every last ounce of strength, he pulled them through the water until they were finally past the current. With his sides splitting, each breath ripping at his lungs, his toes finally touched bits of sand on the sea floor. His body giving out, the surf helped to bring him ashore.

Landing on the beach, Haim gasped for air, but with the sky beginning to lighten in the east there was no time to rest. Crawling on all fours, he pulled on the rope until all forty yolim had made it to shore. He then rolled over onto his back, panting for air as he struggled to untie the rope from around his waist. "Free yourself from the rope!" he ordered, still lying on his back. They would have to stay together, but if spotted they would need to run. Since a rope could easily wash ashore, Haim had them leave it on the beach, but they would have to wear their life jackets. It would be too easy to figure out what transpired if forty life jackets were discovered there.

With the nine good swimmers still responsible for their groups, Haim had them run into the dunes. Under the protection of sea grass and the remaining darkness, he led them up the coast. When they finally neared the landing point, Haim gave the whistle signal to his troops. Hearing no response, he whistled again, but still nothing. Had they already left? With the sun about to rise, how would he now get 40 yolim to the nearest safe house? Suddenly, they stiffened, hearing rustling through the sea grass.

Haim sighed with relief as his unit stealthily appeared through the reeds. Doing as told, the yolim remained quiet while loading into four hidden vans. As Haim helped the young mother she whispered to him in German, "Bless you. We will never forget this." Haim shook his head, whispering back, "It's best we all forget this." With a grateful kiss on his cheek, she boarded the van with her baby and husband. An hour before, while almost drowning, he considered the mission a huge mistake. It now all seemed worth it.

Inside the vans, the yolim changed into farming clothes that had been brought for them. With no indication that they had left the boat it was doubtful that patrols would be searching for them. If stopped they would pretend to be migrant workers. Haim and Ivan, looking out of the window as they drove along the coast road, glimpsed the rising sun lighting the back of the boat as it headed out to sea. The boys cracked a smile. Dutifully following the orders of The High Arab Committee and British Command, the captain departed that morning.

CHAPTER 19

THE VAN DROPPED Haim and Ivan off on a quiet side road bordering on the Ben Shemen Youth Village. They quickly made their way through the brush to a hidden breach in the fence. Following Haim under the barbed wire, Ivan began coughing up dust as he crawled in the dirt. Haim helped cleaning him off while explaining, "Sorry for bringing you in like this, but if they left us off inside the compound people would ask questions. No one can ever know you're an illegal."

After cautiously leading Ivan to the horse stable, Haim made up a bed of hay for him to rest on in the storage stall while he took care of Amon and the other horses. He could have brought Ivan directly to Lehman, but it was past the horses feeding time and it would seem more natural if Ivan was slipped in while there was more activity. As Haim was getting the horse feed, Pearlman appeared: "You're late. And you look like shit." Too exhausted to find an excuse, Haim shrugged, "Sorry, I couldn't sleep." Pearlman reprimanded, "Even if you stay up all night, you still have to do your chores. Next time tell me before ..." Pearlman stopped, alerted by sounds coming from the stall.

Listening in but unable to understand Hebrew, Ivan hid under the hay worried that Pearlman would search for him. Haim anxiously interceded, "That's probably just another mouse. I'll take care of it." Too many supposed mice had made similar sounds from that stall for Pearlman to believe it. In a normal world he might have questioned why a teenage boy would be hiding someone, but even before the Arab elders tried to take Amon, Pearlman was aware that Haim had been working with the Haganah: "Take care of it, and get some sleep. I'll tell your teachers not to expect you today." Haim breathed easier. It was good to know that Pearlman would continue to look the other way.

Breakfast was in full swing when Haim took Ivan to see Lehman. As they entered the boisterous hall, Ivan recoiled. Knowing that Ivan had never been outside of his small German village, Haim assured, "Relax, they yell so loud in Hebrew no one will notice you." They made their way to the headmaster's table, where Haim interrupted Lehman eating his breakfast:" "Professor Lehman, this is a new student, Ivan Sachs." Hearing the name, Lehman almost spit out his milk. Pearlman, at the same table, was unfazed. Covering his surprise, Lehman piped in, "Ivan, yes, yes, I didn't expect you so soon. So good to see you. You were just a small boy when we last met." Haim explained, "His cousin dropped him off early. He must've gotten lost. I found him wandering around the horse stable." As casually as possible, Lehman welcomed Ivan in German, "Please, make yourself at home. And why don't you both drop by my office after you finish your breakfast."

The adrenalin pumping through Ivan kept him awake, but Haim needed sleep. "Stay quiet and eat quickly so we can get out of here," Haim advised in

German. Struggling to focus, he introduced Ivan to the students seated near them at breakfast. To avoid making any mistakes he explained, "He's German, doesn't talk much."

A short time later in the office, Lehman exhaled with relief, "So, how on earth did you get Ivan off of that boat?" Haim questioned, "What boat? As far as I know his cousin dropped him off. He'll need temporary papers, until his cousin returns with his real ones." Taken aback, Lehman questioned, "But, I thought, didn't you get him off of that...?" Haim shrugged, "I don't know what you're talking about. You know we can't do anything that might put the school at risk." Lehman nodded, "Yes, of course. What was I thinking?"

As much as Lehman wanted to know what happened, he would never again broach the subject. Several days later, Haim received Ivan's forged papers through the Haganah, and Lehman could only speculate on what had transpired that night.

∞

Though Ivan knew to never mention it, he was always grateful to Haim for saving his life. Until he became more comfortable with Hebrew, Haim also helped make his introduction into Ben Shemen easier by speaking German with him. Though Ivan would have liked to be close friends, Haim kept a certain distance. Amon still became agitated with others around, and Haim had to keep his friendship with Khalid a secret. The more who knew, the more likely the Arab Militia in Beit Nabala would find out, and label Khalid a traitor.

Most students were anxious to be accepted, eagerly joining in the evening activities. To keep their budding hormones in check, teenaged boys and girls were kept separate unless under supervision, keeping unwanted pregnancies at Ben Shemen almost unheard of. There were several girls that Haim was attracted to, but being an outsider dissuaded him from pursuing them. And he had more important things to do than singing Zionistic songs while holding hands around a campfire. His focus had to be on uniting Arabs and Jews to make life in Palestine more acceptable to his father.

There was little time for him to solve the mid-East crisis. Besides his schoolwork, working on the farm and being part of the Haganah, because of his work at the horse stable he was asked to also take over the cow stable. There had been an outbreak of Hoof and Mouth disease in Palestine, and Lehman was concerned of it reaching the cows at Ben Shemen.

The cow stable foreman had recently emigrated to the United States, and the new foreman, a frail clock maker from Poland, showed Haim around, sighing, "We just don't know what's wrong." Stunned to see the horrid conditions, as the cows were living up to their ankles in manure, Haim questioned how they had survived at all. "When did you last muck?" Haim asked in disbelief. "Muck?" the foreman questioned, as if hearing the word for the first time. Apparently, he had volunteered for the job having no idea what it entailed, and being an undesirable job, no one argued.

Removing several months of manure from over fifty cows was an overwhelming task, but feeling for the suffering animals, Haim went to work. The foreman tried to help, but he was meant for intricate timepieces, not manual labor. Haim watched him struggle with a shovel, barely making a dent. Concerned for the strain it was putting on the older man's heart, Haim asked, "While I'm doing this, why don't you milk the cows. I've never done it before, and you'd really be helping me out." The foreman happily put down the shovel as he nodded with relief, "Sure, no problem."

Over the next several weeks, Haim spent whatever time he could mucking stalls and caring for the cows. To his surprise, by improving their conditions they almost instantly seemed healthier and happier. But his roommates immediately complained about the stench. No matter how much he washed, rubbing his skin until it turned red, the smell seemed to permeate into him. Avi and the twins finally gave him an ultimatum, "It's the cows or us. Quit the stable or find somewhere else to sleep." Haim chose the cows.

Ivan, whose Hebrew was improving, argued for Haim, but for Haim it was an easy decision. He had become attached to the cows as they had come to trust him. Before taking over the cow stable, he would have said that all cows were alike. He soon learned that each was very different in looks and personality. Some were playful, some more serious,

or relaxed, anxious, curious, stronger, weaker...
Some gave a lot of milk, some only a little, but
overall they were extremely kind, gentle animals.
His feelings for them didn't compare to his love for
Amon. Amon was his best friend, but he soon knew
all of their names an could recognize all fifty cows by
face.

For their security, students had to sleep where they
were assigned. But an exception had already been
made for Haim. Since his roommates now told their
housemother that he would have to quit the cow
stable if he wanted to sleep in their room, the faculty
would look the other way as Haim set up a bed in
the tool shed to cover up the fact that he had taken a
stall near Amon. The cover seemed to work, as no
one made fun of him, but Ivan asked if he minded
sleeping in the horse stable. Haim assured, "No, I
have my own room. It's like sharing a house with
good friends." The smell didn't seem to bother
Khalid, who assured, "Compared to my goats, you
smell sweet." And the men at the café happily
slapped Haim on the back applauding him for
bringing in the good aroma of the farm.

Haim kept his clothes and belongings in his dorm
room, but from then on he slept in the stables.
Though he liked being closer to Amon and enjoyed
the privacy, he was glad that his father would never
know, as he could only imagine his father's reaction
to find out that his son was living in a barn.

CHAPTER 20

IN LATE OCTOBER, Haim and Amon were working in the field when in the distance he saw Pearlman walking towards him accompanied by a smaller man with a gate similar to his father's. "That's strange," Haim thought, questioning if his eyes were playing tricks on him. But as they came closer, Haim became convinced that it actually was his father. He jumped up on Amon and galloped to them.

Trotting to a stop, Haim dismounted and ran to Julius. Too stunned by Haim's stench, ragged clothes and lanky six-foot frame, Julius didn't even have a chance to put out his hand before Haim grabbed him in a hug. Haim exhaled in German, "Father, why didn't you tell me you were coming?! Where is mother?! Is she here?!" Julius looked up, perplexed, "Did you not get our letters?" Though Julius and Klara had written many times to inform him of the trip, the Nazis must have confiscated the letters, perhaps to prevent any organized attempt to keep Julius in Palestine.

Slowly adjusting to his son's appearance, Julius assured him that Klara was fine, but the three good German families who had taken over their home, especially the Nazi, Herr Sack, on the top floor, could not spare her. She was now cook and governess. "I would say we are servants, but without pay 'slave' is a more accurate term. Still, your mother fusses over the children, as good slaves do, so in return the children love her, which has undoubtedly made things better for us. If I were alone, I'm sure they would have taken me away by now." Uncertain how to respond by his upsetting words, Haim only asked, "How long can you stay?" Julius admitted, "Only a few days. I'm only here to see your progress." In truth, with Haim's persistent letters, Julius was finally looking into life in Palestine, but he didn't want to raise his son's hopes.

Before Haim could argue for his parents moving to Palestine, Amon began nudging him from behind. Haim introduced Julius to Amon as his "best friend," pointing with pride to the fields of wheat, sunflowers, oats and chickpeas: "We worked those fields together, just the two of us. With you and mother here, we could make a great life." Out of obligation, Julius attempted to pet the horse. Amon immediately reared up whinnying, as if being attacked by a venomous snake, and Julius quickly recoiled. Haim calmed Amon explaining to Julius, "Sorry, he's a little shy. But once you get to know him, I know you'll be good friends."

Julius found that hard to believe, as he and the horse seemed equally repelled by each other. Haim insisted, "He really is a great horse. He was a gift of King Abdullah to Haim Arlosoroff." Seeing Julius's skepticism, Haim looked to Pearlman for corroboration. Standing off to the side to give space to the father and son reunion, Pearlman, still unable to pet Amon, confirmed with, "Either a gift, or it was the best way to get rid of the beast." Haim didn't blame Julius for underappreciating Amon. After all, what great horse would be plowing fields in Palestine?

Julius had far greater concerns than the feelings of his son's horse. The more violent second phase of the Arab revolt had begun. With increasing attacks on British forces, the British army and Palestinian Police brutally suppressed it, killing, wounding or exiling 10% of the adult male Arab population. The Grand Mufti narrowly escaped by disguising himself as a Bedouin, sliding down a rope of the Haram wall that he had been hiding in and fleeing to Lebanon for asylum under the French government.

Having just traveled through what appeared to be a war zone, Julius worried for the safety of his son. Without even knowing that Haim was regularly leading his Haganah unit, Julius questioned whether he should allow his son to remain there. And finding his son appearing as a lowly laborer was another blow. If he had passed Fritz in the street, he never would have recognized him. The odor alone would have made him look the other way. Ideally, he saw Fritz in England preparing for Oxford or Cambridge, where future doors would be opened for him. What possible connections could be made for Fritz in Palestine through his best friend, the horse? But seeing the hope in his son's eyes, Julius decided that he would say nothing until the end of the trip.

Julius was put up in the modest home of Professor Melnick and his wife, Sana. The tall, handsome biology teacher had taken a special interest in Haim, encouraging his interest in plant biology, and trying to give the boy, still considered an outsider, a sense of belonging. Melnick was by far Haim's favorite teacher and the one person at Ben Shemen he most emulated. Though only in his mid-thirties, he had become almost a father figure to him.

Both the Melnicks and Pearlman were surprised to find so little resemblance between Haim and his father, in temperament as well as looks. Haim enjoyed adventure, the outdoors, working with his hands, while Julius was formal, rigid, and with an air of superiority. He thanked the Melnicks whenever appropriate, but he was clearly only tolerating his time there. The first evening, after dinner while Sana and Fritz were washing the dishes, Melnick asked Julius if he would like anything else. "I would not turn down a cognac," Julius answered. Melnick laughed: "Me neither. We have some homemade dandelion wine, made with our own dandelions and citrus fruits. You're welcome to it." Julius politely declined, questioning why Melnick would feel the need to say, "homemade," as if anyone would actually buy dandelion wine.

Julius was not intentionally difficult or rude, but after years of being served, first by maids and then by Klara after Hitler came into power, such things as clearing plates and washing dishes were beneath him. The Melnicks did their best to keep up, trying to make him as comfortable as possible, but had they been in Julius's employ, they would have been dismissed. Once alone in bed, Melnick confided to Sana, "I'm guessing Haim takes after his mother."

As different as they were, both Haim and Julius seemed blind to the other's limitations. It was clear to Melnick that Haim would never turn his father into a contented farmer, and Julius could never make his son a proud businessman, but knowing how important it was to Haim for his parents to move to Palestine, hoping for a miracle, Melnick said nothing.

Since Julius brought only two suits for the trip, Melnick offered his best farming clothes. Julius confided to Fritz, "I can not wear these rags." No matter how inappropriate for Ben Shemen, Julius continued wearing his tie and jacket. Melnick and Fritz showed Julius the best-run farms of the Moshav, but miles of rock walls, ditches and dusty fields only impressed Julius with how quickly they soiled his shoes, shoes that Haim polished each night while Sana cleaned his suits.

His last evening at Ben Shemen, Julius walked with Fritz listening to him enthusiastically talk of their future in Palestine: "You don't have to farm. Amon and I can do it. You'll just take care of the business. You'll see, we'll do just as well here ..." Julius finally interrupted with a somber shake of his head: "I don't want my son to be a farmer." The gravity of Julius's words left Fritz speechless. Julius continued, "There is no future for you here. I am afraid we must send you to London. If you are frugal, the six thousand Swiss francs should be enough to cover your education, but you'll have to work extra hard to make up for..." Fritz interrupted: "You think they want us in London? Why do you think they sent us here? Palestine is Britain's solution to the Jews." Julius insisted, "They will want you. You are my son.

You will earn their respect." Fritz responded in disbelief: "The way you earned the respect of the Nazis who've taken over your home? You can be killed by Nazis in Germany or England, but this is where we belong!" Having enough, Julius put his foot down: "You prefer us killed by Arabs in this wasteland! I am your father. You will do as I say!" Realizing that no good could come from upsetting his father on his last night in Palestine, Fritz said nothing more, but he would have no part of England.

The three years Haim had lived in Palestine taught him to distrust the British. Ruling with an iron fist, several times a year they raided the dorms, turning over room after room with little regard to the damage caused to the students' property. Weapons were then confiscated with the threat of deportation if any more were discovered. Since the boys needed to defend themselves, they would have to rearm and search for better hiding places. The British had thrown Haganah members into jail with no explanation. If found innocent of the supposed crime, they were released again with no apology. Ongoing rumors of British abuse; shooting yolim trying to escape and knowingly sending Jewish refugee back to their likely death, only fueled Haim's distrust and anger towards the British.

And the British press did little to help. Many British politicians publicly expressed support for Hitler. Neville Chamberlain, the recently elected Prime Minister, even recommended restoring to Germany certain territories lost in WWI. The royal families of England and Germany were also known to intermarry and be closely entwined. Only earlier that month, it was well publicized that Edward VIII, the abdicated king, travelled through Germany with his new wife, Baltimore divorcée, Wallis Simpson, in support of his old friend, Adolph Hitler, even giving Hitler the Nazi salute when greeting him at Hitler's Obersalzberg retreat. To Hitler, Edward's abdication was a great blow to Germany, as he stated with regret, "I am certain through him permanent friendly relations could have been achieved."

When war broke out, King Edward VIII was made a British Major-General, but was soon discovered to have leaked Allied war plans to the Germans. Instead of being tried and executed for treason, he was made Governor of the Bahamas, where Churchill felt Edward VIII and his wife could do the least damage to the British war effort. Since Edward VIII disliked blacks as much as Jews, he considered his time in the Bahamas an excessive punishment.

Given the facts, Haim worried that England could join with the Nazis. Jewish refugees in England would then be killed or have to escape all over again. Though his father was right that they could all be killed by Arabs in Palestine, Haim trusted his Arab friends. They had only treated him with respect. He had no British friends. Few British officers even brought their families to Palestine. The barren wasteland, overrun with Arabs and Jews, must have seemed unsuitable for their wives and children.

Having been treated as second-class citizens by the British, most Palestinian Jews and Arabs wanted the British out. They believed they could then work

Palestine out amongst themselves. With the British in Palestine greatly outnumbered and many British officers viewing their time there as only something to endure, it seemed possible. But Haim also knew that the Empire wasn't about to relinquish a small mandate because of a few disgruntled undesirables. And since British rule of Palestine was one of its few appeals to Julius, Fritz kept to himself what he believed to be Palestine's future.

∞

Conversation was sparse the following morning as Fritz drove Julius to Haifa's port. Neither wanted the visit to end badly and both still hoped for the other to come around. It was a good day for sailing, bright and dry, as usual for Palestine. With few cars on the road, parking at the port was easy. Julius reluctantly accepted Fritz's offer to carry his suitcase to the boat. Before the Nazi regime, Julius always travelled with a large trunk, suits hanging on one side and a full chest of draws on the other, requiring a porter to transport it by dolly. He was now restricted to one small suitcase, checked thoroughly to make sure nothing of value was leaving Germany.

Fritz and Julius entered the bustling dock, maneuvering around the many Arab workers and British soldiers loading and unloading crates and bags from the rows of ships, while Jewish and Arab businessmen in suits, tracking their wares, stood on the sidelines talking with officials. From dress alone, everyone's background was easily identifiable. Fritz and Julius stopped to watch several donkeys lowered by sling off of one of the ships. Julius said with a critical eye, "They import Donkeys here? We replaced them long ago with machines." Adding with a snicker, "Next, they will unload spinning wheels and sundials." Fritz said nothing, since not only were donkeys still commonly used for hauling, many farms, especially ones without electricity, often used spinning wheels and sundials.

With its flag of the swastika blowing full mast, Julius's boat was easy to spot. "I'll carry your bag on board?" Fritz offered. Julius shook his head with concern: "It's best that you don't. A possible misunderstanding could lead to your not being allowed off." Fritz was surprised to hear Julius express concern for the actual situation. It was the first time his father had during the entire trip, making clear that Julius was determined to go back to Germany to protect his property, but would not risk the life of his son.

Fritz had planned to say nothing confrontational that morning, but with sudden apprehension of what his father was heading back to, he urged, "Please talk to mother about coming here. Don't rule it out just yet." Julius acquiesced with a slight nod as he picked up his valise while grabbing his lower back to ease the pain: "And you give some thought to London. You're future is what matters most." Julius put out his hand to shake, and Fritz took it. But seeing Julius's eyes moisten, Fritz hugged his father one last time. And Julius hugged him back.

After their fight from the night before, neither expected there to be tears on Julius's departure. But with the world on the brink of war, neither knew when or if they would ever see each other again. Suddenly, an argument over which country was safest seemed trivial. Coming out of the hug, both tried hiding their emotions, though neither was very successful. Not wanting to be a bad example after such a display, Julius firmly shook Fritz's hand one last time, and quickly turned to walk up the ship's ramp.

Fritz waited for his father to reappear on deck. After about half an hour, they waved goodbye one last time as the boat departed and Julius drifted out of view. As Fritz watched the boat sail off into the horizon, he finally realized how much he was asking of his father. What he liked about Palestine; its lack of pretention, the diverse group of friends he had made, working outdoors with Amon, the freedom, it all meant little to Julius. Julius could only view life on the kibbutz as giving up all status, cleaning latrines, digging ditches, toiling the soil in filthy rags from morning to night, all while fighting Arab rebels. How different would that be from Julius's perception of the Nazi concentration camps? Having suffered through the Great War, Julius had worked hard to protect himself from that kind of life. And with the Nazis boasting a thousand year Reich, exile to Palestine meant dying penniless in a hostile, foreign land with little chance of returning to the life that he had cherished.

Fritz struggled to think of how he would now get his parents out of Germany. Even if he went to England, as his father wished, without resources his parents would never follow him there. For Julius, being poor in England would be worse than life on a kibbutz, where at least everyone was poor. Fritz could see no alternative than to somehow make life in Palestine more desirable to his father. But if nothing else came from Julius's trip, Fritz finally had a better understanding of his father's strengths and weaknesses, and that Julius loved him as only a father could.

CHAPTER 21

A MONTH LATER, Haim was in biology class when he received a message to report immediately to Lehman's office. As he walked over, he tried coming up with every possible argument for his many offenses, but nearing the open office door he believed to hear Lehman casually say in German, "You can be very proud of Fritz. He has become quite an asset to the school." Haim questioned what 'Fritz' Lehman could be referring to, but Lehman then signaled him to enter: "Ah, here he is now." A well-dressed man, seated facing Lehman, immediately turned to Haim. A broad smile spread across Rudolf Schank's face.

Haim had received a strange letter from Rudy offering to pay for his schooling and suggesting, like his father, that he go to England. He assumed that his mother had set it up. Why else would her friend from the café want to pay his tuition? But being Christian wouldn't Rudy have had to end his friendship with Klara, just as all of Haim's Christian friends had with him? Stunned to see him in Palestine, Haim asked in disbelief, "Onkel Rudy?" Rudy beamed as he got up to shake hands, "Fritz, my boy!" You are a hard one to find." After Julius's initial disgust at first seeing Haim only the month before, Haim was surprised that Rudy seemed unaffected by his ragged clothes and barnyard smell, though the smell had mostly dissipated since he had improved the living conditions for the cows.

Seeing no other reason for Rudy to be there, Haim asked with concern, "Are my parents okay?" Placing a warm arm around his shoulder, Rudy assured, "They're fine, or, as well as can be expected. I don't know if I told you, but I have factories producing doors, windows, glass roofs, all with steel frames. Since I had to see a major supplier in Istanbul, I thought, being in the area why not stop off here to see you?" Istanbul being a several-day trip from Palestine, it hardly seemed in the area, but before Haim could say anything Lehman interjected, "Since Herr Schank must be back on his boat tonight in Tel Aviv, why don't you take the day off of class to show him around? I will inform your teachers."

As Haim led him out into the compound, Rudy indicated the large brown box under his arm: "I brought this for you, Fritz." Thinking the worst, Haim asked with concern, "What is it?" Rudy laughed: "That will spoil the surprise. Shall we go to your room to open it?" While walking, Haim told Rudy that he had taken the Hebrew name 'Haim', "After Haim Arlosoroff. It means 'life.'" Rudy pondered a moment, "Haim ... Life ... It's good. Suits you." Haim, still bewildered, led on.

Inside the dorm room, Rudy noticed the wooden planks surrounding the beds for protection: "I'm glad to see you're careful. Have these boards come in handy?" Haim nodded: "But I usually sleep on a bed in the horse stable." Rudy indicated the box, asking, "Where should I put it?" Having him set it down on the desk, Haim opened it up and looked inside. Haim said in disbelief: "A long wave radio?" Rudy nodded,

"I remember how much you enjoyed the music at the café. Plug it in. Let's see how it works." The radio hummed and buzzed as they searched through static filled stations. Finding one from Berlin, Haim eagerly listened to hear the news from home.

Rudy became anxious as the commentator expounded, "Know, dear Christian, and have no doubts, that next to the Devil you have no more bitter, poisonous and determined enemy than a genuine Jew..." Rudy began to turn the station, but Haim stopped him. The commentator continued: "If they do something good for you, it is not because they love you, but because they need room to live with us. But their true goal is to drive thousands of German businessmen to bankruptcy, to starve German woman and children. Know for a fact, that Jews have never produced a single creative man, but that all great men in every country have been implacable opponents of the Jews..." Ignoring Haim's desire to listen, Rudy turned it off, "I'm sorry. The world is filled with many stupid people." Trying to change subjects, Rudy asked, "Would you mind showing me around? I'd like to know about your life here."

Leaving the dorm, they ran into Ivan, Avi, the twins and several other boys on their way to their next class. "This your father?" Avi asked Haim in English, the common language. "Of course not," Haim scoffed. "You saw my father a month ago." "Oh, right. I forget." As the boys headed off to class, concerned that Rudy was offended, Haim apologized: "Sorry, he didn't know what he was saying." Rudy assured,

"Not at all. I'm honored he would think I'm you're father." That surprised Haim, not only because Rudy was Christian, but because only a month earlier his actual father had been clearly embarrassed by the appearance of his son. Perhaps Julius felt it was his duty as a father to be more critical of his son.

Out in the grazing field next to the cow stable, Haim introduced Rudy to some of his favorite cows. Rudy commended: "I'm amazed you can tell them all apart." Haim shrugged, "Can't you tell your friends apart?" Rudy conceded, "True. Though most of my friends are much more unscrupulous."

Haim then brought Rudy to the cow stable and asked if he wouldn't mind relaxing while he mucks: "I don't want to risk them getting sick again." As Haim worked, Rudy changed into an old pair of overalls that he found hanging on the stable wall. He then picked up a shovel and surprised Haim by helping him muck. As they piled cow dung into the wheelbarrow and loaded it onto the manure pile Haim asked, "You sure you don't mind?" Rudy shook his head: "No, feels good. Reminds me of when I was a boy working my father's farm." With Rudy's size and strength, the two finished in no time.

Rather than join the other students in the Mess Hall for lunch, Haim wrapped up sandwiches, stealthily stuffed carrots into a small burlap sack, and quickly led Rudy out again. "I see you like carrots," Rudy said, trying to keep up. Haim nodded, "Not as much as my best friend."

Walking past the horse stable, Haim called out to Amon grazing in the field, Amon quickly looked up, surprised to see Haim there early. Letting out a whinny, he galloped towards him. Cracking a smile, Rudy said, "So this is your carrot-loving friend." Haim nodded, "He's a little shy. It's probably best if you don't try to pet him." Quickly handing Rudy the sandwiches and carrots, Haim ran to meet Amon.

Rudy stayed back watching as Amon affectionately greeted Haim. Though they had just seen each other that morning, Amon nuzzled Haim's chest while Haim scratched behind his ears. Haim then jumped up on Amon and trotted over to Rudy. Genuinely impressed, Rudy took in Amon: "He's magnificent. How did such a horse come to be here?" Haim explained while dismounting, and Rudy didn't seem surprised that Amon was a gift from King Abdullah.

As they made their way to have lunch in the shade of an old oak tree, Haim played with Amon hiding carrots behind his back before feeding them to him. Perhaps because of Rudy's admiration, Amon seemed relaxed enough for Rudy to pet him, but Haim saw no reason to test it.

When they finished eating, Rudy asked, "What would you do now if I weren't here?" Haim pointed to a field: "Amon and I are preparing that, but it's okay. It'll be there tomorrow." Rudy offered, "No, I'd like to help. Running factories doesn't leave much time to be outdoors."

Rudy suggested that they first remove a large boulder, "Otherwise you'll always struggle to plow around it. Do you have dynamite?" Haim's eyes widened as he shook his head: "With the terrorist attacks, if we're caught with dynamite they'd close down the school." Rudy nodded with assurance: "There are other ways. Most would break their backs with a sledgehammer and chisel, but there is Hannibal's method." From history class, Haim knew that the 3rd Century BC Carthaginian ruler, Hannibal, was considered one of the greatest military generals of all time, marching an entire army with Elephants over the Alps into Italy. But he heard nothing about him breaking up boulders. Rudy explained, "My father taught me that whenever a boulder blocked Hannibal's path he'd have his men build a fire around it until it was smoldering hot. They would then pour cold water on it forcing the stone to fracture into pieces."

Sounding like a good idea, they set to work gathering wood and buckets of water. With the kindling and timber around the boulder, they set it on fire and stood back as it became engulfed in flames. Checking his pocket watch, Rudy suggested working the field as it burned. About an hour later, with the embers still glowing, they tested the boulder with a sledgehammer. The now brittle, smoldering rock easily chipped away with each stroke. On Rudy's command, they threw on buckets of water, and the entire boulder cracked down the middle. Over the next hour they took turns smashing it to pieces with the sledgehammer until the entire boulder was reduced to ruble. To Haim's surprise, not only had Hannibal's method worked, but it also cracked the stone along its grains, making flat pieces good for stacking.

Exhausted and sweaty, Rudy and Haim stood back to admire their work. "We make a good team," Rudy commended as he patted Haim on the shoulder. Smiling, Haim nodded in agreement. Rudy threw what little water was left onto the ruble. It hissed and steamed as it hit the still smoldering rocks: "Looks like it won't cool off in time for me to help you move it." Haim shrugged: "That's okay. The hard part's done." Soberly checking his watch, Rudy nodded, "I'll have to head back soon. Is there a place to wash up?" Haim was about to take Rudy to the showers, but then thought better of it.

At the water tower where Haim swam every evening, they stripped down to their underwear. "You sure it's okay?" Rudy asked. "Do people drink this water?" Haim joked as he dove in, "I hope not!" Popping his head out of the water, Haim smiled, "No, it's used at night to irrigate the fields." They swam, raced and played in the water washing off the dirt and soot. Rudy used his pocket watch to time Haim swimming underwater. "Two minutes, six seconds!" Rudy announced as Haim gasped for air. Though used to swimming alone, Haim felt completely at ease with Rudy. There was something reassuring knowing that they both learned to swim in the same bend of the Rhine.

Once Rudy was dried off and changed back into his suit, he awkwardly admitted, "Before I go, there is something I would like to talk to you about." Haim waited as Rudy found his words: "When your father returned from war, he was a changed man. War can do that. All of his energy went into rebuilding the business, and I believe you're mother felt very neglected. It wasn't her fault. It wasn't anyone's fault. But I want you to know that I don't regret it. Not one bit. Do you understand what I'm trying to say?" Having no idea, Haim shook his head. Rudy struggled to continue, "Would you find it... Would it be so very bad to discover that your mother and I developed feeling for each other, feelings that perhaps were stronger than what was proper?" Not liking where this was going, Haim cut it off with: "It's none of my business..." "Yes, it is," Rudy interjected. "Not the affair, but what I'm trying to tell you. I think you already know." Rudy exhaled before saying, "I came here to tell you that I'm your father."

The words were like a punch to Haim's gut, leaving him speechless. With a reassuring hand on Haim's shoulder, Rudy pressed: "You must see it, too." Pushing his hand away, Haim shook his head, "No, I don't see anything." Rudy insisted, "I'm not trying to replace your father. But things are worse in Germany than probably anything you've heard. You're father won't leave because of his business and you're mother won't go without him. If something were to happen, I want you to know that I'm here for you." Rudy was disheartened at seeing Haim shaken to his core. "I'm sorry," he offered. "But I felt I had to tell you. Now, we've had a good day. Let's leave it at that?"

Little was said as they walked back to the compound. Rudy tried breaking the silence: "Is there anything you'd like to ask?" But the last thing Haim wanted was to probe. He wished that Rudy would take it back, to say that he was joking, but he knew that wasn't about to happen.

The car was waiting as they came to the main entrance. Rudy awkwardly hugged Haim goodbye, stressing before getting into the back seat: "Please try to think about what I've told you." Still stunned, Haim watched the car disappear down the driveway. *Try* to think about what he told him? As if he had a choice. Had his mother known that Rudy was coming to Palestine to see him? Could he write to her about it without risking informing his father? He decided that in no way would he jeopardize his parents' marriage over the possibly deranged rantings of a guilt-ridden ex-lover.

At the time, Haim didn't choose to not believe. It was impossible for him to believe. With no one to explain that the parent is the one who raises you, who loves you, accepting Rudy as his father meant rejecting Julius and believing that his entire life had been a lie. Julius may have been demanding, but he always acted in what he believed to be his son's best interest. In the recesses of Haim's mind, before a time that he could remember, Julius had gazed down on his son with pride and joy. That cherishing gaze was one of the greatest gifts. Etched into Haim's mind, like a first language, it helped define him. Knowing deep down that he was loved helped to give him the courage to set off on his own, to become his own person. Could he suddenly erase something that had become an internal part of him?

Needing time to think, he went back to his dorm room. On opening the door, he found Ivan, his roommates and some of the other boys huddled around the radio. Seeing Haim, Avi blurted out, "Hey, that man give you this? Is okay we listen?" "Why ask?" Haim said as he grabbed several books and headed out.

As he made his way to the Horse stable, Ivan ran up from behind. Haim had made his intro into Ben Shemen much easier: "No more tricks on newcomers," he had told the other boys. "It's our job to make him feel welcome." To Haim's surprise, they listened. Ivan was soon working at the Falhar and showed a natural talent for machinery. Catching his breath, Ivan asked, "Are you upset we were playing the radio?" Haim, looking straight ahead, shook his head as he pressed on: "No, you can burn it for all I care."

"What happened?" Ivan said, trying to keep up. Haim slowed down enough for Ivan to ask, "Who was that man? What'd he say?" Haim sneered, "He said he's my father." Ivan was taken aback: "What do you mean? He's your real dad?" Haim glared at him, "Of course not. He's Christian. Christians are crazy." Wide-eyed, Ivan agreed, "Yeah, but why would he say that?" Haim bitterly spat, "Ask my mother." Ivan hesitated: "But what if it's true? I mean, you do kind of look like him. That's not a bad thing. He's a good looking guy." Haim rolled his eyes while Ivan struggled to help: "Hey, it's tough to have no father, but this could be good. You'll have one to spare."

Seeing that he wasn't helping Haim's spirits, Ivan assured, "Don't worry. I won't tell anyone." Ivan didn't want to make Haim any more of an outsider than he already was, and having a Christian father wouldn't be helpful at Ben Shemen. Upset, wanting time to think, Haim accepted with a quiet nod.

CHAPTER 22

Einat's determination was revived by the discovery of the Haim Hausman magic lanterns, showing that he was the actual illustrator of 'AND THERE WAS EVENING'. Drawn into the many illustrations, she could feel a tenderness, beauty, humor, and love of children and animals. How could somebody who had survived so much suddenly vanish? In a strange way, finding him became part of her survival. She wasn't finished until her mission was accomplished.

Now armed with the elderly Enoch's testimony that Haim Hausman taught art to the children of Ben Shemen, along with the book on botany stating that he was a Ben Shemen graduate, she once again prepared for battle with the archivist. To her relief, a young woman picked up the phone, informing her, "I'm sorry, she's out for a few weeks. I'm subbing. Is there something I can help you with?" "I'm so sorry to hear that," Einat said as sincerely as possible. "She's familiar with my research."

As Einat began to explain, the young woman jumped in, "Yes, of course. I've heard about it. I'm Nisa. How can I help?" Nisa would not only open the files to Einat she would even begin the search while Einat drove there. Apparently, the mystery still wanted to be solved.

Nisa's thick-rimmed glasses and unkempt dark, curly hair only slightly masked her natural beauty.

She warmly greeted Einat, and led her to the files: "I couldn't find Haim Hausman, or any Hausman, on the school's payroll, but that's not surprising. If he had just graduated when he illustrated the book on botany, they could have paid him with room, board and a little cash under the table. After the war, if he had a paying job with the publishing house, he probably volunteered to teach art to the students." That made sense to Einat, as she had sensed that the magic lanterns were a gift to them.

Unfortunately, the archivist was right. There were no files for Haim Hausman, only a 'Fritz Huysman.' And with the notes in Hebrew, there was no German spelling of the name, 'Hausman'. Nowhere did the teachers write his first name. Einat asked, "Do you have any idea when he arrived?" Nisa shook her head, "His files must have been destroyed in the fire of '36. Since there's a question mark after his date of arrival '1934/1935?' I'm guessing it was rewritten very quickly. The notes stop after spring of 39. He probably graduated then, which means he would have been born around 1920-22."

When Nisa left Einat to search on her own, she found the notes to be consistent: "He's an outsider," "keeps to himself." But he was good at school, especially in biology and botany, and exceptional in languages; German, French, Italian, English, Hebrew, and Arabic. The main complaint of the teachers was that, unlike most of the other children, he rarely participated in outside activities, such as the dances and nightly campfires. No reason was given, but

Einat imagined that had his family been there, things might have been different.

To her dismay, there was no mention of an interest in art. How could he then be Haim Hausman? Her heart sank as she realized that she might be on the wrong track. Had another student, for some reason, later taken the name, Haim Hausman? Discouraged, she decided to change her search for only those students excelling in art. For over an hour, through file after file of students before 1939, she was surprised to find absolutely no mention of art anywhere.

Nina admitted as she looked through the Ben Shemen database, "You're right. There are no art teachers or art classes before World War 2. Maybe Haim Hausman introduced them after the war. Who knows? But if he had a passion for art, he might've taught himself. I wouldn't give up on our Fritz just yet." Somewhat hopeful, Einat added, "It does say he excelled in botany. That could have led to his illustrating the Dr. Gottlieb book?

After several more hours of searching, it was time for Einat to leave in order to be home before her children. While gathering her things, Nisa came over carrying a pad of stapled pages: "I printed out a list of students from 1934 to 1948. We don't know how complete it is. They may not have listed all of the students who were here illegally." Surprised, Einat warmly thanked her as she took the list. "There's a check by the ones we've had some contact with," Nisa explained. "And I've crossed out the ones that we know have died. Hopefully, someone on there can tell you more." Appreciative of her kindness, Einat admitted, "I should probably tell you, I might have misled you a little about the archivist's willingness to help with this." Nisa cracked a smile: "I'm sure I'll be far too busy to mention it to her."

For the next several days, Einat tried tracking down every living student on the list. Most who had survived WWII, the Palestinian war of 1948, and the Six-Day war of 67, had either died from natural causes or their whereabouts were unknown. And the few she actually made contact with couldn't recall a Fritz or Haim Hausman. She had left several with question marks after their names, intending to get back to them, including an Ivan Sachs. After several failed attempts of reaching Ivan at his home, she tired the garage that he had once owned. "Sure, I've know Ivan since I was a kid," said the current owner. "Worked here thirty years before buying the place from him." Hopeful, Einat briefly explained her mission. But he brushed it off, "No, never mentioned a Haim Hausman. Doubt he can help." Einat stressed, "But they were in school together." The garage owner chuckled at the absurd notion, "Ivan's gotta be ninety. I can't remember kids from my school. How many you think he remembers? He did say Shimon Peres went to his school, but don't think he met him either." He assured Einat that she had the right home number, but saw no point in bothering him: "He's a mechanic. This garage was his life. What's he gotta do with an artist?"

After their talk, she tried Ivan's home one more time, but still no answer. She told herself that she would get back to him, but she believed that the current garage owner was probably right. They were in very different worlds. And with a sixty-year ongoing search, if Ivan Sachs had known Haim Hausman he would have come forward.

She made contact with a few more students enrolled after WWII, but none remembered Haim Hausman. One suggested, "Tamar Duvdevani, if you find her, I bet she'll know." Tamar Duvdevani had worked in the publishing house in the 1950's, and Einat remembered seeing her signature on almost all of their letters from that period. Convinced that finding Duvdevani was the key, Einat went at it. But after being led through a series of calls, an older woman, Gala, responded: "I don't know a Tamar Duvdevani, but I certainly remember Haim Hausman." Einat thought that she must have misunderstood: "You mean you know his work?" "Yes, and him," Gala assured. "Can you actually describe him?" "Very well," Gala said. "He was quite tall, maybe 6'3", quite handsome, and had quite a body."

Gala's husband, listening in from another phone, cut her off: "How do you know this?" Gala stated matter-of-factly, "How do you think? We looked." Her husband was shocked: "You what? What does that mean? Did he also look at you?!" Einat, still stunned, listened in as she could feel Gala rolling her eyes: "No, I assure you, he never saw me naked. And I say that with the deepest regret." The husband demanded, "So, how did you see him naked? He just took his clothes off for you?" She shrugged him off: "Don't be silly. There were communal showers. We kept track of his schedule so we could peek. He didn't even know we were watching. Where's the harm?" The husband was outraged: "Me? How about you harmed me?! That's shameful!" She chided, "Are you telling me you've never looked at a beautiful naked girl?" The husband yelled, "No! Never! I've only seen you!" Gala stated, "Well, I promise, you will never have to suffer through that again. Now may I please go back to my *private conversation*?!"

The husband slammed down the receiver. Einat remained silent, questioning if she should still be on the line. But Gala calmly asked, "Good, so where were we?" Einat began: "I'm sorry, if this is a bad time..." Gala cut her off: "Don't be silly. A little jealousy keeps him young." Einat, hoping that Gala could give some insight into the Haim Hausman drawings, asked if it would be possible to meet.

The following afternoon in a little Tel Aviv coffee shop near to where Gala was shopping, Einat stared, fixated at Gala as she looked through the magic lantern drawings. "No, sorry, I don't remember any story with a smiling horse," Gala said, shaking her head. She continued looking, admitting that they looked familiar, but saw nothing specifically recognizable: "These magic lanterns were for young children. I was a teenager then."

Einat opened the book 'AND THERE WAS EVENING' and turned to an illustration of the father: "They say artist draw themselves. Could this be Haim Hausman with blonde hair?" Gala looked at the picture, but quickly shook her head: "No, he's handsome, but the features are too delicate. Haim

Hausman was larger, more manly." Einat pressed, "Do you see him in any of the drawings, even if only a slight resemblance? Take your time." Gala rejected drawing after drawing until she suddenly stopped on a picture of a strong, handsome, dark-haired man holding wheat stalks in one hand and a glowing loaf of bread in the other. "Well I'll be, here he is." Excited, Einat asked, "Are you sure? Is it a self-portrait or just a strong likeness?" Gala chuckled, "My dear, it's a cartoon. But it does bring him back. I remember his face as more handsome, but the muscular arms, the hair, that's him."

Gala didn't know if his name had been Fritz before Haim, if he had been in the war, or even his approximate age. Then it suddenly hit her: "Wait, a friend of his told us that he was madly in love with some older Italian woman and was trying to get back to her. I was devastated. How could a fifteen-year-old girl compete with that? I'm pretty sure she was in her early thirties, which to us was ancient. I remember we were shocked because she was eight years older than him. Back then that just didn't happen. So I guess he was in his mid-twenties.

Gala promised to call if anything else came to her. She also gave Einat the number of one of the other girls who had spied on Haim Hausman: "She's still clever and was there before me. Hopefully she can tell you more."

Gala's friend was 8-years-old when she arrived at Ben Shemen in the summer of 39: "I remember he worked in a sort of lab where children went for biology classes. It may have been the closest thing

Palestine had to a natural history museum, and all in one room." Besides that, she could add nothing more to what Gala had said, and could think of no reason why Haim Hausman would be erased from history. "He was a good guy. If not, we wouldn't have liked him so. I don't recall a scandal, but it was a long time ago. And people did have a way of disappearing back then."

Einat, determined, finally tracked down Tamar Duvdevani: "He left before I was at the publishing house. I remember when the book became so popular, we hoped to hear from him, but I don't think we ever did. I'm sorry. I wish I could tell you more. But I just can't think of anyone still alive who might have known him."

Einat sat looking at the cartoon of Haim Hausman: "Okay, good-guy, where to now?"

CHAPTER 23

November 7, 1938:

THE 17-YEAR-OLD Herschel Grynszpan, having escaped to Paris from Germany two years earlier, received word that his family was arrested with 12,000 other Polish Jews living in Germany, stripped of their property and herded aboard trains for Poland. Since the Polish government refused them entry, they were forced to live in the horrid conditions of refugee camps along the border.

Herschel, an unemployed, undocumented alien youth living in Paris, desperate to help his family, entered the German embassy, and asked to see "His Excellency, the ambassador" to hand over "the most important document." When presented to the 29-year-old Ernst vom Rath, Herschel shot vom Rath five times. On his immediate arrest, Herschel confessed that it was an act of desperation to avenge the Jews and bring public awareness to actions already taken by the Germans.

November 9, 1938: hours after vom Rath's death, Kristallnacht began. Named after the shards of glass littering the streets from smashed windows of Jewish-owned stores, buildings, and synagogues, many consider it to be the beginning of the Holocaust. 30,000 Jews were arrested and incarcerated in Nazi concentration camps. Jewish homes, hospitals, and schools were ransacked as the Nazis and German civilians demolished buildings with sledgehammers. Over 1,000 synagogues were burned, 95 in Vienna alone, over 7,000 Jewish businesses were destroyed or damaged.

As the most widely reported event of German Jews while it was happening, accounts from foreign journalists working in Germany sent shock waves around the world. "No foreign propagandist bent upon blackening Germany before the world could outdo the tale of burnings and beatings, of blackguardly assaults on defenseless and innocent people, which disgraced that country yesterday," wrote The Times.

Haim huddled around the radio with the other boys listening to the German announcer tell the world that the Jews had "fired the first shot! ... We understand the challenge, and we accept it!" Only Avi cheered, "Herschel do right thing!" To believe the Nazis, the actions of this 17-year-old boy were the sole cause of the Holocaust. Goebbels even kept Herschel alive for the trail that would prove the Jews' guilt to the world. However, the Nazis discovered that vom Rath was a known homosexual, often referred to in the Parisian gay community as "Madame Ambassador". Goebbels, whose hatred of gays equaled that of Jews, cancelled the trail to avoid a scandal. How the Nazis disposed of Herschel is still unknown.

Fearing the worst, Haim desperately tried to get word on his parents, but with the Nazis dictatorship came the end of civil liberties. Though Hitler never won the election, having at most only 37% of the vote compared to Hindinburg's 50%, in 1933 he took power by force and intimidation, claiming that the Dutch communist, Marinus van der Lubbe, set fire to the Reichstag building as the beginning to the communist take over. Though the Nazis probably framed Van der Lubbe, and may have even started the fire themselves, skilled in fear tactics, they publicized the "evil" intents of the communists, and implemented the Reichstag fire decree. All communists were placed in concentration camps, along with anyone else in opposition to the Nazis. All publications considered "unfriendly" were suppressed. With phone tapping common practice, Rudy Schank didn't dare to call Palestine directly. Several days after Kristallnacht, while he was at the factory talking on the phone to one of his trusted suppliers in Turkey, Rudy took the chance of asking if he would relay a message.

Lehman called Haim into his office, grimly informing, "Herr Schank has word from one of your parents' boarders." Herr Becker, a choirmaster, was living with his wife, Elisabeth, and two small children, Paul and Trudi on the second floor of the Hausmann's home. Unlike Professor Sack, the Nazi living on their the third floor, the Beckers treated the Hausmanns with respect, even expressing gratitude for being allowed to stay there. In return, Klara doted over the Becker children, who would later write of their wonderful life in a Jewish home - until that terrifying night.

The evening of Kristallnacht, six men forced their way into the Hausmann's home, taking bats and sledgehammers to everything made of glass and porcelain. The Beckers fled into the garden with Klara, hiding her behind one of the large boxwoods. As one of the men came outside to scan the garden with a flashlight, the Beckers quickly crouched down, hiding in front of the boxwood. They remained frozen as the beam passed over their heads. Seeing nothing suspicious, the man turned to head inside, but little Paul, chilled by the cold night air, let out a sneeze. Within moments the flashlight was shining in their faces. "Jews?" the man demanded. "No," Mrs. Becker said anxiously shaking her head. "My husband is the choir master." Herr Becker handed over his papers. The man studied them with his flashlight: "Then why hide?" "Why?!" Elizabeth asked in disbelief. "Look at how you've frightened the children." Shining the light on a terrified Paul and Trudi, the man softened slightly: "You will take us to the Jews." Elizabeth argued, "Herr Hausmann is far too ill with a flu. He must rest." "He will rest plenty in prison," the man informed.

Klara remained frozen behind the boxwood as the man escorted the Beckers inside. Fortunately, Professor Sack, undoubtedly out destroying other Jewish homes and establishments, was not there to give her away. Against the Beckers' protests, Julius was escorted to Bingen Nazi party headquarters for assignment to a concentration camp. Fortunately, one of the sergeants, a former friend of Julius's, declared him too ill and Julius was sent back home. "You're parents were very lucky," Lehman assured. "However, Herr Schank insists that you must convince them to leave Germany."

What had Haim been trying to do since before he left for Palestine? But perhaps now they would listen. "Can they stay here?" Haim asked. Lehman confirmed, "We'll make room for them." Though Haim was only 17, the same age as Herschel Grynszpan, having led Haganah missions for over two years, Lehman could no longer view him as a boy. Though still considered an outsider at Ben Shemen, on nightly guard duty he had become the unspoken leader. Even Avi respected his authority.

At almost his full height of 6' 2.5", he had grown to become a strong leader. Having hated people lauding their power over him, Haim rejected his British training of ruling with an iron first. He considered his men as equals, all working together for the same cause, risking their lives for what they believed in. With their survival depending on the strength of the unit as a whole, he saw maintaining a good relationship with his men as crucial.

Though the British had crushed the first phase of the Arab revolt, they had instilled in the Arabs a deep seeded hatred and mistrust. On July 7, 1937, the Peel commission, as a solution to the Arab/Jewish problem, recommended partitioning Palestine into a smaller Jewish state and larger Arab state, with Jews receiving some of the best land, including 80% of the citrus crop. Peel also proposed transferring 225,000 Arabs from the new Jewish state into Transjordan.

As outrage spread through the Arab communities, the Grand Mufti promoted death to all British and Jews. The much more violent, peasant-led second phase of the revolt was triggered. The British police tried to arrest the Grand Mufti, but having been tipped off he managed to escape. For three months he led the revolt while hidden within a Haram.

On September 26, 1937 Arab gunmen assassinated the Acting District Commissioner of the Galilee, Lewis Andrews. British officials immediately deposed the Grand Mufti from the presidency of the Muslim Supreme Council, though he evaded arrest by escaping into Lebanon. The British then arrested and deported the top five Palestinian Arab leaders, disbanded the Arab Higher Committee, dismantled all Palestinian paramilitary units, closed off all frontiers to Palestine, withdrew telephone connections with all neighboring countries, and introduced press censorship. With every British casualty by Arab insurgents the more Arab civil rights were chipped away at.

But to appease Arab demands to control Jewish immigration, the British opened the Atlit concentration camp in Palestine, the first of their concentration camps for illegal Jewish refugees. Surrounded by barbed wire and watchtowers, it eerily resembled the German concentrations camps. Jewish inmates at Atlit were equally humiliated as men and women were separated, stripped naked and sprayed with DDT. But unlike the German camps, shut down by the end of WWII, the British camps continued all the way up to the formation of the State of Israel in 1948. Though never outright death camps, due to their horrid condition many Jews died there, including some who had miraculously survived the Nazi concentration camps.

(Atlit was finally closed in 1945 after Jewish leaders got word that 40 captured Jewish Iraqi refugees were being sent back to almost certain death. Six Palmachniks (pre-State commandos,) infiltrating in the guise of Hebrew teachers, informed the prisoners of the plan, and enlisted the help of two Jewish sentries to disable all of the sentries' rifles. Quietly cutting the barbed-wire fences to let in a larger Palmach force, including future Israeli Prime Minister, Yitzhak Rabin, they stealthily climbed the watchtowers to tie up and gag the guards. At 1:00 am, the Palmach fighters woke the already packed prisoners, and with babies and toddlers on their backs they led 200 detainees in the cover of darkness.

It was crucial to climb the Carmel Mountains to the shelter of kibbutz Beit Oren before sunrise, as dawn would mean certain capture by the British. But as Yitzhak Rabin stated, "Refugees are not soldiers." With the Palmach carrying as many children and bags as possible, their pace was still too slow to make it in time. The soldiers begged the refugees to leave their bags, promising to buy them new clothes. But it was not clothes that the refugees were hanging on to. In their suitcases were photos, letters, and mementos of their murdered families, all they had left of them. Having somehow kept them through the war, they couldn't let go now, even if it meant recapture.

As the sun rose, hearing the distant rumble of British vehicles in pursuit, the soldiers knew that their rescue mission was doomed. Like so many others, they would end up for years in British camps. But as they scaled the final ridge to kibbutz Beit Oren, they witnessed a miracle. Thousands of Jews, woken from their sleep by bullhorns announcing the plight of the escaping refugees, converged on Beit Oren. Piling out of cars, busses and trucks, they massed around the yolim as a human shield.

Through the sea of Jews, the British police found it impossible to distinguish the escapees. After several hours, they gave up. All of the inmates unable to escape that night were sent to British concentration camps in Mauritius or Cypress, while the escapees -- with their suitcases -- were dispersed throughout Palestine.)

∞

Throughout the Arab revolt of 1936-'39, while the British fought the Arabs, Haim and his men worked hard to save the yolim. Orde Charles Wingate, a fervent Christian Zionist, had incorporated the Haganah into British defense. Haim's unit was often ordered to patrol and set ambushes near Arab villages. But being only 17 and still in school, the British accepted that he was not allowed to stay out late, leaving Haim and the younger members responsible for slipping in yolim.

October 1938, stakes became higher as Bernard Montgomery took command of the 8th Infantry Division in Palestine. Committing over 20,000 professional soldiers, Montgomery mercilessly suppressed Arab uprisings as he had to the uprisings in India. Haim had befriended some of the Indian regiments and was surprised to learn that they weren't allowed to use the same bathrooms as the British soldiers. "We may die for them, but never pee with them," confided one Indian soldier. With Montgomery in charge, if caught bringing in yolim Haim was sure to be sent to Atlit concentration camp.

One evening patrol, Haim was in the third of four jeeps when the road ahead of them blew up. Arab rebels, appearing from both sides of the road, began firing on them. Blocked by the first jeep trapped in the blown-out trench and the last jeep behind them, Haim and his men scrambled to the ground. Using the jeeps for cover, they fired back. When almost out of ammunition, they were about to make a run for it, but the Arab rebels, also low on ammunition, suddenly scattered into the hills. Along with the many wounded, a British Sergeant and two Indian soldiers were killed.

Though it was far too dark for Haim to make out any of the faces of the men firing at them, he was ordered to go with British troops to identify possible suspects in the nearby village. Fearing that he would be spotted by one of his Arab friends, he tried staying in the background as he watched the men of the Arab village forced to strip naked in the square before being whipped while interrogated. Haim was then ordered to stand guard over them as they were placed behind metal fencing. Though there was no evidence of any guilt, for their refusal to name names, the British took pickaxes to their homes, smashing all of the windows, mirrors, furniture, cabinets of glass and porcelain. Grains and produce were thrown into sheets and dosed in olive oil. After their homes were destroyed, the village men were then sent to prison camps.

Haim wanted to help the villagers, but if the British found out that he was fluent in Arabic he would be used for endless interrogations, and Haim was determined to never participate in any other similar operations. As a British officer was about to set fire to the homes, Haim called out, "Wait! I think I know these men. I'm pretty sure they've warned us of attacks on Ben Shemen." Fortunately, one of the Arab prisoners spoke some English. After translating for Haim, each prisoner was prompted to nod when asked if they had warned students at Ben Shemen of possible rebel attacks. With each nod, Haim confirmed that he remembered him.

The British commander was dubious: "You know these rebels are mindful of massacring all you Jews?" Haim awkwardly shook his head, "They're terrorized by the rebels, too. That's why they've helped us." The commander exhaled with frustration as he scanned the pathetic, naked Arabs. Whether he believed Haim or not, after finding no weapons in any of their homes, he decided to let them off, warning them: "You're just lucky you have a friend here."

British soldiers were known to surround villages, usually before dawn so that they could catch suspects before they fled, then forcing men and women from their homes, separating them into wire cages, and after a weapons search, destroying everything. One British soldier explained to Haim's unit, "With a punitive raid, you can knock the place about. Anything you see you smash. If they're perfectly intact, all those houses you've just searched, you are not doing your stuff." New recruits were usually reluctant at first to destroy the homes of innocent people, but in surprisingly little time they quickly adjusted.

After an attack by Arab rebels on a British patrol in the village of Kawkab Abu Haija, the British army destroyed the entire village. When a British army vehicle ran over a mine near Kafr Yasif, British soldiers burned down seventy houses and machine-gunned nine villagers. Demolishing homes of Arab civilians, shooting handcuffed prisoners, using local Arabs for testing minefields are just some of the descriptions from official British documents of methods used by British authorities to combat Arab terrorism.

Arab informers, hidden under hoods, screened the men, nodding when a 'suspect' was found. If no informers were available, papers were checked against a list of suspects. Any amount of destruction was justified as "insurgents and weapons search." While the British carried out arms searches in the village of Halhūl, ten Arab men, kept in an open-air-pen for several days with little water, died of heat prostration. The cause of death was attributed to "unfortunate circumstances" of the abnormally hot weather and low resistance of the older men.

The brutality Haim experienced during British weapons searches at Ben Shemen was nothing to what he now saw. And with the censoring of the Arab press, it all went unreported. Montgomery even banished reporters so that his men could carry out their work unfettered by the media.

Some British officials spoke out against the abuse, but most agreed with Lord Dufferin: "I do not feel we have the right to interfere. British lives are being lost and I don't think that we, from the security of Whitehall, can protest squeamishly about measures taken by the men on the frontline." Sir John Shuckburgh agreed: British authorities in Palestine are not faced "with a chivalrous opponent playing the game according to the rules, but with gangsters and murderers."

By the end of the Arab revolt, 5,000 Arabs were dead. The British army and police had killed more than 2,000 in combat. 108 were hung for terrorist activities. Many more died trying to surrender, even some who were only 12-years-old. Around 20,000 in total, over ten percent of the adult male Palestinian Arab population between 20 and 60, were killed, wounded, imprisoned or exiled. Estimates for fatalities of Palestinian Jews were much less, ranging from only 91 to several hundred.

Through all of the second phase of the revolt, Haim went every Saturday on the bus from Lydda to spend the afternoon with his friends at the café in

Jaffa. Though always the only non-Arab, he never felt any animosity. In fact, his friends on the bus seemed more afraid than he was of Arab rebels. Trapped between two factions, they would be killed as traitors if suspected of informing, but by not informing the British viewed them as the enemy.

In October of 1938, Haim walked to the bus stop in Lydda to find that the town had been devastated by British troops. Twenty-one homes were destroyed; including one belonging to Tarek and Luja, the parents of Sabah, the little girl that Haim first sketched on his early trips to Jaffa. Cordoned off with the other women, Luja helplessly watched as Tarek was forced to strip naked in the street and kneel down on a bed of thorns while being brutally interrogated by the British. His back bloodied from caning, he still refused to talk. With rebel informers likely watching, naming names was equal to a death sentence. Without being read his rights or told any charges he was sent with the other arrested Arab men from Lydda to a detention camp.

Luja only learned later that his arrest might have been in connection to a recent attack on British military police. She knew that he could not have participated. Wanting to raise Sabah in peace, he had done his best to avoid the insurgents, and exhausted after long hours of construction work in Tel Aviv, his free time was either spent with his family or sleeping.

But guilt often had little to do with arrest. There were many incentives to inform; rewards, settling a score, procuring a neighbor's land, and it was safer to denounce an illiterate Arab worker with little recourse than an actual rebel who would get revenge if the informant's identity was ever uncovered.

Tarek and Luja had protected Haim when he went to check on his friends at the café in Jaffa. They had risked their lives pretending that he was part of their family when stopped by Arab insurgents and British police. Not only were they now homeless, the British police had imposed heavy fines on the families of the arrested men while Arab rebels also fined many of them for non-compliance with the revolt. With their livestock taken away, homes destroyed, long curfews imposed and the men sent to detention camps, the fines were impossible to pay. The rebels then took whatever they wanted from the ruined families while British police confiscated chickens, eggs, grains and anything else they could sell in Haifa.

For the first time, Haim asked for help from his friends at the café in Jaffa. On their own, they had used their contacts to arrange a position for Julius as administrator of one of the Rothschild wineries in Palestine. If anything could lure Julius to Palestine it would be the late Baron Edmond de Rothschild, producer of some of the finest wines in the world.

Considered by many the father of Zionism, Rothschild spent an estimated $50 million in establishing a Jewish homeland in Palestine. Acquiring over 125,000 acres, he built the first Palestinian power plants, converting the barren land into settlements with businesses, synagogues, farms and schools. (By advocating spoken Hebrew, "I have heard many French poems in France. Here I will be delighted to hear Hebrew poetry," he also inspired the early kibbutz artists in creating their first children's books.)

Like Arlosoroff, Rothschild stressed the importance of good relations between Arabs and Jews. Shortly before his death in 1934 he wrote to the League of Nations: "The struggle to put an end to the Wandering Jew, could not have as its result, the creation of the Wandering Arab." Never overlooking the Arab cultivators of the land that he bought, through development he made it capable of supporting ten times the population. On Rothschild's land, even in the worst periods of the revolt, Jews and Arabs lived together in peace.

Shihab glumly shook his head, "Your father is a successful Jewish wine merchant. Placing him on a Rothschild estate was nothing. Asking the British to release a possible rebel will put us on their watch list." Haim stressed, "But I know he's innocent." Shihab shot back, "You think that matters? British kill poor innocent Arabs all the time just to teach resistance a lesson!" Sensing Haim's determination, Rasul interjected, "If we promise to find living quarters for his wife and daughter will you drop this?" Haim shook his head: "Luja and Sabah have been taken in by family. Tarek is the one who needs help." Rasul tried to hide his frustration: "But why you? One more stunt like getting the British to release all those naked peasants will have you sent back to Germany. Is that what you want?" Before

Haim could respond, Rasul assured, "Trust me, you will only do more harm than good." With his glare intact, Shihab left little room for argument: "If you must help, you're only move is to find someone with true influence over the British."

∞

The next day, Haim and Khalid shared their Sunday lunch with Amon at their hiding spot near the stables. Their old spot ran too much risk of their being seen together by Arab rebels, and they still couldn't risk Khalid being suspected of having informed on the rebels' plan to kill Amon. Avi and a few of the other boys knew that they were indebted to Khalid. If they had spied on Haim and Khalid having lunch near the stables nothing was ever said.

Needing a plan to save Tarek, Haim was more anxious than usual to see Khalid. Though Khalid had no connections with the British, he had a way of seeing things clearly. But before Haim had a chance to bring it up, Khalid surprised him with, "It appears I'm getting married." "Married?" Haim asked in disbelief. "Last week you didn't even have a girlfriend." Khalid shrugged, "It was just decided by our families. It won't be for another year. She's young, only fifteen. But she should make a good wife." Baffled, Haim asked, "Why's that? How well do you know her?" Khalid shook his head: "Hardly at all." Haim prodded, "So it's in the contract? If she isn't a good wife you can sue?" Khalid laughed: "If she heard us she'd probably sue me. I can't talk to her the way we talk. She would think I'm crazy. But she's quiet, and seems nice. I knew you wouldn't like this." Haim shook his head: "I didn't say that. It's just, you're spending the rest of your lives together and it sounds like you've spent more time picking out a goat." Khalid confided: "I'm not like you. You can travel the world to meet women from all over. But no women wander into Beit Nabala looking to marrying a shepherd."

Other than Khalid's future appearing more certain, Haim didn't see them as different. They were best friend, talking freely about anything. Both planned to spend the rest of their lives in Palestine, hoping to one-day be open about their friendship and openly discussing politics or whatever while raising their families on nearby farms.

"It's good news," Haim allowed. "You'll be the first one of us to have sex." Khalid laughed: "Maybe, but we haven't even kissed yet." Haim laughed: "It'll be okay. I'm guessing she knows even less than us. So it'll be the best sex either of you ever had." Though sex was one of their favorite topics, in 1938 Palestine, a Jewish boy in a kibbutz and an Arab boy in small peasant village had little chance to experience it. There were several girls that Haim was attracted to, but in a time when women were expected to marry as virgins, they were all strictly guarded under their housemother's stern watch.

While on guard duty, Haim had actually kissed Sheila and after vowing to absolute silence she allowed him to feel her breasts. Sheila was no longer the innocent girl he had met shortly after his arrival. But she now made it clear that anything more than kissing and petting would require marriage, and she wasn't sure if she felt that way about Haim. He had only confided in Khalid, and since Sheila soon moved on to a more popular boy, both boys agreed that Sheila's breasts were the only thing that Haim truly loved about her.

Other than marriage, their only viable option for experiencing sex was with a prostitute. Besides not having the money, in a time before penicillin, the grotesque images of incurable venereal diseases shown to the students had worked well enough as a deterrent.

When Haim finally got around to telling Khalid about Tarek, he was surprised by his advice: "Tell Professor Lehman." Haim asked incredulously, "Lehman? What can he do?" Khalid shrugged, "You know there is resistance in Beit Nabala. Why do you think the British have left us alone?" Haim assumed that the small village had slipped under British radar. Dumbfounded, he asked, "Professor Lehman?"

The year before, when the Grand Mufti ordered all supplies routes cut off to Jewish settlements, the people of Beit Nabala worked together to get food to Ben Shemen. Haim thought it was solely due to their concern for the children. Khalid informed him, "Sure, they care about the children, but without Professor Lehman's friendship, they would not have helped. It is because he told the British that Beit Nabala is a friend to the Jews that they leave us alone. I can think of no other who might be able to help you."

Haim never fully forgave Lehman for allowing the elders of Beit Nabala to almost kill Amon. His offer to help get his parents out of Germany seemed a vain attempt at reconciliation: "Convince your father that he could be of great help to the school. Perhaps he could start a winery here." Having met his father, Haim questioned if Lehman was serious. Running one of Rothschild's wineries couldn't lure Julius to Palestine. How would he be tempted by a winery manned by children?

∞

Seeing no other choice, Haim swallowed his pride and went to Lehman for help. "I'll see what I can do," Lehman said, though he clearly preferred to not get involved. Lehman had walked a fine line gaining the trust of both British and Arabs, even earning the support of Orde Charles Wingate. He was not about to jeopardize it. But if convinced of Tarek's innocence, Haim was sure that Lehman would feel compelled to help. As if reading Haim's mind, Lehman advised, "Don't get your hopes up. There's probably little I can do."

Lehman was waved through the barbed wired entrance gate of the local police station to meet with his friend, the local chief of police. The chief responded in disbelief: "A lad of yours went off alone to Lydda to see family in Tel Aviv? Lucky the blokes still alive." Lehman nodded: "Yes, it was foolish, but fortunately Tarek and his wife were there to protect him." The chief nodded: "But one good turn won't excuse a rebel. Don't see what can be done." Lehman insisted: "We're convinced there is a mistake. With all of the attacks on the school, if he were a rebel why risk his life for a student he might later kill?" As the chief pondered, Lehman added: "And Tarek works for a Jewish owned Construction Company in Tel Aviv. They also vouch for him, claiming he puts in far too many hours to be part of the revolt."

With Lehman's determination, the chief finally agreed to arrange a meeting with the detention camp's supervising colonel. But it would take repeated calls on Lehman part to finally set a date. "The middle of November is several weeks away," Lehman said over the phone to the colonel. "Tarek's wife and child are extremely anxious to have him home. Is there nothing sooner?" The colonel explained that for Tarek to participate forms would have to be filled out and steps taken to release him from work duty, all of which would take time. "It's rather important to keep their days full. Last thing we want are idle rebels." Lehman conceded, "I understand." He understood too well the abuses of the labor camps, but reproaching the colonel would not help Tarek.

With the many horrific stories of inmates being tortured, killed or simply disappearing, Luja was distraught hearing that it would be several more weeks before Tarek's possible release. Haim assured her that Lehman was doing everything he could, but he only hoped that to be true.

Several weeks later, Lehman approached the imposing detention camp surrounded by barbed wire and sentries in towers positioned to easily pick off anyone around the compound. Lehman was frisked at the gate, his papers carefully checked, and driven to the entrance of the seemingly impenetrable, concrete building. He then waited for several minutes in the entrance hall until the colonel came down to greet him. While shaking hands with the tall, handsome colonel, Lehman wondered what the colonel had done to deserve this forsaken outpost. "We have placed Tarek in a holding room," the colonel informed. "He appears to only speak Arabic. Will you need a translator?" Lehman shook his head, assuring the colonel that his stilted Arabic should suffice."

A bright ceiling lamp hung over the gray folding table of the holding room, now doubling as an interrogation room. Seated behind the table was an unkempt, dark, lean, handcuffed man. Though malnourished, the intensity of his gaze seemed to pierce through Lehman.

"Tarek? I almost didn't recognize you," Lehman said in Arabic. Though the colonel and guard claimed to speak only English, Lehman preferred taking no chances: "Haim and your wife have been worried sick. Every day they tell me, 'Professor Lehman, you must get Tarek out of there.' Apologies for my Arabic, as always, but I hope you understand?" To Lehman's relief, Tarek played along, assuring him with a nod.

The colonel glanced over several papers while sitting with Lehman on the other side of the table. "Sorry to have wasted your time," the colonel said to Lehman. "But please explain to Tarek that unfortunately we will have to detain him a little longer for his own safety. My superiors have decided that his release would trigger suspicion that he informed for his freedom. He would then stand little chance on the outside." Though Lehman was dubious of the reasoning, he translated as accurately as possible. To avoid the colonel from understanding his response, Tarek spoke with little emotion: "They care nothing for my safety? They are sons of dogs turning innocent men into slaves."

Lehman was aware that many innocent Arab workers were taken as prisoner to work as slave labor for building the British mandate's roads and infrastructure, but for the moment he needed Tarek to let that go. Lehman explained to the colonel, "He says that he truly appreciates your concern, but not to worry. He will be safe with his Jewish employers in Tel Aviv. And I can assure you that if for some reason that doesn't work out he is welcome at Ben Shemen." Concerned that the colonel understood Tarek, Lehman added: "I'm a little rusty with the language, but I believe that was the gist." The colonel offered, "I appreciate that, but he is under arrest for suspicion of working with the rebels."

Tarek responded to Lehman's translation: "I help Arab resistance no more than I help British swine. Both filthy pigs deserve to be penetrated by a thousand penises." Lehman translated to the Colonel: "Tarek assures that he would never aid the Arab rebels." The colonel dismissively nodded: "That's all quite fine, but …" Lehman interjected: "Tarek and his family have suffered greatly at the hands of the rebels. I give my word that he will have nothing to do with them." Tarek knowingly questioned, "You tell him what I say." Lehman calmly reprimanded, "Of course not. If you don't care about your own life, think of your wife and child. The British are not broad minded. Act accordingly." The colonel interrupted: "What's that you're saying?" Lehman quickly covered: "He's concerned about his wife and child. I assured him they are fine. Can you tell me what evidence there is against him?" The colonel shook his head: "Obviously we can't disclose anything of our informant." Lehman insisted: "I'm certain that the informant was mistaken. Tarek is a friend of Ben Shemen, and as the head of the school you must know that I would never deliberately help to free an insurgent."

The colonel would only agreed to look into the matter, which was undoubtedly his way of placing it on a back burner. But then convinced of Tarek's innocence, Lehman became his champion, checking each week to see if any progress had been made on his release. Though little ever was, Lehman's weekly calls alerted the British that if something were to happen to Tarek it would not go unnoticed.

The greatest fear was that Tarek would die due to the horrid living conditions. With inmates sleeping crowded together on hardwood bunks stacked three high, disease quickly spread. The longer Tarek remained there the more likely he would end up like the other unfortunate victims, quickly removed and disposed of.

At the end of January 1939, Lehman made his weekly call to find out that Tarek, delirious with a fever, might not make it through the night. With the detention camp's infirmary little more than a sick room for isolating dying inmates, Lehman insisted on moving Tarek to the Ben Shemen infirmary, where they could care for him. Prepared for a battle, Lehman was surprised how easily the colonel agreed to the release. Perhaps he saw it as the most efficient way of removing the body. On the condition that Lehman return Tarek to the camp if he were to recover, Lehman assured: "I swear on the Entire British Empire."

At the Ben Shemen's infirmary, Luja and Haim watched over Tarek through the night, keeping him hydrated with what little chicken broth he could keep down, drying off the sweat from his malnourished body, and every hour changing him into dry bedclothes and sheets.

The next morning, a haggard, gaunt Lehman met with the colonel to inform him of Tarek's death. Tears welled as he invited the colonel to the service set for that afternoon: "As you know, Muslims bury their dead as soon as possible, leaving no time for a viewing. But if you'd like to see the body to confirm, you must come as soon as possible. Tarek's family is with him, but I'm sure they'll be civil." As far too much of his time had already been spent on an inconsequential detainee, the colonel checked his schedule: "I'm sorry, at the moment I can't possibly get away."

Lehman hobbled away as if carrying the weight of the world. After passing the barbed wired gate, the corners of his mouth cracked into a smile. Though Tarek was written off as dead, with Luja's persistent care, the fever had broken. Taking no chances of the

British finding out, a service was performed over a mock grave while Tarek had been moved to a nearby safe house.

Luja was spoon-feeding Tarek while Haim was teaching Sabah to read from an Arabic children's book as their eyes fixed on Lehman who somberly shook his head while entering the room of the safe house: "I'm afraid I missed my calling," Lehman confessed. Fear flooded Luja: "They do not believe Tarek is dead? They are coming?" Lehman cracked a smile: "No, but considering my performance, I was truly destined for the stage. They should not bother you again."

CHAPTER 24

ONCE FULLY RECUPERATED, Tarek, Luja and Sabah moved to Haifa, where Rasul found Tarek a job on the loading docks. Having lost everything, they needed to save money before moving to Transjordan, where there would be no threat of rearrest by the British. Shihab would help Tarek make connections in Transjordan, but advised them to keep a low profile in Palestine. Tarek needed no warning. His heart raced with each site of a British officer. But as war loomed with Germany, the political situation was quickly shifting.

March 1938: Hitler went directly against the Treaty of Versailles to enact the Anschluss: Germany's invasion and annexing of Austria. Despite the Austrian government's pleas for help, Britain and the other allies only voiced disapproval.

September 1938: to prevent Germany taking Czechoslovakia by force, British Prime Minister, Neville Chamberlain, flew to Munich to negotiate the Munich Agreement, allowing only the annexation of the Sudetenland into Germany. After signing the agreement, Chamberlain was granted a private meeting with Hitler, where he pulled from his pocket the "Anglo-German Agreement" stating that the two nations considered the Munich Agreement: "symbolic of the desire of our two people never to go to war again." According to Chamberlain, Hitler enthusiastically nodded, "Ja! Ja!" and the two men signed the paper. The German Foreign Minister reproached Hitler for signing it, but Hitler assured: "Oh, don't take it so seriously. That piece of paper is of no further significance whatsoever."

Chamberlain, however, returned to London a hero for negotiating permanent peace with Germany. From the first floor window of 10 Downing Street he addressed the cheering masses recalling the words of his predecessor, Benjamin Disraeli: "My good friends, this is the second time there has come back from Germany to Downing Street peace with honor. I believe it is peace for our time. We thank you from the bottom of our hearts. Now I recommend you go home, and sleep quietly in your beds."

November 9, 1938: A month later, the horrors of Kristallnacht made clear that Hitler could not be trusted. Many refugees from Germany warned of the incredible force Hitler was amassing. But Chamberlain, fearing that Hitler would view it as an abandonment of their peace agreement, resisted advancing rearmament to a war footing. It was a disastrous mistake.

March 15, 1939: Germany invaded the Czech provinces of Bohemia and Moravia, including Prague. Conceding that war seemed inevitable, Chamberlain sought an agreement with France, the USSR and Poland to defend Poland if their independence was threatened. Polish mistrust of the Soviet Union caused negotiations to fall apart, but Britain committed all possible aid to Poland in the event of a German invasion.

The Soviets continued negotiations with Poland and Romania to aid their defense. But fearing that the Soviets would take control, neither country would allow Soviet troops to be stationed within their borders. Soviets then signed a pact with Germany committing the countries to non-aggression toward each other, along with a secret agreement dividing up Poland in the event of war.

Finally accepting that Hitler had little intention of honoring their peace agreement, Chamberlain wrote to Hitler stating that Britain was fully prepared to live up to its obligations to protect Poland. But Hitler shrugged it off to his generals: "Our enemies are small worms. I saw them at Munich."

Braced for war, Britain now needed their Arab allies, and especially their oil. April 1939, Chamberlain stated: "We are now compelled to consider the Palestine problem from the point of view of its effect on the international situation. If we must offend one side, let us offend the Jews, rather than the Arabs." Colonel Richard Meinertzhagen protested: "His actions of his majesties government in Palestine is very near to that of Hitler in Germany. We have dishonored our promises to the Jews. After 20 years of incredible effort in Palestine the Jews are asked to abandon their National home at the bidding of Arab violence." But his words fell on mostly deaf ears, and Britain's policy towards the Arabs and Jews quickly turned.

British atrocities towards the Arabs were severely cut back and the enforcement of Jewish immigration restrictions increased. With British assurance that

Palestine would maintain an Arab majority, the Arab revolt ended. Tarek and his family could breath easier, but more than ever yolim would have to be snuck in, and Haim was unable to help.

∞

At the end of April 1939, shortly after turning 18 and graduating with top grades, Haim needed a job. Reluctant to ask Lehman for more help, he found one on his own as a farmhand in the Ben Shemen moshav. The farmer seemed almost as indifferent to his wife and two small children as he was to Haim, and with jobs almost impossible to find in Palestine, Haim questioned why this one was available. But since Amon was allowed to join him, he accepted.

Saying goodbye to the cows and other horses was the most difficult part. Even though he had trained several students that he trusted to replace him, they had become part of his family, and the thought of them feeling abandoned by him was crushing. He told himself that he would visit them often, but he would soon find out how difficult that would be.

∞

Life on the small farm of the Moshav was miserable; waking up at 4:00 am, he worked past sundown 7 days a week. Too exhausted to draw or even read, much less explore with Amon and assist his Haganah unit, what little free time he had was spent recuperating. While the farmer and his family had all of their meals in the kitchen, Haim was never invited inside the house. He would eat his meals at the barn with Amon. His only human companionship was when Khalid would occasionally sneak in to join them for lunch.

"When I save enough to start my own farm, everyone working it will be treated as family," he told Khalid. But the 6,000 Swiss francs that his father had put in a trust for him was unavailable until his 22nd birthday, and with his salary under two dollars a week, having his own farm seemed to be a distant dream.

Haim worked the farm for three long months with no days off when Professor Melnick surprised him with a visit while he was eating dinner with Amon. After momentarily questioning if his eyes were playing tricks on him, Haim jumped up to enthusiastically greet Melnick. "Why are you eating in the barn?" Melnick questioned. Not wanting to burden him, Haim assured, "Amon and I always eat together." Melnick didn't press it, but even though Haim's height, strength and demeanor made him appear more mature than his years, he questioned what kind of employer would have an 18-year-old eating dinner in a barn with a horse. "This letter came for you," Melnick said as he handed it to Haim. "Since you haven't come to see us, seemed like a good excuse to see you."

Surprisingly, the letter's return address was Rudy Schank's supplier in Turkey. With Nazi censorship, unless seeking money from family outside of Germany, letters from Jewish homes were often discarded. Knowing that it must be word on his parents, Melnick insisted: "Go ahead. Read it. I'll wait." Haim began reading out loud, "Dearest Haim, being that your parents have received no reply from you to their many letters, I have taken it upon myself to contact you. Do not be concerned. You're parent's are healthy…" Haim exhaled with relief before quickly reading the rest to himself. Stunned, he looked up at Melnick: "In less than two weeks, I'm to meet my family in Bologna, Italy. My parents will be visiting my sister there." Melnick instantly understood the apprehension in Haim's eyes: "Don't worry. We'll find a way to get you passage." Haim shook his head: "There's not enough time." Uncomfortable accepting help, Haim tried to argue, but Melnick was resolute: "It's important you go."

The following afternoon, Haim was plowing a field with Amon when he spotted Melnick in the distance stumbling towards them over rows of furrows. Believing to hear Melnick call out: "Professor Lehman has a job for you!" Haim abandoned the plow, and ran to meet him. "Congratulations," Melnick said. "You'll be assisting me and the other professors in the Botany/Biology Lab. That is, if you're willing to leave all this."

There was no goodbye party, no promises to stay in touch. Haim simply informed the farmer that he was leaving, loaded his few belongings into the Ben Shemen jeep that Melnick had parked there, and he and Amon walked away, never looking back.

∞

With Amon settled back at the Ben Shemen horse stable, Haim found Melnick, who helped carry Haim's bags up to his small room on the second floor of the teacher's quarters. Overwhelmed with gratitude, Haim admitted, "I don't know how to thank you." Melnick shook his head: "If you wanted a job, all you had to do was ask. I believe Professor Lehman was hurt by the way you left." Haim knew that Lehman had hired Ivan and some of the other students, but after the trouble with Tarek, he assumed that his favors were used up. "You need to learn to help yourself," Melnick advised. "You're not a charity case. We need you here."

Being isolated on the small farm of the Moshav, Haim was unaware that the shift of British support to the Arabs left the school with increasing insurgent attacks. Since 1927, Lehman had dedicated his life to protecting the youth village. Unable to now rely on the British, everyone from senior students to elder faculty participated in its defense. Since Haim had proven to be one of their best guards, Lehman wanted him there.

A few days later, Haim was called into Lehman's office: "Here are your letters of transit and round trip passage to Bologna." Bewildered, Haim offered what little money he had saved. Lehman cracked a smile: "Keep that for incidental." Before Haim could argue, Lehman acknowledged: "I understand that you could not possibly accept such a large gift, so we will work it out of your pay." Though Haim's pay was little more than room and board, he accepted. Glancing Haim over, Lehman asked, "Now, do you have anything to wear for the trip?" Haim looked down, indicating his work clothes. Lehman chided,

"Travel like that? You'll give your father a heart attack."

The next day, Lehman took Haim to Tel Aviv for a cheap irregular piece of fabric large enough to make into a summer suit. Settling on a fine charcoal wool pinstripe, he then picked irregular fabrics for two shirts and pleated pants. After fitting Haim into a secondhand pair of size 12 fine leather shoes, they drove to a farm on the Ben Shemen moshav. The farmer, a former tailor in Warsaw, looked over the fabrics: "Any particular style you would like?" Haim unfolded an advertisement that he had torn out of a magazine. Studying the illustration of the suit, the farmer/tailor read the caption out loud: "You too can look like Cary Grant!"

Several days later, Haim picked up the suit and drove back to Ben Shemen. He shaved, washed, put on the suit, and headed to the dining hall. Lehman had asked him to wear it there so that he could check on the fit.

As Haim entered the hall, a hush came over the room. Having only seen Haim in ragged farming clothes, many had to double take before realizing who he was. As Haim made his way to Lehman, the room broke into applauds. Impressed by the transformation, even Lehman admitted: "Apparently, anyone can look like Cary Grant."

CHAPTER 25

HAIM'S BOAT SAILED for three days from Haifa to Venice, making stops in Alexandria, Rhodes, Piraeus, Brindisi, and his debarkation point of Rimini. From Rimini he would take the train to Bologna. While docked at each port to take on passengers, he normally would have loved to explore the sites, but he was now too anxious to see his family.

His first morning on deck, resting on a recliner in his new clothes he seemed transformed into a man of leisure. To pass the time he had planned to study a book on desert botany, but during his first break he pulled out his sketchpad and began to charcoal an older gentlemen resting on a nearby recliner. With little in the way of entertainment, a group quickly formed around him. The man turned over, unaware that his likeness was being drawn, and the group was disheartened, assuming that Haim would not be able to finish. To their surprise, the image was fixed in Haim's mind and he completed the drawing as if the man had never moved. "You must be a professional," said the mother of a little boy and girl. Haim laughed: "Far from it. If you'd like, I could try drawing your children."

Haim's time as a man of leisure was soon over as he quickly changed into work clothes and began charcoal portraits of the passengers. By Rhodes he had to go ashore for more supplies. One gentleman insisted on paying a dollar for his portrait. Haim tore it from the pad and handed it to the man, who looked at it quizzically: "You forgot to sign it." Haim hadn't forgotten. He hadn't seen the point. His father had engrained in him: "Art is a hobby. As a career, you will starve." He obligingly signed with only his first name, 'Haim', making it not only his first time to sell a work of art, but also the first one signed with his Hebrew name. The other passengers quickly asked him to also sign their drawings. It seemed like a silly formality, but he happily signed them all 'Haim'.

∞

Several days later, Haim took in Bologna's two towers and red roofed buildings glowing in the late afternoon sun as the train pulled through the surrounding hills exposing the red city. It left an indelible impression. But as they slowly made their way into the station the toll of WWI and the depression could be seen on the deteriorating facades of the first university town.

For twenty lire, about a dollar, Haim found a ride with several other passengers in the back of an old van. Heading directly south into the old town, he took in the renaissance buildings, medieval palaces and sidewalks covered in columned arcades. After letting off the other passengers, the van climbed the southern most hill stopping in front of an imposing 19th Century villa.

Though only a shadow of its former glory, with terracotta paint crumbling off of its walls and vegetables growing in what once were formal gardens, after five years in Palestine Haim was unaccustomed to such grandeur. Walking past the open cast-iron gate, permanently stuck off of its hinge, he climbed over the broken first marble step and up to a large oak door framed by Doric columns. Striking the brass knocker, a slight commotion emerged from within house. The heavy door creaked opened to Klara looking up at him. Stunned to see a 6' 2 ½" smartly dressed, handsome, young man looking down on her, it took her a moment before asking, "Fritz?"

Before he could answer, Klara exclaimed, "My Fritz!" Taking him in her arms, tears ran down her cheeks, not only overjoyed at seeing her son after so many years, but also distraught over how much of his childhood she had missed. Julius, also emotional, struggled to maintain his demeanor as he shook Fritz's hand. Lotte, at 5'1", exuberantly struggled to reach up to her brother: "What have they been feeding you? I'll need a stepladder!" Fritz shrugged, "Working the cow stable you get all the milk you want." "Well, no more pillow-fights with you," Lotte stated. She anxiously led Fritz to the villa's owners, who had been standing off to the side to allow room for the family reunion. "Fritz, this is Signora Morrisini and her daughter Gabriella."

With one look at Gabriella, Fritz was struck. It was more than just her beautiful, delicate features, silky blonde hair and 5'6" perfect frame. Her crystal blue eyes seemed to pull him in, revealing a kindness, intelligence, passion and sensitivity. He had only imagined admiring such a woman from afar, but here she was staring back at him, as if equally transfixed. His heart raced. Suddenly forgetting all of his Italian, he held out his hand and it suddenly came back to him: "It is a pleasure."

Gabriella's delicate hand fitting perfectly into his seemed to excite sensations throughout his body. Also lost for words, Gabriella hesitated before replying, "The pleasure is mine." Lotte scolded, "Fritz, where are you manners? Everyone knows Gabriella is gorgeous, but Signora Morrisini is your host." Fritz, flustered, immediately turned to La Signora: "My apologies, Signora. My mind is slow from long trip and bad Italian. Thank you so much for allowing me to your home." "You are very welcome, young man." Signora Morrisini held out her hand facedown, as had been the custom. Unsure whether to shake or kiss it, Fritz decided to bow slightly while gently cupping her hand in both of his. Her smile conveyed that, although he had no idea what he was doing, she appreciated the effort.

Lotte teased her brother: "Maybe your slow mind will do better in English. Gabriella is fluent." She then asked Gabriella with a knowing smile, "So, what do you think of my little brother? Is he all you imagined?" Gabriella awkwardly admitted, "I'm afraid much more. You showed me pictures of a little boy." Lotte shrugged, "That's how I left him. Believe me, I'm as surprised as you." Lotte led Fritz to his bags: "It looks as if you swallowed my little brother. Come on, I'll take you to your room."

As Fritz carried his bags, Lotte led him up the grand staircase: "I see you like older women. You do know Gabriella is my age." Fritz shrugged, "I hadn't thought about it." Lotte cracked a knowing smile: "Yes, you were focused on other things. But I knew you'd hit it off. She is wonderful with children." In her letters to Fritz, Lotte had mentioned that Gabriella was a beautiful girl, but he assumed that most women weren't very impartial when it came to the looks of their friends. From then on, he would take Lotte at her word.

Soon after leaving Bern, Switzerland to study in Bologna, Lotte answered Gabriella's ad for a room to rent on the university's bulletin board. Both were working on their doctorates, Gabriella in English, Lotte as an MD specializing in infectious disease. On their first meeting they talked over coffee late into the afternoon. It was as if they were old friends catching up after not seeing each other for a long while. And after living together for several years they thought of each other more as sisters. "I've never had a friend like Gabriella," Lotte confided as she led Fritz down the upstairs hall. "We tell each other anything, without judgment. I hope you've found someone like that in Palestine."

Fritz, nodding slightly, was about to tell her of Khalid, but before having the chance she led him into one of the second floor guest rooms: "Put your bags down anywhere. Now, we need a plan to stop father from returning to Germany." "And mother?" Fritz asked. Lotte assured, "Mother's easy. She'll stay, but not without father." Fritz shrugged: "So, we'll make him." Lotte corrected: "No, we'll make him think it's his decision. Promise me, Fritz, you won't fight with father. We both know how infuriating he can be, but if it becomes a battle he'll dig in." Fritz assured her with a nod. But on Lotte's raised eyebrow, he insisted: "Don't worry, I'm not a child any more. I promise."

Lotte ran the kitchen that evening preparing a true Bolognese dinner. Having become passionate about the cuisine, she made it a mission to master some of her favorite recipes. And everyone appreciated her taking charge. Gabriella and her mother were not raised for domestic work, and Klara was delighted to be assisting her daughter.

"What can I do?" Fritz offered as he walked into the kitchen. Lotte commanded, "Go! Entertain father and Harry." Klara intervened: "Lotte, let your little brother help. Harry's with your father, and we don't want to repeat what happened when Martha and Toni locked Fritz out of the kitchen?" Lotte conceded: "You're right, he'd destroy the place now. Gabriella, help teach my little brother how to roll out and cut the vermicelli." Cracking a smile after eyeing Fritz, she added: "I'm guessing we'll need extra."

Lotte and Harold Oestreicher had been together ever since their escape from Germany in 1933. Through Lotte's letters, Fritz knew that she and Harry were getting their MDs in the same school, but due to their busy schedules and living apart, they didn't see each other that often. That apparently had changed, as Harry seemed perfectly comfortable there. Fritz was glad to have Harry there. Even though he and Lotte were the heads of their school's socialist party in Germany, for some reason Julius got along with Harry. And with Harry's plans of becoming a psychiatrist, Fritz thought he might be helpful in keeping Julius from returning to Germany.

While showing Fritz how to roll out the dough, Gabriella asked, "What happened when you were locked out of the kitchen?" Fritz cracked a smile: "I was four-years-old, and a troublemaker, so the maids locked me out into the garden hoping to get some work done. I was so angry I smashed my fist through the kitchen window and they had to rush me to the hospital for stiches. I guess that taught thcm." Gabriella laughed, "And what did you learn?" Fritz shrugged: "When breaking a window, use a brick."

As they worked together, Fritz forced sad thoughts, such as his parting with Amon several days before, to suppress the arousal by each touch of Gabriella's tender hand. For the first time, he understood the meaning of "Love at first sight." So this was what Shakespeare must have experienced before writing 'Romeo and Juliet'. When he had read the play for class he found it somewhat farfetched. But it now made perfect sense that Romeo would marry the daughter of an archenemy after only one extremely shallow conversation, and why, after sleeping with her one night, he would drink poison on the discovery that she had died for no apparent reason. Unfortunately, his relationship with Gabriella seemed just as doomed, as she was clearly too levelheaded to run off with an 18-year-old Jewish Palestinian farmer. But he told himself that he would at least have a week with her. That would have to last a lifetime.

At dinner, the delectable green vermicelli and other Bolognese specialties only enhanced the thrill Fritz felt being with his family and Gabriella. After five years in Palestine, he had forgotten what it was like to have his mother's unconditional love, his father's protective eye, and to be in cahoots with his devoted co-conspiratorial sister. There was no fighting at the table. The few times Fritz broached the subject of Germany, Julius quickly deflected: "Please, I want to hear more about you." Fritz told the lighter stories of Palestine, such as the practical jokes first played on him, while Lotte continued pressing the advantages of Bologna.

Though Gabriella backed Lotte up, Signora Morrisini, perhaps out of modesty for her hometown, continually contradicted them: "Even into my childhood, Bologna was a terrible place. Have you seen the two towers? At one time there were over 180, all holding supplies for the warring families." Fritz asked, "So, in 'Romeo and Juliette' the Montagues and Capulets would each have had a tower?" La Signora assured, "Of course, Verona was equally brutal. It is no coincidence that Shakespeare placed his tragedy in this area." Trying to deflect the conversation, Lotte added: "But that was a long time ago. It's much friendlier now." La Signora looked at her in disbelief: "You call fascists friendly?" Lotte corrected, "I mean, the towers were torn down and families get along just fine. Isn't that right, Gabriella?" Gabriella nodded: "Yes, our neighbors are very nice. We have no intention of warring with them." La Signora grumbled, "Friendly fascists, really?"

But besides La Signora's feelings for Bologna, dinner went smoothly. It was only when they retired into the drawing room for coffee that Julius, checking his pocket watch, asked Harry, "Should you not be getting back? Is there no curfew?" Harry, suddenly feeling the warm weather, awkwardly pulled on his neck collar as he admitted: "Actually, I thought I might stay here tonight." Gabriella quickly agreed, "Yes, Harry is always welcome." "It seems we've taken over your home," Klara said with concern to la Signora. "If it would help, perhaps Fritz and Harry could share a room?" Gabriella assured; "No, that won't be necessary."

Gabriella anxiously glanced to Lotte, who finally broke the awkward silence: "Mother, father, there is something I've been meaning to tell you. It's not necessary for Harry to share a room with Fritz. You see, we were married several months ago." Julius and Klara looked at her, stunned. She continued: "I know I should have told you earlier, but I didn't want to upset you. You would have wanted to be part of it, and really, it was nothing, just a small civil service. Gabriella and a friend of Harry's were the only ones there. If I believed there was any chance that you could make it ..."

Tears formed in Klara's eyes as she immediately went to hug Lotte: "Of course you shouldn't have to wait for us. You're in love. You deserve to be happy." Lotte's uncomfortable nod suggested that love was not the only issue: "Yes, and it also doubles our chances for going to America." Lotte explained that the quota for legal German immigration into the US that year had quickly filled up, but the law called for sponsors. With Julius's brother, Friedrick, having immigrated to the US the year before, and with Harry also having a cousin in America, by being married they now had two different family members vouching for them. Lotte disclosed: "What's most important is that Uncle Friedrick has found jobs for us, so we'll be able to stay in America until the quota opens up again."

Julius took a moment before questioning: "Friedrich has jobs for you? Doing what?" Lotte stated matter-of-factly, "I believe an acquaintance of his has need for a butler and maid. But we're happy to take anything." Julius bitterly spat: "My daughter, a maid?" Klara tried to calm him: "Father…" But Lotte cut in assuring: "Of course, if you and mother join us I'm sure you'd figure out how to start a business in no time. It would be a great help to us if you were there." Gabriella added, "And I have friends in the underground working at the American Embassy. With Lotte and Harry married and working in American, they believe they can get papers for all of you." Seeing that Julius was about to completely reject the idea, Harry attempted reverse psychology: "Of course, we understand your concerns. America is a modern country. You're methods of distributing wine may seem outdated." "Outdated?!" Julius fired back. "Americans know nothing of wine! In a year I could triple any of their businesses!" Lotte enthusiastically jumped in: "Good, so you'll join us!"

Julius took a moment before dejectedly shaking his head: "Not returning to Germany means losing everything. That was made clear when we received papers for this trip. And there are three good German families waiting like vultures to take over our home." Though Fritz had been determined not to fight, having listened quietly he now asked: "So, you would die for a house." Julius snapped back: "Or we die of starvation in Italy, Palestine, America or God knows where! You think Germans are the only ones to hate Jews?! If we leave Germany now we have nothing!" Fritz argued, "You won't starve! There are six thousand Swiss francs sitting in a bank account in Geneva! Take it and save yourselves!" Julius was adamant: "That money is yours! It is your future! I will die before touching that!" Fritz yelled back, "No, you and mother will die! I don't need it. In Palestine, we share. If you don't take it I'll give it away!" Hearing that, Julius exploded: "Give it away? Give it away?! You will do no such thing! You are a child! I am your father! I am responsible for this family! You will do as I say! End of discussion!!"

Fritz, seething, was silenced by Lotte's glare as she shook her head at him. Julius, regaining his composure, attempted to lift the dark cloud engulfing the room: "Please, things are not so dire. There are over half a million Jews in Germany. The Nazis cannot kill half a million Jews. And if it is any consolation, I promise, should things get any worse, mother and I will leave." Calming down, Fritz respectfully asked: "Have you considered the job on the Rothschild Estate in Palestine? Arabs and Jews live peacefully together there, so you'll have no trouble with insurgents." Julius scoffed: "Communists! I should work the rest of my life for nothing, and then what?!" Fritz assured, "You'll be taken care of. And if you don't like it, you can go back to Germany. View it as a holiday until all this passes over." Julius sardonically stated, "The Nazis have promised a thousand year Reich. That is quite some holiday."

Gabriella tried to reassure Julius: "You can stay with us in Bologna. You will be safe here. I will protect you. And Jews are not persecuted here as they are in Germany. Everyone knows that Mussolini has a Jewish mistress. Even if we can't get papers for you in time to leave with Lotte and Harry, Bologna has a large underground. They will also help." Julius shook his head: "You are very kind, but it is asking too much. Now, all of you should stop worrying. I can assure you that the worst is over. How else would we have gotten papers for this trip?" Fritz shrugged: "Because the Chief of Police who saved you're life on Kristallnacht is now trying to save it again. He probably told you that you'll lose everything as a warning to sneak out whatever you can, because returning to Germany means certain death." Furious, Julius reacted more to the insolence: "What do you know of it? In Palestine you live in the dirt! And you expect your mother and I should do the same?!" Realizing that nothing he could say would make a difference Fritz shook his head in frustration and stormed out.

After an awkward silence, Klara began to get up: "My poor Fritz, I should go to him." Lotte stopped her: "I think Fritz has had enough family for the moment. Maybe Gabriella can go."

∞

Still fuming, Fritz stood on the terrace looking out, unable to appreciate the lights of Bologna under the night sky. How could his father be so blind? Wanting to hit something, he turned to see Gabriella standing on the terrace's entrance, her look of compassion instantly softening his mood. With trepidation, she quietly walked over to him. Leaning back against the terrace wall she offered: "You're father loves you very much. What he does he believes is in your best interest." Fritz bitterly spat: "The pig-headed fool. How's it in my best interest to have my parents murdered by Nazis?"

With a comforting hand, Gabriella confided; "When I was around your age my father died from a heart attack. A broken heart seemed appropriate, as he blamed himself for losing our money in the crash. I've always regretted that nothing I said could convince him otherwise. But more than anything, I wish I could take back my last words to him. He refused to let me go out with a boy. He said that the boy was beneath us. I was furious, called him an idiot living in a dream world, that I was lucky the boy would even associates with my family. I snuck out that night to see a movie with the boy, a silly movie about a tenor with stage fright. I still remember the title, 'Three Lucky Fools'. I don't believe I laughed once. That was the last time I saw my father alive. What I'm trying to say is that, we don't know what the future holds, but if something terrible should happen to your parents, I hope you won't regret your last words to them."

Fritz took a moment before asking: "What happened to the boy?" Gabriella cracked a smile: "I would only have sex with him if we were married, so he asked to marry me and I agreed. But then another girl became pregnant with his child and he had to marry her." Fritz laughed slightly: "Your father was right. He was beneath you." Gabriella demurely smiled before soberly telling him: "Your father's afraid. You're young. You can do anything you want with your life. For a man his age, it's not so easy. He will have to start over, with nothing." Fritz finally gave a consolatory nod. Gabriella encouraged: "But don't give up. We have a week to help him find his courage."

Fritz warmly placed an appreciative hand on hers. Looking into each other's eyes, a passion stronger than both of them pulled them into a kiss. It was a kiss like none he had ever experienced. Holding her in his arms, her arms wrapping around his neck, they became one. Suddenly coming to her senses, Gabriella pulled away: "Fritz, we mustn't." Refusing to looks in his eyes, she implored: "Forgive me. Please forget this ever happened." Speechless, Fritz watched as she rushed back inside, both unaware of Lotte watching from her second floor window.

∞

As Fritz climbed the main staircase, Lotte stared down on him from the second floor landing. "Do you know where Gabriella is?" he asked. Lotte cracked a knowing smile: "Why? Want to borrow more of her lipstick?" Fritz, stunned, quickly rubbed his lips with the back of his hand to see a red smear. Lotte advised: "It's a nice shade, but you might want to wash it off before saying goodnight to father. I'll say goodnight to Gabriella for you."

Gabriella's heart was still racing as she sat in her room in front of the vanity. Lost in thought, she jumped at the knock on her door: "Who is it?" Lotte opened the door a crack: "It's me. Who else would it be?" "Come in," Gabriella said, slightly relieved. Even now that Lotte was married, she and Gabriella continued their nightly ritual of combing each other's hair before going to bed. "My little brother was looking for you," Lotte said as she combed. Gabriella awkwardly asked, "Really? Do you know what he wanted?" Lotte shrugged, "I could imagine, but we didn't talk after I told him to wash the lipstick off of his face."

Gabriella turned to her with wide-eyes as Lotte apologized: "Sorry, I didn't mean to spy. But in his state of mind, I was worried about sending you out there alone. Still, I had a feeling you'd lift his spirits. As usual, I was right." Gabriella's heart sunk: "Lotte, I'm so sorry. I promise, it will never happen again." Lotte seemed unfazed: "Please, you kissed a boy. You didn't burn down Bologna." But Gabriella was still distraught: "Yes, a boy. He's 18. How could I allow myself?" Lotte shrugged: "How could you not? I saw that kiss." Gabriella was bewildered: "How is he so mature? More than most of the boys here our age." Lotte reasoned: "He had to grow up fast. What frightens you most? How good it felt or what people will think? Listen, he looks 23 and you look like a teenager. No one will think anything of it." Gabriella laughed slightly in disbelief: "You would never allow yourself to become involved with an 18-year-old." Lotte shrugged, "Depends if he kissed me like that."

Though both young women laughed, Gabriella knew that passion had never played a great role in Lotte's relationship with Harry. The world was in turmoil. Being of similar minds, over time they came to rely on each other. Marriage was the next logical step. Lotte explained, "In a way being with Harry is reassuring. It's safe, and in this world that means something. But still, I wouldn't mind knowing how it feels to shake the way you are after just one kiss. Can you imagine your wedding night?" Gabriella blushed slightly as Lotte continued: "Maybe you're right. Flying too close to the sun will burn your wings, but don't discard it too quickly." Gabriella shook her head in disbelief: "You are suddenly a hopeless romantic." Lotte put a warm arm around Gabriella's shoulder: "Maybe I just like the idea of you being my sister." Gabriella warmly, but firmly stated: "I like that too, but since someone has to be the adult here, I will assure you, neither your brother's nor my wings will be burnt by the sun."

∞

After a restless night, Gabriella woke to the sound of hammering from outside. Morning sunlight filtered through the trees as she put on her bathrobe and followed the sound to the front of the second floor landing. Opening the window, she looked down to see Fritz, shirtless in workpants, pounding a spike under the broken front marble step. His tanned, muscular body glistened in the early sun as he swung the sledgehammer. "Fritz, what are you doing?" she asked with concern. Fritz smiled up at her, "Fixing this step before they all break off and someone gets hurt."

A short time later, Gabriella was in work clothes assisting him. Though she had just woken up and purposely wore no makeup, he was just as entranced by her. She had planned to apologize again and explain about the kiss, but feeling somewhat aroused by his body, she thought better of broaching anything sexual until he was dressed. To her surprise, they worked well together as he patiently explained whatever he needed.

Klara found Julius observing them from the parlor window. Smiling down on them, she commented: "He does seem quite taken by her." Julius shook his head in disbelief: "Is the boy insane? Does he think he will impress her by behaving like a common laborer? No matter. She is beautiful, but far too old for him." Klara shrugged off Julius's rigidity: "He doesn't seem to mind. And have you noticed the way she looks at him?" Julius nodded: "Of course, he's a Hausman. He takes after my great grandfather, who was also abnormally tall." Knowing better than to argue, Klara nodded slightly as she said with a glint: "Perhaps something will come of it." Julius scoffed, "Don't be ridiculous. Besides being too old, she is Italian and Catholic. I could never allow it." Klara gently reasoned: "The world has changed since our days of arranged marriages. And maybe that's for the best. If they have a chance for happiness, why not take it?" Unwilling to waste anymore time arguing with a hopeless romantic, Julius gave a perturbed shrug.

"It looks beautiful," Gabriella said as they stood back to admire the repaired foundation. Taking her in, Fritz agreed, "Yes, very beautiful." Ignoring the complement, she asked, "How did you learn to do this?" Fritz wiped the sweat off of his body as he explained: "We do all of the construction at Ben Shemen. The elders teach the younger. If you'd like, tomorrow before it gets too hot we can fix the gate." Gabriella shook her head with concern: "Fritz, you shouldn't spend your vacation working." Putting on his shirt, he assured: "With you helping it doesn't feel like work."

With his shirt on, Gabriella felt more comfortable bringing up the kiss: "Fritz, I want to apologize again for last night. You know that Lotte is like a sister to me. I hope that you'll think of me in that way also." Fritz, assuming she knew that he would have married her on the spot, believed this to be her way of letting him down gently. Though hurt, he couldn't be angry with her. Considering his age and situation why would she consider him as anything more than a friend? After showing so much kindness and generosity to his family, he was determined to not make her uncomfortable, especially in her own home. With a brave face, he conceded: "Of course. No need to worry. I promise, it won't happen again."

Though Gabriella tried to appear appreciative, her heart sank. Lotte was right. It would not be easy letting go of that kind of passion. Still, she understood that he had come to his senses and realized that she was far too old for him. He was now letting her down easy. Not wanting him to feel any guilt for making what she believed to be the wise decision, she sensitively assured: "I appreciate that, Fritz. One day, some girl will be very lucky to have you."

During the cooler morning hours, Gabriella continued helping Fritz fix up the villa. Though both hid their true feelings, they developed a strong friendship. Each afternoon Gabriella and Lotte showed Julius, Klara and Fritz the sites of Bologna, always making sure that Julius was having a good time. In the evening, Fritz would draw everyone's portraits, making extras of Gabriella for himself.

Fritz was alone with Klara only once when they walked to the market for provisions. He considered asking her about Rudolf Schank's claim of being his father, but thought better of it. In his heart, he already knew. Why would Rudy have traveled all the way to Palestine with a radio just to deceive him? And how could he deny the resemblance? If confronted, he imagined that his mother would be honest. But guilt-ridden, she may be less likely to argue with Julius about staying in Bologna, and could possibly even confess the truth to him, destroying their marriage. Fritz's battle was to keep his family together, not tear them apart. He decided to accept Ivan's advice of feeling lucky for having two fathers, and never mention Rudy Schank.

To use the time more constructively, Fritz suggested: "If you refuse to go back, maybe that will force father to stay." Klara shook her head: "Your father has already suggested that I stay here while he goes back alone." Before Fritz could encourage her to take him up on it, Klara explained: "But if I hadn't been with him these last years, I don't know that he would still be alive. You know your father, always speaking his mind. For my sake, he's been willing to play sick in bed. But to send him back alone, the Nazis would surely kill him and I would never forgive myself." Bewildered, Fritz asked, "Do you hear yourself? Why would either of you go back to that?" Klara offered, "Germany is our home. Most Germans are good. They are poets and philosophers. They must come to their senses sometime." Fritz soberly asked, "And what if it's too late?"

∞

For their last night in Bologna, Klara insisted on going out: "We must celebrate our time together." American Swing had recently come into vogue, and Lotte found an advertisement boasting: "The best American Swing Band in Bologna." Julius cynically commented: "Some achievement." But Klara was anxious for the experience, and all went except Signora Morrisini, who confided to Gabriella that she would regretfully forego "the pleasure of inebriated fools dancing in a smoked filled room to that dreadful American music."

They toasted away a bottle of champagne as the crowd energetically danced to a heavyset Bolognese woman belting out America Swing in a strong Italian accent. When the band began playing the recently popular Andrews Sisters song, 'Bei Mir Bist Du Schoen' the crowd broke into cheers and began to jitterbug. Klara suggested that she and Julius try the new dance. Julius resisted, but Lotte dragged them onto the dance floor with Harry, assuring that they will teach them how it's done.

Gabriella asked as she sat alone with Fritz, "Do you like to dance?" Having never participated when the students at Ben Shemen danced during evening activities, Fritz admitted, "I never learned." Watching the couples jitterbug on the floor, Gabriella encouraged, "It's never too late. You don't have to be afraid. As you see, no one here is professional. They're just having fun." Julius did little more than lead Klara with his arm as she attempted some of the simpler Jitterbug moves. Surprisingly, Lotte and Harry kept up with the better couples. Since even his proper father made a slight attempt, Fritz felt obliged to try.

As he and Gabriella stepped onto the dance floor the song finished, and the band began playing the Hoagy Carmichael ballad, 'Old Man Moon', made popular in the movie, 'Topper". Appreciating the slower tempo, Gabriela took Fritz's hand as she encouraged, "This is better. Less chance to hurt each other." Moving together, he took her in his arms, and with her body against his, the words seem to take on special meaning:

> "Old man moon wake up 'cause I've
> fallen in love.
>
> So spread the news to all the stars
> above.

Shine for my baby while we're dancing tonight.

And fill her tender eyes with love and dynamite."

Under the song's spell, the champagne and the passion they felt for each other, they were pulled into another kiss. Suddenly aware that they were on the dance floor, Gabriella pulled away. Scanning the room for Julius, Klara and Lotte, she was relieved to find them still too engaged in the dance to have noticed. Regretfully, she acknowledged, "Fritz, we shouldn't. You know that I'm too old for you." Fritz shook his head: "No, you think I'm too young, but I'll wait." Breathless, Gabriella asked, "For what? The difference in our age will never change." Fritz admitted, "True, but in time, maybe you'll find that it doesn't matter." Bewildered, Gabriella asked, "What does matter?" Fritz admitted, "That I love you. That I will always love you."

Having suppressed her feelings for a week, she gave up the battle. Pulled back into his arms, now more than a kiss, it was the uniting of two people in love. Aware that it was their last night together, that they may never see each other again, and that the memory of that kiss might have to last a lifetime, she allowed herself to completely succumb to the passion. As they intertwined, the music, the dance floor and the crowd slowly melted away.

∞

A cold morning rain dampened the already somber mood as Lotte and Gabriella joined Julius, Klara and

Fritz to the train station. Harry was interning at the hospital, and Signora Morrisini chose to not overcrowd the van.

Seeing the train to Germany approaching the station, Julius first went to Gabriella, "We are very much indebted to you, my dear. It was a truly wonderful week, more enjoyable than anything I can remember." Gabriella warmly held Julius's hand: "It doesn't have to end. We would be so honored if you and Klara would stay." Fearful of showing his emotions, Julius warmly patted her hand and turned to Lotte. After kissing and hugging him goodbye, Lotte implored, "Father, reconsider, for our sake." But Julius held his ground: "Everything I do is for your sake." Fritz, remembering Gabriella's advice, was determined to not regret what might be his last words to his parents. But he knew that he would regret not giving it at least one last try. As he shook Julius's hand Fritz beseeched: "Stay, just until you're sure it's safe to go back." Klara tried to help: "Father, maybe we should, for our children. You see how important it is to them." Though Klara's upbringing of finishing schools and ballet lessons made her no more prepared than Julius for the farming life of the kibbutz, Fritz was thankful that she was willing to try. Julius nodded, "Yes, you should stay. I will go back to take care of the business." Refusing to discuss it any further, Julius picked up his bag and turned to board the train.

Klara, conceding, warmly hugged Gabriella: "How can we ever thank you?" Gabriella reiterated her offer, but Klara wouldn't let Julius go back alone.

Hugging Lotte, she reassured her through tears, "Hopefully, we will soon see you in America." Lotte, normally strong, was unable to stop her eyes from welling up as she pleaded, "Don't go. We need you. You must convince father!" Overcome by emotion, Klara firmly hugged Lotte before turning to Fritz.

"My Fritz, please forgive me. Sending you away so young was the most difficult thing I've ever done. But perhaps it was for the best. You have grown into such a wonderful young man." They tenderly hugged as the conductor gave the final boarding call. Fighting through her emotions, Klara said her last words to him: "Wherever you go, always know how much I love you." Unable to say more, she wiped tears away as she boarded the train.

Lotte leaned in on Fritz, who supported her with a consoling arm, but uncertain of ever seeing their parents again, they were clearly supporting each other.

By the time Fritz's train pulled in from the other direction, Lotte was able to maintain her normally strong facade. With war looming, she preferred for her brother to join her to America, but at least he was out of Germany: "Whatever happens, promise me that you won't do anything crazy. You will protect yourself." Fritz nodded his assurance, though both knew that it was a fairly hallow promise. After hugging him one last time, Lotte took Gabriella's hand and placed it in his: "Don't pretend. You two need time alone. I'll be in the station." Giving them a knowing smile, she turned and headed off.

Alone with Gabriella, Fritz asked, "May I write to you?" "Of course," She assured. "But Fritz, promise me, if you should meet a girl, a nice girl your age, you will forget about us." Soberly taking her in, Fritz asked, "How am I supposed to do that? I'm in love with you." Gabriella struggled to help him understand: "I love you, too. Which is why I want you to be happy. We may never see each other again. It's important for me to know that..." Before she could finish he pulled her into another kiss. Steam surrounded them as the train slowly began to move. Tearing himself away, Fritz jumped onto the train's boarding step, calling to her while moving: "Don't worry about me being happy. You love me. That's all I need to know." Gabriella struggled to keep up with him on the platform. Moving out from under the platform's cover, she was hit by the cold rain as they waved goodbye until Fritz was pulled out of view.

CHAPTER 26

"SHE MUST BE quite some girl," a musician on the boat told Haim after accepting a fifth charcoal portrait for playing Hoagy Carmichael's "Old Man Moon'. Haim questioned how he would know that, but quickly realized that his feelings for Gabriella must have been written all over his face. Several passengers grumbled at hearing the same song over and over, but on their two-night trip to Palestine Haim couldn't be sated. He would never hear 'Old Man Moon' again without thinking of Gabriella and the kiss they shared on that dance floor.

Arriving at Ben Shemen, Haim immediately went to find Amon. Calling out to him in the field, Amon whinnied back from over the hill. Moments later he appeared galloping towards him. Having never been apart for so long, Amon shook with excitement as he nuzzled Haim's chest. It was the welcome Haim needed after leaving his family and Gabriella.

Collecting frogs, scorpions, insects, plant samples, or whatever else Melnick and the other professors in the Biology/Botany museum needed, seemed more like fun than a job. Calling it a museum was somewhat of a stretch, as it was really just a lab consisting of a few classrooms, but it was the first of its kind in Palestine. With Saturdays off, Haim was able to see his friends again at the Jaffa café. He and Amon also resumed their covert weekly lunches with Khalid. Though at the end of July, Khalid had married on his wife's sixteenth birthday, their friendship seemed unaffected. Haim, now in love, could relate the research he was doing in the school library on sexual relationships and child rearing while Khalid could help him better understand the needs of a woman.

Haim was also drawing again in his free time. Working under the professors he felt less of a need to hide it. As he was setting up an earthworm display, the botany professor, Dr. Zechariah Gottlieb, discovered his sketchbook and demanded: "Haim, is this yours?" Holding a handful of worms, Haim nervously explained: "It doesn't take away from my work. It's just for my breaks." Gottlieb exclaimed, "These are good! Why didn't you tell us you could draw?" Having struggled over the illustration for his book, 'Anatomy and Morphology of the Plant', Gottlieb was delighted to discover that his assistant could draw. He immediately asked Haim if he would consider illustrating his book. Haim worked extremely hard to make his first job as an artist look professional. Though it didn't pay anything and the budget only allowed for cheap blue ink, the experience and Gottlieb's delight with the work was more than enough for Haim.

Those weeks were some of the happiest for Haim in Palestine. He still had to get his parents out of Germany and find a way to be with Gabriella, but that would be more easily accomplished once he was older and more established.

Time was not on his side. Less than a month after his return from Bologna, the world began its descent into an unparalleled nightmare.

September 1, 1939: Germany invaded Poland, triggering war on an unprecedented scale. Hitler's blitzkrieg (lightning war) showed the world the Nazis' plan of attack. One after the other, the unprepared nations would be ruthlessly crippled by a blitz of bombings; cutting off airfields, railroads, communications, and munitions. A massive land invasion of tanks, troops and artillery would follow, allowing the infantry to easily pick off any remaining resistance.

SS operations immediately formed concentration camps in the conquered nations so that Jews, undesirables and anyone considered an enemy to the Nazis would either be used for slave labor or exterminated. Within a day of invading Poland, the SS Totenkopf "Death's Head" regiments began the reign of terror on the Polish people, enslaving and murdering women, children, elderly for no other crime than being Polish.

September 3, 1939: under Neville Chamberlain, the British government issued an ultimatum demanding the immediate withdrawal of German troops from Poland. When the ultimatum expired at 11:00 am that same day, Great Britain declared war on Germany, as did France.

September 17th, The Soviet Union, having made a treaty with Hitler, invaded Poland from the west. By October 6, Germany and the Soviet Union were dividing and annexing the whole of Poland. But as Neville Chamberlain discovered, Hitler's word was not to be trusted, and less then two years later the German war machine set its blitzkrieg on Russia.

Overnight, the doors for Jewish escape were shut. Knowing the power of propaganda, the Nazis wanted as little word to spread of the atrocities being committed within their borders. In need of funds for the war, they stripped the Jews of everything, even prying the gold from their teeth. Hitler, a vegetarian against cruelty to animals, shifted medical testing and experimentations on to Jews. For Julius and Klara survival now meant a Nazi defeat.

Haim and Melnick immediately went to British headquarters in Jerusalem to enlist in the British Army. Lehman tried to stop them. With the British seeking Arab support, the school was under almost nightly attack by insurgents, and the faculty and older students were left to defend it. As much as Haim and Melnick cared about the school and hated the British, if the Nazis were victorious all would be lost.

To Haim and Melnick's surprise, the British recruiting office turned them down. "We'll call when you're needed," was the only explanation given by the captain in charge. Both being well-trained soldiers, fluent in German and English and with an intimate knowledge of the German mindset, how could they not be needed? Lehman reasoned, "They may believe that, above all, you're German, and your loyalty is to your homeland." As preposterous as that sounded, it was not uncommon for Jewish German and Austrian refugees to be turned down in England when trying to enlist. There was a fear that Nazis, pretending to be Jewish refugees, would infiltrate the armed forces gaining access to critical information. But chances of that were highly unlikely from German Jews who had immigrated to Palestine years before. Lehman assured, "In any case, you are needed here."

To Haim and Melnick's frustration, Avi and the twins were accepted into the British Army that same day. Several days later, Ivan and about ten other graduates working at the school, were also enlisted. Lehman tried to make sense of it to Haim by reasoning: "It's the luck of the draw. Don't be discouraged. You're doing more than your share here."

Haim couldn't help but feel guilty for enjoying his work while the war was going on, but he was getting invaluable experience. Several other teachers asked him to illustrate their scientific books and articles, and for the children he began creating magic lanterns. The first was the Story of Amon: 'The gift colt from King Abdullah to Haim Arlosoroff; the dangerous, untrainable stallion whose love for an outcast refugee boy changed them both, and together they tamed the land of Ben Shemen.'

He questioned if the children would show any interest in the story. But their eyes widened with delight at the first candle-illuminated drawing, and they begged to hear it over and over again, motivating Haim to create more magic lanterns. Wanting them to feel good about their lives in Palestine, all of the stories were based on the children of the kibbutz. All were told by memory, never considering that they would be of any interest to future generations. With none written down, only the illustrations remain.

∞

On one of Haim's Saturday visits to the café in Jaffa, Rasul asked him to follow him again. For the second time in the opulent guest quarters, he met with King Abdullah. Haim sat cross-legged facing the King, this time enjoying the strength of the coffee as he sipped. King Abdullah relaxed into a hint of a smile: "I see you have grown into a man. And Amon, how is he?" Haim assured, "He is well. He has grown very strong. I'm always grateful to call him my friend." King Abdullah nodded his approval: "I have heard of the dangers you faced to help our friends here during the British destruction of Jaffa. Do you still believe that Arabs and Jews can live together in peace?" Haim nodded: "I believe that most of us can." King Abdullah studied him for a moment: "But you wish to fight in this war." Haim nodded again. King Abdullah cautioned: "You can not help unite our people if you are dead." Haim nodded: "Staying alive is preferable." King Abdullah cracked a smile: "So you will honor my request not to fight." Though no one was to ever contradict a king, Haim sensed honesty was more important to Abdullah: "You're Highness, I'm greatly honored that you would show any concern for my safety, but my parents are in Germany. If the Nazis win, they will die. I must do whatever I can." King Abdullah considered before allowing: "If you insist on fighting, get word to me of your regiment. I will try to protect you, but do not make my job too difficult." Bowing his headed, King Abdullah ended their conversation. Haim bowed his head and again walked out backwards, keeping an eye on the door from behind so as not to bump into it.

∞

Each month Haim and Melnick tried their luck at the British recruiting office. They became so used to being rejected it took a moment to register when the new recruiting officer welcomed them into the British Army. Handing over the forms to fill out, he disclosed: "It appears an agreement was made between my predecessor and your headmaster. By offering up a dozen young men, he was able to secure the two of you." Confused, Haim asked, "Professor Lehman offered up a dozen men?" The recruiter shrugged: "His obligation was apparently fulfilled. You knew nothing of this?" Baffled, Haim and Melnick shook their heads. Though they said nothing to the recruiting officer, that explained why Ivan, an admitted pacifist, enlisted several days after they had been turned down. Lehman must have fired him along with eleven other former students. With so few jobs in Palestine they had little choice but to enlist. The officer added, "Fortunately for you, I would make no such agreement. Records show you to be excellent soldiers of the Haganah. It's good to have you on board. "

When Haim and Melnick handed in their forms at the registration office, the officer behind the desk smirked as he read Haim's full name, "Fritz Sigmund Hausmann? Can't very well call you that can we? Fritzies are the enemy." Haim offered, "My Hebrew name is Haim." The officer looked at him skeptically:

"Sounds as if you're clearing your throat. How about Freddy? That's a rather good name. Freddy Hausmann. Should do you well." Haim nodded as the officer noted it on the file and slipped it into a folder. It made little difference to Haim, as it was only for the short while until they won the war. Melnick's name was changed to Melville, but Haim would continue only calling him 'Professor'.

Haim and Melnick were then asked to swear allegiance to King George VI promising to protect the King from all of his enemies. Though it seemed like a tall order, they both swore to it, and were scheduled to report for duty in two weeks.

On the drive back, they decided to forgive Lehman for preventing their enlistment. Knowing how important the school was to Lehman, and considering all of the lives that he had saved, including their own, confronting him seemed pointless. They would simply hope for his best wishes and thank him again for all he had done for them.

Several days later, British soldiers invaded the school turning everything over in a massive search. On the discovery of a large arms cache, Lehman was arrested. Haim and Melnick tried to go with him to make sure that he would be all right, but Lehman insisted, "Stay here and protect the school. I can take care of myself."

Several days later, determined to free Lehman from being torture by the British, Haim and Melnick ignored his orders and went to the prison to negotiate his release. But on their arrival, they found Lehman relaxing in the main office with the Warden and several officers. "Welcome!" Lehman beamed as he greeted them. "What brings you here?" Confused, Melnick suggested, "We came to save you?" Melnick laughed: "My heroes! Just in time! I believe we are about to secure my release."

Before starting the Youth Village, Lehman had been a doctor in Germany. With a natural ability to sway people, as he had the Arab leaders in the surrounding communities, he quickly had the new British authorities supporting his efforts to protect the Jewish refugee children in his care. For the good part of the day, he had checked over the officers' charts before giving each one medical advice. After a few calls by the warden, Lehman was allowed to return with Haim and Melnick to Ben Shemen.

∞

The last Saturday before entering the army, Haim went as usual to see his friends at the Jaffa café. For his send off, Rasul bought everyone a round of coffee, a generous move for Rasul. He asked for all of the details of where Haim would be stationed, but Haim only knew that he was in the 8th Army training at Sarafand. "We will investigate," Rasul assured.

When it was time to leave, Shihab firmly shook Haim's hand: "It is a long time since that lost, Jewish boy wandered in here. At the time, I did not think he would survive Palestine. I have never been so glad to be wrong." Shihab choked up as he hugged Haim goodbye. All those years ago, intrigued by Shihab's threatening glare, Haim went into the café only to see if he could find some common ground between them, never guessing how much he would one day look up to him. How small his life in Palestine would probably have been had he listened to all warnings and not taken that first bus trip to Jaffa.

∞

The night before Haim and Melnick were to leave, a farewell party was thrown for them at Ben Shemen. During the party, Sheila pulled Haim aside to give him a long, passionate goodbye kiss. "I'll wait for you," she breathlessly confided. "For what?" Haim asked, thinking that she wanted him to get her a drink or something. Sheila laughed, "For you, Silly, to get back from the war." Caught off guard, having thought that she wasn't interested in him, he agreed. Even though he was still far too in love with Gabriella to fully appreciate Sheila's kiss, it wasn't bad. And with Gabriella insisting that he not commit to her, in a way it felt good to have a girl waiting for him back home.

Haim had invited Khalid to the party, on the condition that he would take no undo risk. It was a nice surprise when he showed up with his young wife. Looking into her kind eyes as she offered a gift of goat cheese and olives from their farm, Haim sensed that she might actually be worthy of his good friend. To Haim's relief they were given a warm welcome by the other faculty and students. Wanting to be accepted in their new homeland and having little chance to meet their Arab neighbors, most were anxious to make friends with a young Arab couple form a neighboring village.

Several years had passed since rumors circulated about an Arab boy warning of the attack on the horse stable. Haim wanted to tell everyone that the boy was actually Khalid, but to protect his friend he would still say nothing. When asked how they knew each other, Haim simply explained, "I ran into Khalid with his lame mule and helped him carry some supplies home." Though that had happened over five years before, the less anyone knew the better.

As Khalid said goodbye to Haim, he confided, "My friend, I wish that I were going with you, but I have news. We are having a baby." Haim lit up: "A baby? That's terrific! Someday I hope to watch our families grow up together." Khalid nodded, "I will miss you." Neither had to say how grateful they were to each other. Their friendship had helped both through a challenging world. They now hugged goodbye, aware that for each new challenges were beginning.

Khalid felt little pressure to join the army, as British recruitment of Palestinian Arabs was nominal. But at the outbreak of the war, along with 21,000 Zionist Jews, 8,000 Palestinian Arabs joined the British Army. It was a large number considering the treatment they had received under British rule. But as bad as the British had been to them, many understood that The Grand Mufti would be worse.

After escaping to Syria, The Grand Mufti changed his policy of executing proven traitors to killing any possible suspect, including members of his own family. As he offered rewards for killing opposition leaders, peace leaders, suspected traitors and Jews, his relationship with French and Syrian authorities deteriorated, and in 1939 he fled to Iraq, where his hatred towards the British and the Jews helped to incite the Anglo-Iraqi war. But with the Iraqi defeat, he made his way to Germany, where, on November 6, 1940, the Grand Mufti arrived in Berlin with a draft proposal to rid the Jews from Palestine. Axis powers readily agreed, but only after the Jews were eliminated throughout Europe. Still, the Grand Mufti was grateful to Hitler for assuring: "Germany's objective would then be solely the destruction of the Jewish element residing in the Arab sphere under the protection of British power".

Axis powers paid The Grand Mufti a fortune as a radio broadcaster, 50,000 marks a month (the equivalent of about $12,000,000 a year today.) Hitler believed The Grand Mufti to be well worth it, attracting Arabs to the Nazi cause by his constant proclamations on Radio Berlin: "Arabs, rise as one man and fight for your sacred rights. Kill the Jews wherever you find them. This pleases God, history, and religion. This saves your honor. God is with you."

In his pamphlet on Islam and Judaism for the 13th SS Handschar division, The Grand Mufti ended with Abu Khurreira's quote: "The Day of Judgment will come, when the Muslims will crush the Jews completely: And when every tree behind which a Jew hides will say: 'There is a Jew behind me, Kill him!" (Even without the help of his anti-Semitic trees The Grand Mufti prided himself for the murder of countless Jews. He successfully collaborated with the Nazis in numerous sabotage and commando operations in Iraq, Transjordan, and Palestine. In September 1943, intense negotiations to rescue 500 Jewish children from the Serbo-Croatian Arbe concentration camp collapsed due to The Grand Mufti's objection, ensuring that all of the children would be murdered.)

His repeated urgings for Germany to bomb Tel Aviv and Jerusalem were denied only because at the time the Nazis considered it unfeasible. But far from uniting all Arabs against the Jews, the Grand Mufti's message of hate, fear and greed received a cold reception by many Palestinian Arabs, swaying Khalid, along with most of Haim's other Arab friends, to side with the British.

∞

In saying goodbye, Haim was able to remain fairly strong until leaving Amon. His repeated requests for he and Amon to enter the cavalry together had all been denied. For six years they had only been separated for the short time when he went to Bologna. In a way, their friendship had saved them both. Pearlman, in his late 40's and probably not going to war, assured Haim that he would look after Amon, which was of some relief. But how would Amon understand that he wasn't being abandoned by Haim, that he would return as soon as possible? And what would become of Amon while he was gone? Haim broke into tears as he hugged Amon around the neck. Seeing how upset Haim was, Amon quietly nuzzled Haim much more affectionately than usual. They walked together to the fence, and as Haim's eyes swelled with more tears he hugged him one last time.

Walking off, Haim felt weak, nauseous, as if punched in the gut. He questioned if he was too sick for the bus ride to the training camp. It didn't matter. He had no choice. His only hope of saving his parents and returning home to Amon was to defeat the Nazis. He then only had to figure out a way for Gabriella to accept them both.

CHAPTER 27

Spring 1940:

HAVING JUST TURNED 19 and nervous of what life would be like in the British Army, Haim/Fred was relieved that he and Melnick were allowed to stay together. Though only 37, Melnick had become somewhat of a father figure to Fred, and with his strong character, he would soon have the other Jewish soldiers also looking up to him.

Once Britain entered the war, Fred's own father and mother were no longer able to write to him, but he received word from Lotte, as they were able to write to her until America also entered the war after the Japanese attacked Pearl Harbor on December 7, 1941. Though she assured him that they were safe, it was far from the truth. Struggling over what to tell her brother, she finally decided there was no point in upsetting him, and possibly pushing him into what would be a suicidal mission in an attempt to save his parents.

Each highly censored letter that Lotte received from her parents, opened and resealed with a stamp of the swastika, contained nothing of their life in Germany. But there were enough first hand accounts to know that they were now forced to wear a yellow star with an inscription of 'Jew' in its center that they had to embroider themselves, their rations were cut, newspaper and telephone access denied, and travel denied. What the Nazis would allow in the letters were Julius's pleas for the equivalent of $1,800 in German franks in return for 2 Cuban visas. Knowing those visas were her parents' only chance, Lotte desperately tried raising the money. But the different branches of the US government and other organizations that she approached, all said the same thing: "It's a Nazi ploy to get money out of Jews from overseas ... With all of the money sent, we know of no Jews who have been given exit visas ... Instead of buying visas, the money will only help fund the Nazi cause." She came to understand that her parents' best chance was for a Nazi defeat, and Fritz was already doing everything he could for that.

At Sarafand training camp, life was perhaps made intentionally miserable to help motivate the soldiers to head off to war. After years of training in the Haganah, there was little for Fred and Melnick to learn there. But Fred didn't have to worry about living with British soldiers. They were segregated from Jewish soldiers and given preferential treatment. Knowing that Fred had a tendency of speaking out, Melnick warned, "Never correct them. We're not here to teach manners. Speak only when spoken to, and focus on training so we can get out of here to fight this war."

Their commanding officer woke them by yelling that first morning: "Come on you yids! On your stinkin' feet!" Melnick quickly silenced Fred with a look and shake of his head. He later explained: "They want to get to you. Don't give them the satisfaction."

The training was not only abusive. It was inadequate. A Scottish Sergeant teaching Fred to shoot missed every shot. When Fred hit all of his, the sergeant only quipped, "That's because I showed you what not to do." Conditions weren't helped by the fly infestation. To help keep it under control anyone with a cigarette tin full of dead flies was given a free ticket to the camp cinema.

What Fred did appreciate at Sarafand was the large pool. He was already a strong swimmer from his daily routine in the Ben Shemen water tower. By practicing in the Sarafand pool whenever allowed, he probably became the strongest swimmer on the compound, but due to segregation could never prove that by racing the British soldiers.

As soon as Fred and Melnick were allowed, they volunteered for the Egyptian front. Instead, they were sent to Port Said (the entrance to the Suez Canal) as drivers: transporting gasoline, food, supplies and ammunition from the harbor to the warehouses. Melnick explained: "It must be the luck of the draw. I'm guessing most soldiers request the front." In reality, few good soldiers were turned down for the front. But King Abdullah had intervened on Fred's behalf: "I have an interest in this young man," Abdullah told British authorities. "I believe that one day he will prove an asset to Arab-Jewish relations, if he remains alive."

∞

At the British Army Base in Port Said, for the first time Fred and Melnick met real British soldiers, who had either been drafted or volunteered. Far from the same disdain that was shown towards Jews in

Palestine, they were surprised to find them decent, upright guys who treated them as equals. And unlike the cold reception that Fred had received at Ben Shemen, the British soldiers went out of their way to make them feel welcome. Fred's only complaint was their smell. Even with a water shortage, Palestinians managed to wash everyday. But when these men undressed, except for their slightly sunburnt faces, necks and hands, their bodies were grey from filth.

An exception was Ray Ellis, a handsome, British gunner, a year older than Fred, who confided, "It's British Army tradition to never wash. Don't worry, in time you'll adjust." Fred asked: "That's a tradition?" Ray laughed, "As you see, it's not one I revere."

Ray also trained at Sarafand: "My first day there I smiled at a Jewish woman passing on the road and she spit on me. What had I done? After all, weren't we fighting the same war? But I soon learned why I wasn't universally loved there. For the record, those training you at Sarafand, that's not who most of us are."

For the first few weeks, Fred and Melnick transported cargo from the harbor to the warehouses. Once proven to be good drivers, they were given their first mission of bringing supplies to the front line. To avoid being seen by Axis fighter pilots, intent on securing the Italian strongholds along the Libyan coast and starving out the British front, they would drive at night with no lights on.

After loading up the truck, they set off on the eight-hour drive. At first they took turns driving, but with Melnick's several near misses of potholes and bombed out craters, he had Fred take over. Years of nighttime missions with Amon seemed to help Fred steer the dark, treacherous roads with only the light of an almost full moon. With Fred's eyes fixed on the dark road, Melnick navigated while watching out for Italian and German fighter planes.

Not long after setting out, they heard a plane heading their way and braced themselves for attack. Melnick scanned out of the window with binoculars, focusing in on what looked like a British fighter. Breathing a sigh of relief, he exchanged a wave with the pilot as it flew by their side. Every hour or so another British fighter plane passed by checking up on them.

By 3:00 am, Melnick was snoring lightly as Fred heard the buzz of another approaching plane. Having become accustomed to the sound it was almost reassuring. But this one seemed different. The other planes had approached on their side. This one sounded as if it were coming up directly behind them. Suddenly a flare lit up the sky. Knowing that had to be the enemy looking for targets, Fred anxiously shook Melnick awake: "We've got company." Coming to, Melnick looked up into the sky behind them with his binoculars and slowly focused in on what appeared to be a German Messerschmitt Bf 109 fighter. Jolted awake, he ordered, "Swerve!" As the plane dived-bombed towards them, Fred floored the gas swinging the truck from one side of the road to the other. With a hand held mirror strapped to a long metal pole Melnick could see behind the truck as machine gun fire rained down in a straight line towards them. "To the right!" Melnick ordered. Fred Swerved to the right out of the line of fire as the plane flew overhead. "Good job," Melnick commended, catching his breath. "Don't give him a target." As the Messerschmitt looped around in the sky, Fred no longer felt fortunate to have a large moon shining down on them: "Too late, he's got one."

Melnick grabbed the machine gun from behind the seat as they braced themselves for another attack. "Get ready," Melnick warned as the plane dive-bombed. Guided by Melnick, Fred raced from side to side between potholes as the Messerschmitt let out another round of bullets. Just as the plane passed overhead, Melnick reached out the window with the machine-gun and fired up at it. The Messerschmitt, seemingly unscathed, flew ahead and began another loop. Fred asked, "What's a Messerschmitt doing here? I thought we only had to worry about Italian fighters." Unsure, Melnick guessed, "Could be Nazi reinforcements, or an Italian pilot in a German plane."

As the Messerschmitt dive-bombed again, they somehow avoided a third stream of bullets. Melnick hung his upper body out of the window and fired up as the plane passed over. Knowing there was little chance of taking out the engine with a machine gun from a moving truck, he aimed for its gas tank. Just when it seemed as if they had made it through the third round, the plane flew ahead and Melnick saw what looked like a bomb dropping from its fuselage. Glistening in the moonlight, Melnick watched the bomb heading towards them for a direct hit. "Go left!" Melnick yelled. Fred swerved left around another pothole, and the bomb exploded to the right of the truck. "Thank the moon for that one," Melnick said with relief. "Only reason I spotted it."

With the moon back in good graces, they braced themselves for a fourth attack. But as the Messerschmitt looped around, instead of coming back for them, they heard its engine disappearing into the distance. Sighing with relief as he wiped sweat from his forehead, Fred asked, "Think he'll come back?" Melnick held up the machine gun: "If he does I'll welcome him." Did Melnick succeeded in hitting the plane's gas tank? Was it out of munitions? They would never know, but from then on, Fred would never again relax at the sound of an approaching plane.

About a half hour later, they spotted three planes heading directly towards them from the west. "What now?" Fred asked. Melnick replied by picking up the machine gun. Watching their approach through the binoculars, Melnick relaxed as he focused in on a British emblem. The three British fighters helped escort them to the depot.

A line of bullet holes crossed the roof and right side of the truck as a British officer showed them where to park: "Looks like a rough trip." They told him of the attack by the Messerschmitt. "Germans have been backing up the Italians. You did well."

As the crew unloaded, Fred and Melnick went to the base for food and much needed sleep. Returning trucks, carrying mostly refuse from the front, were rarely targets, but for fear of being spotted neither Fred nor Melnick even dared to light a cigarette.

∞

While having dinner in the mess hall one evening Melnick pointed out a small, thin, blond soldier staring at Fred. "Don't recognize him," Fred shrugged. "Looks like he's only about 15. You ever see him at Ben Shemen?" Melnick shook his head: "He may be mistaking you for someone else. Probably some British kid who lied about his age to enlist." They headed back to the barracks thinking nothing more of it.

But that evening as Fred headed to the showers, the boy, in undershirt and shorts, followed him. "Excuse me," the boy said in perfect Hebrew. "Were you in Palestine?" Fred nodded with surprise. The boy smiled as he looked up at him in awe: "It is you. You don't remember me." Fred apologetically shook his head: "Sorry." The boy offered: "You saved my life, you and your black horse."

Fred studied the boy. Could it actually be? Fred had given up hope of ever again seeing that first yolim he had hidden, the little Polish boy who bravely rode Amon. But he often thought of him, wondering if he was okay. Gently taking the boy's left arm and lifting the sleeve, there, as he remembered it, was the scar of the Star of David carved into him by boys in Poland. "Jacek?" Fred asked in disbelief. The boy beamed as he nodded: "'Jack' now. Jack Rose, the British changed it from Rosenstein." Jack's German last name came from his grandfather, who had immigrated to Poland. Fred shouldn't have known his first name, as they were told to remain anonymous to lessen the chances of being giving away, but Jack's pretty cousin had let it slip when Fred handed him over to her, and he never forgot it.

Fred exhaled with relief, "It's good to see you." Holding out his hand he introduce himself: "I'm Fred, alias Haim, alias Fritz Houseman, alias Hausmann." Jack smiled as the shook hands: "I'm honored to meet all of you." After becoming emotionally invested by protecting Jack through that night, from then on Fred tried to remain as detached as possible from the yolim he was helping. But seeing Jack now, smiling and healthy, it was all worth it.

Melnick was right, Jack had lied about his age to enlist, but though he looked only 15, he was actually 17, showing just how desperate the British Army was for new recruits. Still feeling responsible for Jack, and knowing how easy it was for a smaller, young, eager soldier to end up on a casualty list, Fred took Jack under his wing. For Melnick, that meant that he now had the two of them to look after. But Fred insisted that even Melnick couldn't know how they met. Though Melnick suspected that Jack was an Aliyah Bet, he would never pursue it. Too many lives were at stake to risk opening up any sort of investigation.

∞

Several weeks later, Fred, Melnick and Jack were about to load up the truck for a trip to the front when an officer informed Fred that he was to bring him to the Colonel's office. Concerned of what trouble Fred had gotten into, and knowing Fred's tendency of speaking out of turn with authority figures, Melnick asked to join them, but was denied.

Fred was escorted into the office, where the Colonel, seated behind his desk, informed him, "You've been requested to drive our visiting Colonel, Colonel Bayley, to Cairo at 1100 hours." "I can't," Fred replied. "We're bringing supplies to the front tonight." Slightly taken aback, the Colonel stated: "That's not a request. It's an order." The Colonel returned to his paper work, believing the discussion was over, but Fred continued: "Who will replace me?" The Colonel begrudgingly allowed, "You and Melville (Melnick) have been training Rose (Rosenstein) so time we put him to the test." Almost involuntarily, Fred responded: "He's not ready. Why not have him drive the Colonel to Cairo? Any fool can do that." The Colonel nodded, "Yes, you've been requested." Before Fred could argue, the Colonel cut him off: "I will remind you, this is the British Army, not a commune of the kibbutz. Insubordination is not tolerated here." Upset, Fred pressed, "But they could be killed. You need someone who knows what they're doing." The Colonel looked at him in disbelief: "Have you not heard a word I've said? You have your orders. Any further discussion will put you in the brig." Fred held his tongue, but seeing the desperation in his eyes, the Colonel felt compelled to add: "It's time for Rose to stand on his own two feet.

I'm sure you've trained him well. Now let's see what he can do."

Fred knew that he hadn't trained him well. Far from ready to drive while under actual aerial attack, Jack had only practiced while under the safety of a British fighter patrol. Had British authorities known that he was only 17 and still just learning to drive, even they wouldn't have allowed it. But he could think of no way to get Jack out of it without giving him away.

Upset, Fred told Melnick and Jack what had transpired. "You're lucky to only get a warning," Melnick reprimanded. "I told you, never talk back to superiors. This isn't Ben Shemen." Fred's begrudging nod wasn't very reassuring. Having seen other soldiers disciplined for far less, Melnick couldn't help but be concerned. But somehow Fred kept getting away with it. Perhaps the British took into account the cultural differences? Or did they appreciate that his intentions were basically good? Neither Melnick, nor Fred, could know that King Abdullah had intervened on his behalf.

Without looking Fred in the eye, Melnick nodded: "Don't worry about us. We'll be okay." With a firm hand on Jack's shoulder, Fred offered some last words of advice: "Remember, never take your eyes off the road. In the dark, anything can come at you. And do whatever Professor Melnick tells you. He's your eyes for everything going on around you." Jack nodded, but Fred could feel his thin body shaking. Trying to calm him, Fred assured: "Just relax, you'll be fine. Professor Melnick and I know you can do this." Jack seemed bolstered, but Fred was far from convinced.

∞

Had Fred not been distraught over the dangers facing Melnick and Jack, the perfect November weather of 1940 would have made for a pleasant 3½ hours drive Southwest along the Nile Delta to Cairo. Angered by the arrogance of this Colonel to pull him off of a mission to make him his chauffer, he had to remind himself of his promise to Melnick to hold his tongue as he listened to the man responsible for the possible death of his friends chatter on about the Arab/Jewish conflict. After replying with only curt responses for over an hour, the Colonel finally gave up on making small talk. Why had he even requested Fred? They had never met, Fred expressed no interest in chauffeuring superiors, and any number of soldiers would have jumped at the chance to see Cairo.

Driving through Cairo, the Colonel had him pull up to the luxurious Shepheard's Hotel, a favorite spot for high-ranking British officials and worldly elite. Fred expected to wait outside when Colonel Bayley asked him to hand the keys to the valet. "Aren't I responsible for the jeep?" Fred questioned. "No," the Colonel corrected. "I'm responsible for bringing you here." Fred stiffened. What he had done for a Colonel to bring him all the way to Cairo? Rather than say something that might get him into more trouble, he hid his anxiety and quietly followed the Colonel in through the grand entrance.

The staff seemed well acquainted with the Colonel as the floor manager greeted him by name and led them through the lobby to the elevator. The small elevator man, in a pressed red wool suit lined with gold buttons, brought them up to the Penthouse. At the penthouse door, the Colonel knocked three times before confiding, "I'll wait for you on the terrace." The Colonel stood back as the door opened, and before Fred could respond, he was ushered inside buy a slim, well-dressed, dark-eyed man in a fez hat. Led into a magnificent salon, Fred stopped at seeing King Abdullah seated between a dozen distinguished looking men. "Welcome my friend," the King said with a subtle nod. "These gentlemen are anxious to make your acquaintance."

Fred instantly recognized Nahhas Pasha, who had already served 3 terms as Prime Minister of Egypt, and Moshe Sneh, the future founder of the Mapam and one of the few Jewish leaders who would later fight for Arab representatives in the Knesset (Israeli parliament.) As he was introduced to the others, he realized that they were all prominent leaders pro Arab/Jewish unity and allied with the British against the Nazis.

Fred quietly listened to the discussion of battling the Nazi fervor growing within the Arab Nations to strategizing Nahhas Pasha's reinstatement as Prime Minister of Egypt. King Abdullah had publicly declared Nahhas Pasha: "The only really effective force among the Egyptians." Being the youngest of the group, Fred spoke only when addressed, but he sensed that King Abdullah's admiration of Pasha was somewhat heightened by his strong dislike of King Farouk.

In 1936, at age 16, King Farouk 1, of the Muhammad Ali dynasty, had succeeded his father, King Fuad 1, to become the last King of Egypt (succeeded only by the short reign of his infant son.) Though schooled in England, King Farouk wanted the British out of Egypt, even sending a note to Hitler saying that an invasion would be welcome.

King Abdullah had still not forgiven the now 20 year-old King Farouk for having just received him with hands in his pockets, drenched in cologne, addressing him with the informal 'you' and offering Abdullah tea in a cup smaller than his own. But all that may have been overlooked had the young king been a benevolent ruler. Farouk, however, was known for being a spoiled, selfish, arrogant Monarch seemingly set on depleting the Egyptian coffers for his own amusement. "As far as his position on the war," King Abdullah scowled, "Mussolini might have well been in Abdeen Palace (King Farouk's Cairo residence.)"

Despite the poverty of most of his subjects, King Farouk had thousands of acres of land, dozens of palaces, and often travelled to Europe for extravagant shopping sprees. His hundreds of cars were all painted red. By forbidding his subjects to have red vehicles he was then free to drive recklessly without threat of being stopped by police. People ran for cover at the site of his red Bentley Mark VI hurtling towards them. An ambulance often followed behind to pick up casualties. It was said that he ate 600 oysters a week (perhaps to rectify his rumored erectile dysfunction), ate caviar directly from the can for breakfast, and by the end of his reign weighed close to 300 lbs.

During the meeting, Nahhas Pasha warned: "If any of you meet King Farouk, make sure to hide your valuables." Known as 'the Thief of Cairo', Farouk was a kleptomaniac and skilled pickpocket. Pasha had attended a state dinner where Farouk even lifted Winston Churchill's priceless Breguet pocket watch right from his pocket. "It was only after the King had retired that Churchill realized his cherished keepsake was missing." One of the King's aides headed off an international crisis by craftily retrieving the watch from the king's bedroom, and returning it to Churchill, placing the blame on a busboy.

(In 1952, at the age of 32, King Farouk was forced to abdicate. Fleeing Egypt in haste, of the many treasures he left behind was one of the world's largest collections of pornography. Farouk died in exile at the age of 45, collapsing in a restaurant in Rome after eating a characteristically heavy dinner. It was rumored that Egyptian intelligence had poisoned his lobster, but few were surprised by his death. No autopsy was conducted, as by then some referred to him as "a stomach with a head.")

With the added hardships of WWII, the Egyptian people were increasingly incensed by King Farouk's lavish lifestyle. King Abdullah stressed: "The time is ripe for a coup." Fred listened as the men devised strategies. When King Abdullah asked what Fred would suggest, he admitted, "I have limited experience with coups, but we've been trained to do missions at night under the cover of darkness." Perhaps it made little difference, but the night of February 4, 1942 British troops and tanks surrounded Abdeen Palace, forcing King Farouk to reinstate Nahhas Pasha as Prime Minister.

As the meeting ended, Nahhas Pasha reminded Fred while shaking his hand, "Remember, King Farouk embodies everything evil in man." Fred bowed his head in respect, even though a spoiled, gluttonous kleptomaniac hardly seemed on par with Adolph Hitler. But he understood that King Farouk was Nahhas Pasha's impediment to being Prime Minister. King Abdullah bowed his head slightly to Fred as they said goodbye: "Thank you, my friend. I hope this will be the first of many such meetings you will attend." Ignoring the fact that he was given little choice, He respectfully bowed his head: "It was my honor."

Though he was in no position to ask, he couldn't help but wonder why King Abdullah would bother with a young, undistinguished private. Was their connection with Amon a sign that he could be trusted? King Abdullah appeared far too pragmatic for that. He could only guess that his friends at the café, in order to secure King Abdullah's protection of him, had overly built him up. As much as he appreciated them for it, he now worried about letting them down.

∞

It was late afternoon when Fred spotted Colonel Bayley on the terrace having drinks with his Lieutenant. Realizing how unfair he had been to the Colonel, who was only following orders and had given up his day to bring him there, Fred approached somewhat sheepishly. After a brief introduction, Colonel Bayley's Lieutenant quickly excused himself, claiming to be overwhelmed with work. Fred wasn't surprised. The Colonel probably had little good to say about him. Out of formality, the Colonel asked, "How did it go?" Fred responded as respectfully as possible, "Okay, thank you. I hope this hasn't been too much of an imposition on you." The Colonel perked up: "It must have gone quite well. You seem to be a changed man." Fred shrugged: "I'm sorry, I was upset about something. It had nothing to do with you." The Colonel questioned, "So, I take it the problem's been resolved." Fred despondently shook his head: "But no point bothering you with it."

"Sit down," the Colonel gently commanded. "What do you say we make a new start?" Over drinks the Colonel got Fred to relay what Melnick and Jack were facing. Leaving out anything that could get them into trouble, Fred ended with: "It's my fault Jack isn't prepared. If they don't make it tonight their deaths will be on my hands."

Feeling Fred's distress, the Colonel thought momentarily: "Perhaps the situation isn't so dire." He summoned a waiter to bring a phone to the table. Fred watched in amazement. Other than in movies, he had never seen anyone making a call from a restaurant table. The Colonel beamed as he was connected: "Bax-old-boy, I have an important task for you..." After discussing the situation, the Colonel smiled as he hung up: "You're friends should arrive intact." The Colonel explained that he was given assurance for Melnick and Jack's truck to have aerial support for their journey out. "Having bypassed certain procedures, it's probably best we keep this to ourselves."

"I don't know how to thank you," Fred said in disbelief. The Colonel offhandedly shrugged: "In a way, I suppose I'm partially responsible. If you're not in a rush to get back, perhaps you'd like to see some of the local sites." Fred guessed that his connection to King Abdullah had something to do with the Colonel's generous offer. Being extremely grateful to him, and not wanting to waste any more of his time, Fred was tempted to confess just how little weight his feedback would carry with the King, but he couldn't pass up seeing the sites of Cairo.

With 1940 Cairo far from the sprawling, congested, urban center of today, they drove through the scenic countryside of the Nile Basin scattered with little villages. The Colonel finally asked: "So, how is it you know King Abdullah?" Fred shrugged: "My best friend was a gift from King Abdullah to Haim Arlosoroff." Confused, the Colonel asked, "A courtesan?" Fred shook his head: "A horse." The Colonel nodded: "So, a horse, not a whore, introduced you?" Fred nodded: "In a way." For whatever reason, the Colonel didn't pursue it.

Half an hour later, Fred looked out in astonishment at the only remaining seven wonders of the ancient world. The Pyramids of Giza and temple of the Sphinx were perhaps even more overwhelming after Sheila had lowered his expectations. "They're tiny," she complained. "Not worth the bother." Looking out at them, he questioned if she had really been there with her family. For 4,500 years, until the building of the Eiffel Tower for the 1889 Paris World's fair, the Great Pyramid of Giza was the tallest building in the world. Bigger and more impressive than he could have imagined, the monuments stood as fitting gates to the immense Sahara.

With few restrictions back then, Fred was free to climb the sacred monuments at will. "Spectacular views from the top," the Colonel acknowledged. "But quite a trek. Hope you forgive me for sitting this one out." Not wanting to make him wait, Fred assured, "If you're busy it's not important." The Colonel corrected: "It's quite important. There is nothing like it. But might I suggest not looking down till you reach the top."

The massive cut stones of the Great Pyramid were more challenging than Fred had expected. Not even halfway up, he paused to catch his breath. Looking down he realized that the Colonel was right. His knees weakened from the dizzying height. Pushing forward, he looked straight ahead scaling stone by stone until he made it to the summit of the massive 455-foot structure.

As he stood in the dry desert wind, he looked out at the breathtaking expanse. To one side was the endless Sahara. To the other, the desert sands abutted the green valley of the Nile, rolling out beyond Cairo and the horizon. He could feel his heart beating as he took in the wonder, astounded by the height and views. Over the millennium how many visitors had taken in the same marvel? It was the closest he had come to an out of body experience, as if he were floating in the sky. Remarkably, what had been his worst day in the army had become the most spectacular.

∞

After the pyramids, they drove past other sites; the Mosques of Mohammed Ali, Ibn Tulun and the Ben Ezra Synagogue. Dining at the Continental Hotel, Fred looked at the menu and his vision blurred at the dizzying prices: "You know I'm only a private." The Colonel chuckled: "Not to worry, it's all taken care of." After months of eating cans of bully beef, consisting of mostly lard turned to liquid by the desert heat, Fred's 19-year-old ravenous metabolism agreed to let the British Government spring for one good meal. Sipping coffee at the end of the dinner, the Colonel informed a sated Fred: "There is one more spot I am to show you."

The Kit Kat Cabaret was famed for catering to Cairo's more licentious elite. Following the Colonel inside, Fred was immediately taken by the stunning belly dancer performing with unusual delicacy and grace in the center of the room. The well-dressed patrons of mixed nationalities, along with about a dozen British officers, seemed equally transfixed as they sat at small square tables surrounding her.

Seeing that he was the only non-commissioned officer, Fred stuck close to the Colonel as they approached the host. A husky, elegant, middle-aged man quickly intervened: "My dear Colonel, what an honor to see you again. And who is our young friend." As the man took in Fred, the Colonel had little choice but to introduce him: "Fred, this is George Calomiris. The proprietor of the Kit Kat." With a glint in his dark, calculating eyes, Calomiris took Fred by the shoulder and escorted them to a front row table: "It is always my pleasure to be of service to our young soldiers." Grabbing a waiter, Calomiris ordered: "Champagne for my friends. Compliments of the house." Confused why he would be given free champagne, Fred guessed that it had something to do with the British trying to make a good impression on King Abdullah.

Calomiris sat down uninvited next to Fred, but was suddenly disturbed by the entrance of a dashing young man with light brown hair and pencil moustache: "Excuse me, a dear friend of my mother's," he said with a slight smile. "Probably here to discuss their needlepoint." As Calomiris headed off, the Colonel confided: "Easy to guess what that's about." But Fred had no idea. The Colonel lifted his glass to what he presumed to be a lovers' tryst, unaware of how far he was from the truth. Though it was years since Fred was on his father's vineyard, he could spot cheap champagne, and this one was undoubtedly saved for less important guests.

The exquisite belly dancer, also unsettled by the dapper young man's entrance, quickly shifted her focus onto Fred. He had never been interested in the dances performed by the students at Ben Shemen, but he was now held spellbound as she sensually gyrated her body for him. If that was also arranged for him to give good feedback to King Abdullah, he thought, "Well done." As she made her final effortless twirls, the Colonel whispered to Fred, "I take it you approve." Mesmerized, Fred could only nod. She finished the set, and with a demure smile moved on to another table. The Colonel informed: "Her name is Hekmet Fahmy, considered by some the most beautiful woman in Egypt. I fear she likes you." Fred shrugged, "No fear there." The Colonel informed, "In Cairo, everything has a price. I believe her going rate is 1,500 piastres a night." At half his yearly wage, Fred almost spat out the cheap champagne.

If he had the money, he may have faced a moral dilemma. Though he was still madly in love with Gabriella, at 19 he felt no pride in still being a virgin. But he had also been conditioned at Ben Shemen on the horrors of venereal disease, backed up with chilling photos forever etched in his mind. His father also drummed into him accounts of soldiers succumbing to V.D. during WWI. (The actual number was 18,000 a day. Through education and early treatments it was greatly reduced by WWII, but it wasn't until 1947 that penicillin was shown to be an effective cure.)

Only the month before, Fred had thought his virgin days might be over when an attractive, young, Egyptian nurse around his age seemed anxious to go out with him. After the movie, she even seemed agreeable to parking in his jeep. But with each move he made beyond kissing, she interrupted with a gruesome story of a V.D. case that she had nursed. Just that day, a syphilis victim apparently had to have his penis amputated. Fred considered calming her by confessing that he was a virgin and she shouldn't worry, but at that point she had sufficiently killed the mood.

To reduce V.D. in German troops, it was said that Hitler had inflatable Aryan sex-dolls created. The project supposedly failed when German troops, too embarrassed to be captured with inflatable sex-dolls, refused to carry them in their packs. But was that really the only reason? Were soldiers truly satisfied by these sex-dolls? The supposed sex-doll factory was destroyed during the bombing of Dresden, eliminating any evidence of its existence, but if true it implies that Hitler was unaware that sex-dolls were not interchangeable with real women, and that most men could effectively masturbate without a large blonde balloon.

The Colonel toasted Fred: "Fortunately, for you money is no issue, at least with King Abdullah picking up the tab." Fred asked in disbelief, indicating Hekmet Fahmy, "King Abdullah told you that he would pay for..." "Not exactly," the Colonel confessed. "But this club, the dinner, we're to submit the bill to his office. I gather he won't mind if..." Fred soberly put down the champagne: "King Abdullah hasn't forgiven King Farouk for greeting him with his hands in his pocket. And you want me to stick him with..." indicating Hekmet. The Colonel shrugged: "Perhaps your mutual friend, the horse, has more influence than you think? We were assured that he would take care of anything you wished." Fred tried to grasp the situation. Maybe it was a test. "Do you know of King Abdullah ever frequenting a place like this?" The Colonel admitted that he didn't. Fred conjectured, "Someone in his office may have recommended this place for a soldier's night out, but I bet the King knows nothing of it. He barely knows me. If I took advantage of him like that, that would be it. And he wouldn't think too highly of you, either." Pulling out his wallet, Fred handed over its contents of 11 pounds. "This is all I have. I hope it covers ..."

The Colonel assured, "Keep your money. The office will take care of it. Didn't mean to upset you." Fred shook his head: "For one amazing moment I thought King Abdullah might actually pay for me to sleep with Hekmet Fahmy." The Colonel offered, "She may still be within reach. George Calomiris clearly likes you, and Fahmy would most likely do anything he asks." Seeing Fred's confusion, the Colonel clarified: "If asked I will deny I said this, but Cairo is not London. We are much more tolerant here, especially for those frequenting the Kit Kat. If George Calomiris entices a young officer for the night, we look the other way." Feeling the need to justify himself, the Colonel explained, "We're at war. We want the best soldiers possible. I believe their sex lives should carry no more weight than the color of their hair. I hope I haven't shocked you." Finding it refreshing, Fred shook his head: "You remind me of my mother.

She didn't judge either. If more were like her I think we'd have a better world." Picking up the champagne, the Colonel toasted, "To your mother."

All eyes suddenly turned to a tall, regally dressed round-faced young man with a thin moustache. As Calomiris effusively greeted the man and his large entourage, the Colonel confided, "King Farouk presently has Calomiris's attention, but with one word I'd wager he'd be by your side." "That's King Farouk?" Fred asked. The Colonel nodded: "Cairo society is small, and the King is a regular at the Kit Kat. In fact, he usually frequents several clubs a night." Observing the so-called 'devil', Fred was surprised that he appeared to be nothing more than a carefree young man.

As Calomiris had tables quickly set up for Farouk and his entourage in front of other patrons, the Colonel continued: "Calomiris is known to be very generous, to his friends. And as his friend I suspect that he would arrange a night for you with Fahmy. I would never suggest such a thing, but the choice should be yours."

Though Hekmet Fahmy was beautiful, she wasn't Gabriella. And even if the possibility amazed him, he was not about to have sex with Calomiris just to get to her. Fred jested, "For peace within our nations, I'll allow Calomiris to focus on King Farouk. Hope he doesn't lose his pocket watch." The Colonel's smile revealed that he was aware of the rumors. Watching Hekmet Fahmy along with several of her friends dance for the king, the Colonel grinned: "At least Fahmy has little chance of being pickpocketed."

(Two years later towards the end of 1942, Hekmet Fahmy would be arrested as one of Egypt's most notorious Nazi spies. Like King Farouk and many other Egyptian nationalists, she believed the Nazi propaganda that the Germans would treat the Egyptians much better than the British elite.

Though she had danced for Hitler, Mussolini and other top Nazi officials, being the most popular belly dancer in Egypt, Fahmy also earned the trust of some of the highest-ranking British officers. The dashing young man with light brown hair and pencil moustache that Calomiris had been engaged with was Johann Eppler, former interpreter for Hitler and the Grand Mufti before becoming a Nazi spy. Now based in Cairo, using an alias, counterfeit British pounds and British officer attire, he enlisted the help of his ex-girlfriend, Hekmet Fahmy. The two recruited other popular belly dancers forming what would become the main German intelligence effort in Cairo.

After Fahmy extracted whatever information she could, the high-ranking British officer slept soundly in her arms as Eppler searched his lodgings for any critical information. With the aid of Anwar Sadat, future president of Egypt, they then fed a continuous flow of high-grade intelligence to Field Marshal Rommel and other top Nazis on the African front.

Though Eppler's Egyptian stepfather had raised him in Alexandria, he had the solid cover of being born to German Jewish parents. It was baffling to Fred why someone with Jewish decent would support the Nazis, but Eppler wasn't alone. In 1934, the year

Fred escaped from Germany, The Association of German National Jews came out in support of Hitler. Though they eventually withdrew that support, even German's joked that they ended their meetings by giving the Nazi salute while shouting 'Down With Us!'

When the British finally uncovered Eppler and his radio operator, Hans Sandstede, they were sentenced to death as spies, but King Farouk intervened and commuted their sentences. Released from prison after the war, Eppler went to Europe and became a successful construction engineer.

Hekmet Fahmy claimed to be an unwitting accomplice; apparently extracting whatever information she could from top British officers and turning it over to Eppler unaware that he was a Nazi spy. Though only sentenced to two and a half years, after her release, she received few movie roles. In an attempt to revive her career she lost all of her own money backing her failed movie, Almotasharidah. The Egyptian Fox, as she became known, then turned to Christianity spending long hours each day in church prayer.)

Though at the time Fred wouldn't have believed it, he was lucky that he couldn't afford Fahmy. Even if he hadn't divulged any information, such as the impending coup, along with every British officer known to have slept with her, he would have been interrogated, suspected, and would have certainly disappointed King Abdullah. As it was, if the King had been testing him, evidently he passed. From then on, wherever stationed, arrangements were made for Fred to meet with any local leaders allied with King Abdullah and the British.

∞

The next day at the base in Port Said, Fred received word from Colonel Bayley that Melnick and Jack had arrived safely to the front. The following morning, he went to meet them on their return from what had been a harrowing trip. While eating their cans of breakfast, adrenaline still raced through Jack as he told Fred of the Italian and German fighter planes. Apparently alerted by the extra aerial support, they had become determined to stop whatever precious cargo was being transported to the front. "Planes kept coming out of the sky," Jack exclaimed. "They were dogfighting all around us. Our fighters shot one down right above us. I froze, and we almost crashed into it, but the Professor grabbed the wheel and swerved us out of the way."

Unwilling to risk having an inexperienced 17-year-old guiding them while under an aerial attack, Melnick saw no choice but for Jack to drive. Jack excitedly continued: "I knew I had to keep my eyes on the road, but how do you do that when Nazis are flying all around you. I could hear a machine gun coming at us, and the Professor told me to go right. I was so nervous I went left. I knew we were done for, but the Professor grabbed the wheel pulling us even more left, and we made it. We even picked up a British pilot whose plane was shot down. I swear, for the rest of the trip he was more scared than me." Melnick shook his head, assuring Fred, "You'd be proud of him. He's now a driver. By the end he had his eyes glued on the road and did everything I said."

Fred gave Jack a reassuring pat on the shoulder: "Congratulations. And for your reward you get a can of spam in monkey grease!" Melnick added: "I still have no idea where all those British fighters came from. Never seen anything like it. The pilot we picked up said they were sent to protect our cargo. You know we only loaded the usual cans of food, weapons and gas." Not at liberty to divulge the Colonel's aid or his meeting with King Abdullah, Fred could say nothing.

Sensing that Fred was holding something back, Melnick helped him out by changing the subject: "How was Cairo?" Fred wanted to tell them of the Great Pyramids, eating at the Continental, seeing Hekmet Fahmy at the Kit Kat Cabaret, but finding no excuse for why a Colonel would have taken a private to those places, he could only shrug: "Not much to say. I was just a driver." Though convinced there was more to the story, Melnick played along: "Consider yourself lucky. A boring trip sounds good right now."

CHAPTER 28

WITH ALL OF ENGLAND on rationing, soldiers lived off of canned Bully Beef, army biscuits, Sweet Tea, and M&V (cans of scrap meat and vegetable packed in what soldiers referred to as monkey grease.) Soldiers occasionally received care packages from their families, but shared by their entire unit they quickly vanished. For Fred, Melnick and Jack, being used to the fresh farm food of the kibbutz, the adjustment was particularly difficult.

So the news of a London cook joining their regiment was greeted with the same enthusiasm as a victory in battle. When the Colonel entered the barracks with the large, burly cook, the soldiers all stood at attention as if welcoming a dignitary: "Men I'd like you to meet Staff Sergeant Claire Potter." Jack, trying to be friendly, naively called out, "Welcome Sergeant Claire, sir!" The laughter quickly subsided as the cook warned in his heavy cockney accent: "Long time since any private had the guts to call me that. I had the Colonel announce my full name so you know I'm not keepin' nothin' from you. But if you value your life, private, you'll address me as, Chef." Jack trembled: "Yes, Chef, sir." From then on no one dared to call Chef anything else.

Determined to control all of North Africa, Mussolini ordered Marshal Graziani to push the Italian Army East through Cyrenaica (now Libya) into Egypt to take Alexandria at all cost. Chef was a tank commander defending the Egyptian Mediterranean port town of Sidi Barrani when his British Crusader took a direct hit from an Italian M13. Sitting on the open hatch, Chef was thrown out by the explosion as the shell pierced into the cabin. Suffering serious leg burns and bruises, he watched helplessly as his tank moved forward in flames, his driver undoubtedly dead with his foot still on the gas as his two other men, unable to escape, screamed from inside the tank as they burnt to death. Another British Crusader took out the Italian M13, saving Chef's life. But once released from the infirmary, with no tank or crew, he was placed on cooking duty until fully recovered.

Volunteers for Chef's team were told to assemble in the mess hall tent. Since being selected meant access to better food, Fred, Melnick and Jack attended with most of the other soldiers. Fred's unit cheered when Fred was announced to be the driver. "Sorry to you other drivers," Chef offered. "But he got the best record." Fred thanked him and asked if he could make a recommendation. As if offended by the insolence, Chef stared him down until informing: "I'm waiting." Fred uncomfortably proposed, "Professor Melnick is my partner. He's a great driver and shot. I wouldn't have my record if it weren't for him." Eyeing Melnick, Chef gave a begrudging nod to Fred: "Right, mate. Glad to have a replacement for you, just in case."

With Fred and Melnick on board, Chef went about choosing the other six men. What appeared to matter most in the selection was the soldier's resourcefulness. Cooking skills were never questioned, and the most distinguished were quickly dismissed. "He may not be so bad," whispered Jack. "Looks like he's leaving the best for more important jobs."

When it came to choosing the last man, Fred awkwardly raised his hand. Chef demanded, "What now?" Fred cleared his throat: "Professor Melnick and I have been training Jack Rose. He's proven to be an admirable soldier." Jack looked up at Fred, surprised and honored. Chef took in the small blond boy: "Admirable is he? How old are you, 12?" Jack lied with conviction: "I'm 18, Chef, sir." Seeing Chef's raised eyebrow, Fred tried to hide his nerves as he interjected: "He's young, but he's agile and determined. He can get into places the rest of us can't. I guarantee, Chef, sir, he's very resourceful." Chef studied Jack until finally warning Fred: "If he don't prove admirable, you're responsible."

Chef dismissed the other men and began the introductory meeting: "So we understand each other, don't none of you ever forget, I'm my only cause. Do anything to cross me, I'll make sure you regret it. Now, I agreed to take over the convoy's cooking and water facilities on two conditions. One: that I have a water tank and a big truck. Two: that I have the fastest driver and best crooks in the company." Chef's glare quickly silenced the laughter: "Any of you disappoint, you won't find it so funny."

On their first outing, Fred discovered Chef's need for a fast driver. After Chef negotiated with the dispatcher, he had Fred drive around the busy Arab market, to get the lay of the land. Finally having him park behind a large tent, Chef ordered, "Leave the motor running and stay put, or you're in tonight's stew." Not daring to move, Fred sat watching through the rearview mirrors. Several minutes passed when he saw Jack furtively pushing a large crate from under the back of the tent. Melnick and several other men quickly followed with more crates and bags. Since Melnick was known to be upright, Fred assumed it was the fasted way of getting supplies to the truck. The rest of the team suddenly ran from the front of the tent with more crates and bags, quickly loading them onto the truck. As the men piled into the back, chef jumped into the front passenger seat ordering Fred: "Go, Go, Go!"

Fred floored it while looking back in the review mirror to see a small, weathered man in a long, white gallibaya chasing after them while screaming in Arabic. When the man finally gave up running, Chef sighed with relief: "That was close." Fred awkwardly asked, "Why? What's wrong with the cinnamon?" Chef looked at Fred bewildered: "Cinnamon? What bloody cinnamon? What the bugger are you talking 'bout?" Fred shrugged, "He was saying we forgot the cinnamon." Chef reprimanded: "You speak Arabic and didn't tell me!? 'Course we need cinnamon! Go back! Back! Now!" Fred threw on the brakes and skidded around.

Chef smiled and bowed to the man, thanking him for the cinnamon, and they drove off again. "What else you holding out on?" Chef demanded. Seeing Fred's bewilderment, Chef articulated: "What other languages you speak?" Fred answered: "Only German, French, Italian and Hebrew." Chef smirked:

"That all?" adding as he looked Fred over: "From now on, you'll do the talking."

Watching Fred maneuver the beaten-up roads, Chef reluctantly admitted, "Glad you drive like a German." Fred firmly corrected: "I drive like a Palestinian." Concerned of how Chef would react to being contradicted, Fred was relieved by Chef's sarcastic response: "Alright, glad Palestinians drive like Germans." Fred later learned that while Chef was bartering with the vendor, he had ordered little Jack to sneak into the back of the tent to make sure that the coast was clear. Melnick and two other men then joined Jack in stealing whatever they could.

From then on, while Fred negotiated with the dispatcher the rest of the team would pilfer food and supplies. "How much corn do we get?" Fred would ask. The dispatcher would tally: "Three-hundred-fifty men gets you twelve boxes." Needing to slow down the process so that Chef's team could steal more, Fred would ask: "Any way to get extra if we cut back on something else." Unaccustomed to haggling over the generally loathed food, the dispatcher was usually caught off guard. When there was no more room for bargaining, Fred was taught to ask, "What do you have that nobody wants?" The dispatcher usually had an inordinate amount of flour. Knowing that few would sacrifice meat for flour, Fred would ask, "How many sacks of flour can we get for a can of corned beef?" By that point, overwhelmed with bargaining, for a few cans of bully beef the dispatcher would give them almost unlimited flour.

Though Chef was the brain of the outfit, to Fred's surprise, Melnick became the unofficial leader, as all of the men looked to him for final orders. Somehow, having Melnick's approval made it okay. For Fred, negotiating became an art. With a new dispatcher, he would sometimes test out his upper crust British accent, finding that he could slow down the process even more by creating stories of life on his family's manor in Manchester.

From the dispatcher, they would then go to a nearby Arab town, open up the goods and Fred would handle in Arabic: "What will you give for one pound of flour?" When word got out to the troops that they were returning with chickens, eggs, lambs, goats, etc., all of the soldiers began volunteering for their convoys.

∞

December 10, 1940: Under General Ritchie, Indian forces with support from British artillery retook Sidi Barrani. One by one the Italian strongholds fell. Overwhelmed by the harsh Sahara and superior British weapons, the Italian Army was pushed back/west along the Cyrenaica (Libyan) coast. To celebrate, Chef prepared a sixteen-course Christmas dinner. Though perhaps not fine cuisine, with dishes such as chicken with Bully Beef, chickpea, olive stuffing, flavored with Egyptian herbs and covered in a white sauce, it was by far the best army meal of these soldiers.

Fred and Melnick continued delivering munitions and supplies to the front, often followed by Jack and his partner in a truck behind them. Usually one or two hours ahead of the huge British convoys, it was an important job, requiring the best drivers, but they found it frustrating to never be part of the actual fighting. Knowing that their jobs often went to British soldiers, Melnick and Jack couldn't understand why three Jewish soldiers were continually turned down for the front.

February 6, 1941: British forces trapped the Italian Army in Benghazi, Libya, taking over 133,00 Italian prisoners. By February 8th, the Libyan coast had been liberated as far west as El Agheila. Churchill praised, "Never before has so much been surrendered by so many to so few."

Even though Hitler had sworn to never repeat Germany's mistake of WWI by dividing the German armies on two fronts, the failed Italian African campaign left him little choice. WWII was a war of machines, which needed oil. (Had the Japanese destroyed the oil reserves at Pearl Harbor, it would have immobilized the American fleet, giving the Japanese a strong path to victory.) With the Nazi reserves of twenty million barrels quickly disappearing, they needed the Russian or Arabian oil fields. Once they had one, the other would be in easier reach.

With the Italian North Africa campaign failing, General Erwin Rommel, soon to be known as 'The Desert Fox', would move in with his newly formed "Afrika Korps". Rommel saw to it that only the best German soldiers from the lauded Nazi Army were recruited and extensively trained for desert warfare.

By March 11, 1941, Germany's fifth Panzer Regiment, with 135 tanks and the most advanced German weaponry, completed its debarkation in Tripoli. On March 24, with British forces spread thin, Rommel's Panzer Regiments and 90th Light Infantry division attacked the weakened British position at El Agheila. By April 1, the Germans had taken Benghazi. Their German Mark III and Mark IV tanks outranged the British tanks in firepower, and commanded with impressive skill, they continued pushing the British east towards Alexandria, Egypt.

Fred and Melnick drove non-stop bringing supplies to the front. As they struggled to stay awake, they feared crashing as much as being hit with a full load of arms. But battles required incredible amounts of munitions. During WWII the Americans alone produced 47 billion rounds of small arms ammunition, approximately 11 million tons. To Fred and Melnick's surprise, Chef was granted permission to join them on one trip.

Since Chef had always seemed extremely critical of them, Melnick questioned him, "You sure you want to do this? It's no joy ride." Chef grumbled: "You think I don't know that? I wanna see what you blokes get way with when I'm not 'round." If he was to report back on their performance, it made no difference. They would do the same job, with or without Chef.

Seated between Fred and Melnick, Chef snored loudly as the first Nazi fighter plane came in to attack. By then, Fred and Melnick were almost indifferent to the danger, working together like a well-oiled machine. As far as they knew, they never did take down a German fighter plane while driving, but they undoubtedly scared off a few. Chef suddenly woke as the fighter tried to pummel them with machine gun fire. Beads of sweat formed on Chef's forehead as his left foot pushed on an imaginary brake and his fingers gripped into the seat. When the plane finally gave up and headed off, Chef exhaled: "Why the bloody hell did I let you bastards talk me into this?"

The next morning, they were unloading when a line of Australians ran past them with fixed bayonets. As Melnick and Chef were carrying off a satchel of munitions, Fred stood on the back of a truck unloading gasoline when an Australian officer yelled up to him: "Hey fellow, why don't you come down and join us?" "What are you doing?" Fred asked. The officer smiled: "Attacking the German line. Gonna get us some Jerries!" Fred shrugged, "I don't have a rifle." The officer threw an extra rifle with a bayonet up to him and smiled: "You do now."

Melnick watched dumbfounded as he saw Fred running off into the desert with the Australians. Following Melnick's gaze, Chef focused in on Fred. In disbelief, he yelled after him: "Where the bloody hell do you think you're going?! Get your scrawny arse back here!" Fred called back, "Right after I get me some Jerries!" Chef screamed, "I mean now! I'm warning you, you stupid Kraut!" But Fred was soon out of hearing range.

Fred ran with the Australians through the desert toward the German trenches amazed by the amount of sandflies popping up all around him. He had never seen anything like it. Holding the bayonet straight in front of him, ready to fire, he continued running as fast as he could confounded that so many flies could live in the hot desert sand. Suddenly coming upon the German trench, he jumped in, held up his bayonet on the Germans in front of him and they all put up their arms. While rounding up the German prisoners, he thanked the Australian officer for allowing him to join in: "Haven't had so much fun since playing war with my gang as a kid. "Thanks fella," the officer said somewhat perplexed. "Glad you liked it."

But as they walked the prisoners back, Fred saw all of the fallen bodies of Australian soldiers strewn across the desert. It suddenly dawned on him that what he thought were sandflies were actually machine gun bullets. They had somehow missed him. His first battle would also be the last that he would enter into without fear.

Chef admonished, "Are you bloody crazy!? I should whip you! Don't you ever do that to me again!" Surprised by Chef's reaction, Fred laughed slightly: "Chef, you look more frightened than me." Melnick joined: "Yeah, careful Chef. It might look like you actually care." Indignant, Chef lashed out: "All I care about is not having to train a new driver! That's all you are to me!" Melnick patted Chef's shoulder: "Chef, we love you too."

∞

Rommel's forces marched across Libya into Egypt crushing each British stronghold. The Australian division in Tobruk was the only hold out, beginning what would become the longest siege in British history. Exasperated by the perseverance of these heroic Australian soldiers, the Nazi dubbed them, 'The rats of Tobruk' or 'Desert Rats'. Given their hellish existence in the bombed out desert town of plain stucco one-story buildings, it seemed an appropriate moniker. But the Australians wore it with pride, even designing from scraps of a downed German plane their own emblems in the shape of a rat.

Those few to miraculously survive both the African and Russian front would usually say that desert warfare was the closer to a living hell. With water always in short supply and no shade whatsoever from the blistering sun, they lived in constant thirst. Voracious flies relentlessly sought blood for their young as scorching hot days turned to bitter cold nights. Survival being the sole focus, all leisurely pleasure was gone. Mirages of sails on the sea and upside down German soldiers enjoying refreshing drinks played games with their minds. But there was never any water, only reflections/mirages caused by the intense glare of the burning sun on the smoldering sand.

When trapped in sandstorms in the open desert there was no place to hide. Sand was everywhere; the eyes, throat, hair. Searing-hot wind blew for hours, choking the soldiers as they lay on the sand covered by their blankets trying to think of anything refreshing to suppress their raging thirsts. During the middle of a blinding sandstorm, Fred knew of one party so desperate of thirst that they went off in search of water. Presumably lost, consumed by the desert, they were never to be heard from again.

April 10, 1941: the German Afrika Korps attacked Tobruk. The noise was deafening as the ground erupted with clouds of dust from German Stuka dive-bombers pummeling the earth. But in a matter of minutes the Australians swung their guns into position cutting off the advance with their shells, and Tobruk held. Rommel ordered more attacks on April 11 and 14 but the Australians somehow persevered. By May 2, 1941, all of Libya had fallen to Rommel's forces, all except the Rats of Tobruk.

With Rommel's Armies surrounding Tobruk, Fred, Melnick and the other drivers were unable to bring supplies in by land. What Tobruk received had to come by air or sea, and the Mediterranean had become a battleground with each side trying to cut off the other's supply lines. The Desert Rats somehow held, but Rommel was unrelenting. He not only needed Tobruk as a supply point close to the front, with the desert town still under British control his armies were forced to move 1,500 tons of supplies daily over the harsh surrounding desert. Churchill ordered Tobruk to be held at all cost. For the soldiers trapped there, water was the most precious commodity. But despite the deprivations, they refused to relent, and by delaying and weakening Rommel's forces, the Desert Rats of

Tobruk played an immeasurable role in stopping the Nazis.

At the end of August, the Australian garrison was finally relieved and the Colonial Empire forces moved in. Throughout September, as the Nazis continued pummeling the town, the siege was strengthened. On the morning of December 4, 1941, Rommel almost broke through, but Allied Forces held, and by the end of the month, having withstood a ninth month siege, Tobruk was finally relieved. That Christmas, Allied troops were celebrating the Nazi retreat.

But their celebration would not last long. As Rommel suddenly began to reconquer stronghold after stronghold, both sides credited him as a military genius with an almost mystic 'fingertip feel', a sixth sense in predicting every move that the British were to make.

For Passover of April 12, 1942, to lift the morale of the Jewish troops, Fred illustrated an entire Haggadah and Chef agreed to prepare the Seder. Fred, Melnick and Jack helped the British cooking-crew prepare the many unfamiliar dishes, such as gefilte fish, unleavened bread and bitter herbs. Out of curiosity, Chef joined for what he called, "the slop." But by the end of the meal he admitted: "Bloody hell, now I see how you blokes suffered."

At the end of May, Rommel launched the Nazi offensive in full force. "Tobruk was a symbol of British resistance," Rommel would state. "We would now finish it for good." For three days and nights the fighting raged around the barren desert crossing southwest of Tobruk, which the British had named, 'Knightsbridge' after the fashionable London district. Chef looked out at the open desert smirking, "Why not call it Buckingham Palace?" As British troops fought desperately to end the siege of Tobruk, Rommel's forces were determined to break through their line and advance towards Egypt.

Ray Ellis, one of the soldiers who first befriended Fred on his arrival at Port Said, manned a 25-pounder field gun with D-troop after his entire B-troop had been wiped out. It was an extremely difficult job. In one day of battle, the two-men team per field gun could fire over 900 shells, each weighing over 25 lbs. Constantly moving the heavy gun in position and loading the shells into the smoldering breech was a challenge for the strongest of men. But even under those conditions, some preferred being a gunner out in the open air than sweltering inside a tank. As Ray and the other gunners fought off over one hundred and fifty 22nd German Panzer Division tanks, which had almost surrounded them, German Stuka dive-bombers joined in the battle. Bombs and shells screamed down in all directions on the British gunners as if all hell had broken loose.

After three days of constant battle, Rommel's troops suddenly pulled back, withdrawing to the south. Believing to have the upper hand, the British prepared to break through the German line in order to end the siege of Tobruk and push the Nazis west until forcing them from the continent. Though the shelling had stopped, the continual air raids made it difficult for the soldiers to catch up on much needed rest, and there was much to do. Despite being pushed to the limits, they had to salvage machinery, resupply arms, food, water, gasoline, and bury the countless dead.

With many tank commanders and their crews killed or critically wounded, Chef was given another tank to command. For his crew, he requested Fred, Melnick and Jack. Both Melnick and Jack were approved, but Chef was informed that he would have to find himself another driver. Distressed, Chef went in search of answers. A friend working under the Colonel explained to him the situation in strictest confidence.

Chef immediately called a meeting with Fred, Melnick and Jack: "You didn't hear this from me, but our boy here can't be our driver. Some bloody King is looking out for him." Finally understanding, Melnick exhaled: "So that's why we keep getting turned down for the Front." Astonished, Jack asked, "You know a King? Can we meet him?" Fred assured: "I barely know him. I would've said something, but wasn't at liberty." Chef admitted: "Count your blessings. I chose you 'cause we had some luck together. Thought you'd be my best chance of getting out of this alive. But you're lucky to be out of it." Fred stiffened: "Who said I'm out?" Chef sneered: "You will, once your roasting all day under the desert sun in a bloody tank with a faulty cooling system. Only a fool wants that, and I don't want no bloody fool driver. You think I'd go if I had some bloody king looking out for me instead of me stupid mum naming me, Claire?"

Fred looked to his friends. Jack was mystified. Not wanting to be separated from Fred, Jack also didn't want to put him in harms way. But Melnick's understanding nod gave Fred full permission to back out. Fred shook his head with determination: "If the Nazis win, we're dead anyway. I'm your driver." Melnick soberly asked Chef: "Will they let him drive?" Chef snickered: "Bloody hell, 'course they will, if he insists. Giving me a tank means troops go back to eating Bully Beef. That's how desperate they are." Knowing how naively most soldiers entered into war, Chef shook his head as he watched the three men enthusiastically shake on it: "Now I gotta train you three bloody fools."

CHAPTER 29

FRED WAS ONLY allowed to join the tank crew after signing a release stating that the decision was of his own volition and against the wishes of his superiors. As desperate as the British were for soldiers, if Fred were to die in combat they didn't want to risk alienating King Abdullah, Britain's most powerful Arab ally.

Chef took over another British Crusader tank. Though faster than the German Panzers Mark III and Mark IV, the Panzers were equipped with the dual-purpose 88-mm anti-aircraft guns, the most feared weapon in North Africa. Extremely accurate, the 88 could stop a tank from over a mile away. With the British Crusader outranged in firepower and its lighter frame more easily penetrated, as Chef had witnessed, they were often turned into 'burning coffins'.

The better Chef trained his crew the better their chances of survival. The harsh desert conditions were challenging for tanks; batteries often didn't work and engines needed constant overhauls due to sand erosion. Chef knew the Crusader inside out, but there was much to teach, and little time. Their first job was to clean out the blood from the last crew. Not knowing what happened, they guessed that during the prior three days of battle the Germans had killed the crew to get the tank before being capture or killed themselves.

Tank crews consisted of four men: commander, gunner, driver and loader. As the driver, Fred would also man the machine gun. Now 21 with a lean, muscular 6' 2 ½" frame, he was large for a tank but still agile enough to fit into the drivers seat. A slender, persnickety, older captain, watching Fred train, reprimanded: "Soldier, who assigned you to this tank? You should be on infantry. King Rules and Regulations strictly specify that tank crew should not exceed the height limit of 6'1"." Chef moved in between Fred and the onerous little man. "Sorry Captain, regulations have been changed," Chef informed. "The Army can now do anything it bloody well likes except give you a baby. And even that's changed. The Army can now give you a baby, they just can't bloody make you love it!" Not daring to argue with Chef, the captain nervously accepted the new regulations, and went on his way.

Chef made Melnick the gunner. Like Fred, he had 20/20 vision and was an excellent shot. That left Jack to be the loader. After two years in the army, Jack was now 19 and though still small he had built up his strength. Lean and lithe, he fitted well into the tank. Even though the shells for the Crusader were lighter than for the 25-pounder field gun, being loader was an extremely tough job. Few would have assigned it to Jack. But Chef, knowing Jack, trusted that he would never give up no matter how heavy the shells or smoldering hot the gun breech.

In the early morning hours of June 5, 1942, an almost full moon lit the quiet Sahara as Ray Ellis and the other gunners waited in position. Having little chance to recuperate from the three days of battle, they would have preferred more rest, but they watched with trepidation as the night sky came alive with a barrage of shells heading towards them from German tanks believed to be within the enormous nearby circular stone depression, known as 'The Knightsbridge Cauldron'. The battle of Knightsbridge would become known as one of the bloodiest of WWII. The battles of Mersa Matruh, Sidi Barrani and the nine-month siege of Tobruk would pale in comparison to the carnage that took place within that Knightsbridge cauldron.

Shells exploded around them as they fired their guns discharging ear-piercing missiles back towards the enemy troops. When the barrage quieted down, they moved forward, surprised to receive no response from the enemy. Making their way up to the wide, circular rim of the depression, there was still no shellfire. Believing to have the German troops in retreat, the plan was to cross the depression to go after them. But topping the rim and entering into the cauldron, the sky suddenly exploded.

Rommel, predicting their every move, had earlier fired the first barrage and quickly withdrew his forces beyond the depression's far rim, causing the retaliating British shells to land on empty ground. Now ready and waiting, Rommel lured the British into a trap. Since the British Royal Air Force (RAF) in North Africa was decimated, both high-altitude German aircraft and dive-bombers were uncontested as they joined in the attack.

Under Chef's command, Fred, Melnick and Jack were the lead tank heading in to support the gunners now trapped in the cauldron. Their much-respected Captain Slinn, who would die in the Knightsbridge's cauldron, gave one last sobering speech to the tank crews. Though still unaware of the full dangers facing them, he prophetically stated: "Many of us will die out there. But if we don't stop the Germans they could go on to conquer Egypt, take the Suez Canal and the door will be open for them to move into the oil fields of the Middle East. With a large percentage of the world's oil at their disposal, they will become virtually invincible. Today, the fate of England and the free world lies in your hands. Gentlemen, may God be with you."

Orders were given from higher up to throw out all unessential equipment and supplies in order to lighten the load. Chef sneered to his crew: "Been at this too long to throw anything out we might need 'cause of some bloody General sipping cocktails in Cairo. What do you say, men?" Fred, Melnick and Jack smiled as they mimicked Chef: "Bloody right!" They made a vain attempt at appearing to throw out some essentials, but in desert warfare it was nearly impossible to be oversupplied with food, water, gasoline and arms.

As the sun broke on the horizon, Fred, leading the line of tanks, cautiously started off. The path was supposed to have been cleared of landmines, but due to the shortage of time, some remained. With the lead tank most likely to hit one, Chef warned: "Keep an eye out for triggers. Don't wanna get us blown up before even making it to battle." At first, Fred safely followed the tracks of the gunners, but they were soon erased by a dessert wind. Half a mile from the depression, a sudden explosion blew the left front of the tank into the air. Crashing down again, Chef regained his equilibrium and called down to his men. Each took a moment before confirming that they were 'Okay'. Chef grumbled to Fred: "Thought I told you to go around the landmines!" If the gas line had been hit, they would be the ones being cleaned out of the tank. Still dazed, Chef climbed out to signal the line of tanks to fold back and go around them.

Jack, struggling to get up, noticed drips of blood landing on his foot. Looking up, he saw a stream of blood oozing from the side of Fred's head: "Fred's been hit!" he yelled to Melnick. Fred asked in disbelief: "What are you talking about? I'm fine..." But looking over his shoulder he saw that his shirt was drenched in blood. Melnick was quickly there with the first aid kit. Panicking, Jack anxiously asked, "What do we do? How do we get him to the infirmary?" Checking that Fred wasn't faint and had little swelling, Melnick assured: "It's okay. Looks worse than it is. There's a lot of blood in the head, but it's a pretty clean tear. Let's stitch him up." Jack disinfected the wound as Melnick threaded the needled. "Guess the old captain was right," Melnick conceded as he stitched. "A little shorter and you probably wouldn't have cut your head." Fred cracked a smile: "Now you tell me."

With the line of tanks moving safely around them, Chef checked back on his crew: "What the bloody hell?!" he said, seeing the interior looking like a crime scene. Melnick explained what happened. Chef sneered: "We just cleaned the place. Hope your head didn't cause too much damage to the tank." Melnick left the wound uncovered to dry, leaving Fred a little weak, but otherwise okay.

With the left chain blown off of its wheels, they worked tirelessly throughout the morning to fix it. Around noon, with the battle still raging on in the distance, they finally had the chain back on, and they anxiously set off to join it. But as Fred reversed to get onto the path another landmine blew off the right chain. Again, the men suffered only minor injuries, and for the rest of the afternoon they struggled to fix the right chain. By early evening they had the tank moving again, but the distant guns had gone silent. The only sound now was the wind blowing across desert. With no radio or communications, they assumed the battle was over.

A huge cloud suddenly appeared on the horizon heading toward Egypt. Chef said, "Must be our lads! Let's join'em." Fred and Jack looked anxiously to Melnick, who shook his head: "Something's wrong." A dust cloud forms behind a tank driving through the desert. The more tanks, the larger the cloud. This one was enormous. Through the dust cloud it was hard to identify the tanks, but they believed them to be British. Strangely, none of the 25-pounder field guns seemed to be in the procession. With their tanks going in to support the gunners, why would they retreat without them? Had the Nazis wiped out the guns and taken the tanks?

With the billowing red smoke growing nearer, they maneuvered their tank off of the path and made their way to the nearest British camp. On entering, a cleric from their division jumped on their tank, urgently asking: "Where'd you come from?! You're the only tank we have left!"

Their entire tank division had been wiped out in Knightsbridge. As the lead tank they were sure to have been one of the first to go. Chef nodded to Fred: "Never thought I'd be saved by a bloody fool driver hitting two landmines." But not knowing if any of their friends had survived, it was hard to feel good about it.

While they had been repairing the left chain as the battle raged on, the German tanks surrounding the rim ceased fire until all 220 British tanks were inside of the cauldron. For Ray Ellis and the other gunners, it was an incredible relief to have the British tanks swarming past them as they joined in the battle. But the relief would soon end. With all the tanks in the cauldron, the Germans once again opened fire with their 88's. The convoy that Chef and his crew had just witnessed was their 70 remaining tanks heading east to build a new line of defense. Fred asked with concern: "What about the gunners? Didn't see any leaving with them." The cleric shrugged: "Hopefully they'll slip out later."

To keep up morale of the retreating troops, they were led to believe that the gunners would follow, but for the gunners, the unfathomable happened. To slow down the Nazis so that the British tanks and infantry could build a new line of defense, the gunners were ordered to fight to the last man and last round. The gunners then watched in disbelief as all of their supporting tanks and infantry turned and retreated past them, leaving the gunners alone to face Rommel's overwhelming forces.

They would wake the next morning knowing that it was probably their last. From what they had heard, death was better than being taken prisoner by the Nazis. With only a slight dusting of sand on the hard stone surface of the cauldron there was no place to dig in for shelter from the upcoming assault. During the carnage, Ray saw only one soldier, an unfit second in command, drive off in terror to save his own life. All others stayed, fighting as their fellow soldiers, some close as brothers, were killed by the relentless shelling from the Nazi tanks.

Late that afternoon, Ray Ellis, firing the last shell from the last working gun, witnessed to the very end his friends being cut in two by enemy shells, incinerated in blazing trucks, blasted apart by screaming Stuka dive-bombers until his entire 107th Regiment of the South Nottinghamshire Hussars was wiped out. As a remaining soldier, a stranger, helped Ray man the last gun, Ray witnessed the young man pummeled to death by machine gunfire. Turning to see the machine gun of the Mark IV aimed directly at his head, Ray accepted death. But for some reason the German behind the gun, stared into his eyes and held his fire.

∞

For the people of Germany, Rommel was legendary as the first Panzer commander to push his way to the English Channel during the Nazi Blitzkrieg invasion of France. It was his most glorious victory, and he proudly took part in the Nazi victory parade through Paris. But his greatest military success, the destruction of the British forces at Knightsbridge, would earn him international fame as the military tactical genius, the Desert Fox. Though often viewed as Hitler's finest General, his status was largely built on myth. Unlike many Nazi generals, who murdered allied soldiers rather than taking them prisoners, Rommel followed the Geneva Convention. But his lack of concern for the welfare of the prisoners implied that his motivation was perhaps the avoidance of possible future charges of war crimes.

As a prisoner under Rommel's command, Ray Ellis witnessed first hand the brutality of the Nazis. Allied prisoners were tortured, beaten, starved and murdered. While Ray and other prisoners from the Battle of Knightsbridge were forced to march several days without food or water over 40-miles of treacherous desert to the coast, they believed to see Rommel drive by. As soldier after soldier fell from heat and thirst, Ray listened helplessly for the gunshots from the Nazi guards driving up from behind in their lorry as they murdered the fallen soldiers.

Could Rommel have been unaware of the crimes being committed by his men? Ray's miraculous survival can be attributed to the kindness of one

German lorry driver who secretly gave him a little water and stale bread before the march. Without that, he would have died with the others leaving no account of the nightmare he suffered through as an Axis prisoner of war.

Some claim that Rommel was not anti-Semitic and prevented the murder of the Jews in North African as he pushed his armies into Egypt, even refusing to comply with Hitler's order to execute Jewish POWs. Though in 1942 the mass executions of Jews had only begun, as Rommel pushed forward, 2,500 Jews in North African concentration camps were already murdered, and there were claims that Rommel used the several hundred thousand other Jews in the camps for slave labor.

From early on, Rommel was a devoted follower of Hitler. As part of Hitler's inner circle, he got along well with Josef Goebbels and other top Nazi officials. There is even a picture of Rommel laughing uproariously with Heinrich Himmler, head of the SS and future architect of the Holocaust. Could he really have been unaware that if his Afrika Korps succeeded in breaking through to the Arab oilfields the Nazis planned to murder all Jews by continuing the holocaust through North Africa and the Middle East, including Palestine? Could an SS Nazi General not know of Hitler's final solution? Returning from a 1937 lecture tour in Switzerland, Rommel commented that the younger Swiss officers often expressed their admiration for "our new Germany", some of them showing "remarkable understanding of our Jewish problem."

The debate will undoubtedly continue on whether Rommel was a ruthless Nazi or a humanitarian Nazi General with a heart of gold. But his mystic 'fingertip feel' can be directly tied to the decoding by German intelligence of the intercepted transcripts of the American attaché in Cairo, Colonel Bonner Frank Fellers.

With little more than the intelligence gathered by Hekmet Fahmy and her belly dancer friends, Rommel's Afrika Korps was in retreat. But that would all change starting January 18, 1942, when for 6 months and 11 days Rommel would receive Bonner Feller's accounts of practically all British activity in and around the Mediterranean.

As military attaché to the U.S. embassy in Cairo, Fellers was given access to the most highly sensitive British military information. And Fellers dutifully sent back volumes of meticulously detailed reports, up to five a day, all read by top U.S. officials, including President Roosevelt. But unbeknownst to Fellers, within hours of sending his dispatches to the Pentagon, the Nazis had them decoded, translated and on their way to Rommel; giving accounts of British strengths, weaknesses, losses, number of tanks, pending commando raids, exact whereabouts of British forces from the night before, etc. For a ruthless, egotistical SS Nazi General with his troops in retreat (or a deceived Nazi SS General with love in his heart for all humanity) Bonner Fellers was a dream come true. Rommel would gloatingly refer to Fellers as: "die gute Quelle (the good source)" and "Our little Fellers." Even

Hitler expressed the hopes that the US attaché would "continue to inform us so well over the English military planning through his badly enciphered codes."

Feller's long, usually pessimistic reports, continually denounced the British as incompetent for losing with superior force, as too many British officers "were sitting on their asses at GHQ ... The Eighth Army has failed to maintain the morale of its troops; its tactical conceptions were always wrong; it neglected completely co-operation between the various arms; its reactions to the lightening changes of the battlefield were always slow."

Rommel undoubtedly took pleasure reading those transcripts knowing that it was Fellers' constant radiograms to Washington that gave his Afrika Korps, with half the tanks and munitions, the ability to dwindle down British forces to practically nothing.

Fellers even boasted: "Many times friendship has produced the information rather than the fact of my official position." Could Fellers really have believed that the British would confide such critically sensitive information because of his charm? With Britain desperate for American aid, they probably would have given the information to anyone in his position.

At one point, when British Intelligence suspected that a leak was coming from Fellers' office, Fellers apparently did use his charm to convince them otherwise. When Fellers then voiced concern to

Washington that the "Black Code" may have been compromised, Washington assured him that the code was unbreakable and ordered him to keep the transcripts coming. Considering the determination to break enemy codes it is remarkable that anyone could think that the 'Black Code', much less any code, was unbreakable? Alan Turing with his team at Bletchley Park invented the computer to break Germany's Enigma code. To break the 'Black Code' it only took a janitor.

September 1941: Late at night at the American embassy in Rome, Loris Gherardi, a cleaner working as a spy for Italian Intelligence, broke into the safe, stealthily removed the 'Black Book', photographed it page by page, and carefully returned without anyone noticing. Why the "Black Code" was kept in the heart of Italian Axis powers is a mystery, especially since the Italian government had keys to the Embassy, but for a short period of time, Mussolini had the upper hand on intelligence. To control the code (so that there was less chance of Washington discovering that it had been broken) Mussolini refused to hand it over to the Nazis. Italian intelligence would only decipher and send on edited versions. But the Nazis, already close to breaking the code, with the deciphered intercepts soon succeeded.

To not miss any messages from their 'Good Source' one hundred and fifty Nazi agents working frantically around the clock searched for all messages from Cairo to Washington. While Fellers transmissions were painstakingly detailed, he made little effort to disguise them from Axis intelligence.

Almost all of his dispatches began with MILID WASH (Military Intelligence Division, Washington) or AGWAR WASH (Adjutant General, War Department, Washington), and all were signed FELLERS, making it easy for the Nazis to pull them from the hundreds of daily coded intercepts. The Desert Fox would then enjoy lunch knowing exactly where the Allied troops stood the evening before.

As one historian noted, the Fellers intercepts "provided Rommel with undoubtedly the broadest and clearest picture of enemy forces and intentions available to any Axis commander throughout the war." After the war, one of Rommel's staff officers confirmed that the stream of intelligence provided by Fellers was "Stupefying in its openness" and "contributed decisively to our victories in North Africa."

But unlike most of Rommel's 'Good Source' the intelligence for the Battle of Knightsbridge didn't come from Bonner Fellers. During the two-day lull while Chef was training his new tank crew, Afrika Korps' Intelligence unit, 621st Radio Intercept Company, headed by Captain Alfred Seebohm, intercepted British 7th Armored Divisions communications giving explicit details of the entire British plan of attack on Rommel's forces at Knightsbridge. With that, Rommel's greatest military success hardly took a tactical genius to trap the British tanks and gunners within the cauldron.

According to Rommel's chief of staff, the British "were quite broad-minded in making speeches during combat, and we had the possibility of making important conclusions from their speeches." On January 21, 1942, aided by intercepts assuring Rommel of temporary front-line armored superiority, the Desert Fox began an offensive advancing his forces 300 miles in just 17 days.

With the defeat of the British at Knightsbridge, Nazi hopes were raised that victory was near. Gaining equipment and supplies with each triumph, on June 13, 1942, Rommel cleared the entire Knightsbridge box, ending the Battle of Gazala. Throughout the Eighth Army the devastating defeat would be known as "Black Saturday". 300 British tanks were reduced to 70. At Rigel Ridge, South African gunners fought to the last man to delay Rommel's forces. All were killed or taken prisoner.

The devastation caused that day by Fellers transcripts was felt around the Mediterranean. The island of Malta, a crucial supply point for the allies, had been under constant attack by the Axis, becoming one of the most intensively bombed areas during WWII. In a full-scale attempt to bring relief to Malta, the British simultaneously sailed in two convoys of supplies. To protect the ships, air raids were scheduled against key Axis bases and airfield, and ground and parachute troops were planned to destroy Axis bombers before they could be flown against the convoys. But in his cable, No. 11119, dated June 11, Fellers' report gave complete details to Italian and German intelligence, which read in part: 'NIGHTS OF JUNE 12TH JUNE 13TH BRITISH SABOTAGE UNITS PLAN SIMULTANEOUS STICKER BOMB ATTACKS AGAINST AIRCRAFT ON 9 AXIS

AIRDROMES. PLANS TO REACH OBJECTIVES BY PARACHUTES AND LONG RANGE DESERT PATROL."

The British and Free French raiders going into action that night were almost all slaughtered. Their only successes were when Fellers' transcripts were ignored, not received, or ineptly handled.

June 16: Fellers reported the full extent of the British tank losses in North Africa: "The British began the present operations on 26 May with 742 tanks ... On 15 June at least 372 had been replaced. A total of 1142 tanks was thus thrown into battle ... The British losses up to the present amount to at least 1009 tanks ... On 10 June there were only 133 tanks of all types in all the depots of the Middle East."

Though Rommel's panzer divisions were exhausted and weakened, he now knew that the British had virtually nothing left to stop his Afrika Korps. On June 20th, Fellers sent one of his most detailed reports back to Washington, providing Rommel with complete operational intelligence needed to attack Tobruk.

Having survived a 9-month siege, another siege was now impossible. On June 21, 1942, Tobruk fell. 33,000 Allied troops surrendered to General Enea Navarrini, gaining Rommel an extraordinary amount of vehicles, equipment, fuel and food, (including the German troops' beloved Egyptian brewed Lowenbrau beer.) He now had the much-needed Mediterranean port and superiority in the central Mediterranean. From then on, eighty percent of

Rommel's transport would consist of captured British vehicles. For Great Britain, the fall of Tobruk was considered a national disaster second only to the loss of Singapore, where 80,000 troops were taken prisoner by the Japanese. Churchill would judge Tobruk as, "worse than a defeat, a disgrace."

With the fall of Tobruk, Rommel was promoted to Field Marshal, though he wrote to his wife that he would have preferred another panzer division.

Since the start of the war the Nazis' seemingly invincible army had never been repulsed. It now appeared that they could conquer anything; Poland, Belgium, the Crimea, much of France, Greece and Yugoslavia, they had laid siege to Leningrad and were marching onto Stalingrad. Along with Singapore, Japan had taken Malaya, Rangoon, Burma, and was poised to invade India. At Pearl Harbor the American Pacific fleet lay in ruins. And in Africa, Rommel was about to take control of the entire Mediterranean, the Suez Canal, and the Persian oil fields. With the Soviets overpowered, Stalin would have little choice but to form a separate peace agreement with Hitler, leaving America allied to a defeated Britain.

On June 22nd, King Abdullah contacted British headquarters in Cairo to discuss possible aid. At the end of the discussion, he inquired about Fred, concerned that his job as driver could now easily prove fatal. A few hours later, he received word that Fred was the driver of the lead tank in the Battle of Knightsbridge, and that his status was unknown. Anyone familiar with King Abdullah would not have found his calm tone reassuring as he reprimanded: "I have asked that this young man be kept off of the front line. You now tell me that he was placed in this most dangerous position of this most disastrous defeat." The Colonel nervously responded to Britain's most important Arab ally: "Apparently, it was at the soldier's insistence. I'm afraid the CO issuing the order was amongst the casualties. We're doing everything in our power to determine the soldier's whereabouts."

The next day King Abdullah was relieved to hear that several landmines had prevented Fred from entering the battle and that his request to continue on the front line had been denied: "We've assigned his tank to the third line." King Abdullah questioned: "And if the first two lines are no longer?" The Colonel soberly responded: "In that case, your Highness, I'm afraid it's the end for all of us."

CHAPTER 30

THOUGH CHEF, MELNICK AND JACK suspected that King Abdullah had a role in placing their tank on the third line, Fred couldn't believe that he would concern himself to that extent with a Jewish private that he barely knew. Having been placed as the lead tank in the battle of Knightsbridge confirmed to Fred that whatever protection King Abdullah had provided at the request of his friends at the Jaffa café, was now over. "We're on the 3rd line because we're the only tank left in our division." Chef raised a skeptical eyebrow, but Fred insisted: "We were sent in to die at Knightsbridge. No one intervened. We're just lucky."

Fred didn't understand that although King Abdullah was a man of science determined to bring his people into the 20th Century, as a religious man he could not overlook that the horse he gave to Haim Arlosoroff in gratitude of their friendship would become the horse of a boy who would take the name Haim, after Arlosoroff, and that this boy would then travel alone to Jaffa to befriend the very men King Abdullah had entrusted with his residency there. It was so implausible that he requested a first meeting to see if the boy had somehow contrived the situation. But King Abdullah was quickly convinced that the boy had no designs, no ulterior motives and in fact wasn't even aware of whose presence he was in. Fred's survival of the Battle of Knightsbridge further convinced King Abdullah that, for whatever reason, this boy had been placed in his life, and he was somewhat responsible for him.

Fred, however, had already witnessed too many lives destroyed, too many children torn from their families, too many butchered young men strewn across the desert to believe in the will of god. He saw his survival as pure luck, which now appeared to be running out. As they watched the convoys of abandoning troops and personnel heading east to put as much distance between themselves and Rommel, it didn't escape Fred, Melnick, Jack and Chef that they were now the ones being left behind to fight to the last man.

British General Neil Ritchie, having commanded the Eighth Army for the last six months, was blamed for the imminent defeat. A captured British officer had the opportunity to see Rommel and Ritchie in action on the same day. While Ritchie had, "thirty aid-de-camps dancing about and an awful lot of paper work. Rommel has two signals vehicles one for outgoing and one for incoming messages. He sits between them in a scout car yapping out orders or writing messages to be transmitted." Though Ritchie may not have been as organized, it seems unfair to put the entire blame of the imminent defeat on his weak command of the Eighth Army. Having started out with more than twice the men and equipment he could have easily cleared the Axis forces out of Africa, had it not been for the decoded transcripts of Bonner Fellers.

On June 25th, Hitler cabled the Italian Army: "Eighth Army practically destroyed ... The historic hour draws near." Mussolini flew to the desert for his triumphant victory parade. With him he brought a military band, 200 cans of black shoe polish for the Italian soldiers boots for the procession, and a mighty white Arabian stallion that he planned to ride through the streets of Cairo for the victory celebration.

That same day, General Ritchie was dismissed and replaced by Field Marshal Sir Claude Auchinleck, Commander and Chief of the Indian Army. Though Auchinleck was a good commander loved by his troops, to stop Rommel now was an overwhelming task for any commander.

June 26: To buy time for his troops to pull back and form a new line, Auchinleck had X Corps (The 10th Indian Infantry Division, 50th Northumbrian Infantry) and XIII Corps (British 7th Armoured Division, Australian 6th Infantry Division, and 4th Indian Infantry Division) make a final stand at Mersa Matruh, the last coastal fortress in Allied possession. After three days and nights of fighting, on June 29, Mersa Matruh fell, giving Rommel 6,000 prisoners, along with more supplies, tanks and arms.

Disorganized and shaken, the remnants of the Eighth Army pulled back 60 miles west of Alexandria, Egypt, to the little coastal desert railway stop of El Alamein. There, the future of the world would be decided.

∞

Having lost most of their armor, Auchinleck chose to make the Eighth Army's last stand where the passage to Cairo narrows to a thirty-eight mile strip; from El Alamein on the Mediterranean coast down to the impassible Qattara Depression (an immense, inhospitable saltpan lying 436 feet below sea level, that no division could cross.)

The northern position at El Alamein was held by South African regiments and covered the coast road and the railway. Indian regiments held the second position, near Deir el Shein. New Zealanders defended the rocky broken ground at Qaret el Abd, and Fred, Melnick, Jack and Chef were sent with Indian regiments to the southern end of the line on the edge of the Qattara Depression.

Knowing that Rommel could attack at any moment, they rushed to build some sort of defense on the high ground overlooking the forbidding depression. About twenty men worked frantically helping them dig in their one tank. With their only gun capable of taking out a Nazi tank, if spotted by Axis forces, the tank would be instantly destroyed.

Exhausted, having worked relentlessly against the clock, to their relief Rommel held off the attack that day. With the soft sand running too much risk of being attacked by scorpions, that night Fred, Melnick, Jack and Chef slept outside on rock slabs by their dug in tank, the closest thing to a home. The convoys that day had little munitions for the 3rd line. Perhaps in consolation they received a mail delivery and cigarettes. With cigarettes viewed as almost legal tender, they saw it as a last wish for the condemned troops.

In the British Army it was customary for the soldiers to read their mail out loud. That night, lying on the rock slabs besides their tank, they smoked cigarettes and listened to each other's letters. Fred always enjoyed hearing from Jack's cousin. The gentleness that he remembered when handing Jack over to her years before was prevalent in her writing. Besides filling Jack in on family and friends, she also kept them abreast of life in Palestine. Not wanting to upset her, Jack's return note mentioned nothing of what he was about to face, only stressing that if Rommel breaks through to Alexandria she must escape to America or someplace outside of the Nazis' reach. The warning was unnecessary. All Jews in Palestine were already in panic of Rommel breaking through.

Fred wondered if Ivan, Avi, the twins and his other enlisted friends from Ben Shemen were aware that the Nazis were about to take the Suez Canal and the Arabian oil fields. With the Germans pushing Russia back, their U-boats starving out Britain, and much of Western Europe under Nazi control, the Afrika Korps would now devastate the Allies supply line, leaving only the long, hazardous route down around the tip of South Africa. The British fleet would have no choice but to abandon the Mediterranean, leaving Malta to fall and turning the sea into an axis lake. Were any of his enlisted friends from Ben Shemen still alive? With Britain's defeat, would there be anyone to stop the murder of the millions of Jews in concentration camps all over Europe and North African? Would that be the end to the Jewish faith?

To get his mind off of it, Fred listened to Melnick's letters from his wife, Sana. She had agreed to check on Amon occasionally, but since he chased her from the barn, it had been over a year since Fred had any word of him. Before Christmas, as the Eighth Army was pushing Rommel's forces back, Fred was unloading supplies on the front when he witnessed the magnificent Indian Cavalry galloping by in the distance. Spotting a black Arabian moving strikingly like Amon, he stared, transfixed, until they disappeared over the dunes. As a horse had little chance against a tank, such sights would soon be gone forever. He regretted that he an Amon weren't allowed to join them, but a few days later he heard that the entire Cavalry had been wiped out by Rommel's troops. Fred consoled himself that at least Amon was back home safe in Palestine.

He continued to receive reassuring letters from Lotte and his Uncle Friedrick. The couple that Lotte and Harry worked for appreciated that their maid and butler also acted as their doctors, and news from Uncle Friedrick assured him that Julius and Klara were still living in their home in Bingen. But both Lotte and Friedrick continued omitting that Julius had been writing Friedrick desperate letters pleading for the equivalent of 1,800 American dollars for Nazis exit visas to Cuba. Lotte and Friedrick tried to raise the money, but it might as well have been a million dollars. Neither would tell Fred. There was nothing he could do, and a soldier on the front already had enough to face.

That night Fred received a letter from Sheila saying that she had met the love of her life, a poet-farmer whose asthma prevented him from entering the war: "I don't want to lead you on, and I know how happy you'll be for me. Enclosed is one of his poems that I thought you'd enjoy." Crumpling up the poem, Fred was about to feed it to the desert when Chef demanded: "Hand it over." Fred reluctantly followed orders. Chef read out loud: "The Imperfection of Beauty: Envied by the world, a rose must have thorns to protect itself..." Knowing that the poem was referring to Sheila, the men's laughter seemed to cheer Fred up. As Chef finished, Melnick conceded, "Pretty heartless letter to send to a soldier on the front." Chef agreed: "Bloody right, good riddance to Sheila. Glad she found her asthma-ridden farmer." They all agreed that Gabriella's sensitive, beautifully written letters were far superior to Sheila's, but Fred was still frustrated that Gabriella would never fully commit. Chef explained: "No bird wants to look older than her fellow. You survive this, no worries. It'll age you ten years, and she's all yours."

"Thanks, Chef. How about reading your letter?" Fred asked. Chef sighed: "Why? It's from me bloody mum." Which meant that it was about her little dog, Elizabeth, named after the princess. When Chef finally wrote to his mother about losing his men in the burning tank, she wrote back: "Elizabeth also had a frightful week." A neighbor had apparently threatened to strangle Elizabeth if she continued barking at him, and an emotionally distraught Elizabeth wet the carpet that evening. According to

Chef, "She always pisses on the rug, but me mum's convinced that it's now 'cause of undue stress."

Along with rationing, at the onset of the war the government issued a pamphlet urging people to kill their family pets. It was a devastating time for a country of animal lovers as parents separated a beloved family member from their children to have them euthanized. As horrible as it was, many considered it their patriotic duty, and in the first week alone 750,000 dogs and cats were slaughtered. Being too difficult for most to even talk about, in time the episode was erased from history.

Chef's mother, unable to murder Elizabeth, refused to comply. To survive, she shared her rations with the little dog. But with so many pets killed and children sent away to the safety of the country, her fears grew that the resentful town's people now had a price on Elizabeth's head. Her battle to protect Elizabeth would grow into an obsession that she believed to share with her son. "Don't know why me daft mum thinks I give a rat's arse. If only the bloody neighbor would feed the bitch some poison and be done with it." Fred warned: "Don't wish that, unless you want your mom to poison the neighbor and end up in prison?" Chef conceded: "She's right daft enough. Know why she named me Claire?" Fred, Melnick and Jack, were too stunned that he brought it up to even respond. "Cause it means 'light'. Me, a bloody twelve-pound baby, and she names me 'light'" Jack offered, "At least she didn't call you Elizabeth." Chef snickered, "Probably 'cause the little princess wasn't born yet. Been called lots of things, but once I got me a job cooking at a local pub, the name 'Chef' stuck." Though pushed to the limits of exhaustion, knowing what they were about to face, sleep came slowly.

Tuesday, June 30: Struggling through the harsh desert heat, they dug ditches, filled sandbags, and fought to keep up morale as the BBC war correspondent announced: "The streets of Cairo are now almost empty ... Navy gone! Alex lost!"

With Rommel so close, the Royal Navy abandoned its base in Alexandria, dispersing its fleet to Haifa and Beirut. Although the BBC announcers presented the El Alamein line as a strongly fortified barrier, the soldiers from the coast down to the Qattara Depression saw the makeshift line as almost indistinguishable from the miles of sand. Reporters who could now drive the short trip out for the day later admitted the badly shaken, dismal state of the Eighth Army as they defended a line that was little more than a widely scattered series of boxes.

Rommel's messages to Berlin of the certain victory were read over German radio. With radio waves heard by all, Fred and Melnick tried to downplay them as they translated for the troops. It would have been better to not hear them at all, but they purposely listened to German radio, hoping for any insight into the enemy. They also wanted to hear Lale Andersen sing what would become the most popular song of WWII, 'Lili Marleen'. Fred always saw Gabriella as he listened to the German lyrics:

"Outside the barracks, by the corner light

I'll always stand and wait for you at night

We will create a world for two

I'll wait for you the whole night through

For you, Lili Marlene

For you, Lili Marlene"

The haunting song transcended language, giving the soldiers a brief respite.

German-Arab radio presented Mussolini as: "the savior and protector of Islam." Adolf Hitler was made relatable to the Egyptians by presenting him, like them, as an ordinary man from a once humiliated nation. Having crushed the French and British imperialists in Europe, Hitler and Rommel would now liberate Egypt from the tyranny of the British elite and save the Arab world from the nefarious plot of a Jewish homeland in Palestine. With the Grand Mufti's constant radio propaganda, the Egyptian army's secret Free Officers Organization, including a young Anwar el Sadat, believed that a Nazi victory would bring them independence. The Muslim Brotherhood urged its member to prepare Molotov cocktails to throw at the British, and a German spy informed Berlin that the Muslim leaders, "planned a reception for Rommel to surpass that of Napoleon's."

Though Fred and the other soldiers were grateful that Rommel had spared them another day, they couldn't help but anxiously wonder why Rommel would wait. Had he attacked immediately, he could have easily broken through. With the Desert Fox seemingly always one step ahead of them, Chef reasoned: "He must have some bloody reinforcements coming in to annihilate us with an all out Nazi blitz."

A sandstorm forced them to take shelter that night in their tank while other soldiers took refuge in their makeshift ditches and pillboxes. The heat inside the crammed tank made it difficult to sleep, but it was better than facing the piercing sand. To fight the heat, Fred imagined that frozen winter in Bingen when he could walk across the Rhine. It made him homesick, but he told himself there was no point. He would never see that world again.

With little sleep, they woke to face the end of Rommel's reprieve. July 1st would become known as 'Ash Wednesday', after the embers of secret British files drifting from the ministry's chimney filled the Cairo sky. Orders to incinerate all classified British documents brought panic in the streets. But not only charred intelligence papers drifted down, the Luftwaffe flew over Cairo dropping facsimiles of pound notes stating in Arabic: "It's not worth even a beggar's time to pick up one of these worthless items."

In Alexandria, German radio broadcast a message to the women: "Get out your frocks, we're on our way!" Italian women prepared a ball while shopkeepers had their Hitler and Mussolini pictures ready in their frames along with red and black Nazi flags to hang outside their shops, some were already hanging. The

Nazis supposedly even had 'victory' postage stamps for Egypt with the portraits of Hitler and Mussolini.

During the Anschluss, Jews were stunned by the number of swastika flags suddenly hanging from the windows as the Nazis paraded through Vienna. Where did they all come from? How long had the Austrians been preparing? It was now believed that the Egyptians would outdo the Austrian's welcome to the Nazis. Citizens yelled at British troops, "Forward Rommel!" Italians waved their flag with pictures of Mussolini. German prisoners taunted the British soldiers: "When Rommel soon rolls through, you'll be our prisoners."

Sir Miles Lampson, the British ambassador, considered by some to be Egypt's true ruler, continued going out publicly. But while at the expensive Mohammad Ali Club, the pro-Nazi Egyptian Prince Abbas Halim stood to loudly toast Rommel's health. Laughing as he added, "Let's hope he does not fall at the last fence."

All British officers were ordered to carry revolvers. A curfew was called for 8pm. Clerks with revolvers replaced fleeing local police or those too afraid to be seen in a British uniform. Abandoned naval stores were looted. German radio announced that the British were retreating in disarray. The British issued an immediate denial, but Cairo roads and trains were flooded with evacuees. With few police, bandit attacks threatened the mass exodus.

Sirens and gunshots rang throughout the night. Hundreds of shell-shocked British and

Commonwealth troops requested sick leave to escape Auchinleck's last stand at El Alamein. When that didn't work, they simply hid or ran. Desertion of Allied troops increased to the point that Auchinleck was asked to reinstate the death penalty for desertion in the face of the enemy. But having been abolished in 1930, Auchinleck turned it down as 'undemocratic.'

Guerillas parachuted into Greece to blow up vital railroad bridges in order to stop Rommel's North African supplies. Many agents there were escaping by train to Palestine but the ones in most danger weren't allowed to join them, as German and Italian Jews working for intelligence as translators and interrogators were barred from entering Palestine because of the British Mandate's control on Jewish immigration.

Dawn reconnaissance flights over the front line reported the Axis to have 1,000 enemy vehicles 15 miles away and moving eastward towards El Alamein. Another 300 were refueling about 20 miles away from Deir el Shein (the upper middle of the line.)

Fred and the other soldiers on the line then received more mail, but this time it came from the sky as German Luftwaffe scattered flyers stating in English: "Single soldiers waving white handkerchiefs are not fired on. Strong German forces have you outnumbered. It is useless trying to escape. You must either surrender or die."

Chef, who had always said, "I'm my only cause," now picked up one of the leaflets sneering: "Should make good toilet paper." His crew was not surprised. They learned to trust his actions more than his words. Having chosen three Jewish soldiers for his tank, making it much more dangerous for him if they were captured, they had been through too much to believe that he would abandon them now. Fred said: "Thanks Chef, you know we love you." Chef snarled back: "Anymore talk like that and I'll be pulling out me bloody white handkerchief."

At the bottom of the El Alamein line, Fred, Melnick, Jack and Chef braced themselves as the enormous dust cloud of two advancing Italian tank cores and multiple divisions loomed towards them. Though clearly outnumbered, there would be no retreat. All Jewish troops also knew that being taken prisoner was not an option. Rommel had hoped that the Allies' defenses would collapse as they had at Mersa Matruh, but the entire line now stood at all cost. As one after another Indian regiment soldiers were killed, others stepped up to take their places behind the guns.

On the Island of Malta the locals had cheered as the sympathetic Italian squadrons had dropped their bombs in the sea and flew away. But now in North Afrika, Italian soldiers fought with equal aggression as the German troops. Breaking through meant winning the war for the Axis and their new Italy. But despite their doggedness, Italian tanks, guns, equipment and training weren't up to German standards. With the Indian regiments dug in on the high ground, they were able to hold, forcing the Italian regiments to finally withdraw without Chef's one tank on the 3rd line ever having to fire a shell.

Along the coast, the powerful German Army devastated the Australian defenses, crushing through late in the day. But coming under heavy fire from three South African brigades they were forced to dig in and the British held along in the north.

In the middle of the line, the 18th Indian infantry Brigade fought desperately throughout the day but by evening were run over by the German tanks. However, their sacrifice bought Auchinleck enough time to bring up defenses, and in combining the remnants of the 18th Indian infantry Brigade with the 1st Armoured Division they held back Rommel's forces.

Chef and his crew were ordered to go up to the fragmented middle of the line, where they spent the night building a new 3rd line of defense, which would again include only their one dug in tank.

July 2nd would see an even more brutal day of battle. Abandoning his planned sweep of the south, Rommel joined his forces to break through the north and middle of the line. By the end of the day, the badly shattered first two lines were down to their last munitions. Had Rommel just pushed a little longer he would have broken through. But the Allies remained concentrated and to their astonishment, Rommel again retreated. Though the line held, with the endless munitions needed for battle, an estimated ten tons per minute, the reserves in

Alexandria were depleted. The majority of the munitions had gone to the 1st line, with the 2nd line getting most of what remained. Over the two days of battle Fred, Melnick, Jack and Chef, ran whatever arms they could to the front lines. With little hope of any more munitions to come, they were down to only six tank shells and one magazine for the tank's machine gun.

Through ULTRA (Alan Turing's group at Bletchley Park who had successfully broken the Nazi's Enigma) British intelligence received word that Rommel planned to deliver an all-out attack the next day along the coast. Chef and his crew were sent north to build a new third line, which would again include only their one dug in tank.

Friday, July 3rd: As the massive tank divisions of Rommel's Afrika Korps advanced toward El Alamein, the Arabic radio station 'Berlin' announced that German and Italian forces were coming to "guarantee Egypt's independence and sovereignty ... to liberate the whole of the Near East from the British yoke." The Grand Mufti went on air to celebrate the Arab nations upcoming freedom from Imperialist Britain and their common enemy, the Jews, by Rommel's "Glorious victory! ... Kill the selfish Jews wherever you find them. This is God's will!" Once Rommel took North Africa, the Grand Mufti prepared to enter Jerusalem as the head of his Muslim Arab Legion squadron of the Third Reich. Near Nablus, Palestine he planned to build a massive Auschwitz-like concentration camp where Jews from Palestine, Iraq, Yemen, Syria, Lebanon and North Africa would be gassed to death.

Fred, Melnick, Jack and Chef stood by their one dug in tank watching the advance of the tremendous dust cloud formed by hundreds of Rommel's tanks. Once almost in range, Chef would have them board the tank and wait for the opportune moment to fire. With only six shells, each one had to count. If lucky, they may take out one tank or two at most. Knowing that any deserters were long gone, and with the enormous line stretching as far the eye could see, the Nazis may have believed that they were facing a formidable foe. But with the first two lines wiped out, what remained were clerks, engineers, secretaries, hospital workers, cooks with knives, mess staff, even patients were released from the hospital to make one last stand against the Nazis. Though they held their guns firmly in the direction of the Germans, few had any bullets. Once Chef gave the order to fire, all would soon be over. Not only would their one tank and crew be quickly obliterated by a barrage of Nazi fire, with fire coming from only one tank Rommel's forces would be alerted to the defenselessness of the entire line.

Fred watched in amazement as Australian soldiers, what remained of the 1st line, took mines in front of their bodies and threw themselves onto German tanks. Though their bravery only slightly slowed down the advance, Fred knew that their turn was next. He told himself that he couldn't complain. At 21 he had lived a rich, full life, and would now end it by trying to stop the Nazis. His biggest regret was ending his life as a virgin. What good did that do him now? He wondered what the other men were thinking as they silently waited. Were they rationalizing their end? Were they praying? Only a miracle could save them now.

When the Nazi tanks began coming into range, Chef said with a final resolve: "Men, it's been an honor." But as they began boarding the tank, they spotted one of the German tanks coming to a stop. Then another. And another. Were they repositioning? Getting stuck in the sand? With other tanks still advancing it didn't make sense.

As more tanks came to a stand still, Chef said in astonishment, "Bloody hell, they're all running outa gas." The 3rd line watched in disbelief as the entire advance came to a stall. Remaining frozen, not daring to move, they waited. The Nazi soldiers only had to abandon their tanks and charge them on foot. Rommel's well armed forces could easily mow them down. But instead of marching over the defenseless 3rd line, driving sixty miles to Alexandria for unlimited gas, taking Egypt, the Suez Canal, the Arabian oil fields, and winning the war by attacking the Soviets on two fronts, the remaining working German tanks turned and retreated, leaving the rest of their tanks abandoned in the sand.

Slowly, cautiously, the line began to relax. Having only one tank and practically no munitions, it was impossible for them to pursue the retreating Axis troops, but accepting that they were somehow spared, the men began to break into cheers. All along the line they celebrated. Chef grabbed Fred in a bear hug: "Okay you dumb Kraut, I'll say it now! I bloody love you, too!" Grabbing Melnick and Jack in the hug, Chef cheered; "The minute I saw this bloke I knew the bloody fool would bring us luck! Gentlemen, from now on, we stick together!"

500 feet from taking El Alamein, Rommel had won the war, but just didn't know it.

CHAPTER 31

THE TRUTH OF ROMMEL'S 'fingertip feel' suddenly going out after burning so brightly at Gazala, Tobruk and Mersa Matruh would have to remain a mystery. Most soldiers on the El Alamein line that day attributed it to inexplicable luck or an act of God. Some even believed that Rommel, suddenly repulsed by Nazi atrocities, chose to lose the war. However, Rommel's letters to his wife expressed continual devastation by his subsequent defeats. When confronted earlier about losing half of his troops at Tobruk, Rommel remarked with indifference: "So what?" Could that same Nazi general suddenly feel more empathy for enemy troops than his own?

Months earlier, Hitler and Mussolini had agreed to postpone an invasion of Egypt until the strategic island of Malta had fallen. Because of Fellers' transcripts, Rommel knew that he had to act fast. On Rommel's insistence Hitler agreed to the invasion.

Just as Rommel's victory seemed certain, on June 27th, 1942, as the Nazis celebrated in Berlin, the Deutschlandsender's 6:00 pm radio broadcast announced: "Tonight we are offering a drama with scenes from the British or American information bureau." German cryptanalysts listened aghast as the radio play featured an actor portraying the U.S. military attaché in Cairo gathering all British military information around the Mediterranean and relaying it to Washington, unaware that it was quickly decoded and in the hands of the Nazis.

How could the prize of Nazi intelligence, what countless Germans had been guarding with their lives, be announced to the world over Nazi controlled German radio? Having brought Germany to the gates of victory, it was unfathomable that Joseph Goebbels would approve of a radio play revealing the Nazis' greatest source of intelligence. However, on June 29th, thirty-six hours later, Rommel's *'fingertip feel'* would end as German intercept operators desperately searched in vain for MILID or AGWAR messages. No more would ever come.

With Fellers' last intercepts pleading for reinforcements: "considerable British panic in Cairo ... The army has been defeated primarily because of the incompetence of its leaders..." Rommel confidently messaged Berlin that victory was soon theirs. But rather than act immediately with the Eighth Army in disarray, Rommel would make the fatal error of waiting for Fellers' usually detailed messages on every aspect of the front. The next day, Rommel still waited, reassured by a transmission from the American Ambassador in Cairo stating that according to Fellers: Rommel will take the delta "unless the British can obtain immediately reinforcements."

On July 1st, with still no word from his 'Good Sources', Rommel saw no choice but to finally attack, hoping for Feller's intercepts to follow. When none did, uncertain of what defenses the Eighth Army had built over the two days, fear seemed to play into the once courageous soldier's every move. Was he now too attached to his godlike status, deserved or not? In ten days he was to be on the cover of Time Magazine. "Heil Rommel" had become a common greeting in Arab Nations. Defeat, being taken prisoner would end the myth.

Each time that he came close to breaking through, he retreated. By July 3rd, after four days with still no word from Fellers, he must have called into question the veracity of Fellers' last intercepts. Had Fellers been aware of the radio play before he wrote them? Were Fellers' last messages a trap to pull the Desert Fox into a well-reinforced line? If Rommel bought into his myth, he would then view his capture as one of the greatest British coups. At the critical moment, with many of his tanks running out of gas as they approached a defenseless 3rd line, too fearful to go forward, he turned back.

A week later, on the night of July 10th, while Rommel waited for reinforcements, Australian troops broke through to German Radio Intercept unit, Kompanie 621, killing its commander, Captain Alfred Seebohm, and capturing 73 of his men. Rommel was furious. Whatever grief he felt over the loss of Captain Seebohm was apparently overshadowed by his fury at losing what remained of his 'fingertip feel'.

Along with the German radio equipment, the British discovered a treasure trove of documents exposing the shocking full extent of Fellers' damage. As stated: "Stupefying in its openness," providing Rommel with "the broadest and clearest picture of enemy forces and intentions available to any Axis commander throughout the war."

With the exposure of the Nazis deciphering the Black Book, and Alan Turing's group at Bletchley Park successfully breaking Germany's Enigma code, the intelligence war took a dramatic shift. Rommel continued struggling to break through at El Alamein until early November, but with little intelligence he finally had no choice but to finally withdraw.

Rommel then received orders from Hitler to fight to the last man and last bullet. Though he had mocked General Ritchie: "What is the advantage of enjoying overall superiority if you allow your enemy to smash your formations one after another?" Without his 'good source' Rommel's superior forces were now pushed back over 1,200 miles into Tunisia. Almost trapped by the Eighth Army, he ignored Hitler's order to "Stand and Die" and ordered the Italian divisions to fight to the last man, allowing him enough time to escape.

Though from early on Rommel had been a devout follower of Hitler, he now lost confidence in a leader who would kill off his generals, especially when he was one of the generals. After Rommel greatly miscalculated the landing of the invasion of Normandy, losing Northern France, he became one of 4,980 implicated in a plot to kill Hitler, including three Nazi field marshals and nineteen Nazi generals. Some, on Hitler's request, were slowly strangled with piano wire. To avoid being executed as a traitor and having his family sent to a concentration camp, Rommel agreed to suicide by cyanide pill.

To cover up that German resistance had undermined the Nazis winning the war, that the Nazi victories in North

Africa were due to the breaking of the Black Code, and that their most celebrated general had betrayed Hitler, the Nazis had to continue the Rommel myth. Spreading word that the Desert Fox had died of either a heart attack or cerebral embolism due to injuries suffered from an earlier car accident, Rommel was given a Nazi hero's funeral. Streets in Germany still bare Rommel's name, as does the military base, Rommel-Kasernes, and a Rommel memorial overlooks his home town of Heidenheim an der Brenz.

Because of US and British officials' belief that the Black Code was unbreakable, 75,000 Allied soldiers needlessly died in North Africa from May to July of 1942 alone. With the people of England suffering constant bombings and strict rationing, the British government already feared a revolt. The senseless death of so many of their sons, bothers, fathers and husbands could easily have been the last straw.

To cover up the incalculable damage done by Bonner Fellers, London and Washington also had no choice but to continue the Rommel myth. To deflect suspicion from Fellers' swift removal from Cairo, Fellers was awarded the Distinguished Service Medal, promoted to Brigadier-General and sent to the Pacific as military secretary under General Douglas McArthur. Though the War Department never exposed the truth, word trickled down to a select few. On hearing Fellers' name mentioned at a Cairo dinner party, Dwight D. Eisenhower stated: "Any friend of Bonner Fellers is no friend of mine."

Churchill was magnanimous, saying nothing, accusing no one. He simply allowed the Fellers disaster to hang in the air. Despite the Japanese bombing of the American fleet in Pearl Harbor on December 7, 1941, the United States sent its first major ground troops to North Africa along with 300 hundred Sherman tanks, the best tanks of the time.

∞

Had it not been for that radio play, history books may now be filled with Nazi victories, British atrocities to the Arabs, and how England lost the war due to the corruption of its ruling elite and one foolish American attaché.

But history is written by the victors.

Considering Goebbels obsession with censorship and propaganda it seems unlikely that through sheer stupidity the radio play made its way on air at that opportune moment. But if the producers of the play were part of the underground while working side by side with Goebbels, as had animator Hans Fischerkoesen, they would have access to privileged information. With phone lines tapped and mail censured, switching radio plays at the last minute may have been their only hope of alerting the Allies to the source of the leak.

When the Gestapo finally caught members of 'The White Rose' (a resistance group of students and their teacher distributing anti-Nazi pamphlets in Germany during WWII) all were beheaded except one last young woman who was about to be tried and executed when the American's broke through in 1945. Had she not been saved, they would have all been erased from history. But with her survival, their identities are known and statues stand in their honor. In the summer of 1942, there would be no Allied troops marching in to save the producers of the radio play.

By switching radio plays in what appears to be a desperate, courageous act, the producers had to know that they were not only giving their lives, but would be erased from history and never acknowledged for their extraordinary sacrifice.

On the evening of July 3rd, Fred and the other soldiers listened in disbelief to BBC radio announcing that British defenses were far too strong for Rommel to break through the El Alamein line. Though stunned by the incredible distortion, they also quickly understood the importance of hiding the truth from the Nazis. There was no choice but to greatly exaggerate their strength, while Rommel would have to underestimate his to deflect blame from his faulty leadership.

Though it would go down on record that Rommel was left with only 26 working tanks, a first hand account tells of 50 Axis tanks alone with 5,000 infantry breaking through the center of the line that day. Shortly after breaking through, they tapped a newly laid 6-inch water pipe, too parched to notice that it was being tested for leaks with saltwater (fresh water being a precious a commodity in the desert.) The almost defenseless British line watched in amazement as the tanks and soldiers turned, and with their hands in the air, their parched, swollen tongues cracked and black from coagulated blood, lumbered back to the British side for fresh water. Had they not tapped that water pipe, they would have been extremely thirsty, but would have probably made it to Alexandria.

Though Fred and the other soldiers of the 3rd line witnessed several hundred Nazi tanks advancing on them that day, to say or do anything that might reveal to the Nazis their utter weakness was viewed as an act of treason. Most never spoke of it until after the war. By then the rewritten history had been accepted as fact.

 To the producers of the radio play, and to all those who gave or risked their lives in slowing down Rommel forces, from North Africa to the enormous Russian front, the world is forever in your debt.

∞

For Fred, surviving the Battle of El Alamein had changed him. Accepting death in the face of an unprecedented evil, he viewed what time he now had as a gift. It was not to be wasted. From that day forward he would become the best soldier possible to help bring an end to the Nazi regime.

THE END

Part 1

THE STOLEN MEDAL

DNW AUCTION HOUSE

In April, 2006, I sat with my father, Fred Hausman, on his deathbed as he asked only one thing of me: "Make sure you get my medals. They're important, especially the DCM." We knew there was no rush. In the 1950's he had corresponded with the British Ministry of Defense (MoD) and was told that his Distinguished Conduct Medal (DCM) was to be given to him by the King or Queen of England in a special ceremony, but that he could get his medals at anytime throughout his life and his family could get them anytime after that. In 1996, when making my first trip to London, he asked me to look into getting his medals. While there, the MoD told me over the phone that my father would first have to fill out a lot of paper work but that his medals were as safe there as in a bank, and confirmed that he, or his family after his death, could get them at anytime.

In fall 2004, I made a video of my father telling his story. He resisted, saying: "No one cares about that." But I pointed out: "If you could hear your grandparents telling their story, wouldn't you want to?" He had to admit that he would, and for 4 hours I recorded him telling his story. 3 ½ hours into it he spoke of his DCM saving his life in Palestine when he was arrested, for reasons he would never know, by British authorities in 1946. On the video he states very clearly that he, "never actually got the DCM, only the ribbon for it." 4 ½ minutes into the following video posted by Einat Amitay:

https://www.youtube.com/watch?v=_aGrOgKPZok&t=322s

In 2014, when finally looking into getting his medals I was then shocked to find this online:

https://www.dnw.co.uk/auction-archive/special-collections/lot.php?specialcollection_id=1&lot_id=199791

Lot 756, 18 May 2011   Dix Noonan Webb   DNW

THE BILL AND ANGELA STRONG MEDAL COLLECTION

Estimate: £6,000 – £7,000   Sold for £11,000

A very rare Second World War Commando operations D.C.M. awarded to Lance-Corporal F. S. Houseman, Royal Army Service Corps, attached No. 2 Commando, a very gallant German-Jew who had earlier served in the "Palestine Brigade" prior to winning his decoration and being twice wounded in No.. 2 Commando.

Distinguished Conduct Medal, G.VI.R. (PAL. 1344 L. Cpl. F. S. Houseman, R.A.S.C.), *minor official correction to unit, edge bruise, good very fine £6000-7000*

Footnote

D.C.M. London Gazette 20 July 1944. The original recommendation - submitted by Lieutenant-Colonel J.M. T. F. "Mad Jack" Churchill, D.S.O., M.C. - states:

'In the Commando raid on Brac Island on the night of 5 March 1944, Driver Hausmann was the leading scout of the section which carried out this raid. The section was seen approaching and two sentries opened fire with schmeiser automatics which pinned them to the ground. Driver Hausmann dashed forward firing his T.S.M.G. and killed one sentry, but the other ran into the house. Hausmann followed, kicked open the door and threw in a hand grenade. When it exploded, he dashed in shouting to the Germans to surrender, and having killed one and wounded two more, the remaining five men gave themselves up.

On the morning of 19 March during the Commando attack on Solta Island, the behaviour of this man was exemplary. In the forefront of the final assualt on the village, he led a small group of men in house-clearing in an area where the German garrison was holding out, and during this operation severely wounded a German who was holding up the advance with a Spandau M.G. which was mounted in an upper window.

Driver Hausmann is a Palestinian of German origin serving in the Commando. He has taken part in three Commando raids in these islands during the last six weeks, and in each of these his behaviour has been outstandingly bold and aggressive. He insists on being the leading scout on all approaches by day or night and is not content to await his tum for this duty. He has set a magnificent example and his conduct under fire is in the highest traditions of the Army.'

Fritz Sigmund Hausmann (a.k.a. Fred Stanley Houseman) was born in Germany, the son of a Wermacht officer. His mother was Jewish and, like her husband, detested the Nazi movement, sentiments that would ultimately result in their arrest by the Gestapo and early demise in a concentration camp. Their son, however, managed to escape the net and make his way to Palestine, where he joined the Haganah organisation, which guarded Jewish settlements against the Arabs.

A well-educated man, who was fluent in English, German, Italian and Yiddish, Houseman made no secret of the fact he hated the British, but since he 'hated the Germans a hell of a lot more', he enlisted in No. 650 Company, R.A.S.C., a component of the "Palestine Brigade", around its formation in November 1942 - a unit whose members openly wore "Star of David" uniform insignia and were accordingly executed on the spot if captured. He did, however, change his name by deed poll to 'Houseman' and adopted a cover story that he was British and from Manchester, facts that appear to have been lost on those responsible for the publication of his name in the London Gazette at the time of his D.C.M. - in the name of Hausmann - an error compounded by the fact the accompanying recommendation had clearly been endorsed, 'No publicity to be given to this citation'.

Having served in North Africa, and survived the sinking of his troop ship, he went on to participate in the Salerno landings in September 1943, but in early 1944 he transferred to No. 2 Commando, a unit of Force 133, charged with holding the island of Vis in the Adriatic, and with mounting regular raids against neighbouring islands off the coast of Yugoslavia.

Thereafter, as vividly outlined in the recommendation for his D.C.M., he displayed notable gallantry in several such Commando raids, his transparent aggression probably only being matched by the likes of his C.O., Lieutenant-Colonel J.M. T. F. "Mad Jack" Churchill, D.S.O., M.C., the sword brandishing, bow and arrow marksman who had recently been recommended for the V.C. in the Sicily operations, or for that matter the Commando's adopted figurehead. 71-year-old Admiral Sir Walter Cowan. Bt., K.C.B., D.S.O., M.V.O., a very ferocious character indeed. A good summary of the events surrounding the raid on the Island of Solta on 19 March 1944, in which Houseman excelled himself again in "house-clearance duties", is to be found in the recommendation for the Bar to "Mad Jack" Churchill's D.S.O.:

'On 19 March 1944. Lieutenant-Colonel Churchill, who commands No. 2 Commando, lead a combined force of Commandos and U.S. Operation Groups in an attack on the German Garrison of Solta Island. The sea approach was made in darkness and disembarkation was completed by 0200 hours. Lieutenant-Colonel Churchill led his heavily laden H.Q. in its rendezvous overlooking the town of Grohote where the enemy garrison was known to be located. The advance was difficult and slow, over rocky ground intersected by walls and piles of stones, and the guides called many halts because of suspected enemy machine-gun posts on the route. Whenever necessary, Lieutenant-Colonel Churchill went forward alone to investigate and when necessary to pick an alternative route. Enemy fire was opened at 0530 hours, by which time the Commandos had surrounded the town. An air bombing attack had been arranged at 0630 hours and the Commandos assault on the town was to follow this bombing ... At 0630 hours the bombing attack by aircraft was carried out, and immediately it was completed the Colonel gave the order to fix bayonets and enter the town. He himself led the advance and directed the house to house searches and street clearance in the face of enemy automatic fire and hand grenades which were thrown from windows and doors. The entire German garrison, consisting of an officer and 108 ranks, was either killed or captured, the Commando party led by the Colonel himself capturing 34 Germans including the Garrison Commander.'

Nor was the last of Houseman's operational outings with No. 2 Commando, his service record revealing that he was wounded by a Spandau bullet in Yugoslavia in April 1944 and by shell and grenade fragments in Albania in August 1944.

Described by one contemporary as something of a loner - and more of the guerilla fighter mould than a regular team-player - Houseman was not very popular with his fellow Commandos, although his courage in battle was undoubtedly appreciated by his C.O. Perhaps as a result of this ongoing unpopularity with his fellow ranks, Houseman returned to duty with the "Palestine Brigade" in August 1944, this time as a despatch rider. Taking his discharge in Italy after the war, he briefly returned to Palestine before settling back 'among dubious friends' in the former country. Little more is known of him, although the fact his D.C.M. first appeared for sale in Los Angeles many years ago suggests he may have emigrated to the U.S.A.

Sold with several letters from ex-members of No. 2 Commando, one of these correspondents adding a great deal of background to Houseman's wartime career, together with hand written service details.

Ex. Dix Noonan Webb. 22 September 2006 {Lot 67), as part of the Ron Penhall Collection.

∞

It seemed impossible. Was the medal a fake? The MoD had assured me personally that his medals "were as safe there as in a bank." Only days before his death, my father told me that he had been talking with the MoD trying to get his medals along with a British military funeral. Sam Ballad, the artist my father was mentoring to replace him as Artistic Director of GAF Corp, remembers hearing him on multiple phone calls with the MoD trying to get his medals: "so my grandchildren can have them." Phone records should confirm that.

Since the MoD knew that my father wanted his medals and they were undoubtedly notified of his death, (as Sam Ballard's uncle, working in the British Embassy in Washington DC, was trying to help my father get a military funeral and his medals) wouldn't they have notified him if his DCM was missing? I now don't believe that it was missing, but alerted of his death thieves within the MoD stole the

DCM and laundered it through DNW's auction of the Ron Penhall collection.

In the auction listing, I was immediately struck by the falseness of the second to last paragraph:

> "Described by one contemporary as something of a loner - and more of the guerilla fighter mould than a regular team-player - Houseman was not very popular with his fellow Commandos, although his courage in battle was undoubtedly appreciated by his C.O. Perhaps as a result of this ongoing unpopularity with his fellow ranks, Houseman returned to duty with the "Palestine Brigade" in August 1944, this time as a despatch rider. Taking his discharge in Italy after the war, he briefly returned to Palestine before settling back 'among dubious friends' in the former country. Little more is known of him, although the fact his D.C.M. first appeared for sale in Los Angeles many years ago suggests he may have emigrated to the U.S.A."

I don't believe that anyone who knew my father could have ever described him as an unpopular guerrilla fighter, especially a fellow commando. Whatever his flaws, he was known for his outgoing, generous and kind nature. His funeral was standing room only with countless people from every walk of life giving testimonials of how much he had gone out of his way to help them. One friend in Israel kept till his death a Haggadah that my father illustrated while in the Eighth Army so that the Jewish troops would be able to have their Passover Seder. Is that the action of an unpopular guerrilla fighter? It also goes completely against the Commando Code. To quote WWII Commando, Peter Masters, from his autobiography, STRIKING BACK:

'Very simple criteria came into play when choosing men for a patrol, "How about Bill?"

"Bill is all right" was an understated solid endorsement. Bill knows his stuff, and if anything happens to you, he won't abandon you if humanly possible. He'll carry you in or hasten to get help. Your life could depend on the three words, "Bill is all right."

Or there was the reply, "Bill is no good," which clearly meant the opposite of the above. This may sound harsh and brusquely judgmental. It had to be. Your life may depend on it.

Or there was the third answer: "I don't know about Bill." This meant I've never been out there with him, or only once, uneventfully. It's too soon to tell. Be careful and alert.'

Would my father's CO, Lieutenant Jack Churchill, known for being loved by his troops, have an unpopular-loner-guerrilla-fighter lead every mission? Who would volunteer? These men were like brothers. They had to know that my father would give his life for theirs or they never would have trusted him to lead. In Yugoslavia Jack Churchill had my father learn Croatian so that they could communicate with the allies. Would Jack Churchill have an unpopular guerrilla fighter doing all of their communications? And of all of these heroic Commandos why would he recommend an unpopular guerrilla fighter for the highest possible honor?

When my father was critically wounded by Nazi fire in Albania, his fellow Commandos carried him down to the beach. He remembers them crying over him, tears running from their eyes as they told him, "You did it Fred. You bought the ticket." Meaning: even if you don't walk again, you'll live. They were right. Several weeks later they were all killed in battle. With his fellow Commandos dead who is this 'one contemporary'? What is his name, rank and serial number?

Reducing my father to an unpopular-guerrilla fighter is almost equally insulting to Jack Churchill, who took extreme care in the protection of his troops; avoiding them being photographed, keeping their names out of the papers for heroic deeds so that the Nazis wouldn't target them, etc. Though the Nazis were taking no prisoners, Jack Churchill survived because the Nazis thought that they had captured Winston Churchill's son, and Jack Churchill allowed them believe it. He would then become connected to the three men to escape from Sachsenhausen Concentration Camp (the basis for the Steve McQueen movie "THE GREAT ESCAPE.) My father, through sheer determination and 26 operations, did walk again.

DNW Auction House and Lord Michael Ashcroft have so far refused to show any of the paperwork connected with the DCM, but Lord Ashcroft did not include 'one contemporary' in his four-page write-up of my father, which further implies that he never existed.

I can only imagine that turning my father into an unpopular-guerrilla-fighter-serial killer alleviated some of the guilt in laundering his stolen medal.

> "Perhaps as a result of this ongoing unpopularity with his fellow ranks, Houseman returned to duty with the 'Palestine Brigade' in August 1944, this time as a despatch rider. Taking his discharge in Italy after the war, he briefly returned to Palestine before settling back 'among dubious friends' in the former country."

Whoever fabricated this now not only felt the need to degrade my father, but also any possible friends, as if only 'dubious' people could have anything to do with him. Other than what is in my father's discharge records, this again is all false. He did not "briefly" return to Palestine, he remained there until 1948. From Palestine he went directly to New York City, never returning to Italy until a family vacation in 1970 when we spent 4 days with Gabriella Morrisini, a beautiful English professor at the University in Bologna. He was very much in love with Gabriella and wanted to marry her. I believe she felt the same for him, but circumstances of the war kept them apart. Is Gabriella one of the 'dubious' friends DNW Auction House is referring to?

> "Little more is known of him, although the fact his D.C.M. first appeared for sale in Los Angeles many years ago suggests he may have emigrated to the U.S.A."

According to Michael Naxton, the curator of the Ashcroft collection, there is no 'fact' of any sale before the auction in September 2006, five months after my father's death. DNW Auction House has refused to show any provenance for the DCM, claiming client confidentiality, but what confidentiality could be broken by supporting statements made public in their auction listing? I believe that if there were any legitimate provenance before my father's death, DNW Auction House would anxiously produce it.

RAY SWAN OF SCOTLAND YARD

Ray Swan of Scotland Yard, the detective in charge of the investigation, has refused to report the DCM as stolen because of a "1948" date stamped on 'despatch' card and a very improbable letter that he apparently has never even asked to see. Though it is of utmost importance that the MoD keep accurate records so that there can be no confusion as to whether or not a war hero received his medals, Ray Swan admits in his email of 11/18/14:

> "Neither card are completed correctly, a fact the MOD point-out themselves. Apparently each card should have clear date / details of either the award ceremony with the King at which the medal was issued or details of the postal address the decorations were issued to via despatch."

Ray Swan is also aware that there is no application from my father for any of his WW2 medals as the MoD admits:

> "The Service Records for Mr Hausmann revealed that he had not previously applied for his Second World War Medals. If the Next of Kin wishes to apply for these awards they still can by printing, completing and signing the attached form."

We now have all of my father's other medals. Ray Swan also knows that there is absolutely no indication that the medal ever left the MoD, that my father never received any of his other medals, that there is no bill of sale from my father, in fact no sale of any kind until the 2006 auction, and that there is a 2004 video of my father stating clearly that he never got his DCM. Since there is no fraudulent application for the medal by someone pretending to be my father, wouldn't the prime suspects then be those guarding the medal from within the MoD?

How then are the prime suspects exonerated by a date stamped on a dispatch card that they could have easily stamped themselves? Does that stamp show anything other than that the medal was struck?

Even the name on the medal is wrong. My father only used the name 'Houseman' to avoid my being killed if caught by the Nazis. His fellow Commandos were then to say that he was Freddy Houseman, a Christian from Manchester, England. He never legally changed his name to 'Houseman', as shown by his discharge records, and I know that 'Fred Hausman' was the name he wanted on his DCM. He would have accepted Fritz Sigmund Hausmann, his legal name, but never 'Houseman'. The thieves apparently read Jack Churchill's citation, and although Jack Churchill was telling the truth to the best of his ability he was mistaken on that point.

Ray Swan also appears to base the entire provenance of the medal on one supposed letter that he was only told of in a conversation with DNW Auction House, the prime suspect in laundering the medal. According to his email of 1/18/14:

> "I have also taken the time to speak to a Director of the Auction firm Dix Noonan Webb who held the first 2006 Auction. Although they do not have a record of where Ron Penhall originally bought

the medal (recollection only is somewhere in the USA) they do have correspondence dated 1988 in which Ron Penhall made an enquiry with them in regard to this medal."

If this was only a phone call, is nothing in writing? Is it only Ray Swan's word against DNW Auction House whether this conversation even took place? And if they did make that statement, shouldn't Ray Swan be aware that DNW Auction House overtly lied in the auction listing by stating: "the fact his D.C.M. first appeared for sale in Los Angeles many years ago..."?

What fact? Why would Ron Penhall write to DNW in 1988 inquiring about a medal without mentioning that he acquired it? What would this strange letter have said? And why would he take the time writing to inquire about the medal in 1988 while writing absolutely nothing of its provenance in 2006 when he was supposedly selling the medal?

Michael Naxton, the curator for the Ashcroft collection (where the stolen medal now resides) admits in his email of 2/12/15:

"I have now been able to carefully examine all the paperwork which accompanied the medals when we purchased them and I regret to say that there is no reference whatsoever to any auction sale in the USA in the 1960s. The only sale mentioned was the much more recent London auction in 2006 and this leaves the trail cold I fear."

As Ron Penhall's widow, brother and daughter will testify, Ron Penhall was known for his integrity and being meticulous about provenance. This is evidenced by the rest of his collection. He travelled all over the world meeting with the war heroes to find out everything he could about the medals in his collection; why they had to sell them, and helping them if needed. Since he lived on the west coast of Canada it seems extremely unlikely that he was laundering stolen medals for a crime ring within the MoD. Who could believe that a serious medal collector like Ron Penhall would acquire my father's DCM without keeping any record of the dealer, pawnshop, auction house, lot #, date, etc.?

Would Ron Penhall acquire my father's DCM somehow, somewhere, sometime in Los Angeles in the 1980's, discard all provenances and wait until 5 months after my father's death to sell his entire collection? Ron Penhall, an elderly Canadian, now passed away, made it clear that it would be too upsetting for him to attend the auction of his enormous collection. What better auction to then launder the stolen DCM?

Why would Ray Swan not even question DNW Auction House for not demanding any provenance in writing? Wouldn't any reputable dealer require that? Was it not suspicious that DNW would save a letter from 1988 but ask for nothing in writing when actually auctioning the medal? Is it plausible that Ron Penhall would even ask DNW Auction House to sell a single gallantry medal without its group of medals and absolutely no provenance? Is there no legal, if not ethical, obligation on DNW's part to make sure that they aren't selling stolen goods?

With my father recently deceased, it would have taken little to contact my family by easily finding his obituary online. Since provenance is so critical with medals, wouldn't DNW want to at least protect themselves by doing that? The fact that they asked for nothing in writing from Ron Penhall convinces me that it was never in the Ron Penhall collection, only laundered through it.

If any other medals with absolutely no provenance were sold through the Ron Penhall collection, I believe that they will also prove to have never actually been in Ron Penhall's collection.

Stunned by Ray Swan's refusal to pursue the case now that he knew there was no legal provenance for the DCM and so much evidence proving that my father never received it, I immediately emailed back on 11/18/2014 telling him that he was leaving us "little choice but to get legal representation..." Ray Swan responded on 11/19/14:

> "As you know I have spent considerable time on this matter. It was always going to be difficult to establish exactly what has happened due to the time that has elapsed. The failure of your father to collect his own medals in his lifetime is also odd. I have found no evidence whatsoever to support your claims of a conspiracy by the Ministry of Defence in this matter. Infact I have found the staff at SO3 Honours & Awards to be dedicated to their role & very concerned to assist ex-servicemen, as you would expect ...
>
> Regards 'vague references' the Auction house DNW state they have written correspondence from Ron

> Penhall that he was in possession of your father's medal in 1988. I think you will find when you take legal representation that this length of time has implications regards proving civil good title of ownership of the medal both on behalf of Ron Penhall and subsequent owners in the UK & presumably in Canada where Ron lived."

Since Ray Swan claims to "have spent considerable time on this matter" why would he not take the time to ask to see this extremely critical, improbable letter, the only apparent evidence implying any sort of provenance before my father's death? Why was this crucial letter not scanned into a computer and included with the medal's other papers? Why would Ray Swan wholeheartedly believe the words of the prime suspects in laundering my father's DCM? As far as: "SO3 Honours & Awards to be dedicated to their role & very concerned to assist ex-servicemen," I believe their dismissive emails and complete disregard to the evidence shows the opposite.

Most importantly, why would Ray Swan want us to believe that going to lawyers would be futile? Obviously, that was a lie, but how else to interpret:

> "I think you will find when you take legal representation that this length of time has implications regards proving civil good title of ownership of the medal both on behalf of Ron Penhall and subsequent owners in the UK & presumably in Canada where Ron lived."

I emailed Ray Swan informing him of the law: "A thief cannot pass good title (no matter how many subsequent owners buy in good faith)." I also asked Ray Swan to site the law he was referring to where "a stolen object goes to the last one to buy it without legal provenance if it has been passed around a lot and stolen a really long time ago."

After sending the email twice, Ray Swan still did not respond. In a later email informing Ray Swan that the DCM was in Lord Ashcroft's collection, and that Lord Ashcroft's curator admits that there is no provenance for the medal before the auction of 2006, Ray Swan emailed on 2/16/2015 "...my investigation in to this matter has now ceased."

After many requests, Ray Swan still refuses, without explanation, to produce this supposed 1988 Ron Penhall letter, which again convinces me that the letter not only doesn't exist, but that it could never have existed because the medal was never in Ron Penhall's collection.

In his email of 11/18, 2014 Ray Swan states:

> "Clearly I cannot investigate a crime where the offence, if it did take place, occurred in 1945 & 1948."

Since Ray Swan questions whether there was even an offense, I call on him to explain his theory of the scheme my father must have devised for his family to somehow get his DCM after his death without having to buy it back from the rightful owner?

His first step must have been in 1948 when the MoD could not have suspected that inserted within all of the documents he had sent to get his DCM were hidden codes that would hypnotize them into throwing away all of these documents, make them forget to fill out the Medal card, and stamp the card without any indication of where the medal was sent, thus making it appear that the DCM was stolen from within the MOD. After getting his DCM at the height of the Arab/Jewish Palestinian war, he then sold it to a pawnshop, only realizing afterwards that he forgot to get his other medals so that they could be sold as an entire group for seven times the amount. Perhaps then hiding in a sarcophagus, late at night he retrieved his signed bill of sale, because as Ray Swan had said early on, provenance with medals is critical.

In the early 1950s, by making my mother believe that he had corresponded with the MOD about getting his medals, and then pretending that the correspondence had fizzled out, my father brilliantly set the stage for the crime he could posthumously carry out in 2014. After the early 1950s he then waited, biding his time, until May of 1996, when I made my first trip to London. By casually asking me to look into getting his medals I would have no idea that he was artfully instilling in me the belief that he never actually got his DCM. Just as my father hoped, I was told that he would have to first fill out a lot of forms, but we needn't worry, they were as safe there as in a bank. He then patiently waited until April of 2006, shortly before his death, to write to the MOD about his medals and also ask my sister and me to make sure that we get them. It was a deviously clever scheme.

Of course that doesn't explain why he didn't just steal the medal back with the bill of sale, and why he never applied for any of his other medals, but who can understands the twisted mind of an unpopular guerrilla fighter?

I actually believe that early on Ray Swan genuinely wanted to know the truth, as he stated in his email of 10/17/14: "Provenance is important and with medals critical..." But his attitude seemed to shift after discovering that there was no provenance and no justification for the medal to have left the MoD.

How does a Scotland Yard detective specializing in stolen arts and antiquities not know the law? Other than a signed confession from the thieves, what will it take for Ray Swan to admit that beyond reasonable doubt my father's DCM was never in his possession and removed improperly from the MoD?

It's curious that in this whole scenario what stands out as odd to Ray Swan is that my father never got his medals in his lifetime. Ray Swan apparently feels it's appropriate to blame the victim. Though I had explained it to him in several emails, and will go into greater detail here.

In 1945, after losing almost everything; his parents, his home, most of his friends, he started over in Palestine. Needing to conserve what little money he had, he could not afford a trip to London to receive his medals. He was given a job as an art director in a new kibbutz-publishing house. He told them that he was only self-taught and unqualified, but because he was a war hero they insisted on him taking the job. It didn't pay much, but he loved art and was lucky to have any job. Few people realize how difficult life in

Palestine was after WW II. For the next three years he worked hard to survive, making a trip to London for his medals was out of the question. He remained in Palestine until 1948, when he went to New York City to be with his sister.

What little money he had went to starting his new life in America. Again, a detour to London was out of the question. He found a low-paying job in New York City, took night courses at Pratt institute of art, and met my mother in 1949. They married and lived in a small, five-story walk-up. Perhaps Ray Swan finds it odd that he didn't drop everything then to take an ocean liner to London for his medals.

Before graduating, he was able to find a job in an ad agency. Being talented, resourceful and extremely hard working, he became successful as a commercial artist. My mother remembers that in the early 50's he then had correspondence with someone in London about getting his medals, probably at the MoD. The correspondence fizzled out, but he was assured that the medals were completely safe and would be waiting for him or his family after his death. Perhaps he should have had the medals sent to him, but that would have meant foregoing the royal ceremony, and I believe a part of him always wanted that.

Though my father became successful, he was extremely generous. As a result, he saved very little. Our first trip to Europe was in 1970 when my mother began working as a librarian and paid for it out of her salary. They discussed going to London for his medals, but decided that it was more important to show my sister and me where we came from in Germany and Austria. My father also wanted to visit Gabriella in Italy and Tito in Yugoslavia, whom he had known through King Abdullah. Tito had saved his life while he was a Commando. His medals would again have to wait.

Perhaps Ray Swan also finds it odd that a year later my father divorced my mother; an intelligent, caring, beautiful woman, especially since it made it financially more difficult for him to get his medals. He then worked for himself running a small commercial art business. With no paid vacation, he rarely took any time off.

In the 1990's the commercial art world was quickly shifting to computers. Many of his associates retired and he lost most of his business. Not having saved enough to retire, he later admitted that it was the most terrifying point in his career. He was in his 70's and had to start all over. But he was a fighter. He worked hard to learn computers and by incessantly making the rounds for work he got a few small jobs from GAF Corp. They were so impressed that at age 76 he became their artistic director. Because of his age, they could only hire him as a consultant, which meant hourly pay with no benefits, but with the long hours it was a well paying job. At his funeral his boss from GAF said that he had never seen anyone work so hard at any age. His commute was 1 ½ hour drive each way. He was first to arrive, the last to leave, and he always brought work home. He again took few vacations and never did make it to England, but he truly loved that job and his team there became like a second family to him.

On Friday, 5 days before his 85th birthday, he drove to work as usual. He had been diagnosed with lung cancer and given only 6 months to live, but he had just started an experimental drug that could possibly give him 1 ½ years. Having a bad reaction to the drug, he drove home early that Friday. The next day he checked into the hospital and he died the following Monday.

We were able to spend that last weekend together. He was fully conscious, and as I've said, the only thing he asked of me was to make sure that I get his medals, especially the DCM. We have his correspondence showing that he was in the process of getting his medals, so no one should assume that they weren't important to him.

If he hadn't been led to believe that they were as safe there as in a bank he would have made sure to have gotten them. The only reason I didn't try to get them earlier is because I would never sell them and the MoD had also led me to believe that having them there was the safest place to keep them for my father's grandchildren. After giving so much and asking for so little I am determined to honor my father's last wish.

My father did not care about getting the medal for himself. He rarely talked about the war. Perhaps Ray Swan finds it odd that he wouldn't want a constant reminder of a nightmare that few could imagine; his parents murdered, his fellow commandos almost all slaughtered, seeing his best friend, Johnny, a British cop, flying through the air with his legs blown off.

When I was a child I asked him why he was a war hero. He simply shrugged: "I was just lucky." That was true, but I took it on face value, unaware that there was so much more to it. I had never seen him fight. He never spanked us, which was common back then. His fights were for peace; the civil rights movement, protesting the Vietnam War. He fought with his art. He created some of the most popular anti-war posters of the time such as, "Suppose They Gave A War And Nobody Came". I believe that the proceeds went to anti-war organizations.

It wasn't until I was in my early twenties that I had any idea what he was capable of. One Sunday when I went to my father's and Stepmom's for our weekly dinner I was taken aback seeing his left eye black-and-blue and looking as if he'd been beaten up. I asked what happened and my stepmom sternly said: "You're dad got into a fight." He then told me that on his commuter train home three football players for the NY Jets had been yelling out racial slurs. Bigotry being a particularly sore spot to him, and seeing all of the other passengers nervously keeping their heads down, he went to the three football players to ask them to stop.

One said, "Who's gonna make us." My father said, "I guess I will, if I have to." When three football players attacked a man in his late-fifties, they probably didn't expect that he would put all three of them into the hospital. All three were also arrested. The story was written up in the Stamford Advocate. Amazed, I asked how he did it. He shrugged: "I was just lucky. With the narrow aisle I could take them on one at a time." I asked in disbelief, "Yeah, but dad, they're football players. Why aren't you in the hospital?" He explained, "With assholes, never fight fair. Knee'em in the balls and smash their nose." That was my first real insight into my father as a commando.

As much as he didn't like to talk, or even think about the war, if he had lived the 6 months that he was given with his lung cancer, I'm sure he would have gotten his DCM, as I don't believe it had yet been stolen. We discussed the risks of the experimental drug. It was his choice and it seemed worth taking the chance. Though he wasn't ready to go, at least he was spared the terrible suffocating death associated with lung cancer.

Whatever Ray Swan wants to believe, had the MoD not led my father, and me, to believe that his medals were much safer there than in our homes, we would have made sure to have gotten his medals. For us, instead of horrific memories, they represent his courage, heroism and incredible survival. They are part of our story. Again, there is no money in it for us. We would never sell my father's medals. This is a matter of justice.

I have no idea how many medals have been stolen from within the MoD, but this may be the first case where the war hero is on video stating clearly before his death that he never received the medal, making this perhaps the one opportunity to expose the crime ring and force an investigation to ultimately unite all of the stolen medals with their rightful owners. No matter what obstacles are put up by the MoD, Scotland Yard, DNW Auction House and Lord Ashcroft, for my father and the other war heroes I am determined to expose the truth.

LORD MICHAEL ASHCROFT

Billionaire Lord Michael Ashcroft must know that he was ripped off by the London Medal Company. Though he has refused to respond, why would his lawyers, curator and assistant hide from him that The London Medal Company evidently bought my father's DCM in its 2011 auction for £11,000, took other war heroes' medals and passed them off as my father's to sell the entire group of medals to him for £78,000 (then about $120,000)? It's a despicable act disassociating the true heroes from their actual medals, but in so doing The London Medal Company increased the DCM's value seven times, in part by making it appear more legitimate, as the sale of a single gallantry medal without its group, and no provenance from the war hero, is extremely suspicious.

Lord Ashcroft must know that we have all of my father's other medals, as it has been stated to him many times. In refusing to address the evidence proving that the medal was never in my father's possession, including the video where my father clearly states that he never got his DCM, it appears that the truth is only a nuisance to Lord Ashcroft, as confirmed by Angela Entwistle's last email, as she responded for Lord Ashcroft, ending with:

> "having satisfied ourselves that the Ashcroft Collection purchased it in good faith … – as, we understand, did its several previous owners – we do not feel under any obligation to continue with

this correspondence. Yours sincerely, Angela Entwistle"

Though Lord Ashcroft may have bought the group of medals in good faith, I believe that anyone buying a WW II medal with absolutely no provenance from the war hero is only buying in the good faith that if it were stolen the rightful owners are now unlikely to come forward. Rather than acting on justice, decency and honor, it would seem that Lord Ashcroft is relying on the MoD's and Scotland Yard's refusal under almost any condition to report the medal as stolen, along with antiquated British laws making it prohibitive for an average person to sue a billionaire.

Perhaps I would feel some sympathy for Lord Ashcroft had he no recourse, but he could easily get his money back from the crooked dealer who sold my father's DCM, along with spurious medals, to him.

Since Lord Ashcroft accredits himself with founding Crimestoppers UK why has he not reported The London Medal Company to the police? Why does he insist on keeping spurious medals along with an extremely questionable DCM? Apparently, he is only against crimes when he doesn't consider it to be in his best interest.

It has been said that excessive greed is synonymous with cowardice, as both are based on selfishness and fear. Perhaps that is why Lord Ashcroft is in such awe of these war heroes who willingly sacrifice their lives for others. What selfless acts has Lord Ashcroft ever performed? In buying war heroes' medals does he believe that he has purchased some of their valor?

My father's DCM should hold no personal value to Lord Ashcroft. He performed no act of courage to earn it. He simply bought it from a crooked dealer. Knowing the deep, personal meaning that it holds to my family, I believe that keeping it makes him as dishonorable as the thieves.

Does Lord Ashcroft deny that the DCM was stolen from within the MoD? If so, I challenge him, the MoD, Scotland Yard, or anyone to give a plausible explanation for why my father at the onset of the 1948 Jewish/Arab Palestinian war, not knowing where he would be from week to week, would apply for his DCM 4 years after earning it while ignoring all of his other medals? Why would he go through all of the trouble of getting one medal without getting the others? And if my father were so desperate for money that he would sell his DCM, why would he not sell it with his entire group of medals? It would have cost him nothing to get the other medals and would have greatly increased the value.

Lord Ashcroft can then also explain why there is no application from my father, no indication of where the medal was sent, no letter from the King accompanying it, no bill of sale from my father or anyone before the 2006 auction, and why my father stated in a video shortly before his death that he never received his DCM.

What does this say about the integrity of a medal collector who shows so little concern for the provenance of a medal in his collection? Does it call into question the integrity of the entire Ashcroft collection? How many other stolen medals has he refused to turn over? Lord Ashcroft speaks of the great debt we owe these war heroes. Is this how he repays it? In my opinion, anyone insisting on keeping a stolen war hero's medal when he can easily get his money back is an enemy to all those who have served.

Though Lord Ashcroft may currently possess my father's stolen DCM, he will never have the entire group. No amount of money will ever tempt any of us to see them within his clutches.

Since my stepmom, sister and I made it clear to my father that we would never sell his medals, my father felt that they should go to his grandchildren. And since my nephew and nieces have also assured me that they would never sell his medals, they will be donated to a worthy cause, such as the Ben Shemen Youth Village, which saved my father's life and I believe still takes in orphaned and refugee children.

Norman Palmer, not one to raise false hope, felt confident that the courts would side in our favor. However, British law seems designed so that the wealthy can steal from the poor, with the poor having little recourse. To sue and lose means paying the legal fees for both sides. To sue and have to pull out due to lack of funds also means paying the legal fees for both sides. Going up against a billionaire, no matter how strong your case, means facing possible bankruptcy. Before proceeding, I've been advised to raise $500,000, a daunting sum.

Perhaps war heroes, who tend to be very generous, are easy targets for those who enjoy buying and selling stolen medals. Perhaps Lord Ashcroft, the MoD, Ray Swan and DNW Auction House feel confident that one insignificant war hero's family is of little concern. But I believe that many are disgusted by these crimes, and together we can make a difference.

I am committed to using all of the proceeds from this book to help unite all of the war heroes' medals stolen from within the MoD with their rightful owners. Any extra money will go to nonprofit veterans organization so that they may be the ones to benefit from these crimes. With your help these brave soldiers who risked and gave their lives for our freedom may finally be shown justice.

CORRESPONDENCE

LORD MICHAEL ASHCROFT

The following is my personal correspondence (from last to first) with Lord Michael Ashcroft, Scotland Yard and the MoD. Though Norman Palmer's hand is clearly evident in the following two emails responded to by Angela Entwistle, and the renowned US restitution lawyer, Tom R. Kline, generously helped with my emails responded to by Michael Naxton (Curator of the Ashcroft Medal Collection), because of lawyer confidentiality I've been advised not to include the exceptional correspondence of Norman Palmer that were sent by Hetty Gleaves to Lord Ashcroft. However, I can assure you that they also received the same dismissive responses.

Angela Entwistle (angela@xxxxxxxxx.com)

6/23/15

To: 'Eric Houston'

Dear Mr Houston Hausman,

With reference to your latest letter (and Annex), I would like to reiterate what has been stated by me and also by Michael Naxton, the Curator of the Ashcroft Collection. The collection purchased your father's medals from the London Medal Company, the UK's largest dealership, in June 2012, at which time we were perfectly aware that the group had previously been sold at public auction by Messrs. Dix Noonan Webb, in London, on 22nd September 2006. According to DNW's sale catalogue – the content of which neither was nor is now our responsibility – it noted that the medals had previously been sold by auction in Los Angeles "many years" before and we had no reason to doubt the veracity of this statement.

One of the points you make (in your Annex) is that your father could not have obtained his DCM "without the contemporaneous transfer of his other medals". This is not in fact the case, because of the system under which all medals are issued. The DCM is a decoration (rather than a medal per se) which would have been presented personally, usually by the sovereign (or dispatched by other means) very soon after it was awarded. By contrast, the wartime service medals (unavailable until well after the end of the War) had to be applied for by the recipient or, in the case of wartime death, his next-of-kin. Thus, no recipient who was granted a gallantry decoration ever received all of his medal entitlement at one and the same time – it was, and always has been, a two-part exercise, often spread over several, if not many, years.

In conclusion therefore, I can only repeat once again that if you furnish us with concrete evidence, in writing, from an official source (be it the MoD or another appropriate source) that the DCM was stolen whilst still in the possession of the authorities and before it was ever issued, we will consider such evidence. Despite all the information you have provided, however, in our opinion there is still no written proof from any official source that the DCM was stolen, and having satisfied ourselves that the Ashcroft Collection purchased it in good faith – as, we understand, did its several previous owners – we do not feel under any obligation to continue with this correspondence

Yours sincerely,

Angela Entwistle

From: Eric Houston [mailto:erichoustonxx@xxxxxxxx.com]
Sent: 15 June 2015 21:19
To: Angela Entwistle
Subject: RE: Fred Hausman's stolen DCM

Dear Ms Entwistle,

Thank you for your letter.

I am surprised that Lord Ashcroft did not think it appropriate to reply to me personally. Given the emphasis that you place on good faith, it would have been instructive to receive Lord Ashcroft's personal account of his state of mind when he purported to buy the medal and of the diligence he exercised (or instructed his staff to exercise) to ensure that the medal was legitimately on the market.

I am also surprised and disappointed that you are not inclined to devote further time to this matter. You appear not to appreciate its importance to my family and me. You also appear unconcerned by the ethical implications of transacting in material which has come into circulation without the owner's consent.

The question of unlawful removal

Your colleague Mr Naxton did not, for reasons which I fail to understand, find it appropriate to inquire further about the available evidence that the medal was unlawfully removed from its original place of custody and put into circulation. Such evidence exists and has already been mentioned in my letters. For the avoidance of doubt, I now recount this evidence in detail in the Annex to this letter.

As to the legality of the matter, I do not propose to tutor you in basic legal principles. Nor do I wish to suggest that you have been unwise enough to express opinions on the legal position without first informing yourself of the law. His Lordship will have his own legal advisers, and he or you will presumably have consulted them before making statements about the legal position. If not, you will have exposed his Lordship to the risk that what you say on his behalf is misleading.

For example, you appear to believe that Lord Ashcroft's purchase of the medal in 2012 operated to confer a good title on him. Perhaps you could cite reasons or authority to substantiate this assertion.

You suggest that I should adduce "clear evidence" to demonstrate that the medal was stolen. Once again, you have already received such evidence in the form of personal statements contained in my last two letters. In addition I have given you the opportunity of further evidence in the form of a video of my father. Neither Mr Naxton nor you has expressed any interest in seeing the video or exploring the matter in any other way. You could have observed this evidence earlier, had Mr Naxton troubled to inquire about the circumstances, rather than dismiss the claim in his own (frankly embarrassing) manner.

I do not, with respect, consider that you have given any credible or acceptable reason for closing the door on this matter. Please consider the following questions.

- Why do you think my family and I are pursuing our claim, if our version of events is not true?

- Do you perhaps consider that my father and I have been lying?

- If so, on what grounds do you base that belief?

- And how do you explain the serious and substantial testimony submitted to you that my father never received the medal and that it entered commercial circulation without his consent?

You also fail to explain why (as you appear to believe) theft is the critical issue. Theft is a criminal offence. My claim is a claim under civil law. This is not a case where the standard of proof is the criminal law standard. The standard of proof is the balance of probabilities.

The position is straightforward. The medal belonged to my father. It never came into my father's possession. It has been placed in circulation and transacted without his authority. Unless you prove otherwise, it is the property of his successor in title.

Further questions and observations

Your letter does at least tell me that the party from whom Lord Ashcroft or the Ashcroft Medal Collection purported to buy the medal is the London Medal Company. For that I am grateful. I had already put this question to Mr Naxton, who did not consider it necessary to answer. Perhaps you could tell me why Mr Naxton found it appropriate to withhold this fact from me.

Perhaps you might now answer another question which I put (without response) to Mr Naxton. I wish to know the identity of the current possessor of the medal: in other words, whether it is currently in the possession of the Ashcroft Medal Collection as a distinct legal entity, or of Lord Ashcroft personally, or of a museum or other institution by way of bailment from the Collection or Lord Ashcroft. Clearly the current location of the medal and the identity of its possessor are relevant to any future action on my part.

A final question is this. You refer to many previous transactions relating to the medal. Your colleague Mr Naxton, on the other hand, told me that there is no available provenance of any kind before the 2006 auction. Why did he say that if it was not true?

Conclusion

The attitude which your employer, your colleague and you have adopted towards this matter is not one which commands my respect.

The medal in question is a chattel of highly symbolic personal significance to a particular family, namely the widow and descendants of my father, including myself. It has further significance to students of Jewish history concerned with the role of Jewish combatants in the Second World War. My family's circumstances are modest. We are not motivated by financial gain.

You, on the other hand, are acting on behalf of a significant public figure, a former member of the House of Lords and a person still admitted to its privileges. The medal has no significant personal and subjective association with Lord Ashcroft, beyond the fact that it is part of a large collection which he has amassed.

One might fairly and reasonably expect that a person in that position would show greater concern for the merits of the claim, the feelings of the family affected and the truth of the situation. In the moral environment to which my family and I belong, any honourable and decent person would at least feel obliged to reflect upon the ethical merits of the matter rather than to take refuge in dismissive and defensive black-letter positions.

I regret that my efforts to approach this matter in a responsible and conciliatory manner have proved unavailing. On behalf of my family I hereby demand the return of the medal.

Please advise me where and when it may be collected on my behalf.

Yours,

Eric Hausman Houston

ANNEX TO LETTER

EVIDENCE THAT MY FATHER DID NOT RECEIVE HIS DCM

AND DID NOT CONSENT TO ITS DEPARTURE

FROM THE POSSESSION OF THE MINISTRY OF DEFENCE

In 2004, I video recorded my father telling his life story. 3 ½ hours into it, he states that he never received the DCM that he was awarded in 1944. The clear inference is that he never travelled to London to receive it and that it never arrived by post. This is first hand evidence, given by the only living person directly concerned in the matter who could give a clear and authoritative recollection of the matter.

I can further testify that my father told me unequivocally on numerous occasions that he never received the medal.

The evidence that my father never received his DCM is supported by other less direct but nonetheless compelling evidence.

According to emails which I have received from Detective Constable Ray Swan of Scotland Yard and officials at the British Ministry of Defense (MOD) my father's service records reveal that he had not previously applied for his Second World War Medals, and that the MOD were still in possession of one decoration and four more of his medals. The MOD also concedes that both dispatch cards were completed incorrectly with no "date / details of either the award ceremony with the King at which the medal was issued or details of the postal address the decorations were issued to via despatch."

I have asked Scotland Yard in an email dated February 17, 2015 and the MOD in an email dated March 13, 2015 to disclose the circumstances (if any) in which my father's DCM could have been transferred to him without the contemporaneous transfer of his other medals, which my family has just received, and whether there is any precedent for such an event. I have received no response to this inquiry. The 'medal application form' offers no option for a person who has been awarded several decorations to specify which individual medals are to be sent on any particular occasion and/or the order in which the relevant medals are to be sent. These circumstances support a clear and reasonable inference that a sequenced or partial receipt of medals is effectively unknown and virtually impossible. There is at the very least no known occasion on which a war hero has received, several years after service, only one of his medals without receiving the rest. It is therefore (again, at the very least) highly improbable that my father would have received only the DCM, particularly as there is no documentary or other evidence that he requested it, whether jointly with or separately from his other awards.

The fact that my father never applied for any of his medals serves only to render all the less credible the assertion that he received the DCM. A few simple, and in my opinion obvious, questions further demonstrate the sheer improbability of the official version.

-    If the medal was posted to my father in January 1948, at the time of the onset of the Palestinian war, to which address would the medal have been sent? The MOD is of course uninformative on this point, contending that the records have been lost or destroyed. But an alternative and more persuasive inference is that such records never existed because the alleged despatch simply never occurred.

- Again, has the MOD paid due regard to (or independently inquired into) the evidence of my father's residential circumstances over the period in question? My father was uncertain where he would be from week to week. Is it contended that he somehow made the arduous trip from Palestine to London to receive his DCM, an occasion which has utterly vanished from the records, but that he did not at the same time trouble to collect his other medals? Such an explanation defies common sense.

Further evidence that my father's DCM never came into his possession may be derived from certain unreliable statements that have, through undisclosed sources, found their way into the commercial record. Since Mr. Naxton has chosen to ignore my request for copies of the paperwork associated with my father's DCM, I am left uninformed as to the evidence, if any, on which the supposed "one contemporary" source based these assertions, and I hereby invite you once again to disclose that evidence. According to the 2006 and 2011 DNW auction listings, my father was believed to be in Italy in 1948: "Houseman returned to duty with the "Palestine Brigade" in August 1944, this time as a despatch rider. Taking his discharge in Italy after the War, he briefly returned to Palestine before settling back 'among dubious friends' in the former country." With all respect to its anonymous author, this statement appears wholly fictitious. My father did not return to the "Palestine

Brigade" in August 1944. After extensive surgery in Italy, in order to enable him to walk again, he was discharged in Sarafand in 1946. Through video testimony by my father and the records of the Kibbutz publishing house in Tel Aviv (where he worked as a commercial artist, and in 1948 illustrated what has become an Israeli children's classic) it is now well documented that my father was in Palestine at the material time. He would not return to Italy until a family trip there in 1971, where we spent several days with Professor Gabriella Morosini, who had been his closest friend there. One is left wondering whether Professor Morosini, a professor of English at the University in Bologna, qualified as one of the "dubious friends" to whom 'one contemporary' refers. It goes without saying that not one of these "dubious" associates is identified in the DNW literature. Nor does the DNW literature cite any single fact that would justify their being stigmatized as "dubious". One marvels at the credulity of the sort of people for whom this species of material is produced.

The garrulous "One contemporary" also refers to my father as: "more of the guerilla fighter mould than a regular team-player - Houseman was not very popular with his fellow Commandos… Perhaps as a result of this ongoing unpopularity with his fellow ranks …" This characterization again appears utterly without authority or foundation. For the record, my father has many surviving friends who can testify that there were few people as generous, outgoing and popular as Fred Hausman. This includes testimony to that effect from those who were friends both during the war and during his postwar years in Palestine. Whatever my father's disagreements with the British authorities, he was highly respected by his commanding officer and loved the British men alongside whom he fought. He declares in the video that these men were like brothers to him.

The revisionist and unsubstantiated characterization of my father as a socially difficult and unpopular combatant calls into question the veracity of other assertions made in the DNW Auction House listing. This includes the following exercise in hallucinatory logic "... the fact his D.C.M. first appeared for sale in Los Angeles many years ago suggests he may have emigrated to the U.S.A." Once again, the author of the statement that the medal appeared for sale at Los Angeles "many years ago" adduces no evidence to substantiate that statement, which is in fact irremediable nonsense. To someone in possession of the facts the statement appears no more than a bare-faced and unmitigated invention.

It is at the very least a credible inference that the existence of the omniscient 'One contemporary' was itself a fabrication, confected by an unknown author, and published to prop up an imaginary account of my father's experiences after the war.

Whatever the motivation behind these falsehoods, the DNW narrative conspicuously fails to attribute them to any identifiable person. On the contrary, the narrative bears the appearance of having been cynically confected. One might fairly assume that its purpose was (a) to provide a plausible provenance for the medal in place of the decades-long factual vacuum existing before 2006, and thus (b) to vindicate the legal validity of the sales in 2006 and 2011.

A further material factor therefore is the total absence from the commercial records of any corroborated provenance showing the trajectory of the medal before its first public auction in September 2006, an event which occurred five months after my father's death (a date which is itself susceptible to adverse inference). If my father's DCM were at some earlier date already part of the "Ron Penhall collection" (another hypothesis which is wholly unverified) it is clear *either* (a) that Ron Penhall himself did not want anyone to know where, when or how he came by the medal in the years before he disposed of it, *or* (b) that DNW did not find it expedient to repeat what Ron Penhall told them. The more feeble and less credible the purported provenance ascribed to an object, the harder it becomes to sustain any assertion that the object was transacted in good faith.

I need hardly say that we have seen no documentation from the MOD to corroborate the suggestion that the medal was in commercial circulation before 2006. On the contrary, the MOD assured me as late as 1996 that all my father's medals remained in the MOD's possession and were as safe as in a bank. I can hardly assume that the MOD officials were lying when they said this. Whatever the means (if any) by which Ron Penhall came into possession after 1996, this cannot have been with my father's consent and will necessarily have involved a violation of my father's right to possession.

I am happy to give explicit reasons as to why my father was never able to make it to London to get his medals. However, I am sure that he would have been more determined had he not been assured by the MOD in the 1950s, and again through me after conversing with the MOD in May 1996, that his DCM and other medals were as safe there as in a bank, and that he, or his family after his death, could get them at any time.

In 2006, several weeks before his death, my father wrote to the MOD in order to get his medals (an email we still have). Not having heard back, he asked my sister and me to make sure that we get them. It was the dying wish of an extremely loving father. I hope you understand why I feel obligated to take whatever action is necessary to get his DCM.

Sincerely,

Eric Hausman Houston

Angela Entwistle (angela@xxxxxxxx.com)

6/03/15

To: 'Eric Hausman Houston'

Dear Mr Houston Hausman,

Thank you for your e-mail to Lord Ashcroft to which, in his absence overseas, he has asked me to respond.

The Ashcroft Collection purchased your father's DCM from the London Medal Company, the UK's largest dealership, in June 2012, at which time we were already aware that the medal had previously been sold at public auction by Messrs. Dix Noonan Webb, in London, on 22nd September 2006. According to DNW's sale catalogue, the medal had also been sold in Los Angeles "many years" before and there is ample evidence that it has, in fact, changed ownership on numerous occasions in the past thirty years or so.

In the absence of any conclusive proof that it was stolen therefore, and having satisfied ourselves that the Ashcroft Collection purchased it in good faith – as did its many previous owners – we do not feel under any obligation to continue this matter. If your own enquiries are able to produce clear evidence of a past theft before the medal was ever issued, please inform us and we will look at the matter again.

Yours sincerely,

Angela Entwistle

-----Original Message-----
From: Eric Hausman Houston

[mailto:erichoustonxx@xxxxxx.com]
Sent: 01 June 2015 21:16
Subject: Fred Hausman's stolen DCM

Message Body:
Eric Hausman Houston
22 Riverside Dr., #11A
New York, NY 10023
email: erichoustonxx@xxxxxx.co

Dear Lord Ashcroft,

I have pasted the attached email below. Is there a business
address to send a hard copy?

I have been in correspondence with your Medals Curator
concerning the DCM awarded to my father Fred Hausmann
in recognition of his acts of gallantry in 1944.

My father died in 2006. He never received this medal and I
am now seeking its delivery to my family, on whose behalf
and with whose authority I am now writing to you.

The medal left the possession of the Ministry of Defense (or
its governmental predecessor) without my father's
authority or consent. There is no formal record of its
dispatch to my father. Nor is there any evidence of an
address to which the medal was dispatched. There is also no
accompanying letter to my father or receipt from my father,
and there is no follow-up correspondence.

I have video evidence of my father, recorded shortly before his death in 2006, in which he states unequivocally that he did not receive the medal.

While my family and I are reluctant to draw adverse conclusions, we cannot discount the possibility that the medal was stolen, either from the relevant ministry by an outsider or from within the ministry by an employee.

While my family and I have cause to believe that the medal was acquired either by your Collection (as a distinct legal entity) or by you in your personal capacity, we do not know whether the medal is currently possessed by your Collection, or by you personally, or by a museum or other institution by way of bailment from your Collection or you. Indeed I should be grateful if you would enlighten me on this point.

I appreciate that you will need time to consider this matter and I wish you to know that I will be happy to furnish whatever information I can on your request. If given sufficient notice I could travel to London to confer with you personally on the matter.

My family takes great pride in my father's achievements. In due course this sense of pride will be shared by generations who never knew him. I am sure that you will appreciate the strength of our desire to retrieve this tangible emblem of his heroism.

There is no question of our selling this treasured artifact

once we recover it. If my family did ever vacate possession, this would be only by donation to a Jewish museum. We believe that the medal has added significance as a very rare – perhaps unique – example of a DCM awarded to a Jewish soldier during World War II.

I apologize for troubling you personally with this matter, but you will see from the attached correspondence that your medals curator has intimated his refusal to correspond further on this point. I wish to be courteous in pursuing our claim. This desire leaves me no option but to approach you on a personal level.

While on the subject of my short and (I regret to say) uninformative exchange of letters with your medals curator, might I respectfully request that your office refrain in future from characterizing my requests and inquiries in derogatory terms? Words like "outburst" and "tirade" are not in my respectful opinion conducive to a conciliatory and constructive dialogue.

I wrote to your medals curator in a business-like fashion, with no wish to cause offence. At my age it is undignified to be addressed as if one were a recalcitrant school-boy, particularly on a matter of such sensitivity and importance to my family and to historians of my faith.

Yours,
Eric Houston Hausman

RE: DCM

Michael Naxton

2/12/15

To: Eric Houston

Dear Mr Houston,

Further to my e-mail on Monday, I have now been able to carefully examine all the paperwork which accompanied the medals when we purchased them and I regret to say that there is no reference whatsoever to any auction sale in the USA in the 1960s. The only sale mentioned was the much more recent London auction in 2006 and this leaves the trail cold I fear. In a spirit of helpfulness however, I would like to make the following comments:-

1.   The information about the US auction sale was presumably provided by the vendor at the London sale in 2006. If it was verbally, he can longer be asked since he has subsequently died. If it was in writing and that paper was indeed sold with the medals, it must have been lost or removed sometime between the auction and when we purchased the medals – I know for a fact that the group has changed hands at least twice between 2006 and when we acquired it.

2.   As far as the service medals and the MID emblem are concerned, none of these were ever issued bearing the name of the recipient as with the DCM. Since you already seem to have confirmation that your father's service medals were neither claimed nor issued, it is clear that the ones we

have with the DCM are spurious although this is a situation we are used to.

I regret there is nothing further we can do and I can only repeat my initial suggestion that you involve the police authorities. I also regret that there will not be any further communications from my office and we regard the matter as now closed.

Michael Naxton

Curator, Ashcroft Medal Collection..

From: Michael Naxton [mailto:michaelxxxxx@xxxxx.co.uk]
Sent: 09 February 2015 18:29
To: 'Eric Houston'

Subject: RE: DCM

Dear Mr Houston,

Your e-mail on Friday afternoon arrived when I was away from my office and I have been extremely busy today. However, rather than show any civilised patience, your latest outburst below does absolutely nothing to help your cause. Do you think I and my colleagues have nothing else to do but answer your intemperate e-mails?

Given that you are asking for our assistance in this matter of your father's DCM, your tirades are quite extraordinary. Despite them, I have nevertheless requested that the documentation which came with the DCM when we purchased it be retrieved from storage so that I can see exactly what information it contains – if any – about the auction in the 1960s. I am trying to help you but if you carry on in this manner, I shall simple cease to respond.

Michael Naxton

Curator, Ashcroft Trust Medal Collection.

From: Eric Houston [mailto:erichoustonxx@xxxxxx.com]
Sent: 09 February 2015 17:37
To: Michael Naxto

Subject: RE: DCM

Dear Mr Naxton,

Since you have not replied to my email requesting copies of all of the paper work accompany my father's stolen DCM, am I to assume that you are denying this request?

Has Lord Ashcroft seen my correspondence with you and approved of your responses? If not, I would like to appeal to him directly. No reply within a timely fashion will be taken as confirmation that Lord Ashcroft is indeed in accordance with you on this subject.

Eric Hausman-Houston

RE: DCM

Eric Houston

2/06/15

To: Michael Naxton

Dear Mr. Naxton,

Thank you for confirming that my father's DCM is in the Ashcroft collection. You refer to the DCM as part of a group. Are there other medals of my father's in this group? Does it include the MID that was to go with his DCM? The MoD confirmed that my father never applied for any of his WW2 medals, and that they still have four of his medals and one decoration. They also confirmed that the dispatch cards for his DCM and MID were completed incorrectly. "Apparently each card should have clear date / details of either the award ceremony with the King at which the medal was issued or details of the postal address the decorations were issued to via despatch."

Since my father never got his DCM and other medals it may appear that they weren't important to him. That's far from the case. He was assured by the MOD in the 1950's and again in the 1990's that his DCM and other medals were completely safe there, and that he, or his family after is death, could get them at anytime. In 2006, several weeks before he died, he wrote to the MOD in order to get his medals. Having not heard back, he asked my sister and me to make sure that we get them. It was the dying wish of an extremely loving father.

When I finally looked into getting his medals, I was shocked to find that his DCM had been auctioned off several times. Surely you can understand why I feel obligated to take whatever action is necessary to get his DCM, and I'm happy to share everything we have on it with you.

As I am unable to replicate your research can you confirm the auction house, date and lot # of its first auction in the 1960's? I'm hopeful that the identity of the first seller may lead to a better understanding of how it left the MOD. Would you be willing to share the paperwork that accompanies his DCM? It would mean a lot to us, as we have never seen it, and it may help to explain some of the incongruities in its last write-ups.

Sincerely,

Eric Hausman-Houston

From: mailto:michaelxxxxx@xxxxx.co.uk
To: erichoustonxx@xxxxxx.com
Subject: DCM
Date: Thu, 5 Feb 2015 12:56:50 +0000

Sir,

Further to my previous e-mail concerning your late father's DCM group, I confirm that these medals are, in fact, now owned by the Ashcroft Collection.

We purchased the group from this country's most respected medal dealer who had bought it from an equally reputable private collector along with several other gallantry medals.

I have now ascertained that this group has appeared at public auction on two occasions, the first as long ago as the 1960s, and has also changed hands commercially at least several times and probably more.

In the circumstances therefore, we believe that we have absolute legal title to these medals and, if you wish to pursue this matter, you should address your claim to the police authorities.

Michael Naxton

Curator, Ashcroft Trust Medal Collection

Hausman DCM

Michael Naxton (mailto:michaelxxxxx@xxxxx.co.uk)

2/04/15

To: erichoustonxx@xxxxxx.com

Dear Mr Hausman-Houston,

Your e-mail received today is so rude and aggressive that it deserves nothing more than the wastepaper basket.

However, the Ashcroft Medal Collection prides itself upon the integrity and scrupulous fair dealing with which it has been formed over the past thirty years and I will therefore investigate your claim to see if has any merit.

I will contact you again in due course.

Michael Naxton

Curator, Ashcroft Medal Collection.

Sent to: http://www.lordashcroft.xxxxxxxxx

Subject: RE: Fred Hausman DCM request.DOCX
Date: Tue, 3 Feb 2015 18:40:22 +0000

As the son of Fred Hausman, Fritz Sigmund Hausmann, I am representing my family with this email. My father never received his DCM, and we now have overwhelming evidence that it was stolen from within the British Ministry of Defense. Having written-up my father in your recent book, SPECIAL OPS HEROES, I'm requesting that you confirm that you are in possession of my father's stolen DCM. If so, I request that it be immediately given to my family, as we are the rightful owners. Please respond as promptly as you can, but in any event, if I do not hear from you by the end of February, I will assume that if you have my father's DCM or other medals, you are refusing to return them.

Sincerely yours,

Eric Hausman-Houston

RAY SWAN

(As of yet, Ray Swan has not responded to this last email.)

Re: Hausman DCM

Eric Houston

Ray.Sxxxxxxxxx.police.uk

Dear Ray,

This is completely unsatisfactory. DNW Auction House has evidently lied to you in a police investigation about having a 1988 letter from Ron Penhall inquiring about my father's stolen DCM. Since you are unwilling to produce this letter, it seems that you are aware of this. Otherwise, please explain why Ron Penhall would write a letter only inquiring about my father's DCM in 1988, but give absolutely no provenance for the medal in 2006 when he was actually selling the medal. Judging from the integrity of the Penhall collection it is clear that my father's DCM was never in his collection, but only laundered through it.

Thus, there is nothing to show any provenance for my father's DCM until after his death in 2006. There is nothing to show that it was legally removed from the MoD, or that it was legally placed on the open market. You are well aware that the MoD has nothing to show that my father ever applied for his DCM or any of his medals, no application, no indication of where it was sent, no letter from the King, no bill of sale from my father. The MoD has now sent us all of his other medals. Please explain why my father would apply for his DCM in 1948 while ignoring all of his other medals. Please explain why my father would sell his DCM without his other medals. Please explain why a war hero would split up his group of medals when it would cost him nothing to get the other medals and would greatly increase the total value.

You also have a video of my father shortly before his death stating very clearly that he never received his DCM, only the ribbon for it. It appears that you are now basing your entire case for my father's DCM not being stolen on a 1948 date stamped on a dispatch card that the prime suspects could have easily stamped themselves. If not, please explain. Other than a signed confession from the thieves, what will it take for you to report my father's DCM as stolen?

I will take your refusal to answer my questions as confirmation that you never requested to see this crucial piece of evidence, and that nothing was put into writing by DNW Auction House of this highly improbable 1988 letter. Though I am yet far from satisfied, I assure you, this is only the beginning.

Eric Hausman Houston

From: Ray.Sxxxxxxxxx.police.uk

Sent: Friday, February 10, 2017 4:39 AM
To: erichoustonxx@xxxxxx.com
Subject: RE: Hausman DCM

Good Morning Eric

Hope you are well. Apologies for not coming back promptly but not always in the office. I also had to take time to refresh my memory re this matter, dating from November 2014 and our last corres 15 months ago.

Clearly it would not be productive to repeat the previous emails sent regards the course of my enquiry in to this matter. However in summary I have found no evidence of Theft being committed by an employee of the MOD or the MOD itself, as per your original complaint in 2014, in regards to the DCM of Lance-Corporal F. S. Houseman, Royal Army Service Corps.

I hope this is satisfactory.

Respectfully

DC Ray SWAN

Art & Antiques unitSCO7

The Metropolitan Police Service

From: Eric Houston <erichoustonxx@xxxxxx.com>
Sent: Friday, February 3, 2017 9:02 AM
To: Ray.Sxxxxxxxxx.police.uk

Fw: Hausman DCM

Eric Houston

Dear Ray Swan,

I am sending this email a 3rd time to have on record that you are refusing to respond to my request to ask to see the very improbable letter of 1988 from Ron Penhall to DNW Auction House only inquiring about my father's DCM. As this is the only piece of evidence indicating any provenance of my father's DCM before his death in April 2006, and since it is extremely strange that Ron Penhall would write inquiring about my father's DCM in 1988 but say nothing about it when he was actually selling it with his entire collection in September 2006, and since it is not with the medal now, it seems unreasonable to trust wholeheartedly the words of DNW Auction House, the prime suspects in the laundering of my father's DCM . Your refusal to respond to this email will lead me to believe that you are well aware of the letter's nonexistence. Best,

Eric Hausman Houston

From: Eric Houston <erichoustonxx@xxxxxx.com>
Sent: Thursday, February 2, 2017 9:31 AM
To: Ray.Sxxxxxxxxx.police.uk

Subject: Re: Hausman DCM

Dear Ray,

I'm preparing to go forward with the case of my father's stolen DCM. From your last emails, I'm under the impression that DNW Auction House only stated in a phone conversation, never putting it in writing, that they have correspondence from Ron Penhall in 1988 in which he only inquired about my father's DCM, never stating in writing that he was in possession of it. Is that correct? Michael Naxton, currator for Lord Michael Ashcroft collection, where my father's stolen DCM now resides, admits in an email that there is nothing to show any provenance before the Ron Penhall auction in September 2006. I believe this calls into question this crucial piece of evidence. Did you ask to see this supposed correspondence? If not, would you please reopen the case and ask DNW to produce this letter. Though DNW has been unwilling to comply to my lawyers' request, DNW has indicated that they will comply to a police investigation. You're help in this matter would be greatly appreciated as it will save me around $10,000 - $15,000 in getting a court order, a Norwich Pharmacal, which I'm prepared to do. Thank you in advance for your assistance in this matter. Best,Eric

From: Ray.Sxxxxxxxxx.police.uk
To: erichoustonxx@xxxxxx.com
Subject: RE: Hausman DCM
Date: Mon, 16 Feb 2015 17:04:32 +0000

Good Morning Eric

As per my last email copied below my investigation in to this matter has now ceased. I have found no evidence that the medal was stolen. There would also appear to be a history of the medal being bought and sold at Auction since at least 1986. This clearly has implications regards good title possession both in Canada & in the UK.

I hope this is satisfactory.

Respectfully

DC Ray SWAN

From: Eric Houston [mailto:erichoustonxx@xxxxxx.com]
Sent: 15 February 2015 22:19
To: Swan Ray P - SCO7

Subject: RE: Hausman DCM

DC Ray Swan, Scotland Yard:

It has recently come to my attention that the stolen Distinguished Conduct Medal (DCM) of my father, Fritz Sigmund Hausmann, aka Fred Hausman, is now in the possession of Lord Michael Ashcroft. Due to the fact that Lord Ashcroft refuses to turn over the stolen medal (see attached email) and that we now have overwhelming evidence that the medal was taken improperly from within the British Ministry of Defense (MOD) and never received by my father, I insist that his DCM be immediately reported as stolen and impounded, along with all of its accompanying paperwork, so that its proper title can be determined by a court of law.

Eric Hausman-Houston

(DC Ray Swan did not reply to the following email, which was sent twice.)

RE: Hausman DCM

To: Ray.Sxxxxxxxxx.police.uk

From: Eric Houston (erichoustonxx@xxxxxx.com)

Sent:Tue 2/17/15 2:13 PM

To: Ray.Sxxxxxxxxx.police.uk

DC Ray Swan, Scotland Yard:

"Under Anglo-American law and the law of some (but not all) European countries, a thief cannot pass good title (no matter how many subsequent owners buy in good faith)."
http://www.artnet.com/magazineus/news/spencer/spencers-art-law-journal7-26-10.asp

 Please site the law you are referring to where a stolen object goes to the last one to buy it without legal provenance if it has been passed around a lot and stolen a really long time ago.

Otherwise, please explain how an inspector of Scotland Yard's Art and Antiques unit has no knowledge of the law?

Given your position, you must know that most people will take your words on this subject as fact. You also know that most are reluctant to hire lawyers due to the prohibitive cost. Therefore, your intent of misleading us can only be interpreted as and attempt to cover up the crime by getting my father's family to drop the case.

You also state: "Clearly I cannot investigate a crime where the offence, if it did take place, occurred in 1945 & 1948. After approx 60 years having passed it is therefore impossible for me to conduct a criminal investigation in to this matter."

As the (attached) Flamenbaum decision states: "To place the burden of locating stolen artwork on the true owner and to foreclose the rights of the owner to recover its property if the burden is not met would … encourage illicit trafficking in stolen art."

I am not asking that you solve the crime. Though it may be the most important WW2 medal of a Palestinian soldier in the British army, and the theft of war medals from within the MOD should merit investigation. I am only asking that you acknowledge the crime and report it as stolen, as has been done with 45,000 other stolen objects from the 1940's.

Since, in fact, you have investigated it, the MOD now admits that my father's service records reveal that he had not previously applied for his Second World War Medals, and that they are still in possession of one decoration and four more of his medals. Since Lord Ashcroft claims to have bought the complete set from the most reputable Medals dealer in England, it calls into question the actions of this most reputable Medals dealer. The MOD also admits that both dispatch cards were completed incorrectly with no "date / details of either the award ceremony with the King at which the medal was issued or details of the postal address the decorations were issued to via despatch."

Please explain how, in 1945, my father's MID (a small oak leaf cluster for the ribbon of the DCM, and awarded after the DCM) was dispatched with no request or authorization from my father. And three years later, in 1948, again with no request from my father, his DCM was then dispatched. Why would they not be given at the same time, along with all of his other medals? Why would he go through the trouble of getting one medal and leave the rest? Has that ever been done? Is it even possible? In the medal application form there is no options for requesting which medals you want and in which order.

And where would they have been sent? According to the auction house listing, at that time he was believed to be in Italy. But my father went back to Palestine after WW2, and it is now well documented that in 1948, during constant war and uncertainty of where he would be from week to week, he illustrated a children's book which (unbeknownst to him) would become an Israeli classic now in it 42nd edition.

As far as buying in good faith, as you state in your email of October 17, 2014, "provenance is important and with medals critical..." With all of the paperwork that has been saved with the DCM, why is there no legal provenance? If my father had sold his DCM that signed bill of sale would be the most critical piece of paper. Without legal provenance, Lord Ashcroft can only claim that he bought the medal in the good faith that if it had been stolen the rightful owners were now doubtful to come forward.

You also have my father's actual testimony. As you know, in 2005 I video recorded my father telling his story. 3 ½ hours into it (4 minutes into the attached video) he states very clearly that he never got his DCM, only the ribbon for it. I believe you will find that he makes a very credible witness.

https://www.youtube.com/watch?v=_aGrOgKPZok#t=109

Since you have extolled on the virtues of the MOD's dedication to assisting ex-servicemen, then please explain why it required so much time and work from you to get the two dispatch cards? Please explain your email of October 3, 2014 where the MOD claims that, "They have no record of the despatch of the medal as your father was apparently attached to the Palestine Army (although fighting within the British Army) and therefore the Medal office would not have been responsible for it." Who at the MOD is unaware that the DCM is to be given by the King or Queen of England at anytime throughout the recipient's lifetime? Again, that can only be interpreted as a blatant lie designed to get my father's family to drop the case.

Though I have already answered in response to your email of September 22, 2014, if you would like, I'm happy to give explicit detail of why my father was unable to make it to London to collect his medals. However, I am certain he would have been more determined had he not been assured by the MOD in the 1950's, and again through me in the 1990's, that his DCM and other medals were as safe there as in a bank, and that he, or his family after is death, could get them at anytime. In 2006, several weeks before he died, he wrote to the MOD (letter attached) in order to get his medals. Having not heard back, he asked my sister and me to make sure that we get them. It was the dying wish of an extremely loving father. I hope you understand why I feel obligated to take whatever action is necessary to get his DCM.

Since this crime as been reported, what action has been taken to assure that my father's DCM and its accompanying paperwork will not be sold, damaged, lost or passed around until proper title is settled?

There is much more evidence that my father's DCM was stolen from within the MOD, which I'm happy to share with you, but at this point it seems superfluous. If you can give no justification for why my father's DCM and MID were removed from within the MOD, then immediately report them as stolen and impound my father's DCM. Otherwise, please explain what it will take for you to act on behalf of the victims of this crime rather than the criminals.

Sincerely,

Eric Hausman-Houston

From: Ray.Sxxxxxxxxx.police.uk
To: erichoustonxx@xxxxxx.com
Subject: RE: Hausman DCM
Date: Wed, 19 Nov 2014 10:57:50 +0000

Morning Eric

Thank you for your email. As you know I have spent
considerable time on this matter. It was always going to be
difficult to establish exactly what has happened due to
the time that has elapsed. The failure of your father to
collect his own medals in his lifetime is also odd. I have
found no evidence whatsoever to support your claims of a
conspiracy by the Ministry of Defence in this matter. Infact I
have found the the staff at SO3 Honours & Awards to be
dedicated to their role & very concerned to assist ex-
servicemen, as you would expect.

I am unsure what you mean by the medal cards being
partial images & your allegation that they are forgeries? I
think it would be constructive if you made contact with SO3
Honours & Awards directly for clarification of the images
provided. My understanding is that they are simply two
paper cards scanned to an email.

Regards 'vague references' the Auction house DNW state
they have written correspondence from Ron Penhall that he
was in possession of your father's medal in 1988. I think you
will find when you take legal representation that this length
of time has implications regards proving civil good title of
ownership of the medal both on behalf of Ron Penhall and

subsequent owners in the UK & presumably in Canada where Ron lived.

I hope this is of help.

Respectfully

Ray

From: Eric Houston [mailto:erichoustonxx@xxxxxx.com]
Sent: 18 November 2014 18:04
To: Swan Ray P - SCO7

Subject: RE: Hausman DCM

Hi Ray,
This doesn't make any sense. Why are we seeing only partial pictures of the cards? Since it's taken so long to get these, how do we know these aren't forged. I see nothing that says the DCM was sent to Italy in 1948. And why would it be sent there. After the war, my father didn't go back to Italy until the 1970's. In 1948 he left Palestine to go to the United States. If my father never applied for the medal, what legal right did the MOD have to send it to a country where hadn't been for 3 years? Why were my father and I lied to about it being safe at the MOD. Why the mysterious references in the Auction house listing: the contemporary who clearly never met my father, the vague reference to an LA auction many years ago?

At this point I don't know what to believe, except that my father never got his medal, and it was sold in an auction in 2011.

It seems that we're left with little choice but to get legal representation to sue for the medal. I imagine the crooks who stole the medal will get away with it, but I'm not convinced that they aren't still there in the MOD. Of course we want the other medals, but the DCM was the one most important to him and most valuable. What justification does the MOD give for not having it. Again, I don't know why I'm only being shown partial pictures of the cards, but I'd like all possible information to explain who stole my father's DCM to figure out what legal steps to take. Best.
Eric

From: Ray.Sxxxxxxxxx.police.uk
To: erichoustonxx@xxxxxx.com
Subject: Hausman DCM
Date: Tue, 18 Nov 2014 16:57:32 +0000

Good Morning Eric

Apologies for not coming back last week.

Please find below and attached an image of the documentation the MOD have been able to find in the National Archives re this matter. The image 'DCM card Hausmann' is of the two medal cards relating to these two of your father decorations, the DCM & one 'Mention in

Despatches'. Apparently this would be a cluster attached to the medal ribbon.

As previously discussed neither card are completed correctly, a fact the MOD point-out themselves. Apparently each card should have clear date / details of either the award ceremony with the King at which the medal was issued or details of the postal address the decorations were issued to via despatch. This is the first piece of physical evidence Ive received from the MOD and it is obviously crucial. Although the postal addresses are not shown the cards have been marked with the dates that the medal and the decoration were issued (posted) to your father. The MOD have summarised this information below:

Please find attached a copy of two medal cards held by the Ministry of Defence Medal Office which show that the Distinguished Conduct Medal (DCM) and Mention in Despatches (MID) have previously been issued by the Ministry of Defence.

The first card shows that Mr Hausmann was awarded an MID on the 11 Jan 1945 this was issued on the 23 May 1945.

The second card shows that the DCM was awarded on the 20 Jul 1944 and issued on the 26 Jan 1948.

The Service Records for Mr Hausmann revealed that he had not previously applied for his Second World War Medals. If the Next of Kin wishes to apply for these awards they still can by printing, completing and signing the attached form.

Clearly I cannot investigate a crime where the offence, if it did take place, occurred in 1945 & 1948. After approx 60 years having passed it is therefore impossible for me to conduct a criminal investigation in to this matter.

I have also taken the time to speak to a Director of the Auction firm Dix Noonan Webb who held the first 2006 Auction. Although they do not have a record of where Ron Penhall originally bought the medal (recollection only is somewhere in the USA) they do have correspondence dated 1988 in which Ron Penhall made an enquiry with them in regard to this medal. It would seem reasonable therefore that he bought the medal at least 18 years before selling it in 2006. Sadly Ron Penhall has since passed-away.

Your father apparently is entitled to four more medals and one decoration. I have attached the MOD medal application form above for you to complete, for you to be awarded these medals on behalf of your father. The contact address for the relevant MOD department is:

SO3 Honours & Awards | Defence Business Services | Ministry of Defence Medal Office | Innsworth House | Imjin Barracks | Gloucester | GL3 1HW |

I hope the above is satisfactory.

Respectfully

DC Ray SWAN

Art & Antiques unit

SCO7

The Metropolitan Police Service

Ray.Sxxxxxxxxx.police.uk

To: <u>erichoustonxx@xxxxxx.com</u>

Sent:Wed 11/12/14 3:15 AM

To: erichoustonxx@xxxxxx.com

Good Morning Eric

Eric you are a suspicious man, would make an excellent Police Officer. Unless you are already one of NYPD's finest???

Ray

From: Eric Houston [mailto:erichoustonxx@xxxxxx.com]
Sent: 11 November 2014 17:11
To: Swan Ray P - SCO7

Subject: RE: DCM

Thanks Ray,
My guess it that if they had a truly legitimate reason for not having the medal, they would get right back. Best,
Eric

From: Ray.Sxxxxxxxxx.police.uk
To: erichoustonxx@xxxxxx.com
Subject: RE: DCM
Date: Tue, 11 Nov 2014 16:55:26 +0000

Evening Eric

Ive been running around all day, and just got in and and
nothing from the MOD. Don't know why, not my fault but
sorry anyway. Will phone them tomorrow and bell or email
you.

Respectfully

Ray

From: Eric Houston [mailto:erichoustonxx@xxxxxx.com]
Sent: 11 November 2014 15:01
To: Swan Ray P - SCO7
Subject: RE: DCM

Hi Ray, let me know if we're talking today. Best,
Eric

From: Ray.Sxxxxxxxxx.police.uk
To: erichoustonxx@xxxxxx.com
Subject: RE: DCM
Date: Mon, 10 Nov 2014 16:48:06 +0000

Thank you Eric, you've probably told me that already but Id forgotten. My team totals 3 people and we cover the whole of London and any International Art requests that come in and pretty much anything else that affects the London Art Market...keeps us busy! Auctions sending an email to a buyer and leaving it up to them if they choose to make contact seems to be pretty standard practise. I will get the Info from the MOD and come back to you, want to make progress with this.

Speak tomorrow.

Ray

From: Eric Houston [mailto:erichoustonxx@xxxxxx.com]
Sent: 10 November 2014 16:38
To: Swan Ray P - SCO7
Subject: RE: DCM

Hi Ray,
Sure, appreciate anything he can find out. The auction house knows who has it. They're willing to send them an email from me, but won't tell me who it is. If it's a Jewish museum, wouldn't mind donating it, as we would never sell it. I see nothing to say that it was ever auctioned before 2010, so I believe that the auction house new there was no legitimate provenance. I have no qualms with them having to return the money to the winning bidder, and getting there money back from the thief/theives.

From: Ray.Sxxxxxxxxx.police.uk
To: erichoustonxx@xxxxxx.com
Subject: RE: DCM
Date: Mon, 10 Nov 2014 16:17:11 +0000

Hello Eric

Still not got anything from the MOD & I have chased,
presume will be tomorrow now. I'm out of the office all day
but will come back in by 4 and phone you. My colleague
Alan is trying to establish who has the DCM now. He knows
the medal collecting world very well and if anyone can he
can.

Hope ok. Best wishes,

Ray

From: Eric Houston [mailto:erichoustonxx@xxxxxx.com]
Sent: 10 November 2014 13:11
To: Swan Ray P - SCO7

Subject: RE: DCM

Hi Ray,
Let me know whenever is good for you to talk. Very anxious
to hear what the MOD has to say. As you can imagine, I
have many questions. What I do know is that my father
never got his DCM medal, the MOD lied to my father and
me saying that it was safe, and the first provenance for it in

the auction house listing is Sept, 2006, 5 months after his death.

Would be great to meet for a drink and pick up my father's other medals. But if my father's DCM isn't put into the data base as stolen, it will also be to meet with lawyers, the press and possibly Jewish agencies to take actions to retrieve his stolen DCM.

All the best,
Eric

From: Ray.Sxxxxxxxxx.police.uk
To: erichoustonxx@xxxxxx.com
Subject: RE: DCM
Date: Mon, 10 Nov 2014 09:53:05 +0000

Hi Eric

Hope you are well. I'm out and about most of the day but would like to call you this afternoon, better with your time difference anyway. I've got to be careful what I say about MOD procedures (50 years ago!!!) because its not my field and don't want to mislead you. They made clear from the beginning however there is a difference between a Gallantry medal and campaign medals. Campaign are mass produced and issued whereas Gallantry are individually struck and allocated, in this case personally by the King or Queen. I presume this is why they are so valuable?

Eric if I don't get the documents from the MOD I wont phone today, no point. I want to give you a full update. Also they are going to advise me how many more medals your father is eligible for. Apparently its five or six. If you fly over to pick them up maybe we could meet for a Pint or Coffee?

Respectfully

Ray

From: Eric Houston [mailto:erichoustonxx@xxxxxx.com]
Sent: 07 November 2014 18:18
To: Swan Ray P - SCO7
Subject: RE: DCM

Sorry to rant, but one last big question: why would the MOD have his other medals and not his DCM?

From: Ray.Sxxxxxxxxx.police.uk
To: erichoustonxx@xxxxxx.com
Subject: DCM
Date: Fri, 7 Nov 2014 16:25:06 +0000

Hello Eric

Not forgotten you, hope all is well. The MOD came back to me this morning, they've been looking at this all week. They think they've finally retrieved postal despatch records from 1948 of your fathers medal being sent-out, even though the medal card itself is blank. They want to put everything they have together and send to me on Monday so I can understand it.

When Ive got all the evidence clear will call you to discuss. Please email me on Monday when you are up and able to talk. If there are aspects to this I cannot clarify will put you in touch with the Director of the Honours and Awards section of the MOD department concerned. They are very keen to assist. Their remit is not just medals but appears to be also HR issues re serving / retired military personnel injured or killed right upto today.

I hope this is satisfactory.

Respectfully

Ray

From: Eric Houston (erichoustonxx@xxxxxx.com)

Sent: Tue 11/04/14 1:35 PM

To: Ray.Sxxxxxxxxx.police.uk

Hi Ray,

Thanks for getting back. I'm not surprised that the MOD has

no record, as I believe it was most likely stolen from inside the department. If not, it would sure make a great who-done-it because I don't see how anyone from the outside could have taken it.

The MOD initially told you that they were not responsible for his DCM because he was a Palestinian resident. They now admit to having other of his medals. Why would they not also have his DCM?

It is terrific to hear that they have other medals that my father never collected. My sister and I remember playing with a box of his ribbons, but we don't remember there being any actual medals with them. I only focused on the DCM because he specifically stated that he never received it. Of course, we would love to get all of them, and hope that no others have been stolen.

Even if a private buyer has it, at least we'll know that, and once it's listed as stolen it should be harder to sell in an auction. And I believe then we can also then be issued a replacement medal.

Again, we really appreciate all you're doing on this. All the best,
Eric

From: Ray.Sxxxxxxxxx.police.uk
To: erichoustonxx@xxxxxx.com
Subject: RE: DCM
Date: Tue, 4 Nov 2014 16:46:20 +0000

Hi Eric

Ive heard back from the MOD but its not good news,
they've got no records of where it went and they are going
to have to look further into it. Apparently the medal card is
not filled-out. Will find out when the last entry was made on
it. I will speak to the officer dealing asap and get the full
picture.

As an aside apparently there are other medals your father
never collected that they still have, I will get the details. Im
know you will be interested. My colleague Alan is going to
try and find-out for me where the medal is now, if with a
dealer should be easy. Less so if its owned by a private
buyer. Will bell you when I have some proper information /
facts.

Respectfully

Ray

From: Eric Houston [mailto:erichoustonxx@xxxxxx.com]
Sent: 27 October 2014 12:01
To: Swan Ray P - SCO7
Subject: RE: DCM

Hi Ray,
Thanks! Really appreciate it.
Eric

From: Ray.Sxxxxxxxxx.police.uk
To: erichoustonxx@xxxxxx.com
Subject: RE: DCM
Date: Mon, 27 Oct 2014 09:58:34 +0000

Hi Eric

My colleague Alan was talking to the MOD on Friday about
it but he didn't come back to me. Will phone him today. He
will get the records and is keen to help. You are right you
can get medal replacements, apparently they have the
letter R next to the serial numbers. Don't think he did due
to cost but I don't think its prohibitive. Perhaps its the sort
of issue you address as you mature in years?

Will come back to you this week. Want to make progress
with this.

Regards

Ray

From: Eric Houston [mailto:erichoustonxx@xxxxxx.com]
Sent: 24 October 2014 19:34

To: Swan Ray P - SCO7
Subject: RE: DCM

Hi Ray,

Guessing my father's military record didn't come in yet. I've been thinking about your brother-in-law's stolen medal. Couldn't he get replacements after reporting them as stolen? I was given that impression from the quote at the bottom of the site below. And at least that way they'll be in a data base as stolen so they can't be too easily sold. We may try to do that with all of my father's missing medals. We would try to do that with his DCM, but it appears that since he never got it, it wasn't stolen from him. All the best, Eric

http://www.paulfrasercollectibles.com/section.asp?catid=179&docid=1066

"Townsend's medals were stolen in 1988, and the lot includes the replacements he was given before the originals were returned."

From: Ray.Sxxxxxxxxx.police.uk
To: erichoustonxx@xxxxxx.com
Subject: RE: DCM
Date: Fri, 17 Oct 2014 11:38:14 +0000

Hi Eric

Just been advised we are getting his military record next week from the National Archive. My colleague Alan

is primed for us both to view it asap. I get your drift re
'Fact'. You are right provenance is important and with
medals critical, so many are stolen by Burglars. Soldiers
tend to have little money and their homes are wide open.
My brother-in-law lost his Falklands medals that way, stolen
just a few years after the War.

When I see the record call you next week.

Ray

From: Eric Houston [mailto:erichoustonxx@xxxxxx.com]
Sent: 08 October 2014 14:29
To: Swan Ray P - SCO7
Subject: RE: DCM

Hi Ray,

Thanks for the update. From the blurb of the last auction,
the first actual date of its appearance seems to be the Ron
Penhall Collection, 22 September 2006. The auction house
stated, "... the fact his D.C.M. appeared many years ago in
Los Angeles..." leaves me curious why they would say
"fact". I'm guessing that provenance is very important. If
there were an actual earlier dated receipt, wouldn't the
auction house have stated that? Anxious to know what the
service record turns up. Thanks again. All the best,
Eric

From: Ray.Sxxxxxxxxx.police.uk
To: erichoustonxx@xxxxxx.com
Subject: DCM
Date: Wed, 8 Oct 2014 09:36:51 +0000

Good Morning Eric

Quick update; Ive requested the National Archive records for your father's military service but will take some time to retrieve. Apparently WW2 military records are not cleared for public access under the Official Secrets Act so no reason to put them onto computer yet. When the paper copies are delivered to London I will review with my colleague who is a medal expert. He has also offered to start working back through the Auction Houses concerned for us. Im hoping the service record will give me a steer as to where it went first & save a great deal of time.

Respectfully

Ray

From: Ray.Sxxxxxxxxx.police.uk

Sent: Mon 10/06/14 12:04 PM

To: erichoustonxx@xxxxxx.com

Hello Eric

As per our telephone conversation, your father's War records have been requested from the National Archive and I will review them when I receive copies. I think this is a sensible approach. As regards procedure re medals issued 65 odd years ago clearly I have no idea.

Will keep you updated however please give me time.

Regards & best wishes

Ray

From: Eric Houston [mailto:erichoustonxx@xxxxxx.com]
Sent: 06 October 2014 16:57
To: Swan Ray P - SCO7
Subject: RE: Stolen WWII DCM medal

Hi Ray,

Have you found out who was responsible for my father's medal? Do you know who in the medal office would have had access to it? At this point I wouldn't trust any of them. For someone at the medal office to say that my father was attached to the Palestine Army and therefore they are not responsible seems like an outright lie. I would even question if they hadn't had involvement with its theft. My father's commanding officer, Frank Churchill, submitted the recommendation, and as you said, if my father were alive today it would be presented to him by the Queen of England. How could it be the responsibility of a government that has been defunct since 1948? What about DCM's awarded to citizens of Australia, New Zealand, India, and South Aftrica? Are those governments also responsible for those medals?

Since there are no dispatch records for the medal, it seems obvious to me that it was stolen from inside the medal office. If someone from outside had pretended to be my father there would be a record of it. And if one medal was stolen in that way, there may be more. The first one could have just opened the door. In any case, I'm sure whoever stole this one believed that they would be safe as it would never be claimed.

Clearly, that's not the case. Again, we would like it to be reported as stolen and given a thorough investigation so that this can be resolved. Hopefully, that will help prevent this happening again. Thanks again. Best,

Eric

From: Eric Houston (erichoustonxx@xxxxxx.com)

Sent: Fri 10/03/14 12:04 PM

To: Ray.Sxxxxxxxxx.police.uk

Hi Ray,

Thanks for talking earlier. Really appreciate it. Unfortunately I don't have anything. When I was in London I got a phone card to save money and called (I believe) the medal or war department. I think it was on my first day there, which may have been Thursday, 22nd of May, 1996. I was transferred several times before being told that my father would have to fill out forms, send them in and they would have to be approved before I could pick up the medal for him. I was concerned that after a period of time the medal would be sold or disposed of, and I was assured that would never happen, that it was as safe in a bank. That really is all i remember. I wish I could tell you more. I didn't take notes and don't recall the name of the person I talked to. Since I had called the department that had the medal it gave both my father and I a false sense of security, and we didn't worry about it since. Let me know if you need me to resend any of the info he had sent to the war department. Best,

Eric

From: Ray.Sxxxxxxxxx.police.uk
To: erichoustonxx@xxxxxx.com
Subject: RE: Stolen WWII DCM medal
Date: Fri, 3 Oct 2014 15:08:54 +0000

Hi Eric

My colleague Alan asks do you have anything written down (even your own notes will do) from you and your Dad's conversations with the Medal Office here re the DCM in the 1990's? Even just names & dates might help us get closer to what happened. Im off till Monday, please take the weekend to recall what you can.

Thank you

Ray

From: Eric Houston [mailto:erichoustonxx@xxxxxx.com]
Sent: 03 October 2014 15:15
To: Swan Ray P - SCO7
Subject: RE: Stolen WWII DCM medal

Thanks Ray, calling now is good.

From: Ray.Sxxxxxxxxx.police.uk
To: erichoustonxx@xxxxxx.com
Subject: RE: Stolen WWII DCM medal
Date: Fri, 3 Oct 2014 14:09:58 +0000

Hi Eric

Sorry, but I assume my email was not clear. I do not think the medal is in Israel. I am trying to establish how it came to Auction as you have asked me to. I am hoping your father's own medal record will assist me, I think that is logical. Happy to talk this through on the phone. Im on duty here for another hour. Please advise if convenient to call you. Otherwise Monday?

Regards

Ray

From: Eric Houston [mailto:erichoustonxx@xxxxxx.com]
Sent: 03 October 2014 14:41
To: Swan Ray P - SCO7
Subject: RE: Stolen WWII DCM medal

Hi Ray,

My father was told that he not only had to go to England to receive the medal, but that it would be given to him by the King (or Queen) of England. When I looked into it in May, 1996 I was told that he was the one who should can get it, but that it was as safe there as in a bank. Now you're telling me that it's in Israel. That doesn't make sense. He was in Palestine from 1945-1948. It seems unlikely that it would have been sent to Palestine without his request or knowledge. I'm not surprised there is no record of it being dispatched as thieves don't usually leave receipts for stolen good. Obviously the medal department (or wherever it was kept) would now like to evade all responsibility, but that doesn't change the fact that it was stolen, and we would like it to be reported as such. What do we have to make that happen? Do we have to hire lawyers? Go to the press? I'm writing a book on my father now, and I'm not about to let it drop.

Since we know the last auction house it should be possible to trace it it back, hopefully to whomever stole it as there will be no legitimate provenance. If auction houses are made aware that they can't just sell stolen war medals without any consequences, maybe it will help prevent future such crimes.

I'm sorry if I seem frustrated, but since my childhood my father had told of the medal he had rights to receive from the King or Queen of England. Knowing that it has been stolen and sold in auction has left me in disgust and we would like it resolved. Thanks again for taking time on this. All the best,
Eric

From: Ray.Sxxxxxxxxx.police.uk
To: erichoustonxx@xxxxxx.com
Subject: RE: Stolen WWII DCM medal
Date: Fri, 3 Oct 2014 08:16:41 +0000

Morning Eric

A colleague is kindly pursuing this matter for me and has already been in touch with a liaison officer in the Medal office. They have no record of the despatch of the medal as your father was apparently attached to the Palestine Army (although fighting within the British Army) and therefore the Medal office would not have been responsible for it. They have requested a physical copy of your father's service record and medal card from the National Archives in Kew. My understanding is this will detail exactly what happened regards the mechanics of the medal being issued to your father.

I have no knowledge of the structure of the Palestine Army vis-a-vis the British Army in WW2. Clearly it was an exceptionally complicated period of history, Eric you may well have more knowledge that me on the subject? As an observation however perhaps you should get in touch with the Israeli Army medal department to see if they have any records of any of this? As soon as I here back from the National Archive will get in touch. Finally I have found no evidence of any Theft to date.

Regards

Ray

From: Eric Houston [mailto:erichoustonxx@xxxxxx.com]
Sent: 02 October 2014 20:16
To: Swan Ray P - SCO7
Subject: RE: Stolen WWII DCM medal

Hi Ray,
Any news? Any idea how someone could have stolen my father's D.C.M. from the medal department? The last auction house said that it "first appeared for sale in Los

Angeles many years ago ..." If that were true wouldn't they list the date and the auction house? The first date they actually have is: "Ex. Dix Noonan Webb, 22 Septemeber 2006 (lot 67), as part of the Ron Penhall Collection." My father died on 25th of April, 2006. It seems strange that the medal was listed so soon after his death. He had written to the medal department shortly before his death stating what medals he had earned. I know that he did that in order to obtain the medal/medals, but forgot to explicitly state that in the letter. I don't know which ones he had. As a child I remember seeing the ribbons for the medals, and there is a picture of him wearing the ribbons, but the only one he stated that he never received was the D.C.M. Someone at the medal department may have been made aware of his D.C.M. by his letter and taken it after they saw that he had died. Shouldn't the medal department have some record of it. Again, really appreciate any help on this. Best,
Eric

From: Eric Houston (erichoustonxx@xxxxxx.com)

Sent: Wed 9/24/14 9:34 AM

To: Ray.Sxxxxxxxxx.police.uk

Hi Ray,

That's not the case here. I don't believe there will be any fighting over the medal. I remember my father wanted the medal to go to my nephew, but that was before he or any of us knew its value. Legally it should go to his widow, my stepmom, Jessica Hausman. We're very close, and I believe it should be hers to do with as she pleases. I know that my father was very proud of the medal, having the right to get it actually saved his life when he went back to Palestine (explained in the video,) so it's upsetting to us that it's been stolen and sold in auctions. Again, thank you so much for looking into this. All the best,

Eric

From: Ray.Sxxxxxxxxx.police.uk
To: erichoustonxx@xxxxxx.com
Subject: RE: Stolen WWII DCM medal
Date: Wed, 24 Sep 2014 08:41:59 +0000

Hi Eric

Ive asked a colleague who happens to be a medal collector to assist me re the best contact at the MOD / War Office. Its something I should know how to do anyway, we get UK medal referrals every six months or so. They are always problematic as they were worth comparatively little when awarded after the War but are now extremely valuable. The last one turned out to be a civil dispute between relatives who haven't spoken for years and disliked each other! When I have more I will contact you.

Respectfully

Ray

From: Eric Houston [mailto:erichoustonxx@xxxxxx.com]
Sent: 23 September 2014 16:53
To: Swan Ray P - SCO7
Subject: RE: Stolen WWII DCM medal

Hi Ray, if it would be helpful to discuss, I can cam on skype or talk on the phone whenever is good for you. All the best,

Eric

From:Eric Houston (erichoustonxx@xxxxxx.com)

Sent: Mon 9/22/14 10:43 AM

To: Ray.Sxxxxxxxxx.police.uk

Hi Ray,
Thanks for getting back so soon after your vacation. My mother told us that my father tried to contact someone in London in the 1950's to get the medal, but after some correspondence, it was never followed through. He planned to get the medal on a trip to London, but he never made it there. Since I had been told when I was there in May of 1996 that it was as safe as in a bank, and he was the only one who could get it, unless he filled out a lot of forms in advance, he felt more secure about it. Since he never went to London and never got the medal, as he states in the video, we can only assume that it was stolen from wherever it was supposed to be. We believe whoever got the medal, got it illegally.

The auction house claims that it first appeared in an auction in Los Angeles, CA. I question that. I imagine if there was any legitimate provenance the auction house would have stated that. In any case, how could there be any legitimate provenance, since my father and no one in the family ever got it? Until I saw it on the auction house site, it never even occurred to any of us that it might be stolen. I know that he meant to get the medal before his death, as he told me that he wanted it to eventually go to my nephew, Billy Bradley. He was close to his death when he wrote to the war office, and looks like he focused on getting a military funeral and forgot to actually ask for the medal. But I don't see how that changes the fact that it was stolen. If the War Office refutes it, hopefully they can tell us who got it, or will have the fraudulent claim of someone pretending to be my father. Please let me know whatever I can do from here. My sister and I are willing to go to London if that would help to resolve this. Thanks again for your help. All the best,
Eric

From: Ray.Sxxxxxxxxx.police.uk
To: erichoustonxx@xxxxxx.com
Subject: RE: Stolen WWII DCM medal
Date: Mon, 22 Sep 2014 13:38:20 +0000

Good Afternoon Eric

Hope you are well, no probs re the delay getting back. I understand your email and the points you raise re NYPD jurisdiction but you have me at a complete disadvantage on one point. Both you and Renee have stated the medal was stolen from the Medal Department in London. I do not know how you know this? Please advise. I suspect the War Office will refute this allegation with some vigour but I am happy to get in touch with them & follow this up.

What contact did your father have with the Medal Department prior to his death regards collecting his medal? Do you have any copies of correspondence that could assist me? Also why did your father never collect his medal?

Thank you for your help with this.

Regards & very best wishes

DC Ray SWAN

Art & Antiques unit SCO7

From: Eric Houston [mailto:erichoustonxx@xxxxxx.com]
Sent: 16 September 2014 22:21
To: Swan Ray P - SCO7
Subject: FW: Stolen WWII DCM medal

Hi DC Ray Swan,

Sorry I'm just getting back. My sister, Renee Bradley, forwarded to me your email below. I waited to talk to detectives here in New York City before contacting you. Detective Mark Fishstien, who recently retired from NYPD, felt that since my father's D.C.M. was stolen from the Medal Department in London, it should reported as stolen from them. Can you help with that? Do we need to apply for the medal first? If so, whom we should contact?

Detective Fishstien and Detective Diaz in New York both feel that since it was never in our possession or in the USA, it's out of their jurisdiction, but they would like to be of help and are happy to talk ith you about it.

I went to London in May of 1996 and looked into getting my father's D.C.M for him. I was told that while he was alive he was the only one who could get it, but that it was as safe there as if it were in a bank. He died in 2006. I was making plans this summer to get it when I found it online, sold in an auction in 2011. (page in the emails below.) In 2005, a year before he died, I recorded him telling his story. A woman in Israel posted it, and about 4 1/2 minutes into the video below he talks about never getting the actual medal.

https://www.youtube.com/watch?v=_aGrOgKPZok

He had intended to get it himself, but never made it to England. He was very proud of that medal, and at the least we would like it put into a database as 'stolen' so that it can be investigated and kept from being sold in auctions.

Much appreciation for any help on this. All the best,

Eric Hausman-Houston

To: erichoustonxx@xxxxxx.com
Subject: Fwd: Stolen WWII DCM medal
From: momxxxxxx@xxx.com
Date: Tue, 5 Aug 2014 08:46:39 -0400

-----Original Message-----
From: Ray.Swan (Ray.Sxxxxxxxxx.police.uk)
To: mommucks <momxxxxxx@xxx.com>
Sent: Tue, Aug 5, 2014 8:18 am
Subject: Stolen WWII DCM medal

Hello Renee

My name is DC Ray SWAN and Im covering for Virginia
whilst she is off unexpectedly. Im aware of this matter
although not all the facts. Can I please clarify some points?
Sincere apologies if you have already covered them with
Virginia.

- Has this matter been reported to the Police in the USA as a
Theft, either historically by your father or recently by
yourself or other family members?

- What is the earliest date you are aware that the medal was sold at Auction, and where was that Auction? You refer to LA & Bill and Angela Strong in your email.

- In your email you state that 'someone within the medal department took the medal'. Please advise your evidence for this.

- Please advise when & where your father settled in the US and rough dates.

- If you know, please advise why your father never collected the medal, did he explain at all? Also did he apply for replacements for the medal not collected? I understand they are provided free of charge although they are marked as replacements.

Many thanks for your help with this. Clearly we always wish to help / advise in such matters however to take this on as a potential criminal investigation we would need a referral through the US Police dealing with a Theft or Fraud allegation. Timescales regards the date the medal was originally sold at Auction are also important regards if this is civil or criminal. I am not familiar with US property law in this regard.

Respectfully

Ray SWAN

Art & Antiques unit SCO7

From: Hutcheon Claire L - SCO7 On Behalf Of Dodd Virginia
M - SCO7
Sent: 05 August 2014 12:43
To: Swan Ray P - SCO7
Subject: FW: Stolen WWII DCM medal

From: momxxxxxx@xxx.com [mailto:momxxxxxx@xxx.com]
Sent: 14 July 2014 17:03
To: Dodd Virginia M - SCO7
Subject: Re: Stolen WWII DCM medal

Virginia, Thank you so much for getting back to me.

My father never got his medal from the British Government.
He made several attempts and was never given it. I'm
afraid he never went to London personally, he just sent
letters from the US. His last attempt was just before he died
and someone within the medal department in 2006 was
kind enough to give us the paperwork for the DMC but they
didn't have the Medal. They did tell my brother that the
medal would never be given to anyone beside my father or
his family. I believe that the medal was taken by someone
who worked where the medal was stored. I would like to
find out how someone could take his medal and all the
correspondence about it? I understand people have spent a
lot of money on his medal but it was stolen and was never
given to my dad. My step mother has the correspondence
for the citation and we could provide that. We received
that just before he died in 2006.

From the auction description of my dad's medal it said that it had been up for auction in LA where the owners of the medal, Bill and Angela Strong purchased it for their collection. I don't know if it is possible to back tract to find out who originally put the medal up for auction but if we could we probably could find out how this could have happened.

Again, any help in finding my dad's medal would be appreciated.

Thank you,

Renee Bradley

http://www.dnw.co.uk/auction-archive/special-collections/lot.php?specialcollection_id=1&specialcollectionpart_id=2&lot_id=77811

-----Original Message-----
From: Virginia.Dodd (Virginiaxxxxx@xxxxxxpolice.uk)

To: Renee Bradley momxxxxxx@xxx.com
Sent: Mon, Jul 14, 2014 4:12 am
Subject: RE: Stolen WWII DCM medal

Dear Renee

Thank you for this enquiry. You did not state when your father actually lost the medal., although you mention that he made attempts in 1950's while in New York. Obviously if it has been missing for the past

60 years this will cause problems as to ownership. What attempts were made by your father over the original lost, was it reported to police. Because of the time that has passed since the loss any attempt to reclaim the medal would enter into civil law. The present owner would have bought the medal in good faith and therefore have some right to claim ownership; you would need to be able to provide proof of ownership, paperwork such as the citation.

Hope this has been of some help

Virginia Dodd

Art and Antiques Unit

New Scotland Yard

From: momxxx@xxx.com [mailto:momxxx@xxx.com]
Sent: 11 July 2014 19:17
To: SCO9 - Art and Antiques
Subject: Stolen WWII DCM medal

I have been doing research on my father, Fred Hausman, I found that his D.C.M medal was auctioned off in 2011. He had tried to get the medal for my son, his grandson, before he died in 2006. He also made attempts in the 1950's while living in New York City, and had my brother look into finding it when he spent a week in London in 2000. He was given a run around, but he was assured that nobody could get the medal except for my father or a family member. I have no idea who stole it. I'm guessing it was someone with access to wherever it was stored. This medal meant a lot to him, and I'd like to do whatever it takes to get it back. Below is the link for the auction.

Thanks so much for helping me out. If I have contacted the wrong division, could you please guide me and let me know, who I should contact.

Regards,

Renee Hausman Bradley

http://www.dnw.co.uk/auction-archive/special-collections/lot.php?specialcollection_id=1&specialcollectionpart_id=2&lot_id=77811

THE MOD

The much more detailed letters from Norman Palmer and Hetty Gleave received the same unwavering response from the MoD, basically refusing any responsibility on the bases of Ray Swan's investigation and the statement of provenance in the DNW Auction House listing.

Our Ref: DBS/Sec/Medals

Ministry of Defence

DBS RES-Sec-DO3 (Butler, Elaine D)
(DBxxxxxxxxxDO3@mod.uk)

7 September 2015

Dear Mr Hausman,

Thank you for your e-mail of 3 August, in which you express your continuing concerns about your late father's Distinguished Conduct Medal (DCM) and raise further questions regarding the award of the DCM.

I am sorry it has taken so long to provide a reply to the issues you have raised.

Regarding the issue of the DCM to your late father, I can confirm that the Department has now conducted a full review of the case and the position taken by the Ministry of Defence Medal Office regarding the issue of the Medal has been maintained.

You enquired as to how many DCM were issued to Jewish Palestinian soldiers in the British Army during World War Two. I am sorry to say that it is not possible to provide an answer to this question as the Medal cards held do not record information of the religious faith of medal recipients.

In answer to your final question regarding the numbers of personnel involved in the despatch of a DCM to its rightful recipient. The Ministry of Defence Medal Office took the administration of medals over from the individual Service Medal Offices in April 2005, and records are no longer held as to how many people would have been involved in this process prior to this time.

I am sorry to provide a further disappointing response to your concerns, but hope it explains the position.

Yours sincerely

DBS Secretariat Team

Ministry
of Defence

DBS RES-Sec-DO3 (Butler, Elaine
D) (DBxxxxxxxxxDO3@mod.uk)

8/03/15

To: Eric Houston

I am out of the office until 5 August your e-mail has not
been forwarded if it is urgent please send to the Secretariat
Group Mailbox, otherwise I will action on my return. If you
wish to speak to someone please call my line manager
Sandra Lloyd on 01253 xxxxxx who is in office.

Eric Houston

8/03/15

To: DBS RES-Sec-DO3 Butler, Elaine D

Dear Ms Butler,

I'm still waiting to hear on the status of my father's DCM. As
you know, I was told there would be an answer by the end
of June. I believe you have ample proof that my father
never received his DCM, and that without any application
from my father for any of his medals, including his DCM,
or address where the medal could have been sent, it was

clearly removed improperly from within the MOD. I note with concern that I have still received no credible alternative explanation for its disappearance, and certainly none that exonerates your Department. In the absence of such explanation, doing my utmost to approach this matter objectively and reasonably and having regard to the burden of proof as outlined in my earlier letter, I remain convinced that there is no possible version of events that is consistent with an absence of fault in your Department.

On another note, I would sincerely appreciate it if you would answer two questions for me.

1. How many Palestinian soldiers in the British Army during WW2, and specifically Jewish Palestinian soldiers, received the DCM.

2. What is the protocol to assure that a DCM is given to its proper recipient. Since I was assured by the MOD in 1996 the my father's DCM was as safe there as in a bank, I can't believe that anyone working within the MOD can easily remove a DCM by just stamping a date on a dispatch card. How many people would have had to be involved in its removal?

I'm happy to discuss/answer any questions. Is there a good number to reach you?

Sincerely.

Eric Hausman

20150630-RESPONSE TO REQUEST FOR MEETING TO DISCUSS DCM OF YOUR LATE FATHER

DBS RES-xxx-DO3 (Butler, Elaine D)
(DBxxxxxxxxxDO3@mod.uk)

6/30/15

To: erichoustonxx@xxxxxx.com

Dear Mr Hausman,

Following our telephone conversation of 29 June, I have spoken to my colleagues regarding your request to meet with them in London next week.

Unfortunately, they are unable to arrange this for you. However I wish to assure you that the case is receiving their full consideration.
Kind Regards

Elaine Butler

DBS Secretariat Team

DBS-MODMO Honours and Awards

6/04/15

To: Eric Houston

Mr Hausman Houston,

Thank you for your email.

I am afraid due to security collection of these awards would not be possible. I have confirmed with our dispatch team that the Second World War awards will be dispatched your stepmother Jessica Hausman shortly. My sincere apologies for the delay in the delivery of these awards.

Yours sincerely,

Catherine

Miss CE Lawrence | SO3 Honours & Awards | Defence Business Services | Ministry of Defence Medal Office | Innsworth House | Imjin Barracks | Gloucester | GL3 1HW

From: Eric Houston [mailto:erichoustonxx@xxxxxx.com]
Sent: 02 June 2015 17:13
To: DBS-MODMO Honours and Awards

Subject: RE: Fred Hausman's - WW2 Medals & DCM, MID

Catherine,

My family is still waiting for my father's medals. If they have not been sent, I will be in London 6-9 July, and can pick them up on Tuesday or Wednesday, 7-8 July. Please let me know if that's possible and if my stepmother, Jessica Hausman, will have to fill out forms to approve it.

Best,

Eric Hausman Houston

RE: Fred Hausman's DCM

Parli Branch-Min Correspondence (MULTIUSER) (ParliBranch-MinCorrespondence@mod.uk)

6/02/15

To: Eric Houston

For information: this has been logged under case ref: MC2015/04814 – to be answered by 30th June 2015.

Kind regards

MOD

Parliamentary Branch

RE: Fred Hausman's DCM

Parli Branch-Min Correspondence (MULTIUSER)
(ParliBranch-MinCorrespondence@mod.uk)

6/02/15

To: Eric Houston

Address is fine, although we can action from this soft copy if
you prefer.

Parliamentary Branch

From: Eric Houston [mailto:erichoustonxx@xxxxxx.com]
Sent: 01 June 2015 21:57
To: Parli Branch-Min Correspondence (MULTIUSER)
Subject: re: Fred Hausman's DCM

Eric Hausman Houston

1st June 2015

Rt Hon Earl Howe

UNDER SECRETARY OF STATE

D/USofS/JA MC2015/02603e

MINISTRY OF DEFENCE

FLOOR 5 ZONE B MAIN BUILDING

WHITEHALL LONDON SW1A 2HB

Telephone: 020 7218 9000

Email: parliBranch-MinCorrespondence@mod.uk

Dear Earl Howe,

This email is in response to the attached letter received from Lord Astor of Hever DL. Please let me know if there is a better address to send the hard copy.

Introduction

I am in receipt of your letter of the 23rd March 2015 addressed to my sister Ms Renee Hausman Bradley.

I regret to inform you that I do not consider your response satisfactory and I do not intend to allow the matter to rest where you propose to leave it.

I have now consulted Professor Norman Palmer QC (Hon) CBE FSA on the matter. Professor Palmer is a senior barrister practising at 3 Stone Buildings Lincoln's Inn London and a leading authority on the law relating to personal property, cultural property and objects of historical interest.

In the light of leading counsel's advice I now state my position as follows.

The legal status of the medal

It is common ground that my father was awarded the DCM on the 20th July 1944 for exceptional courage in action.

By virtue of that award my father became entitled to possession of the medal struck in his name. He had a right of possession superior to that of the government departments or agencies which successively held possession of the medal pending delivery to him.

It is my contention

(i)   That the medal was stolen by a person or persons unknown.

(ii) That the medal was thereafter made the subject of various transactions.

(iii) That all of these transactions were concluded without my father's authority.

(iv) That before the medal became the subject of commerce the medal was in the possession of the

Ministry of Defence, and that possession was held voluntarily.

(v) That my father's right to possession of the medal persisted for at least the whole of the time that the medal was in the voluntary possession of the Ministry of Defence.

(vi) That for the whole of the period during which the medal was in the possession of the Ministry of Defence (and probably beyond that period) the Ministry of Defence was my father's bailee.

(vii) The relationship of bailment arose from the fact that the Ministry was voluntarily in possession of a chattel to which my father had the superior reversionary right of possession.

My father did not collect or otherwise receive possession of the medal during his lifetime.

The medal did not leave the possession, custody or control of the Ministry of Defence in consequence of any act or omission on the part of my father.

In particular:

(i)   The medal did not depart from the possession, custody or control of the Ministry of Defence by way of delivery to or collection by my father, or otherwise at his instance or instigation.

(ii) Any departure of the medal from the possession, custody or control of the Ministry of Defence occurred without my father's authority, whether express or implied, actual or ostensible.

(iii) Any departure of the medal from the possession, custody or control of the Ministry of Defence constituted a violation of my father's right of possession.

A few weeks before his death my father wrote to the Ministry of Defence, requesting the delivery of his medal. He received no reply to that request.

The medal left the possession, custody or control of the Ministry on a date unproven. It has since been the subject of a purported sale at auction by the firm of Dix Noonan and Webb on at least two occasions: in 2006 and 2011.

I am given to understand that the medal is currently in the possession of one of the following: Lord Ashcroft's Medal Collection (in so far as that is a distinct legal entity), or Lord Ashcroft in his personal capacity, or a museum or other institution holding by way of bailment from the Collection or from Lord Ashcroft. Such possession is wholly without my family's consent and an affront to our own right of possession.

In these circumstances:

(i)   I now call on the Ministry of Defence, as bailee of my father's medal, to prove on a balance of probabilities that the departure of the medal from the possession, custody or control of the Ministry, and/or its loss by the Ministry, did not occur by reason of the Ministry's default.

(ii) In the absence of such proof, and without prejudice to other applicable heads of liability or available forms of recourse, I propose to regard the Ministry as liable for such departure and loss

(iii) In the absence of due satisfaction from the Ministry I will seek redress from the Ministry on grounds of (a) breach of bailment, (b) conversion, both statutory and at common law, (c) negligence, and (d) such other head of liability as appears to me appropriate in the light of such matters as emerge.

For the avoidance of doubt, this letter is without prejudice to any further form of redress or recourse that might be available to me. I reserve my right to exert all appropriate measures both at law and otherwise to enforce my rights against the Ministry.

Absence of proof of delivery

In your letter of 23rd March 2015 to my sister Ms Renee Hausman Bradley you contend that the medal was "issued" to my father on 26th January 1948. From this and the following sentence in your letter I presume that you intend to convey that the medal was despatched to him on that date.

You do not however disclose any document to corroborate your assertion that the medal was despatched to my father, whether on 26th January 1948 or at any other time. In particular you adduce no covering letter to him, nor any receipt signed by him. Nor do you adduce any documentation to disclose the address to which the medal was despatched or to explain how your Department obtained any such address. On the contrary you state that such particulars are no longer available. By this I presume you to mean that the relevant documentation has been misplaced, destroyed or stolen by or from your Ministry or one or more of its predecessors.

Your last statement does of course raise the question whether such particulars were ever available, in other words whether the medal was ever in fact despatched to my father. I emphatically assure you that whether or not such despatch occurred (which I do not admit) my father did not receive his medal. That is corroborated by video evidence from my father himself.

Furthermore I do not (in the absence of compelling evidence from you) accept that the medal was ever despatched or that, if it was despatched, it was despatched to an appropriate address. The burden of proof in that respect is on the Ministry as successor to the Department which held the medal at the time of such despatch.

If the medal was despatched, but only to an inappropriate address, the relevant Department will have committed the tort of conversion by misdelivery.

If the medal was not despatched at all, but was unlawfully removed from the possession of the relevant Department, the Ministry is liable to my family as a bailee unless it can prove either absence of fault or the lack of any causal connection between its actual or presumed fault and the disappearance of the medal. Theft by in-house personnel who have been entrusted with any part of the Ministry's duty of care towards the medal will count as theft on the part of the Ministry.   Again, the burden of proof lies with the Ministry.

It would have been impossible for your Ministry or its predecessor to have known in January 1948 where to despatch the medal because:

(i)   My father gave you no address, and indeed entered into no communication with the relevant officials on this or any other matter, and

(ii) My father was himself living in various places in the early post-War years and had no fixed or suitable address to which the medal could have been sent.

You mention that, owing to "the passage of time" the officials at the Medals Office "can only assume that the late Mr Hausmann received his awards, as there is no evidence to suggest that they were ever returned." But with the greatest respect to those officials and you, that is not the only inference that can be drawn from the circumstances. Moreover, it is by no means the most persuasive inference. The more persuasive inference is that the medal was clandestinely and unlawfully removed from the Ministry's possession.

To sum up, there is no serious evidence that:

(i)   The medal was ever despatched to my father.

(ii) The medal, even if despatched, was correctly addressed.

(iii) The medal was ever received by my father.

(iv) The responsible officials ever sought to confirm that the medal was correctly addressed and received.

In these circumstances I respectfully suggest that your officials have chosen to adopt an analysis of the position which is unwarrantably limited and self-exonerating, and which would not, absent cogent and positive rebutting evidence from your department, stand up to judicial scrutiny.

The foregoing circumstances point, in my respectful view, to the conclusion that the medal was stolen or otherwise removed from the Ministry in violation of my father's right and interest: either from the relevant Ministry by an outsider or (more probably) by someone employed at the relevant Ministry itself. I call upon you now to rebut both this presumption and the presumption of fault that would also attach in law to that or any other cause of disappearance (such as an erroneous despatch to an unauthorised address).

If your Department cannot rebut the burdens of proof to which it is subject, it is liable to my family for the value of the medal. The technical inheritor is my mother in law, Ms Jessica Hausman, but the entire family is united on her behalf. The liability of your Department will include a sum to represent distress and vexation at the loss of a cherished family emblem. I would remind you that this medal symbolises and reflects our memory of a heroic soldier and father whose life had notable significance both historically and to the Jewish faith. It is a crucial element in our family history and it belongs without question with our family.

In these circumstances the Ministry of Defence might consider it appropriate to mitigate its liability by retrieving the medal at its own expense from the current holder and returning it to my family forthwith.

I await your response.

Yours,

Eric Houston Hausman

(I received no response to the follow email)

From: Eric Houston (erichoustonxx@xxxxxx.com)

Sent: Fri 3/13/15 4:27 PM

To: DBS-MODMO Honours and Awards MULTIUSER (dbs-modmohonoursandawards@mod.uk)

Catherine,

Thank you for issuing my father's, Fred Hausman's, campaign medals in the near future.

As far as his DCM and MID are concerned, there is now overwhelming evidence that they were stolen from within the MOD. It appears that his DCM may have been in circulation without any legal provenance since the late 1980's. Its first public auction was in September of 2006, 5 months after my father's death, and it is currently held in Lord Michael Aschcroft's collection.

According to Ray Swan, the MOD admits that both dispatch cards were completed incorrectly with no "date / details of either the award ceremony with the King at which the medal was issued or details of the postal address the decorations were issued to via despatch." I would like to know all information the MOD gave to Scotland Yard when the matter was referred to Detective Swan.

Since it was never in my father's possession, and removed inappropriately from the MOD without any authorization from my father, it is the MOD's responsibility to report it as stolen. Please do so immediately so that a police report can be filed for both his DCM and MID.

Otherwise, please explain how, in 1945, my father's
MID was dispatched with no request or authorization from
my father. And three years later, in 1948, again with no
request from my father, his DCM was then dispatched. Why
would they not be given at the same time, along with all of
his other medals? Why would he go through the trouble of
getting one medal and leave the rest? Has that ever been
done? Is it even possible? In the medal application form
there is no options for requesting which medals to receive
and in which order.

Please explain where they would have been sent? According
to the auction house listing, at that time he was believed to
be in Italy. But it is now well documented that my father
went back to Palestine after WW2, and in 1948, during
constant war and uncertainty, even he did not know where
he would be from day to day.

You also have my father's testimony, around 4 minutes in
the video below:
https://www.youtube.com/watch?v=_aGrOgKPZok#t=109

He states very clearly that he never got his DCM, only the
ribbon for it. I believe you will find that he makes a very
credible witness.

Before the dispatch cards were revealed, Ray Swan's email
of October 3, 2014 states that the MOD claims, "They have
no record of the despatch of the medal as your father was
apparently attached to the Palestine Army (although
fighting within the British Army) and therefore the Medal

office would not have been responsible for it." I contested that, and it was never brought up again. How could someone at the MOD, after researching and answering to Scotland Yard on this subject, be unaware that the DCM is to be given by the King or Queen of England at anytime throughout the recipient's lifetime?

I can give explicit detail of why my father was never able to make it to London to collect his medals. However, I'm sure he would have been more determined had he not been assured by the MOD in the 1950's, and again through me in the 1990's, that his DCM and other medals were as safe there as in a bank, and that he, or his family after is death, could get them at anytime. In 2006, several weeks before he died, he wrote to the MOD (letter attached) in order to begin the process of getting his medals. Having not heard back, he asked my sister and me to make sure that we get them. It was the dying wish of an extremely loving father. I hope you can understand why I feel obligated to take whatever action is necessary to get his DCM.

Due to mishandling within the MOD, and without my father's or his family's consent, my father's DCM and its accompanying paper work, which should have been uncirculated, has now been passed around, damaged and some of the paper work is apparently even missing.

There is more evidence that my father's DCM was stolen from within the MOD, but If you can give no justification for why my father's DCM and MID were removed from within the MOD, then immediately report them as stolen so that proper title can be established. I'm happy to discuss this with you and can be reached in New York City at tel #: (917) 660-2380

As a side-note, the last attachment shows that my father was also awarded (or recommended for) the BEM. Can you give any insight into this?

Sincerely,

Eric Hausman-Houston

Subject: RE: Fred Hausman's - WW2 Medals & DCM, MID
Date: Thu, 12 Mar 2015 10:33:53 +0000
From: DBS-MODMOHonoursandAwards@mod.uk
To: 'erichoustonxx@xxxxxx.com'

Mr Hausman-Houston,

Thank you for your email dated 15 January 2015 in respect of your Father's medals.

I am pleased to confirm that our records show that your father had not previously applied for any Second World War campaign medals. As such, I can confirm that the MOD Medal Office (MODMO) can issue the following medals to the official Next of Kin, Mrs J C Hausman, as confirmed on the completed application form:

1939/45 Star

Africa Star with 8th Army Clasp

Italy Star

War Medal 1939-45

Your father was awarded the Mention in Despatches (MID) on 11 Jan 1945 and this was issued to him on the 23 May 1945. The Distinguished Conduct Medal (DCM) was also awarded to him on 20 July 1944 and issued on the 26 January 1948.

As the DCM and MID have already been issued, the MODMO cannot issue replacement without a Police Crime Ref number or successful Insurance claim following a loss through house fire or flood.

I can confirm that DCI Ray Swann was informed of this information on 13 November 2014.

The MOD Medal Office do not hold the citations for MIDs or DCMs. Any further surviving documentation concerning these awards are held at The National Archives.   If you wish to obtain copies of these records you will need to contact The National Archives at the following address:

www.nationalarchives.gov.uk

Or, alternatively in person or in writing at:

Advice and Records Knowledge Department

The National Archives

Ruskin Avenue

Kew

Richmond

Surrey

TW9 4DU

Tel: +44 20 8 876 3444

If you wish to obtain copies of your father's service records please write to the following address:

Army Personnel Centre

Historical Disclosures

Mailpoint 555

Kentigern House

65 Brown Street

Glasgow

G2 7EX

We will issue the Second World War campaign medals listed above in the very near future.

Kind regards

Catherine

Miss CE Lawrence | SO3 Honours & Awards | Defence Business Services | Ministry of Defence Medal Office | Innsworth House | Imjin Barracks | Gloucester | GL3 1HW

From: DBS-MODMO Honours and Awards (MULTIUSER)
Sent: 22 January 2015 10:32
To: 'erichoustonxx@xxxxxx.com'
Cc: DBS-MODMO Hons Awards SO3 (Lawrence, Cath D)
Subject: Fred Hausman's - WW2 Medals & DCM, MID

Mr Hausman-Houston,

Many thanks for your email below along with the above attachments.

I can confirm that this has now been passed onto the relevant department for action and, they will be in contact in due course.

Regards.

Mrs Clare West

DBS MODMO Honours & Awards E1a

DBS-Medals@mod.uk (Group Mailbox)

DBS-MODMOHonsAwardsE1a@mod.uk (Personal)

Internal: 95471 7310

External: 01452 712612 Ext 7310

From: Eric Houston [mailto:erichoustonxx@xxxxxx.com]
Sent: 15 January 2015 21:04
To: DBS-Medals (MULTIUSER)
Subject: re: Fred Hausman's DCM, MID and other

British Ministry of Defense, medal department:

As Fred Hausman's son, I'm writing to request that the family of Fritz Sigmund Hausmann, aka Fred Hausman, receive all of his WW2 medals, including his DCM and the MID that goes with it, all of which he never received nor authorized to be taken from the MOD.

A completed application for these medals is attached. Is there anything else we will need to submit for my father's DCM and missing MID?

We have been in touch with DC Raymond Swan of Scotland Yard, Art & Antiques unit SCO7, who has been unable to find any proof that the DCM and MID were ever presented to Mr. Hausmann during his lifetime or to his heirs, which is consistent with our understanding. Thus, application for issuance of an original set of medals and associated citations and other documents is both timely and appropriate.

A medal identified as Mr. Hausmann's DCM was sold through DNW Auction house in 2011 [in London]. An email dated July 21, 2014 DNW affirmed that they have been in contact with the current owners. Mr. Hausmann's family also asks that you locate and reclaim the missing MID.

Finally, we would also like to receive all of the original citations/documentations that go with all of the medals to assure that there is no chance that they will ever be again in circulation without our approval.

Please inform me that immediate action is being taken to issue an original set of medals to Mr. Hausmann's family and to recover my father's DCM and to locate and reclaim his missing MID.

All the best,

Eric Hausman-Houston

Thomas R. Kline
Of Counsel

AUTHOR'S NOTE:

If you enjoyed this book and want to help unite the war heroes' stolen medals with their rightful owners, please help to spread the word by posting a short review on Amazon or any other social network. Thanks for your support.

About The Author

Eric Houston is the recipient of the KEY WEST THEATER FESTIVAL AWARD. His play, BECOMING ADELE, was produced and directed by Gerry Cohen at The Court Theatre, LA, produced Off-Broadway by the GOTHAM STAGE COMPANY, directed by Victor Maog, and was optioned by Warner Bros. Television. His play, SWEET DELIVERANCE was quoted to be "The funniest play to come out of the Barter theatre", was given an extended run at the Hudson Theatre, LA, and was the last play optioned by legendary Broadway producer, Alexander Cohen. After working as a ghostwriter, 'THE LOST ARTIST' marks Eric Houston's first book written in his own voice and name.

Quotes from LA production of 'BECOMING ADELE'

"Impressive! Razor-sharp performance consistently surprises and delights!" – LA TIMES, July 11 2003

"Wasilewski, in a funny, wise, and poignant script, displays an awesome talent that brings tears as easily as laughter" - Greg Owen, IN MAGAZINE, Vol. 6, Issue 11 – July 15-28, 2003

"Audrey Wasilewski completely mesmerizes the audience for over two hours!" – TOLUCAN TIMES

"Recommended – Heartfelt! Engaging! Witty! Tender! Most enjoyable! – LA WEEKLY

"Entertaining! Funny! Sheer joy!" – BACKSTAGE WEST

"Captivating! Mesmerizing! Perfection! ... Weight on the roof is a sure bet!" – BEVERLY HILLS COURIER

"Tour de force performance! Wasilewski is funny, intelligent, and endearing! She is a delight! – BEVERLY HILLS OUTLOOK

"Vibrant! Wonderful! Wasilewski is a charmer! A refreshing summertime tonic!" - Les Spindle, FRONTIER MAGAZINE, August 1, 2003

"Remarkable! So very funny! Her experiences give people a chance to laugh a lot, and cry a little, too!" - CULVER CITY NEWS REVIEW

For more info and photos, visit:

THE LOST ARTIST on Facebook.com

70735090R00295

Made in the USA
San Bernardino, CA
06 March 2018